THE LIFE OF REASON

By George Santayana

THE LIFE OF REASON (*One-volume edition*)

THE POET'S TESTAMENT: POEMS AND TWO PLAYS

THE BACKGROUND OF MY LIFE: *Vol. I of Persons and Places*

THE MIDDLE SPAN: *Vol. II of Persons and Places*

MY HOST THE WORLD: *Vol. III of Persons and Places*

DOMINATIONS AND POWERS: REFLECTIONS ON LIBERTY, SOCIETY
    AND GOVERNMENT

THE IDEA OF CHRIST IN THE GOSPELS, OR GOD IN MAN

REALMS OF BEING

THE REALM OF SPIRIT

THE REALM OF TRUTH

THE PHILOSOPHY OF SANTAYANA:
    SELECTIONS FROM THE COMPLETE WORKS OF GEORGE SANTAYANA

OBITER SCRIPTA: LECTURES, ESSAYS AND REVIEWS

THE LAST PURITAN: A MEMOIR IN THE FORM OF A NOVEL

SOME TURNS OF THOUGHT IN MODERN PHILOSOPHY

THE GENTEEL TRADITION AT BAY

THE REALM OF ESSENCE

THE REALM OF MATTER

PLATONISM AND THE SPIRITUAL LIFE

DIALOGUES IN LIMBO

POEMS

SCEPTICISM AND ANIMAL FAITH

EGOTISM IN GERMAN PHILOSOPHY

SOLILOQUIES IN ENGLAND AND LATER SOLILOQUIES

CHARACTER AND OPINION IN THE UNITED STATES

THE SENSE OF BEAUTY

INTERPRETATIONS OF POETRY AND RELIGION

THE HERMIT OF CARMEL AND OTHER POEMS

WINDS OF DOCTRINE

THE LIFE OF REASON: OR THE PHASES OF HUMAN PROGRESS
    I.   INTRODUCTION AND REASON IN COMMON SENSE
    II.   REASON IN SOCIETY
    III. REASON IN RELIGION
    IV. REASON IN ART
    V.   REASON IN SCIENCE

LITTLE ESSAYS DRAWN FROM THE WORKS OF
GEORGE SANTAYANA
    BY LOGAN PEARSALL SMITH, *with the collaboration of the author*

CHARLES SCRIBNER'S SONS

THE
LIFE OF REASON

OR

The Phases of Human Progress

BY GEORGE SANTAYANA

ONE-VOLUME EDITION

Revised by THE AUTHOR *in Collaboration*
with DANIEL CORY

ἡ γὰρ νοῦ ἐνέργεια ζωή

CHARLES SCRIBNER'S SONS

New York

COPYRIGHT, 1953, BY DANIEL M. CORY

COPYRIGHT, 1905, 1906, BY CHARLES SCRIBNER'S SONS;

RENEWAL COPYRIGHT, 1933, 1934, BY GEORGE SANTAYANA.

CHARLES SCRIBNER'S SONS

*All rights reserved. No part of this book may be reproduced
in any form without the permission of Charles Scribner's Sons*

E–2.66[V]

PRINTED IN THE UNITED STATES OF AMERICA

B
945
523
L7
1953

PREFACE

In the autumn of 1951, when I returned to Rome to pass the winter as usual with Santayana, he showed me a letter he had just received from America. John Hall Wheelock of Scribner's had sounded him on the possibility of a new and abridged one-volume edition of *The Life of Reason*.

"It must not only be abridged," Santayana told me at once, "but *revised* as well. Take that word 'mechanical', for example, that I use so frequently in these books. It suggests that I believe the world is composed of a lot of little wheels and springs like an enormous Swiss watch. I may be a materialist, but I hope I am not as naive as all that."

I know that Santayana welcomed an opportunity to revise what many critics consider is his *chef d'oeuvre*, and he felt that a discreet condensation of the five volumes might make the work more congenial to the mind (and purse) of the young student. After all, an enthusiast could always find the original volumes in a public library.

"Did I ever tell you," Santayana continued, "that about forty-five years ago G. E. Moore wrote a review of *The Life of Reason* for *Mind*, in which he said words to the effect that the work was so confused it was not worth discussing. I think he complimented me on my style, but that was about all."

I have not checked on this old review by the distinguished English philosopher, but I am convinced that it was one of those things which leave a sediment in a man's mind, and which he feels he would like to clear up someday. Be that as it may, here in the late evening of life was a final opportunity to settle old accounts—to purify once and for all the sustaining wine of reason. But was he able, physically and mentally, to do it? No, not alone. And if the reader will forgive me, here I had another chance to justify my rather ambiguous existence. It was decided that we would tackle the task of revision and abridgement *insieme*, as Santayana put it, and he immediately wrote to Mr. Wheelock saying that I was to edit the new edition "in collaboration with the author."

In my mind's eye I can see that frail shell of a body, clad in an old brown dressing-gown, sitting in an armchair with a rug across his knees. In one hand a volume of the Triton edition of his Works

T.S. 6-9-67

60986

v

(the print is larger in this *de luxe* edition), and in the other the magnifying glass to assist the sight of the one good eye. A large red crayon lies handy on the desk beside him to mark boldly the amputations in the body of reason. How I bless that red crayon! As I hesitate over the fascinating fair flesh of writing in these five volumes, I ask myself, like some nervous assistant surgeon at a major operation, how I could ever proceed with my delicate work, if the Master had not first guided me in the interstices of redundant sentences, and around the corners of many a fat paragraph! Yes, and there were plentiful revisions of text in the spacious margins, and even new footnotes scrawled on the bottom of some pages.

In due course, Santayana's own work on *The Life of Reason* was finished. He had pruned the five volumes carefully, and the faithful red crayon was in action until the last chapter of *Reason in Science*. A sustained effort was made to dispel those early mists of idealism from the realistic body of his philosophy, and to make clear to the reader that our *idea* of a natural world can never be *that world itself*. Science might reveal the mathematical skeleton of things, but the bulk of human experience is incorrigibly poetical, and only remotely representative of its actual conditions.

It gave Santayana a great deal of satisfaction to feel that he had lived to complete his last task.

"What I have yearned for all my life," he told me, "is not so much cosmic unity—like Whitehead, but simply 'completion'. If I see a circle half-drawn, I yearn to complete it."

If we consider for a moment this passion for completion, I think we will agree that it is in perfect accord with a fundamental principle of all Santayana's philosophy. He desired above all that everything, be it a plant, or an animal, or a human being, or a nation, should fulfil or complete its own inherent potentiality. And in this he was very Hellenic in spirit. What saddened him was the inevitable spectacle of some budding power blighted by an alien domination. If only the life of reason could become a mastering ideal in the hearts of the responsible administrators of the affairs of this world, then we might all enjoy that variety and development of culture which is the true goal of civilised society. I like to think that this book (one of the philosophical classics of the twentieth century) may help to sustain such a wise tolerance.

DANIEL CORY

Rome, 1952–53.

CONTENTS

CONTENTS

I

REASON IN COMMON SENSE

CHAPTER 1

THE BIRTH OF REASON

HUMAN LIFE, when it begins to possess intrinsic value, is an incipient order in the midst of what seems a vast though, to some extent, a vanishing chaos. This retreating chaos can be deciphered and appreciated by man only in proportion as the order in himself is confirmed and extended. For man's consciousness is evidently realistic; it clings to his fate, registers, so to speak, the higher and lower temperature of his fortunes, and, so far as it can, represents the agencies on which those fortunes depend. When this dramatic vocation of consciousness has not been fulfilled at all, consciousness is wholly confused; the world it envisages seems consequently a chaos. Later, if experience has fallen into shape, and there are settled categories and constant objects in human discourse, the assumption is made that the original disposition of things was also orderly and indeed mechanically conducive to just those feats of instinct and intelligence which have been since accomplished. A theory of origins, of substance, and of natural laws may thus be framed and accepted, and may receive confirmation in the further march of events. It will be observed, however, that what is credibly asserted about the past is not a report which the past was itself able to make when it existed nor one it is now able, in some oracular fashion, to formulate and to impose upon us. The report is a rational construction based and seated in present experience; it has no cogency for the inattentive and no existence for the ignorant. Although the universe, then, may not have come from chaos, human experience certainly has begun in a private and dreamful chaos of its own, out of which it still only partially and momentarily emerges. The history of this awakening is of course not the same as that of the environing world ultimately discovered; it is the history, however, of that discovery itself, of the knowledge through which alone the world can be revealed. We may accordingly dispense ourselves from preliminary courtesies to the real universal order, nature, the absolute,

3

and the gods. We shall make their acquaintance in due season and better appreciate their moral status, if we strive merely to recall our own experience, and to retrace the visions and reflections out of which those conceptions have grown.

To revert to primordial feeling is an exercise in mental disintegration, not a feat of science. We might, indeed, as in animal psychology, retrace the situations in which instinct and sense seem first to appear and write, as it were, a genealogy of reason based on circumstantial evidence. Reason was born, as it has since discovered, into a world already wonderfully organised, in which it found its precursor in what is called life, its seat in an animal body of unusual plasticity, and its function in rendering that body's volatile instincts and sensations harmonious with one another and with the outer world on which they depend. It did not arise until the will or conscious stress, by which any modification of living bodies' inertia seems to be accompanied, began to respond to represented objects, and to maintain that inertia not absolutely by resistance but only relatively and indirectly through labour. Reason has thus supervened at the last stage of an adaptation which has long been carried on by irrational and even unconscious processes. Nature preceded, with all that fixation of impulses and conditions which gives reason its tasks and its *point-d'appui*. Nevertheless, such a matrix or cradle for reason belongs only externally to its life. The description of conditions involves their previous discovery and a historian equipped with many data and many analogies of thought. Such scientific resources are absent in those first moments of rational living which we here wish to recall; the first chapter in reason's memoirs would no more entail the description of its real environment than the first chapter in human history would include true accounts of astronomy, psychology, and animal evolution.

In order to begin at the beginning we must try to fall back on uninterpreted feeling, as the mystics aspire to do. We need not expect, however, to find peace there, for the immediate is in flux. Pure feeling rejoices in a logical nonentity very deceptive to dialectical minds. They often think, when they fall back on elements necessarily indescribable, that they have come upon true nothingness. If they are mystics, distrusting thought and craving the largeness of indistinction, they may embrace this alleged nothingness with joy, even if it seem positively painful, hoping to find rest there through self-abnegation. If on the contrary they are rationalists they may reject the immediate with scorn and deny that it exists at all, since in their books they cannot define it satisfactorily. Both mystics and rationalists, however, are deceived by their mental agility; the immediate exists, even if dialectic cannot explain it. What the rationalist calls nonentity is the substrate and locus of all ideas, having the obstinate reality of matter, the crushing irrationality of existence itself; and one who attempts to override it becomes to that extent an irrelevant rhapsodist, dealing with thin after-images of being. Nor has the mystic who sinks into the immediate much better appreciated the situation. This immediate is not God but chaos; its nothingness is pregnant, restless, and brutish; it is that from which all things emerge in so far as they have any permanence or value, so that to lapse into it again is a dull suicide and no salvation. Peace, which is after all what the mystic seeks, lies not in indistinction but in perfection. If he reaches it in a measure himself, it is by the traditional discipline he still practises, not by his heats or his languors.

The seed-bed of reason lies, then, in the immediate, but what reason draws thence is momentum and power to rise above its source. It is the perturbed immediate itself that finds or at least seeks its peace in reason, through which it comes in sight of some sort of ideal permanence. When the flux manages to form an eddy and to maintain by breathing and nutrition what we call a life, it affords some slight foothold and object for thought and becomes in a measure like the ark in the desert, a moving habitation for the eternal.

Life begins to have some value and continuity so soon as there is something definite that lives and something definite to live for. The primacy of will, as Fichte and Schopenhauer conceived it, is a mythical way of designating this situation. Of course a will can have no being in the absence of realities or ideas marking its direction and contrasting the eventualities it seeks with those it flies from; and tendency, no less than movement, needs an organised medium to make it possible, while aspiration and fear involve an ideal world. Yet a principle of choice is not deducible from mere ideas, and no interest is involved in the formal relations of things. All survey needs an arbitrary starting-point; all valuation rests on an irrational bias. The absolute flux cannot be physically arrested; but what arrests it ideally is the fixing of some point in it from which it can be measured and illumined. Otherwise it could show no form and maintain no preference; it would be impossible to approach or recede from a represented state, and to suffer or to exert will in view of events. The irrational fate that lodges the transcendental self in this or that body, inspires it with definite passions, and subjects it to particular buffets from the outer world—this is the prime condition of all observation and inference, of all failure or success.

Those sensations in which a transition is contained need only analysis to yield two ideal and related terms—two points in space or two characters in feeling. Hot and cold, here and there, good and bad, now and then, are dyads that spring into being when the flux accentuates some term and so makes possible a discrimination of parts and directions in its own movement. An initial attitude sustains incipient interests. What we first discover in ourselves, before the influence we obey has given rise to any definite idea, is the working of instincts already in motion. Impulses to appropriate and to reject first teach us the points of the compass, and space itself, like charity, begins at home.

The guide in early sensuous education is the same that conducts the whole Life of Reason, namely, impulse checked by experiment, and experiment judged again by impulse. What teaches the child to distinguish the nurse's breast from sundry blank or disquieting presences? What induces him to arrest that image, to mark its associates, and to recognise them with alacrity? The discomfort of its absence and the comfort of its possession. To that image is attached the chief satisfaction he knows, and the force of that satisfaction disentangles it before all other images from the feeble and fluid continuum of his life. What first awakens in him a sense of reality is what first is able to appease his unrest.

Had the group of feelings, now welded together in fruition, found no instinct in him to awaken and become a signal for, the group would never have persisted; its loose elements would have been allowed to pass by unnoticed and would not have been recognised when they recurred. Experience would have remained absolute inexperience, as foolishly perpetual as the gurglings of rivers or the flickerings of sunlight in a grove. But an instinct was actually present, so formed as to be aroused by a determinate stimulus; and the image produced by that stimulus, when it came, could have in consequence a meaning and an individuality. It seemed by divine right to signify something interesting, something real, because by natural contiguity it flowed from something pertinent and important to life. Every accompanying sensation which shared that privilege, or in time was engrossed in that function, would ultimately become a part of that conceived reality, a quality of that thing.

The same primacy of impulses, irrational in themselves but expressive of bodily functions, is observable in the behaviour of animals, and in those dreams, obsessions, and primary passions which in the midst of sophisticated life sometimes lay bare the obscure groundwork of human nature. Reason's work is there undone. We can observe sporadic growths, disjointed fragments of rationality, springing up in a moral wilderness. In the passion of love, for instance, a cause unknown to the sufferer, but which is doubtless the springflood of hereditary instincts accidentally let loose, suddenly checks the young man's gayety, dispels his random curiosity, arrests perhaps his very breath; and when he looks for a cause to explain his suspended faculties, he can find it only in the presence or image of another being, of whose character possibly, he knows nothing and whose beauty may not be remarkable; yet that image pursues him everywhere, and he is dominated by an unaccustomed tragic earnestness and a new capacity for suffering and joy. If the passion be strong there is no previous interest or duty that will be remembered before it; if it be lasting the whole life may be reorganised by it; it may impose new habits, other manners, and another religion. Yet what is the root of all this idealism? An irrational instinct, normally intermittent, such as all dumb creatures share, which has here managed to dominate a human soul and to enlist all the mental powers in its more or less permanent service, upsetting their usual equilibrium. This madness, however, inspires method; and for the first time, perhaps, in his life, the man has something to live for. The blind affinity that like a magnet draws all the faculties around it, in so uniting them, suffuses them with an unwonted spiritual light.

Here, on a small scale and on a precarious foundation, we may see clearly illustrated and foreshadowed that Life of Reason which is simply the unity given to all existence by a mind *in love with the good*. In the higher reaches of human nature, as much as in the lower, rationality depends on distinguishing the excellent; and that distinction can be made, in the last analysis, only by an irrational impulse. As life is a better form given to force, by which the universal flux is subdued to create and serve a somewhat permanent interest, so reason is a better form given to interest itself, by which it is fortified and propagated, and ultimately, perhaps, assured of satisfaction. The substance to which this form is given remains irrational; so that rationality, like all excellence, is something secondary and relative, requiring a natural being to possess or to impute it. When definite interests are recognised and the values of things are estimated by that standard, action at the same time veering in harmony with that estimation, then reason has been born and a moral world has arisen.

CHAPTER 2

FIRST STEPS AND FIRST FLUCTUATIONS

CONSCIOUSNESS IS a born hermit. Though subject, by divine dispensation, to spells of fervour and apathy, like a singing bird, it is at first quite unconcerned about its own conditions or maintenance. To acquire a notion of such matters, or an interest in them, it would have to lose its hearty simplicity and begin to reflect; it would have to forget the present with its instant joys in order laboriously to conceive the absent and the hypothetical. The body may be said to make for self-preservation, since it has an organic equilibrium which, when not too rudely disturbed, restores itself by growth and co-operative action; but no such principle appears in the soul. Foolish in the beginning and generous in the end, consciousness thinks of nothing so little as of its own interests. It is lost in its objects; nor would it ever acquire even an indirect concern in its future, did not love of things external attach it to their fortunes. Attachment to ideal terms is indeed what gives consciousness its continuity; its parts have no relevance or relation to one another save what they acquire by depending on the same body or representing the same objects. Even when consciousness grows sophisticated and thinks it cares for itself, it really cares only for its ideals; the world it pictures seems to it beautiful, and it may incidentally prize itself also, when it has come to regard itself as a part of that world. Initially, however, it is free even from that honest selfishness; it looks straight out; it is interested in the movements it observes; it swells with the represented world, suffers with its commotion, and subsides, no less willingly, in its interludes of calm.

Natural history and psychology arrive at consciousness from the outside, and consequently give it an artificial articulation and rationality which are wholly alien to its essence. These sciences infer feeling from habit or expression; so that only the expressible and practical aspects of feeling figure in their calculation. But these aspects are really peripheral; the core is an irresponsible, ungoverned, irrevocable dream. Psychologists have discussed perception *ad nauseam* and become horribly entangled in a combined idealism

9

and physiology; for they must perforce approach the subject from the side of matter, since all science and all evidence are external; nor could they ever reach consciousness at all if they did not observe its occasions and then interpret those occasions dramatically. At the same time, the inferred mind they subject to examination will yield nothing but ideas, and it is a marvel how such a dream can regard those natural objects from which the psychologist has inferred it. Perception is in fact no primary phase of consciousness; it is an ulterior practical function acquired by a dream which has become symbolic of its conditions, and therefore relevant to its own destiny. Such relevance and symbolism are indirect and slowly acquired; their status cannot be understood unless we regard them as forms of imagination happily grown significant. In imagination, not in perception, lies the substance of experience, while knowledge and reason are but its chastened and ultimate form.

Every actual animal is somewhat dull and somewhat mad. He will at times miss his signals and stare vacantly when he might well act, while at other times he will run off into convulsions and raise a dust in his own brain to no purpose. These imperfections are so human that we should hardly recognise ourselves if we could shake them off altogether. Not to retain any dulness would mean to possess untiring attention and universal interests, thus realising the boast about deeming nothing human alien to us; while to be absolutely without folly would involve perfect self-knowledge and self-control. The intelligent man known to history flourishes within a dullard and holds a lunatic in leash. He is encased in a protective shell of ignorance and insensibility which keeps him from being exhausted and confused by this too complicated world; but that integument blinds him at the same time to many of his nearest and highest interests. He is amused by the antics of the brute dreaming within his breast; he gloats on his passionate reveries, an amusement which sometimes costs him very dear. Thus the best human intelligence is still decidedly barbarous; it fights in heavy armour and keeps a fool at court.

If consciousness could ever have the function of guiding conduct better than instinct can, in the beginning it would be most incompetent for that office. Only the routine and equilibrium which healthy instinct involves keep thought and will at all within the limits of sanity. The predetermined interests we have as animals fortunately focus our attention on practical things, pulling it back, like a ball with an elastic cord, within the radius of pertinent matters. Instinct alone compels us to neglect and seldom to recall the irrelevant infinity of ideas. Philosophers have sometimes said that all ideas come from experience; they never could have been poets and must have forgotten that they were ever children. The great difficulty in education is to get experience out of ideas. Shame, conscience, and reason continually disallow and ignore what consciousness presents; and what are they but habit and latent instinct asserting themselves and forcing us to disregard our midsummer madness? Idiocy and lunacy are merely reversions to a condition in which present consciousness is in the ascendant and has escaped the control of unconscious forces. We speak of people being "out of their senses," when they have in fact fallen back into them; or of those who have "lost their mind," when they have lost merely that habitual control over consciousness which prevented it from flaring into all sorts of obsessions and agonies. Their bodies having become deranged, their minds, far from correcting that derangement, instantly share and betray it. A dream is always simmering below the conventional surface of speech and reflection. Even in the highest reaches and serenest meditations of science it sometimes breaks through. Even there we are seldom constant enough to conceive a truly natural world; somewhere passionate, fanciful, or magic elements will slip into the scheme and baffle rational ambition.

An imaginative life may therefore exist parasitically in a man, hardly touching his action or environment. There is no possibility of exorcising these apparitions by their own power. A nightmare does not dispel itself; it endures until the organic strain which caused it is relaxed either by natural exhaustion or by some external influence. Therefore human ideas are still for the most part sensuous and trivial, shifting with the chance currents of the brain, and representing nothing, so to speak, but personal temperature. Personal temperature, moreover, is sometimes tropical. There are brains like a South American jungle, as there are others like an Arabian desert, strewn with nothing but bones. While a passionate sultriness prevails in the mind there is no end to its luxuriance. Languages intricately articulate, flaming mythologies, metaphysical perspectives lost in infinity, arise in remarkable profusion. In time, however, there comes a change of climate and the whole forest disappears.

It is easy, from the stand-point of acquired practical competence,

to deride a merely imaginative life. Derision, however, is not interpretation, and the better method of overcoming erratic ideas is to
trace them out dialectically and see if they will not recognise their
own fatuity. The most irresponsible vision has certain principles of
order and valuation by which it estimates itself; and in these principles the Life of Reason is already broached, however halting may
be its development. We should lead ourselves out of our dream, as
the Israelites were led out of Egypt, by the promise and eloquence
of that dream itself. Otherwise we might kill the goose that lays
the golden egg, and by proscribing imagination abolish science.

Visionary experience has a first value in its possible pleasantness.
Why any form of feeling should be delightful is not to be explained
transcendentally: a physiological law may, after the fact, render
every instance predictable; but no logical affinity between the formal quality of an experience and the impulse to welcome it will
thereby be disclosed. We find, however, that pleasure suffuses certain states of mind and pain others; which is another way of saying
that, for no reason, we love the first and detest the second. The
polemic which certain moralists have waged against pleasure and
in favour of pain is intelligible when we remember that their chief
interest is edification, and that ability to resist pleasure and pain
alike is a valuable virtue in a world where action and renunciation
are the twin keys to happiness. But to deny that pleasure is a good
and pain an evil is a grotesque affectation: it amounts to giving
"good" and "evil" artificial definitions and thereby reducing ethics
to arbitrary verbiage. Not only is good that adherence of the will
to experience of which pleasure is the basal example, and evil the
corresponding rejection which is the very essence of pain, but when
we pass from good and evil in sense to their highest embodiments,
pleasure remains eligible and pain something which it is a duty to
prevent. A man who without necessity deprived any person of a
pleasure or imposed on him a pain, would be a contemptible knave,
and the person so injured would be the first to declare it, nor could
the highest celestial tribunal, if it was just, reverse that sentence.
For it suffices that one being, however weak, loves or abhors anything, no matter how slightly, for that thing to acquire a proportionate value which no chorus of contradiction ringing through all the
spheres can ever wholly abolish. An experience good or bad in itself
remains so for ever, and its inclusion in a more general order of

things can only change that totality proportionately to the ingredient absorbed, which will infect the mass, so far as it goes, with its own colour. The more pleasure a universe can yield, other things being equal, the more beneficent and generous is its general nature; the more pains its constitution involves, the darker and more malign is its total temper. To deny this would seem impossible, yet it is done daily; for there is nothing people will not maintain when they are slaves to superstition; and candour and a sense of justice are, in such a case, the first things lost.

Here we come upon a crisis in human development which shows clearly how much the Life of Reason is a natural thing, a growth that a different course of events might well have excluded. Laplace is reported to have said on his death-bed that science was mere trifling and that nothing was real but love. Love, for such a man, doubtless involved objects and ideas: it was love of persons. The same revulsion of feeling may, however, be carried further. Lucretius says that passion is a torment because its pleasures are not pure, that is, because they are mingled with longing and entangled in vexatious things. Pure pleasure would be without ideas. Many a man has found in some moment of his life an unutterable joy which made all the rest of it seem a farce, as if a corpse should play it was living. Mystics habitually look beneath the Life of Reason for the substance and infinity of happiness. In all these revulsions, and many others, there is a certain justification, inasmuch as systematic living is after all an experiment, as is the formation of animal bodies, and the inorganic pulp out of which these growths have come may very likely have had its own incommunicable values, its absolute thrills, which we vainly try to remember and to which, in moments of dissolution, we may half revert. Protoplasmic pleasures and strains may be the substance of consciousness; and as the sea and the flat waste to which all dust returns have a certain primordial life and a certain sublimity, so all passions and ideas, when spent, may rejoin the basal note of feeling, and enlarge their volumes as they lose their form. Though to acquire or impart form is delightful in art, in thought, in generation, in government, yet a euthanasia of finitude is also known. All is not affectation in the poet who says, "Now more than ever seems it rich to die"; and, without any poetry or affectation, men may love sleep, and opiates, and every luxurious escape from humanity.

The step by which pleasure and pain are attached to ideas, so as to be predictable and to become factors in action, is therefore by no means irrevocable. It is a step, however, in the direction of reason; and though reason's path is only one of innumerable courses perhaps open to existence, it is the only one that we are tracing here.

When consciousness begins to add diversity to its intensity, its value is no longer absolute and inexpressible. The felt variations in its tone are attached to the observed movement of its objects; in these objects its values are imbedded. A world loaded with dramatic values may thus arise in imagination. If a dog, while sniffing about contentedly, sees afar off his master arriving after long absence, the change in the animal's feeling is not merely in the quantity of pure pleasure; a new circle of sensations appears, with a new principle governing interest and desire; instead of waywardness subjection, instead of freedom love. But the poor brute asks for no reason why his master went, why he has come again, why he should be loved, or why presently while lying at his feet you forget him and begin to grunt and dream of the chase—all that is an utter mystery, utterly unconsidered. Such experience moves wholly by inspiration; every event is providential, every act unpremeditated. Absolute freedom and absolute helplessness have met together: you depend wholly on divine favour, yet that unfathomable agency is not distinguishable from your own life.

The story which such animal experience contains, however, needs only to be better articulated in order to disclose its underlying machinery. *Felix qui potuit rerum cognoscere causas*, said a poet who stood near enough to fundamental human needs and to the great answer which art and civilisation can make to them, to value the Life of Reason and think it sublime. To discern causes is to turn vision into knowledge and motion into action. It is to fix the associates of things, so that their respective transformations are collated, and they become significant of one another. In proportion as such understanding advances each moment of experience becomes consequential and prophetic of the rest. The calm places in life are filled with power and its spasms with resource. No emotion can overwhelm the mind, for of none is the basis or issue wholly hidden; no event can disconcert it altogether, because it sees beyond. Means can be looked for to escape from the worst predicament; and whereas each moment had been formerly filled with nothing but its own adventure and surprised emotion, each now makes room for the lesson of what went before and surmises what may be the plot of the whole.

At the threshold of reason there is a kind of choice. Not all impressions contribute equally to the new growth; many, in fact, which were formerly equal in rank to the best, now grow obscure. Attention ignores them, in its haste to arrive at what is significant of something more. Nor are the principles of synthesis, by which the aristocratic few establish their oligarchy, themselves unequivocal. The first principles of logic are like the senses, few but arbitrary. They might have been quite different and yet produced, by a now unthinkable method, a language no less significant than the one we speak. Twenty-six letters may suffice for a language, but they are a wretched minority among all possible sounds. So the forms of perception and the categories of thought, which a grammarian's philosophy might think primordial necessities, are no less casual than words or their syntactical order. Why, we may ask, did these forms assert themselves here? What principles of selection guide mental growth?

To give a logical ground for such a selection is evidently impossible, since it is logic itself that is to be accounted for. A natural ground is, in strictness, also irrelevant, since natural connections, where thought has not reduced them to a sort of equivalence and necessity, are mere data and juxtapositions. Yet it is not necessary to leave the question altogether unanswered. By using our senses we may discover, not indeed why each sense has its specific quality or exists at all, but what are its organs and occasions. In like manner we may, by developing the Life of Reason, come to understand its conditions. When consciousness awakes the body has, as we long afterward discover, a definite organisation. No syllogism is needed to persuade us to eat, no prophecy of happiness to teach us to love. On the contrary, the living organism, caught in the act, informs us how to reason and what to enjoy. The soul adopts the body's aims; from the body and from its instincts she draws a first hint of the right means to those accepted purposes. Thus reason enters into partnership with the world and begins to be respected there; which it would never be if it were not expressive of the same physical forces that are to preside over events and render them fortunate or unfortunate for human interests. Reason is significant in action only because it has begun by taking, so to speak, the body's side; that sympathetic bias enables her to distinguish events pertinent to the chosen interests, to compare impulse with satisfaction, and, by representing a new and circular current in the system, to preside over the formation of better habits, habits expressing more instincts at once and responding to more opportunities.

CHAPTER 3

THE DISCOVERY OF NATURAL OBJECTS

AT FIRST sight it might seem an idle observation that the first task of intelligence is to represent the environing reality, a reality actually represented in the notion, universally prevalent among men, of a cosmos in space and time, an animated material engine called nature. In trying to conceive nature the mind lisps its first lesson; natural phenomena are the mother tongue of imagination no less than of science and practical life. Men and gods are not conceivable otherwise than as inhabitants of nature. Early experience knows no mystery which is not somehow rooted in transformations of the natural world, and fancy can build no hope which would not be expressible there. But we are grown so accustomed to this ancient apparition that we may be no longer aware how difficult was the task of conjuring it up. We may even have forgotten the possibility that such a vision should never have arisen at all. A brief excursion into that much abused subject, the psychology of perception, may here serve to remind us of the great work which the budding intellect must long ago have accomplished unawares.

Consider how the shocks out of which the notion of material things is to be built first strike home into the soul. Eye and hand, if we may neglect the other senses, transmit their successive impressions, all varying with the position of outer objects and with the other material conditions. A chaos of multitudinous impressions rains in from all sides at all hours. Nor have the external or cognitive senses an original primacy. The taste, the smell, the alarming sounds of things are continually distracting attention. There are infinite reverberations in memory of all former impressions, together with fresh fancies created in the brain, things at first in no wise subordinated to external objects. All these incongruous elements are mingled like a witches' brew. And more: there are indications that inner sensations, such as those of digestion, have an overpowering influence on the primitive mind, which has not learned to articulate or distinguish permanent needs. So that to the whirl of outer sensations we must add, to reach some notion of what consciousness may contain before the advent of reason, interruptions and lethargies caused by wholly blind internal feelings; trances such as fall even on comparatively articulate minds in rage, lust, or madness. Against all these bewildering forces the new-born reason has to struggle; and we need not wonder that the costly experiments and disillusions of the past have not yet produced a complete enlightenment.

The onslaught made in the last century by the transcendental philosophy upon empirical traditions is familiar to everybody: it seemed a pertinent attack, yet in the end proved quite trifling and unavailing. Thought, we are told rightly enough, cannot be accounted for by enumerating its conditions. A number of detached sensations, being each its own little word, cannot add themselves together nor conjoin themselves in the void. Again, experiences having an alleged common cause would not have, merely for that reason, a common object. Nor would a series of successive perceptions, no matter how quick, logically involve a sense of time nor a notion of succession. Yet, in point of fact, when such a succession occurs and a living brain is there to acquire some structural modification by virtue of its own passing states, a memory of that succession and its terms may often supervene. It is quite true also that the simultaneous presence or association of images belonging to different senses does not carry with it by intrinsic necessity any fusion of such images nor any notion of an object having them for its qualities. Yet, in point of fact, such a group of sensations does often merge into a complex image; instead of the elements originally perceptible in isolation, there arises a familiar term, a sort of personal presence. To this felt presence, certain instinctive reactions are attached, and the sensations that may be involved in that apparition, when each for any reason becomes emphatic, are referred to it as its qualities or its effects.

Such complications of course involve the gift of memory, with capacity to survey at once vestiges of many perceptions, to feel their implication and absorption in the present object, and to be carried, by this sense of relation, to the thought that those perceptions have a representative function. And this is a great step. It manifests the mind's powers. It illustrates those transformations of consciousness the principle of which, when abstracted, we call intelligence. We must accordingly proceed with caution, for we are digging at the very roots of reason.

The chief perplexity, however, which besets this subject and makes discussions of it so often end in a cloud, is quite artificial. Thought is not a mechanical calculus, where the elements and the method exhaust the fact. Thought is a form of life, and should be conceived on the analogy of nutrition, generation, and art. Reason, as Hume said with profound truth, is an unintelligible instinct. It could not be otherwise if reason is to remain something transitive and existential; for transition is unintelligible, and yet is the deepest characteristic of existence. Philosophers, however, having perceived that the function of thought is to fix static terms and reveal eternal relations, have inadvertently transferred to the living act what is true only of its ideal object; and they have expected to find in the process, treated psychologically, that luminous deductive clearness which belongs to the ideal world it tends to reveal. The intelligible, however, lies at the periphery of experience, the surd at its core; and intelligence is but one centrifugal ray darting from the slime to the stars. Thought must execute a metamorphosis; and while this is of course mysterious, it is one of those familiar mysteries, like motion and will, which are more natural than dialectical lucidity itself; for dialectic grows cogent by fulfilling intent, but intent or meaning is itself vital and inexplicable.

The process of counting is perhaps as simple an instance as can be found of a mental operation on sensible data. The clock, let us say, strikes two: if the sensorium were perfectly elastic and after receiving the first blow reverted exactly to its previous state, retaining absolutely no trace of that momentary oscillation and no altered habit, then it is certain that a sense for number or a faculty of counting could never arise. The second stroke would be responded to with the same reaction which had met the first. There would be no summation of effects, no complication. However numerous the successive impressions might come to be, each would remain fresh and pure, the last being identical in character with the first. One, one, one, would be the monotonous response for ever. Just so generations of ephemeral insects that succeeded one another without transmitting experience might repeat the same round of impressions—an everlasting progression without a shadow of progress. Such, too, is the idiot's life: his liquid brain transmits every impulse without resistance and retains the record of no impression.

Intelligence is accordingly conditioned by a modification of both structure and consciousness by dint of past events. To be aware that a second stroke is not itself the first, I must retain something of the old sensation. The first must reverberate still in my ears when the second arrives, so that this second, coming into a consciousness still filled by the first, is a different experience from the first, which fell into a mind perfectly empty and unprepared. Now the newcomer finds in the subsisting One a sponsor to christen it by the name of Two. The first stroke was a simple 1. The second is not simply another 1, a mere iteration of the first. It is 1^1, where the coefficient represents the reverberating first stroke, still persisting in the mind, and forming a background and perspective against which the new stroke may be distinguished. The meaning of "two," then, is "this after that" or "this again," where we have a simultaneous sense of two things which have been separately perceived but are identified as similar in their nature. Repetition must cease to be pure repetition and become cumulative before it can give rise to the consciousness of repetition.

The first condition of counting, then, is that the sensorium should retain something of the first impression while it receives the second, or (to state the corresponding mental fact) that the second sensation should be felt together with a survival of the first from which it is distinguished in point of existence and with which it is identified in point of character.

Now, to secure this, it is not enough that the sensorium should be materially continuous, or that a "spiritual substance" or a "transcendental ego" should persist in time to receive the second sensation after having received and registered the first. A perfectly elastic sensorium, a wholly unchanging soul, or a quite absolute ego might remain perfectly identical with itself through various experiences without collating them. It would then remain, in fact, more truly and literally identical than if it were modified somewhat by those successive shocks. Yet a sensorium or a spirit thus unchanged would be incapable of memory, unfit to connect a past perception with one present or to become aware of their relation. It is not identity in the substance impressed, but growing complication in the phenomenon presented, that makes possible a sense of diversity and relation between things. The identity of substance or spirit, if it were absolute, would indeed prevent comparison, because it would exclude modifications, and it is the survival of past modifications within the present that makes comparisons possible. We may impress any number of forms successively on the same water, and the identity of the substance will not help those forms to survive and accumulate their effects. But if we have a surface that retains our successive stampings we may change the substance from wax to plaster and from plaster to bronze, and the effects of our labour will survive and be superimposed upon one another. It is the actual plastic form in both mind and body, not any unchanging substance or agent, that is efficacious in perpetuating thought and gathering experience.

Were not Nature and all her parts such models of patience and pertinacity, they never would have succeeded in impressing their existence on something so volatile and irresponsible as thought is. A sensation needs to be violent, like the sun's blinding light, to arrest attention, and keep it taut, as it were, long enough for the system to acquire a respectful attitude, and grow predisposed to resume it. A repetition of that sensation will thereafter meet with a prepared response which we call recognition; the concomitants of the old experience will form themselves afresh about the new one and by their convergence give it a sort of welcome and interpretation. The movement, for instance, by which the face was raised toward the heavens was perhaps one element which added to the first sensation, brightness, a concomitant sensation, height; the brightness was not bright merely, but high. Now when the brightness reappears the face will more quickly be lifted up; the place where the brightness shone will be looked for; the brightness will have acquired a claim to be placed somewhere. The heat which at the same moment may have burned the forehead will also be expected and, when felt, projected into the brightness, which will now be hot as well as high. So with whatever other sensations time may associate with this group. They will all adhere to the original impression, enriching it with an individuality which will render it before long a familiar complex in experience, and one easy to recognise and to complete in idea.

In the case of so vivid a thing as the sun's brightness many other sensations besides those out of which science draws the qualities attributed to that heavenly body adhere in the primitive mind to the phenomenon. Before he is a substance the sun is a god. He is beneficent and necessary no less than bright and high; he rises upon all happy opportunities and sets upon all terrors. He is divine, since all life and fruitfulness hang upon his miraculous revolutions. His coming and going are life and death to the world. As the sensations of light and heat are projected upward together to become attributes of his body, so the feelings of pleasure, safety, and hope which he brings into the soul are projected into his spirit; and to this spirit, more than to anything else, energy, independence, and substantiality are originally attributed. The emotions felt in his presence being the ultimate issue and term of his effect in us, the counterpart or shadow of those emotions is regarded as the first and deepest factor in his causality. It is his divine life, more than aught else, that underlies his apparitions and explains the influences which he propagates. The substance or independent existence attributed to objects is therefore by no means only or primarily a physical notion. What is conceived to support the physical qualities is a pseudo-psychic or vital force. It is a moral and living object that we construct, building it up out of all the materials, emotional, intellectual, and sensuous, which lie at hand in our consciousness to be synthesised into the hybrid reality which we are to fancy confronting us. To discriminate and redistribute those miscellaneous physical and psychical elements, and to divorce the god from the material sun, is a much later problem, arising at a different and more reflective stage in the Life of Reason.

When reflection, turning to the comprehension of a chaotic experience, busies itself about recurrences, when it seeks to normalise in some way things coming and going, and to straighten out the causes of events, that reflection is inevitably turned toward something dynamic and independent, and can have no successful issue except in mechanical science. When on the other hand reflection stops to challenge and question the fleeting object, not so much to prepare for its possible return as to conceive its present nature, this reflection is turned no less unmistakably in the direction of ideas, and will terminate in logic or the morphology of being. We attribute independence to things in order to normalise their recurrence. We attribute essences to them in order to normalise their manifestations or constitution. Independence will ultimately turn out to be an assumed constancy in material processes, essence an assumed constancy in ideal meanings or points of reference in discourse. The one marks the systematic distribution of objects, the other their settled character.

We talk of recurrent perceptions, but materially considered no perception recurs. Each recurrence is one of a finite series and holds for ever its place and number in that series. Yet human attention, while it can survey several simultaneous impressions and find them similar, cannot keep them distinct if they grow too numerous. The

mind has a native bias and inveterate preference for form and identification. Water does not run down hill more persistently than
attention turns experience into constant terms. The several repetitions of one essence given in consciousness will tend at once to be
neglected, and only the essence itself—the character shared by those
sundry perceptions—will stand and become a term in mental discourse. After a few strokes of the clock, the reiterated impressions
merge and cover one another; we lose count and perceive the
quality and rhythm but not the number of the sounds. If this is
true of so abstract and mathematical a perception as is counting, how
emphatically true must it be of continuous and infinitely varied
perceptions.

The senses in their natural play revert constantly to familiar
objects, gaining impressions which differ but slightly from one another. These slight differences are submerged in apperception, so
that sensation comes to be not so much an addition of new items to
consciousness as a reburnishing there of some imbedded device. To
catch the passing phenomenon in all its novelty and idiosyncrasy is
a work of artifice and curiosity. Such an exercise does violence to
intellectual instinct and involves an aesthetic power of sinking into
the stream of sensation, having thrown overboard all rational ballast
and escaped at once the inertia and the momentum of practical life.
Normally every datum of sense is at once devoured by a hungry
intellect and digested for the sake of its vital juices. The result is
that what ordinarily remains in memory is no representative of particular moments or shocks—but rather a logical possession, a sense
of acquaintance with a certain field of reality, in a word, a consciousness of *knowledge*.

But what, we may ask, is this reality, which we boast to know?
May not the sceptic justly contend that nothing is so unknown and
indeed unknowable as this pretended object of knowledge? The
sensations which reason treats so cavalierly were at least something
actual while they lasted and made good their momentary claim to
our interest; but what is this new ideal figment, unseizable yet ever
present, invisible but indispensable, unknowable yet alone interesting or important? Strange that the only possible object or theme of
our knowledge should be something we cannot know.

An answer to these doubts will perhaps appear if we ask ourselves what sort of contact with reality would satisfy us. Is it a
verification of truth in sense? It would be unreasonable, in that

case, after all the evidence we demand has been gathered, to complain that the supersensible substance, reality, or independent object, does not itself descend into the arena of immediate sensuous
presentation. Knowledge is not eating, and we cannot expect to
devour and possess *what we mean*. Knowledge is recognition of
something absent; it is a salutation, not an embrace. It is an advance
on sensation precisely because it is representative. The terms or
goals of thought have for their function to subtend long tracts of
sensuous experience, to be ideal links between fact and fact, invisible wires behind the scenes, threads along which inference may
run in making phenomena intelligible and controllable. An import
that should become an image would cease to be indicative. Now
external objects are thought to be principles and sources of experience; they are accordingly conceived realities on a deeper plane.
We may look for all the evidence we choose before we declare our
belief to be warranted; but we must not ask for something more
than evidence, nor expect to know realities without conceiving them
anew. They are revealed only to understanding. We cannot cease
to think and still continue to know.

Now the practical burden of such understanding, if you take
the trouble to analyse it, will turn out to be what the sceptic says
it is: assurance of eventual sensations. But as these sensations, in
memory and expectation, are numerous and indefinitely variable,
you are not able to hold them clearly before the mind; indeed,
the realisation of all the potentialities which you vaguely feel to lie
in the future is a task absolutely beyond imagination. Yet your
present impressions are far from representing adequately all that
might be discovered or that is actually known about the object
before you. This object, then, to your apprehension, is not identical
with any of the sensations that reveal it, nor is it exhausted by all
these sensations when they are added together; yet it contains nothing assignable but what they might conceivably reveal. As it lies in
your fancy, then, this object, the reality, is a complex and elusive
entity, the sum at once and the residuum of all particular impressions. With this hybrid object, sensuous in its materials and ideal
in its locus, each particular glimpse is compared, and is recognized
to be but a glimpse, an aspect which the object presents to a particular observer.

Such are the primary relations of reality and appearance. A
reality is a term of discourse based on a psychic complex of mem

ories, associations, and expectations, but constituted in its ideal independence by the assertive energy of thought. An appearance is a passing sensation, recognised as belonging to that group of which the object itself is the conceived representative, and accordingly regarded as a manifestation of that object.

Thus the notion of an independent and permanent world is an ideal term used to mark and as it were to justify the cohesion in space and the recurrence in time of recognisable groups of sensations. This coherence and recurrence force the intellect, if it would master experience at all or understand anything, to frame the idea of such a reality. If we wish to defend the use of such an idea and prove to ourselves its necessity, all we need do is to point to that coherence and recurrence in external phenomena. That brave effort and flight of intelligence which in the beginning raised man to the conception of reality, enabling him to discount and interpret appearance, will, if we retain our trust in reason, raise us continually anew to that same idea, by a no less spontaneous and victorious movement of thought.

CHAPTER 4

NATURE UNIFIED AND MIND DISCERNED

THE THEORY that all real objects and places lie together in one even and homogeneous space, conceived as similar in its constitution to the parts of extension of which we have immediate intuition, is a theory of the greatest practical importance and validity. By its light we carry on all our affairs, and the success of our action while we rely upon it is the best proof of its truth. The imaginative parsimony and discipline which such a theory involves are balanced by the immense extension and certitude it gives to knowledge. It is at once an act of allegiance to nature and a Magna Charta which mind imposes on the tyrannous world, which in turn pledges itself before the assembled faculties of man not to exceed its constitutional privilege and to harbour no magic monsters in unattainable lairs from which they might issue to disturb human labours. Yet that spontaneous intelligence which first enabled men to make this genial discovery and take so fundamental a step toward taming experience should not be laid by after this first victory; it is a weapon needed in many subsequent conflicts. To conceive that all nature makes one system is only a beginning: the articulation of natural life has still to be discovered in detail and, what is more, a similar articulation has to be given to the psychic world which now, by the very act that constitutes Nature and makes her consistent, appears at her side or rather in her bosom.

That the unification of nature is eventual and theoretical is a point useful to remember: else the relation of the natural world to poetry, metaphysics, and religion will never become intelligible. Lalande, or whoever it was, who searched the heavens with his telescope and could find no God, would not have found the human mind if he had searched the brain with a microscope. Yet God existed in man's apprehension long before mathematics or even, perhaps, before the vault of heaven; for the objectification of the whole mind, with its passions and motives, naturally precedes that abstraction by which the idea of a material world is drawn from the chaos of experience, an abstraction which culminates in such atomic

26

and astronomical theories as science is now familiar with. The sense for life in things, be they small or great, is not derived from the abstract idea of their bodies but is an ancient concomitant to that idea, inseparable from it until both became abstract.

What enables men to perceive the unity of nature is the unification of their own wills. A man half-asleep, without fixed purposes, without intellectual keenness or joy in recognition, might graze about like an animal, forgetting each satisfaction in the next and banishing from his frivolous mind the memory of every sorrow; what had just failed to kill him would leave him as thoughtless and unconcerned as if it had never crossed his path. Such irrational elasticity and innocent improvidence would never put two and two together. Every morning there would be a new world with the same fool to live in it. But let some sobering passion, some serious interest, lend perspective to the mind, and a point of reference will immediately be given for protracted observation; then the laws of nature will begin to dawn upon thought. Every experiment will become a lesson, every event will be remembered as favourable or unfavourable to the master-passion. At first, indeed, this keen observation will probably be animistic and the laws discovered will be chiefly habits, human or divine, special favours or envious punishments and warnings. But the same constancy of aim which discovers the dramatic conflicts composing society, and tries to read nature in terms of passion, will, if it be long sustained, discover behind this glorious chaos a deeper consecutive order. Men's thoughts, like the weather, are not so arbitrary as they seem and the true master in observation, the man guided by a steadfast and superior purpose, will see them revolving about their centres in obedience to quite calculable instincts, and the principle of all their flutterings will not be hidden from his eyes. Belief in indeterminism is a sign of indetermination. No commanding or steady intellect flirts with so miserable a possibility, which in so far as it actually prevailed would make virtue impotent and experience, in its pregnant sense, impossible.

We have said that those objects which cannot be incorporated into the one space which the understanding envisages are relegated to another sphere called imagination. We reach here a most important corollary. As material objects, making a single system which fills space and evolves in time, are conceived by projection from the flux of sensuous experience, so, *pari passu*, the rest of experience, with all its other outgrowths and concretions, withdraws into the sphere of mind, the sphere of memory, fancy, and the passions.

Mind, in this proper sense of the word, is the residue of existence, the leavings, so to speak, and parings of experience when the material world has been cut out of the whole cloth. Reflection underlines in the chaotic continuum of sense and longing those aspects that have practical significance; it selects the efficacious ingredients in the world. The trustworthy object which is thus retained in thought, the complex of connected events, is nature, and though so intelligible an object is not soon nor vulgarly recognised, because human reflection is perturbed and halting, yet every forward step in scientific and practical knowledge is a step toward its clearer definition. At first much parasitic drapery clings to that dynamic skeleton. Nature is drawn like a sponge heavy and dripping from the waters of sentience. It is soaked with inefficacious passions and overlaid with idle accretions. Nature, in a word, is at first conceived mythically, dramatically, and retains much of the unintelligible, sporadic habit of animal experience itself. But as attention awakes and discrimination, practically inspired, grows firm and stable, irrelevant qualities are stripped off, and the mechanical process, the efficacious infallible order, is clearly disclosed beneath. Meantime the incidental effects, the "secondary qualities," are relegated to a personal inconsequential region; they people the realm of appearance, the realm of mind.

Mind is therefore sometimes identified with the unreal. We oppose, in an antithesis natural to thought and language, the imaginary to the true, fancy to fact, idea to thing. But this thing, fact, or external reality is, as we discern it, a completion and hypostasis of certain suggestions of experience. The idea of external reality is therefore continuous with the rest of our own minds. Their common substance is the immediate flux. This living worm has propagated by fission, and the two halves into which it has divided its life are mind and nature. Mind has kept and clarified the crude appearance, the dream, the purpose that seethed in the mass; nature has appropriated the order, the constant conditions, the causal substructure, disclosed in reflection, by which the immediate flux is explained and controlled. The chemistry of thought has precipitated these contrasted terms, each maintaining a recognisable identity and having the function of a point of reference for memory and will. Some of these terms or objects of thought we call things and marshal in all their ideal stability—for there is constancy in their motions and transformations—to make the intelligible external world of practice and science. Whatever stuff has not been absorbed in this construction, whatever facts of sensation, ideation, or will, do not coalesce with the newest conception of reality, we then relegate to the mind.

Raw experience, then, lies at the basis of the idea of nature and approves its reality; while an equal reality belongs to the residue of experience, not taken up, as yet, into that idea. But this residual sensuous reality often seems comparatively unreal because what it presents is entirely without practical force apart from its material organs. This inconsequential character of what remains over follows of itself from the concretion of whatever is constant and efficacious into the external world. If this fact is ever called in question, it is only because the external world is vaguely conceived, and loose wills and ideas are thought to govern it by magic. Yet in many ways falling short of absolute precision people recognise that thought is not dynamic or, as they call it, not real. The idea of the physical world is the first flower or thick cream of practical thinking. Being skimmed off first and proving so nutritious, it leaves the liquid below somewhat thin and unsavoury. Especially does this result appear when science is still unpruned and mythical, so that what passes into the idea of material nature is much more than the truly causal network of forces, and includes many spiritual and moral functions.

The material world, as conceived in the first instance, had not that clear abstractness, nor the spiritual world that wealth and interest, which they have acquired for modern minds. The complex reactions of man's soul had been objectified together with those visual and tactile sensations which, reduced to a mathematical baldness, now furnish terms to natural science. Mind then dwelt in the world, not only in the warmth and beauty with which it literally clothed material objects, as it still does in poetic perception, but in a literal animistic way; for human passion and reflection were attributed to every object and made a fairy-land of the world. Poetry and religion discerned life in those very places in which sense and understanding perceived body; and when so much of the burden of experience took wing into space, and the soul herself floated almost visibly among the forms of nature, it is no marvel that the poor remnant, a mass of merely personal troubles, an uninteresting distortion of things in individual minds, should have seemed a sad and unsubstantial accident. The inner world was all the more ghostly because the outer world was so much alive.

This movement of thought, which clothed external objects in all the wealth of undeciphered dreams, has long lost its momentum and yielded to a contrary tendency. Just as the hypostasis of some terms in experience is sanctioned by reason, when the objects so fixed and externalised can serve as causes and explanations for the order of events, so the criticism which tends to retract that hypostasis is sanctioned by reason when the hypostasis has exceeded its function and the external object conceived is loaded with useless ornament. The transcendental and functional secret of such hypostases, however, is seldom appreciated by the headlong mind; so that the ebb no less than the flow of objectification goes on blindly and impulsively, and is carried to absurd extremes. An age of mythology yields to an age of subjectivity; reason being equally neglected and exceeded in both. The reaction against imagination has left the external world, as represented in many minds, stark and bare. All the interesting and vital qualities which matter had once been endowed with have been attributed instead to an irresponsible sensibility in man. And as habits of ideation change slowly and yield only piecemeal to criticism or to fresh intuitions, such a revolution has not been carried out consistently, but instead of a thorough renaming of things and a new organisation of thought it has produced chiefly distress and confusion.

What helps in the first place to disclose a permanent object is a permanent sensation. There is a vast and clear difference between a floating and a fixed feeling; the latter, in normal circumstances, is present only when continuous stimulation renews it at every moment. Attention may wander, but the objects in the environment do not cease to radiate their influences on the body, which is thereby not allowed to lose the modification which those influences provoke. The consequent perception is therefore always at hand and in its repetitions substantially identical. Perceptions not renewed in this way by continuous stimulation come and go with cerebral currents; they are rare visitors, instead of being, like external objects, members of the household. Intelligence is most at home in the ultimate, which is the object of intent. Those realities which it can trust and continually recover are its familiar and beloved companions. The mists that may originally have divided it from them are gladly forgotten so soon as intelligence avails to pierce them, and as friendly communication can be established with the real world. Moreover, perceptions not sustained by a constant external stimulus are apt to be greatly changed when they reappear, and to be changed unaccountably, whereas external things show some method and proportion in their variations. Even when not much changed in themselves, mere ideas fall into a new setting, whereas things, unless something else has intervened to move them, reappear in their old places. Finally things are acted upon by other men, but thoughts are hidden from them by divine privilege.

Existence reveals reality when the flux discloses something permanent that dominates it. The brain, though mobile, is subject to habit; its formations, while they lapse instantly, return again and again. These ideal objects may accordingly seem in a way more real and enduring than things external. Hence no primitive mind puts all reality, or what is most real in reality, in an abstract material universe. It finds, rather, ideal points of reference by which material mutation itself seems to be controlled. An ideal world is recognised from the beginning and placed, not in the immediate foreground, nearer than material things, but much farther off. It has greater substantiality and independence than material objects are credited with. It is divine.

When agriculture, commerce, or manual crafts have given men some knowledge of nature, the world thus recognised and dominated is far from seeming ultimate. It is thought to lie between two others, both now often called mental, but in their original quality altogether disparate: the world of spiritual forces and that of sensuous appearance. The notions of permanence and independence by which material objects are conceived apply also, of course, to spirits. They come and go; they govern nature or, if they neglect to do so, it is from aversion or high indifference; they visit man with obsessions and diseases; they hasten to extricate him from difficulties; and they dwell in him, constituting his powers of conscience and invention. Sense, on the other hand, is a mere effect, either of body or spirit or of both in conjunction. It gives a vitiated personal view of these realities. Its pleasures are dangerous and unintelligent, and it perishes as it goes.

Such are, for primitive apperception, the three great realms of being: nature, sense, and spirit. Their frontiers, however, always remain uncertain. Sense, because it is insignificant when made an object, is long neglected by reflection. No attempt is made to describe its processes or ally them systematically to natural changes. Its illusions, when noticed, are regarded as scandals calculated to foster scepticism. The spiritual world is, on the other hand, a constant theme for poetry and speculation, which are naturally as shifting and self-contradictory as they are persistent. They acquire no fixed character until, in dogmatic religion, they are defined with reference to natural events, foretold or reported. Nature is what first acquires a form and then imparts form to the other spheres. Sense admits definition and distribution only as an effect of nature and spirit only as its principle.

The form nature acquires is, however, itself vague and uncertain and can ill serve, for long ages, to define the other realms which depend on it for definition. Hence it has been common, for instance, to treat the spiritual as a remote or finer form of the natural. Beyond the moon everything seemed permanent; it was therefore called divine and declared to preside over the rest. The breath that escaped from the lips at death, since it took away with it the spiritual control and miraculous life that had quickened the flesh, was itself the spirit. On the other hand, natural processes have been persistently attributed to spiritual causes, for it was not matter that moved itself but intent that moved it. Thus spirit was barbarously taken for a natural substance and a natural force. It was identified with everything in which it was manifested, so long as no natural causes could be assigned for that operation.

If the unification of nature were complete sense would evidently fall within it; since it is to subtend and sustain the sensible flux that intelligence acknowledges first material objects and then their general system. The elements of experience not taken up into the constitution of objects remain attached to them as their life. In the end the dynamic skeleton, without losing its articulation, would be clothed again with its flesh. Suppose my notions of astronomy allowed me to believe that the sun, sinking into the sea, was extinguished every evening, and that what appeared the next morning was his younger brother, hatched in a sun-producing nest to be found in the Eastern regions. My theory would have robbed yesterday's sun of its life and brightness; it would have asserted that during the night no sun existed anywhere; but it would have added the sun's qualities afresh to a matter that did not previously possess them, namely, to the imagined egg that would produce a sun for tomorrow. Suppose we substitute for that astronomy the one that now prevails: we have deprived the single sun—which now exists and spreads its influences without interruption—of its humanity and even of its metaphysical unity. It has become a congeries of chemical substances. The facts revealed to perception have partly changed their locus and been differently deployed throughout nature. Some have become attached to operations in the human brain. Nature has not thereby lost any quality she had ever manifested; these have merely been redistributed so as to secure a more systematic connection between them all. They are the materials of the system, which has been conceived by making existences continuous, whenever this extension of their being was needful to render their recurrences intelligible. Sense, which was formerly regarded as a sad distortion of its objects, now becomes an original and congruent part of nature, from which, as from any other part, the rest of nature might be scientifically inferred.

Spirit is not less closely attached to nature, although in a different manner. Taken existentially it is a part of sense; taken ideally it is the form or value which nature acquires when viewed from the vantage-ground of any interest. Individual objects are recognisable for a time not because the flux is materially arrested but because it somewhere circulates in a fashion which awakens an interest and brings different parts of the surrounding process into definable and prolonged relations with that interest. Particular objects may perish yet others may repeat them, like the series of suns imagined by Heraclitus, to perform the same office. The function will outlast the particular organ and the power attributed to spirit would be the part of nature's fertility by which such expression was secured.

CHAPTER 5

DISCOVERY OF FELLOW-MINDS

WHEN A ghostly sphere, containing memory and all ideas, has been distinguished from the material world, it tends to grow at the expense of the latter, until nature is finally reduced to a mathematical skeleton. This skeleton itself, but for the need of a bridge to connect calculably episode with episode in experience, might be transferred to mind and identified with the scientific thought in which it is represented. But a scientific theory inhabiting a few scattered moments of life cannot connect those episodes among which it is itself the last and the least substantial; nor would such a notion have occurred even to the most reckless sceptic, had the world not possessed another sort of reputed reality—the minds of others—which could serve, even after the supposed extinction of the physical world, to constitute an independent order and to absorb the potentialities of being when immediate consciousness nodded. But other men's minds, being themselves precarious and ineffectual, would never have seemed a possible substitute for nature, to be in her stead the background and intelligible object of experience. Something constant, omnipresent, infinitely fertile is needed to support and connect the given chaos. Just these properties, however, are actually attributed to one of the minds supposed to confront the thinker, namely, the mind of God. The divine mind has therefore always constituted in philosophy either the alternative to nature or her other name: it is *par excellence* the seat of all potentiality and, as Spinoza said, the refuge of all ignorance.

In all social life we envisage fellow-creatures conceived to share the same thoughts and passions and to be similarly affected by events. What is the basis of this conviction? What are the forms it takes, and in what sense is it a part or an expression of reason? This question is difficult, and in broaching it we cannot expect much aid from what philosophers have hitherto said on the subject. For the most part, indeed, they have said nothing, as by Nature's kindly disposition most questions which it is beyond a man's power to answer do not occur to him at all. The suggestions which have actually been made in the matter may be reduced to two: first, that we conceive other men's minds by projecting into their bodies those feelings which we immediately perceive to accompany similar operations in ourselves, that is, we infer alien minds by analogy; and second, that we are immediately aware of them and feel them to be friendly or hostile counterparts of our own thinking and effort, that is, we evoke them by dramatic imagination.

The first suggestion has the advantage that it escapes solipsism by a reasonable argument, provided the existence of the material world has already been granted. But if the material world is called back into the private mind, it is evident that every soul supposed to inhabit it or to be expressed in it must follow it thither, as inevitably as the characters and forces in an imagined story must remain with it in the inventor's imagination. When, on the contrary, nature is left standing, it is reasonable to suppose that animals having a similar origin and similar physical powers should have similar minds, if any of them was to have a mind at all. The theory, however, is not satisfactory on other grounds. We do not in reality associate our own grimaces with the feelings that accompany them and subsequently, on recognising similar grimaces in another, proceed to attribute emotions to him like those we formerly experienced. Our own grimaces are not easily perceived, and other men's actions often reveal passions which we have never had, at least with anything like their suggested colouring and intensity. This first view is strangely artificial and mistakes for the natural origin of the belief in question what may be perhaps its ultimate test.

The second suggestion, on the other hand, takes us into a mystic region. That we evoke the felt souls of our fellows by dramatic imagination is doubtless true; but this does not explain how we come to do so, under what stimulus and in what circumstances. Nor does it avoid solipsism; for the felt counterparts of my own will are echoes within me, while if other minds actually exist they cannot have for their essence to play a game with me in my own fancy. Such society would be mythical, and while the sense for society may well be mythical in its origin, it must acquire some other character if it is to have practical and moral validity. But practical and moral validity is above all what society seems to have. This second theory, therefore, while its feeling for psychological reality is keener, does not make the recognition of other minds intelligible and leaves our faith in them without justification.

Now the fact that crude experience is innocent of modern philosophy has this important consequence: that for crude experience all data whatever lie originally side by side in the same field; bodies are passionate, desire moves them, thought broods in space and is constituted by a visible metamorphosis of its subject matter. Animism or mythology is therefore no artifice. Passions naturally reside in the object they agitate—our own body, if that be the felt seat of some pang, the stars, if the pang can find no nearer resting-place. Only a long and still unfinished education has taught men to separate emotions from things and ideas from their objects. This education was needed because crude experience is a chaos, and the qualities it jumbles together do not march together in time. Reflection must accordingly separate them, if knowledge (that is, ideas with eventual application and correct transcendence) is to exist at all. In other words, action must be adjusted to certain objects and not to others, and those chiefly regarded must have a certain interpretation put upon them by trained apperception. The rest must be treated as moonshine and taken no account of except perhaps in idle and poetic reverie. In this way crude experience grows reasonable and appearance becomes knowledge of reality.

The fundamental reason, then, why we attribute consciousness to animal bodies is that those bodies, before they are conceived to be merely material, are conceived to possess all the qualities which our own consciousness possesses when we behold them. Such a supposition is far from being a paradox, since only this principle justifies us to this day in believing in whatever we may decide to believe in. The qualities attributed to reality must be qualities found in experience, and if we deny their presence in ourselves (*e.g.*, in the case of omniscience), that is only because the idea of self, like that of matter, has already become special and the region of ideals (in which omniscience lies) has been formed into a third sphere. But before the idea of self is well constituted and before the category of ideals has been conceived at all, every ingredient ultimately assigned to those two regions is attracted into the perceptual vortex for which such qualities as pressure and motion supply a nucleus. The moving image is therefore impregnated not only with secondary qualities—colour, heat, etc.—but with qualities which we may call tertiary, such as pain, fear, joy, malice, feebleness, expectancy. Sometimes these tertiary qualities are attributed to the object in their fulness and just as they are felt. Thus the sun is not only bright and warm in the same way as he is round, but by the same right he is also happy, arrogant, ever-young, and all-seeing; for a suggestion of these tertiary qualities runs through us when we look at him, just as immediately as do his warmth and light. The fact that these imaginative suggestions are not constant does not impede the instant perception that they are actual, and for crude experience whatever a thing possesses in appearance it possesses indeed, no matter how soon that quality may be lost again. The moment when things have most numerous and best defined tertiary qualities is accordingly, for crude experience, the moment when they are most adequately manifested and when their inner essence is best revealed; for it is then that they appear in experience most splendidly arrayed and best equipped for their eventual functions. The sun is a better expression of all his ulterior effects when he is conceived to be an arrogant and all-seeing spirit than when he is stupidly felt to be merely hot; so that the attentive and devout observer, to whom those tertiary qualities are revealed, stands in the same relation to an ordinary sensualist, who can feel only the sun's material attributes, as the sensualist in turn stands in to one born blind, who cannot add the sun's brightness to its warmth except by faith in some happier man's reported intuition. The mythologist or poet, before science exists, is accordingly the man of truest and most adequate vision. His persuasion that he knows the heart and soul of things is no fancy reached by artificial inference or analogy but is a direct report of his own experience and honest contemplation.

More often, however, tertiary qualities are somewhat transposed in projection, as sound in being lodged in the bell is soon translated into sonority, made, that is, into its own potentiality. In the same way painfulness is translated into malice or wickedness, terror into hate, and every felt tertiary quality into whatever tertiary quality is in experience its more quiescent or potential form. So religion, which remains for the most part on the level of crude experience, attributes to the gods not only happiness—the object's direct tertiary quality—but goodness—its tertiary quality transposed and made potential; for goodness is that disposition which is fruitful in happiness throughout imagined experience. The devil, in like manner, is cruel and wicked as well as tormented. Uncritical science still attributes these transposed tertiary qualities to nature; the mythical notion of force, for instance, being a transposed sensation of effort. In this case we may distinguish two stages or degrees in the transposition: first, before we think of our own pulling, we say the object itself pulls; in the first transposition we say it pulls against us, its pull is the counterpart or rival of ours but it is still conceived in the same direct terms of effort; and in the second transposition this intermittent effort is made potential or slumbering in what we call strength or force.

It is obvious that the feelings attributed to other men are nothing but the moral suggestions of their behaviour. In beings of the same species, however, these qualities are naturally exceedingly numerous, variable, and precise. Nature has made man man's constant study. His thought, from infancy to the drawing up of his last will and testament, is busy about his neighbour. A smile makes a child happy; a caress, a moment's sympathetic attention, wins a heart and gives the friend's presence a voluminous and poignant value. In youth all seems lost in losing a friend. What the mystic beholds in his ecstasy and loses in his moments of dryness, what the lover pursues and adores, what the child cries for when left alone, is much more a spirit, a person, a haunting power, than a set of visual sensations; yet the visual sensations are connected inextricably with that spirit, else the spirit would not withdraw when the sensations failed. We are not dealing with an articulate mind whose possessions are discriminated and distributed into a mastered world where everything has its department, its special relations, its limited importance; we are dealing with a mind all pulp, all confusion, keenly sensitive to passing influences and reacting on them massively and without reserve.

This mind is feeble, passionate, and ignorant. Its sense for present spirit is no miracle of intelligence or of analogical reasoning; on the contrary, it betrays a vagueness natural to rudimentary consciousness. Those visual sensations suddenly cut off cannot there be recognised for what they are. The consequences which their present disappearance may have for subsequent experience are in no wise foreseen or estimated, much less are any inexperienced feelings invented and attached to that retreating figure, otherwise a mere puppet. What happens is that by the loss of a sustained stimulus the whole chaotic mind is thrown out of gear; the child cries, the lover faints, the mystic feels hell opening before him. Then we feel that we are surrounded by unutterable and most personal hatreds and loves. We allow the half-deciphered images of sense to drag behind them every emotion they have awakened. We endow each overmastering stimulus with all its diffuse effects; and any dramatic potentiality that our dream acts out under that high pressure—and crude experience is rich in dreams—becomes our notion of the life going on before us. We cannot regard it as our own life, because it is not felt to be a passion in our own body, but attaches itself rather to images we see moving about in the world; it is consequently, without hesitation, called the life of those images, or those creatures' souls.

There is evidently one case in which the "pathetic fallacy" is not fallacious, the case in which the object observed happens to be an animal similar to the observer and similarly affected, as for instance when a flock or herd are swayed by panic fear. The emotion which each, as he runs, attributes to the others is, as usual, the emotion he feels himself; but this emotion, fear, is the same which in fact the others are then feeling. Their aspect thus becomes the recognised expression for the feeling which really accompanies it. So in hand-to-hand fighting: the intention and passion which each imputes to the other is what he himself feels; but the imputation is probably just, since pugnacity is a remarkably contagious and monotonous passion. It is awakened by the slightest hostile suggestion and is greatly intensified by example and emulation; those we fight against and those we fight with arouse it concurrently and the universal battle-cry that fills the air, and that each man instinctively emits, is an adequate and exact symbol for what is passing in all their souls.

Whenever, then, feeling is attributed to an animal similar to the percipient and similarly employed the attribution is mutual and correct. Contagion and imitation are great causes of feeling, but in so far as they are its causes and set the pathetic fallacy to work they forestall and correct what is fallacious in that fallacy and turn it into a vehicle of true and, as it were, miraculous insight.

Let the reader meditate for a moment upon the following point: to know reality is, in a way, an impossible pretension, because knowledge means significant representation, discourse about an existence not contained in the knowing thought, and different in duration or locus from the ideas which represent it. But if knowledge does not possess its object how can it intend it? And if knowledge possesses its object, how can it be knowledge or have any practical, prophetic, or retrospective value? Consciousness is not knowledge unless it indicates or signifies what actually it is not. This transcendence is what gives knowledge its cognitive and useful essence, its transitive function and validity. In knowledge, there-fore, there must be some such thing as a justified illusion, an irrational pretension by chance fulfilled, a chance shot hitting the mark. For dead logic would stick at solipsism; yet irrational life, as it stumbles along from moment to moment, and multiplies itself in a thousand centres, is somehow amenable to logic and finds uses for the reason it breeds.

Now, in the relation of a natural being to similar beings in the same habitat there is just the occasion we require for introducing a miraculous transcendence in knowledge, a leap out of solipsism which, though not prompted by reason, will find in reason a con-tinual justification. For tertiary qualities are imputed to objects by psychological or pathological necessity. Something not visible in the object, something not possibly revealed by any future examina-tion of that object, is thus united with it, felt to be its core, its meta-physical truth. Tertiary qualities are emotions or thoughts present in the observer and in his rudimentary consciousness not yet con-nected with their proper concomitants and antecedents, not yet relegated to his private mind, nor explained by his personal endow-ment and situation. To take these private feelings for the substance of other beings is evidently a gross blunder; yet this blunder, with-out ceasing to be one in point of method, ceases to be one in point of fact when the other being happens to be similar in nature and situa-tion to the mythologist himself and therefore actually possesses the very emotions and thoughts which lie in the mythologist's bosom and are attributed by him to his fellow. Thus an imaginary self-transcendence, a rash pretension to grasp an independent reality and to know the unknowable, may find itself accidentally rewarded. Imagination will have drawn a prize in its lottery and the patho-logical accidents of thought will have begotten knowledge and right reason. The inner and unattainable core of other beings will have been revealed to private intuition.

This miracle of insight, as it must seem to those who have not understood its natural and accidental origin, extends only so far as does the analogy between the object and the instrument of percep-tion. The gift of intuition fails in proportion as the observer's bodily habit differs from the habit and body observed. Misunderstanding begins with constitutional divergence and deteriorates rapidly into

false imputations and absurd myths. The limits of mutual understanding coincide with the limits of similar structure and common
occupation, so that the distortion of insight begins very near home.
It is hard to understand the minds of children unless we retain
unusual plasticity and capacity to play; men and women do not
really understand each other, what rules between them being not so
much sympathy as habitual trust, idealisation, or satire; foreigners'
minds are pure enigmas, and those attributed to animals are a
grotesque compound of Æsop and physiology. When we come to
religion the ineptitude of all the feelings attributed to nature or the
gods is so egregious that a sober critic can look to such fables only
for a pathetic expression of human sentiment and need; while, even
apart from the gods, each religion itself is quite unintelligible to
infidels who have never followed its worship sympathetically or
learned by contagion the human meaning of its sanctions and formulas. Hence the stupidity and want of insight commonly shown
in what calls itself the history of religions. We hear, for instance,
that Greek religion was frivolous, because its mystic awe and momentous practical and poetic truths escape the Christian historian
accustomed to a catechism and a religious morality; and similarly
Catholic piety seems to the Protestant an aesthetic indulgence, a
religion appealing to sense, because such is the only emotion its
externals can awaken in him, unused as he is to a supernatural economy reaching down into the incidents and affections of daily life.

Language is an artificial means of establishing unanimity and
transferring thought from one mind to another. Every symbol or
phrase, like every gesture, throws the observer into an attitude to
which a certain idea corresponded in the speaker; to fall exactly
into the speaker's attitude is exactly to understand. Every impediment to contagion and imitation in expression is an impediment to
comprehension. For this reason language, like all art, becomes pale
with years; words and figures of speech lose their contagious and
suggestive power; the feeling they once expressed can no longer be
restored by their repetition. Even the most inspired verse, which
boasts not without a relative justification to be immortal, becomes
in the course of ages a scarcely legible hieroglyphic; the language
it was written in dies, a learned education and an imaginative effort
are requisite to catch even a vestige of its original force. Nothing is
so irrevocable as mind.

Unsure the ebb and flood of thought,
The moon comes back, the spirit not.

There is, however, a wholly different and far more positive
method of reading the mind, or what in a metaphorical sense is
called by that name. This method is to read character. Any creature
with which we are familiar teaches us to divine its habits; slight
indications which we should be at a loss to enumerate separately,
betray what changes are going on and what promptings are simmering in that organism. Hence the expression of a face or figure;
hence the traces of habit and passion visible in a man and that indescribable something about him which inspires confidence or mis-
trust. The gift of reading character is partly instinctive, partly a
result of experience; it may amount to foresight and is directed not
upon consciousness but upon past or eventual action. Habits and
passions, however, have sensuous names, though indicating dispositions rather than particular acts (a disposition being mythically
represented as a sort of wakeful and haunting genius waiting to
whisper suggestions in a man's ear). We may accordingly delude
ourselves into imagining that a pose or a manner which really indicates habit indicates feeling instead. In truth the feeling involved,
if conceived at all, is conceived most vaguely, and is only a sort
of reverberation or penumbra surrounding the pictured activities.

It is a mark of the connoisseur to be able to read character and
habit and to divine at a glance all a creature's potentialities. This
sort of penetration characterises the man with an eye for horse-
flesh, the dog-fancier, and men and women of the world. It guides
the born leader in the judgments he instinctively passes on his subordinates and enemies; it distinguishes every good judge of human
affairs or of natural phenomena, who is quick to detect small but
telling indications of events past or brewing. As the weather-
prophet reads the heavens so the man of experience reads other
men. Nothing concerns him less than their consciousness; he can
allow that to run itself off when he is sure of their temper and
habits. A great master of affairs is usually unsympathetic. His observation is not in the least dramatic or dreamful, he does not yield
himself to animal contagion or re-enact other people's inward experience. He is too busy for that, and too intent on his own purposes. His observation, on the contrary, is straight calculation and
inference, and it sometimes reaches truths about people's character

and destiny which they themselves are very far from divining. Such apprehension is masterful and odious to weaklings, who think they know themselves because they indulge in copious soliloquy (which is the discourse of brutes and madmen) but who really know nothing of their own capacity, situation, or fate.

If Rousseau, for instance, after writing those Confessions in which candour and ignorance of self are equally conspicuous, had heard some intelligent friend, like Hume, draw up in a few words an account of their author's true and contemptible character, he would have been loud in protestations that no such ignoble characteristics existed in his eloquent consciousness; and they might not have existed there, because his consciousness was a histrionic thing, and as imperfect an expression of his own nature as of man's. When the mind is irrational no practical purpose is served by stopping to understand it, because such a mind is irrelevant to practice, and the principles that guide the man's practice can be as well understood by eliminating his mind altogether. So a wise governor ignores his subjects' religion or concerns himself only with its economic and temperamental aspects; if the real forces that control life are understood, symbols that do not represent those forces may be disregarded. But such a government, like that of the British in India, is more practical than sympathetic. While wise men may endure it for the sake of their material interests, they will never love it for itself. There is nothing sweeter than to be sympathised with, while nothing requires a rarer intellectual heroism than willingness to see one's equation written out.

Nevertheless this same algebraic sense for character plays a large part in human friendship. A chief element in friendship is trust, and trust is not to be acquired by reproducing consciousness but only by penetrating to the constitutional instincts which, in determining action and habit, determine consciousness as well. Fidelity is not a property of ideas. It is a virtue possessed pre-eminently by nature, from the animals to the seasons and the stars. But fidelity gives friendship its deepest sanctity, and the respect we have for a man, for his force, ability, constancy, and dignity, is no sentiment evoked by his floating thoughts but an assurance founded on our own observation that his conduct and character are to be counted upon.

The expression of habit in psychic metaphors is a procedure known also to theology. What is conceived is the god's operation, not his emotions. In this way God's goodness becomes a symbol for the advantages of life, his wrath a symbol for its dangers, his commandments a symbol for its laws. The deity spoken of by the Stoics had exclusively this symbolic character; it could be called a city— dear City of Zeus—as readily as an intelligence. And that intelligence which ancient and ingenuous philosophers said they saw in the world was always intelligence in this algebraic sense, it was intelligible order. Nor did the Hebrew prophets, in their emphatic political philosophy, seem to mean much more by Jehovah than a moral order, a principle giving vice and virtue their appropriate fruits.

CHAPTER 6

CONCRETIONS IN DISCOURSE AND IN EXISTENCE

IDEAS OF material objects ordinarily absorb the human mind, and their prevalence has led to the rash supposition that ideas of all other kinds are posterior to those of bodies and drawn from the latter by a process of abstraction. The table, people said, was a particular and single reality; its colour, form, and material were parts of its integral nature, qualities which might be attended to separately, perhaps, but which actually existed only in the table itself. Colour, form, and material were therefore abstract elements. They might come before the mind separately and be contrasted objects of attention, but they were incapable of existing in nature except together, in the concrete reality called a particular thing. Moreover, as the same colour, shape, or substance might be found in various tables, these abstract qualities were thought to be general qualities as well; they were universal terms which might be predicated of many individual things. A contrast could then be drawn between these qualities or ideas, which the mind may envisage, and the concrete reality existing beyond. Thus philosophy could reach the familiar maxim of Aristotle that the particular alone exists in nature and the general alone in the mind.

Such language expresses correctly enough a secondary conventional stage of conception, but it ignores the primary fictions on which convention itself must rest. Individual physical objects must be discovered before abstractions can be made from their conceived nature; the bird must be caught before it is plucked. To discover a physical object is to pack in the same part of space, and fuse in one complex body, primary data like coloured form and tangible surface. Intelligence, observing these sensible qualities, identifies them in their operation although they remain for ever distinct in their sensible character. It is altogether erroneous, therefore, to view an object's sensible qualities as abstractions from it, seeing that, for us, they are its original and component elements.

The immediate continuum may be traversed and mapped by two different methods. The prior one, because it is so very primitive and rudimentary, and so much a condition of all mental discourse, is usually ignored in psychology. The secondary method, by which external things are discovered, has received more attention. The latter consists in the fact that when several disparate sensations, having become recognisable in their repetitions, are observed to come and go together, or in fixed relation to some voluntary operation on the observer's part, they may be associated by contiguity and merged in one portion of perceived space. Those having, like sensations of touch and sight, an essentially spatial character, may easily be superposed; the surface I see and that I touch may be identified by being presented together and being found to undergo simultaneous variations and to maintain common relations to other perceptions. Thus I may come to attribute to a single object, the term of an intellectual synthesis and ideal intention, my experiences through all the senses within a certain field of association, defined by its practical relations. That ideal object is thereby endowed with as many qualities and powers as I had associable sensations of which to make it up. This object is a concretion of my perceptions in space, so that the redness, hardness, sweetness, and roundness of the apple are all fused together in my practical regard and given one local habitation and one name.

This kind of synthesis, this superposition and mixture of images into notions of physical objects, is not, however, the only kind to which perceptions are subject. They fall together by virtue of their qualitative identity even before their spatial superposition; for in order to be known as repeatedly simultaneous, and associable by contiguity, they must be associated by similarity and known as individually repeated. The various recurrences of a sensation must be recognised as recurrences, and this implies the collection of sensations into classes of similars and the apperception of a common nature in several data. Now the more frequent a perception is the harder it will be to discriminate in memory its past occurrences from one another, and yet the more readily will its present recurrence be recognised as familiar. The perception in sense will consequently be received as a repetition not of any single earlier sensation but of a familiar and generic appearance. This will be the one habitual *idea* with which recurring sensations will be henceforth identified. Such a living concretion of similars succeeding one another in time, is the idea of a nature or quality, the universal falsely supposed to be an abstraction from physical objects, which in truth are conceived by putting together these very ideas into a spatial and permanent system.

Here we have, if I am not mistaken, the origin of the two terms most prominent in human knowledge, ideas and things. Two methods of conception divide our attention in common life; science and philosophy develop both, although often with an unjustifiable bias in favour of one or the other. They are nothing but the old principles of Aristotelian psychology, association by similarity and association by contiguity. Only now, after logicians have exhausted their ingenuity in criticising them and psychologists in applying them, we may go behind the traditional position and apply the ancient principles at a deeper stage of mental life.

Intellectual dominion of the conscious stream begins with the act of recognising these pervasive entities, which having character and ideal permanence can furnish common points of reference for different moments of discourse. Save for ideas no perception could have significance, or acquire that indicative force which we call knowledge. For it would refer to nothing to which another perception might also have referred; and so long as perceptions have no common reference, so long as successive moments do not enrich by their contributions the same object of thought, evidently experience, in the pregnant sense of the word, is impossible. No fund of valid ideas, no wisdom, could in that case be acquired by living.

Ideas are creatures of intelligence, goals of thought, ideal terms which cogitation and action circle about. As the centre of mass in a body, while it may by chance coincide with one or another of its atoms, is no atom itself and no material constituent of the bulk that obeys its motion, so an idea, the centre of mass of a certain mental system, is no material fragment of that system. The peculiarity of life is that it lives; and thought also, when living, passes out of itself and directs itself on the ideal, on the eventual. It is an act. An act does not consist in velocity of change but in constancy of purpose; in the conspiracy of many moments and many processes toward one ideal harmony and one concomitant ideal result. The most rudimentary apperception, recognition, or expectation, is already a case of indicative cognition, of transitive thought resting in a permanent essence. Memory is an obvious case of the same thing; for the past, in its truth, is a system of events in relation, a

system now non-existent and never, as a system, itself experienced,
yet confronted in retrospect and made the ideal object and standard
for historical thinking.

These arrested and recognisable ideas, concretions of similars
succeeding one another in time, are not abstractions; but they may
come to be regarded as such after the other kind of concretions in
experience, concretions of superposed perceptions in space, have
become the leading objects of attention. The sensuous material for
both concretions is the same; the perception which, recurring at
different moments otherwise not retained in memory gives the idea
of roundness, is the same perception which helps to constitute the
spatial concretion called the sun. Roundness may therefore be
carelessly called an abstraction from the real object "sun"; whereas
the peculiar optical and muscular feelings by which the sense of
roundness is constituted—probably feelings of gyration and perpetual unbroken movement—are much earlier than any solar observations; they are a self-sufficing element in experience which, by
repetition in various accidental contests, has come to be recognised
and named, and to be a characteristic by virtue of which more complex objects can be distinguished and defined. The idea of the sun
is a much later product, and the real sun is so far from being an
original datum from which roundness is abstracted, that it is an
ulterior and quite ideal construction, a spatial concretion into which
the logical concretion roundness enters as a prior and independent
factor. Roundness may be felt in the dark, by a mere suggestion of
motion, and is a complete experience in itself. When this recognisable experience happens to be associated by contiguity with other
recognisable experiences of heat, light, height, and yellowness, and
these various independent objects are projected into the same portion of a real space; then a concretion occurs, and these ideas being
recognised in that region and finding a momentary embodiment
there, become the qualities of a thing.

A conceived thing is doubly a product of mind, more a product
of mind, if you will, than an idea, since ideas arise, so to speak, by
the mind's inertia and conceptions of things by its activity. Ideas
are mental sediment; conceived things are mental growths. A concretion in discourse occurs by repetition and mere emphasis on a
datum, but a concretion in existence requires a synthesis of disparate
elements and relations. An idea is nothing but a sensation apper-

ceived and rendered cognitive, so that it envisages its own recognised character as its object and ideal: yellowness is only some sensation of yellow raised to the cognitive power and employed as the symbol for its own specific essence. It is consequently capable of entering as a term into rational discourse and of becoming the subject or predicate of propositions eternally valid. A thing, on the contrary, is discovered only when the order and grouping of such recurring essences can be observed, and when various themes and strains of experience are woven together into elaborate progressive harmonies. When consciousness first becomes cognitive it frames ideas; but when it becomes cognitive of causes, that is, when it becomes practical, it perceives things.

Concretions of qualities recurrent in time and concretions of qualities associated in existence are alike involved in daily life and inextricably ingrown into the structure of reason. In consciousness and for logic, association by similarity, with its aggregations and identifications of recurrences in time, is fundamental rather than association by contiguity and its existential syntheses; for recognition identifies similars perceived in succession, and without recognition of similars there could be no known persistence of phenomena. But physiologically and for the observer association by contiguity comes first. All instinct—without which there would be no fixity or recurrence in ideation—makes movement follow impression in an immediate way which for consciousness becomes a mere juxtaposition of sensations, a juxtaposition which it can neither explain nor avoid. Yet this juxtaposition, in which pleasure, pain, and striving are prominent factors, is the chief stimulus to attention and spreads before the mind that moving and variegated field in which it learns to make its first observations. Facts—the burdens of successive moments—are all associated by contiguity, from the first facts of perception and passion to the last facts of fate and conscience. We undergo events, we grow into character, by the subterraneous working of irrational forces that make their incalculable irruptions into life none the less wonderfully in the revelations of a man's heart to himself than in the cataclysms of the world around him. Nature's placid procedure, to which we yield so willingly in times of prosperity, is a concatenation of states which can only be understood when it is made its own standard and law. A sort of philosophy without wisdom may seek to subjugate this natural life, this blind budding of existence, to some logical or moral necessity; but this very attempt remains, perhaps, the most striking monument to that irrational fatality that rules affairs, a monument which reason itself is compelled to raise with unsuspected irony.

Active life and the philosophy that borrows its concepts from practice have thus laid a great emphasis on association by contiguity. Hobbes and Locke made knowledge of this kind the only knowledge of reality, while recognising it to be quite empirical, tentative, and problematical. It was a kind of acquaintance with fact that increased with years and brought the mind into harmony with something initially alien to it. Besides this practical knowledge or prudence there was a sort of verbal and merely ideal knowledge, a knowledge of the meaning and relation of abstract terms. In mathematics and logic we might carry out long trains of abstracted thought and analyse and develop our imaginations *ad infinitum*. These speculations, however, were in the air or—what for these philosophers is much the same thing—in the mind; their applicability and their relevance to practical life and to objects given in perception remained quite problematical. A self-developing science, a synthetic science *a priori*, had a value entirely hypothetical and provisional; its practical truth depended on the verification of its results in some eventual sensible experience. Association was invoked to explain the adjustment of ideation to the order of external perception. Association, by which association by contiguity was generally understood, thus became the battle-cry of empiricism; if association by similarity had been equally in mind, the philosophy of pregnant reason could also have adopted the principle for its own. But logicians and mathematicians naturally neglect the psychology of their own processes and, accustomed as they are to an irresponsible and constructive use of the intellect, regard as a confused and uninspired intruder the critic who, by a retrospective and naturalistic method, tries to give them a little knowledge of themselves.

Rational ideas must arise somehow in the mind, and since they are not meant to be without application to the world of experience, it is interesting to discover the point of contact between the two and the nature of their interdependence. This would have been found in the mind's initial capacity to frame objects of two sorts, those compacted of sensations that are persistently similar, and those compacted of sensations that are momentarily fused. In empirical philosophy the applicability of logic and mathematics remains a miracle or becomes a misinterpretation: a miracle if the process of nature independently follows the inward elaboration of human ideas; a misinterpretation if the bias of intelligence imposes *a priori* upon reality a character and order not inherent in it. The mistake of empiricists—among which Kant is in this respect to be numbered —which enabled them to disregard this difficulty, was that they admitted, beside rational thinking, another instinctive kind of wisdom by which men could live, a wisdom the Englishmen called experience and the Germans practical reason, spirit, or will. The intellectual sciences could be allowed to spin themselves out in abstracted liberty while man practised his illogical and inspired art of life.

Here we observe a certain elementary crudity or barbarism which the human spirit often betrays when it is deeply stirred. Not only are chance and divination welcomed into the world but they are reverenced all the more, like the wind and fire of idolaters, precisely for not being amenable to the petty rules of human reason. In truth, however, the English duality between prudence and science is no more fundamental than the German duality between reason and understanding. The true contrast is between impulse and reflection, instinct and intelligence. When men feel the primordial authority of the animal in them and have little respect for a glimmering reason which they suspect to be secondary but cannot discern to be ultimate, they readily imagine they are appealing to something higher than intelligence when in reality they are falling back on something deeper and lower. The rudimentary seems to them at such moments divine; and if they conceive a Life of Reason at all they despise it as a mass of artifices and conventions. Reason is indeed not indispensable to life, nor needful if living anyhow be the sole and indeterminate aim; as the existence of animals and of most men sufficiently proves. In so far as man is not a rational being and does not live in and by the mind, in so far as his chance volitions and dreamful ideas roll by without mutual representation or adjustment, in so far as his body takes the lead and even his galvanised action is a form of passivity, we may truly say that his life is not intellectual and not dependent on the application of general concepts to experience; for he lives by instinct.

The Life of Reason, the comprehension of causes and pursuit

of aims, begins precisely where instinctive operation ceases to be merely such by becoming conscious of its purposes and representative of its conditions. Logical forms of thought impregnate and constitute practical intellect. The shock of experience can indeed correct, disappoint, or inhibit rational expectation, but it cannot take its place. The very first lesson that experience should again teach us after our disappointment would be a rebirth of reason in the soul. Reason has the indomitable persistence of all natural tendencies; it returns to the attack as waves beat on the shore. To observe its defeat is already to give it a new embodiment. Prudence itself is a vague science and science, when it contains real knowledge, is but a clarified prudence, a description of experience and a guide to life. Speculative reason, if it is not also practical, is not reason at all. Propositions irrelevant to experience may be correct in form, the method they are reached by may parody scientific method, but they cannot be true in substance, because they refer to nothing. Like music, they have no object. They merely flow, and please those whose unattached sensibility they somehow flatter.

Hume, in this respect more radical and satisfactory than Kant himself, saw with perfect clearness that reason was an ideal expression of instinct, and that consequently no rational spheres could exist other than the mathematical and the empirical, and that what is not a datum must certainly be a construction. In establishing his "tendencies to feign" at the basis of intelligence, and in confessing that he yielded to them himself no less in his criticism of human nature than in his practical life, he admitted the involution of reason—that unintelligible instinct—in all the observations and maxims vouchsafed to an empiricist or to a man. He veiled his doctrine, however, in a somewhat meager and satirical nomenclature, and he has paid the price of that indulgence in personal humour by incurring the immortal hatred of sentimentalists who are too much scandalised by his tone ever to understand his principles.

If the common mistake in empiricism is not to see the omnipresence of reason in thought, the mistake of rationalism is not to admit its variability and dependence, not to understand its natural life. Parmenides was the Adam of that race, and first tasted the deceptive kind of knowledge which, promising to make man God, banishes him from the paradise of experience. His sin has been transmitted to his descendants, though hardly in its magnificent and simple enormity. "The whole is one," Xenophanes had cried, gazing into heaven; and that same sense of a permeating identity, translated into rigid and logical terms, brought his sublime disciple to the conviction that an indistinguishable immutable substance was omnipresent in the world. Parmenides carried association by similarity to such lengths that he arrived at the idea of what alone is similar in everything, viz., the fact that it is. Being exists, and nothing else does; whereby every relation and variation in experience is reduced to a negligible illusion, and reason loses its function at the moment of asserting its absolute authority. Notable lesson, taught us like so many others by the first experiments of the Greek mind, in its freedom and insight, a mind led quickly by noble self-confidence to the ultimate goals of thought.

Such a pitch of heroism and abstraction has not been reached by any rationalist since. No one else has been willing to ignore entirely all the data and constructions of experience, save the highest concept reached by assimilations in that experience; no one else has been willing to demolish all the scaffolding and all the stones of his edifice, hoping still to retain the sublime symbol which he had planted on the summit. Yet all rationalists have longed to demolish or to degrade some part of the substructure, like those Gothic architects who wished to hang the vaults of their churches upon the slenderest possible supports, abolishing and turning into painted crystal all the dead walls of the building. So experience and its crowning conceptions were to rest wholly on a skeleton of general natures, physical forces being assimilated to logical terms, and concepts gained by identification of similars taking the place of those gained by grouping disparate things in their historical conjunctions. The eye was to be trained to pass from that particoloured chaos to the firm lines and permanent divisions that were supposed to sustain it and frame it in.

Rationalism is a kind of builder's bias which the impartial public cannot share; for the dead walls and glass screens which may have no function in supporting the roof are yet as needful as the roof itself to shelter and beauty. So the incidental filling of experience which remains unclassified under logical categories retains all its primary reality and importance. The outlines of it emphasised by logic, though they may be the essential vehicle of our most soaring thoughts, are only a method and a style of architecture. They neither absorb the whole material of life nor monopolise its values. And as each material imposes upon the builder's ingenuity a different type of construction, and stone, wood, and iron must be treated on different structural principles, so logical methods of comprehension, spontaneous though they be in their mental origin, must prove themselves fitted to the natural order and affinity of the facts. Nor is there in this necessity any violence to the spontaneity of reason: for reason also has manifold forms, and the accidents of experience are more than matched in variety by the multiplicity of categories. Here one principle of order and there another shoots into the mind, which breeds more genera and species than the most fertile terrestrial slime can breed individuals.

Language, then, with the logic imbedded in it, is a repository of terms formed by identifying successive perceptions, as the external world is a repository of objects conceived by superposing qualities that exist together. Being formed on different principles these two orders of conception—the logical and the physical—do not coincide, and the attempt to fuse them into one system of demonstrable reality or moral physics is doomed to failure by the very nature of the terms compared. When the Eleatics proved the impossibility— *i.e.*, the inexpressibility—of motion, or when Kant and his followers proved the unreal character of all objects of experience and of all natural knowledge, their task was made easy by the native diversity between the concretions in existence which were the object of their thought and the concretions in discourse which were its measure. The two do not fit; and intrenched as these philosophers were in the forms of logic they compelled themselves to reject as unthinkable everything not fully expressible in those particular forms. Thus they took their revenge upon the vulgar who, being busy chiefly with material things and dwelling in an atmosphere of sensuous images, call unreal and abstract every product of logical construction or reflective analysis. These logical products, however, are not really abstract, but, as we have seen, concretions arrived at by a different method than that which results in material conceptions.

Thus the many armed with prejudice and the few armed with logic fight an eternal battle, the logician charging the physical world with unintelligibility and the man of common-sense charging the logical world with abstractness and unreality. The former view is the more profound, since association by similarity is the more elementary and gives constancy to meanings; while the latter view is the more practical, since association by contiguity alone informs the mind about the natural occasions of its own experience. Neither principle can be dispensed with, and each errs only in denouncing the other and wishing to be omnivorous, as if on the one hand logic could make anybody understand the history of events and the conjunction of objects, or on the other hand as if cognitive and moral processes could have any other terms than constant and ideal natures.

CHAPTER 7

ON THE RELATIVE VALUE OF THINGS AND IDEAS

IT IS a remarkable fact, which may easily be misinterpreted, that while all the benefits and pleasures of life seem to be associated with external things, and all certain knowledge seems to describe material laws, yet a deified nature has generally inspired a religion of melancholy. Why has man's conscience in the end invariably rebelled against naturalism and reverted in some form or other to a cultus of the unseen?

We may answer in the words of Saint Paul: because things seen are temporal and things not seen are eternal. And we may add, remembering our analysis of the objects inhabiting the mind, that the eternal is the truly human, that which is akin to the first indispensable products of intelligences, which arise by the fusion of successive images in discourse, and transcend the particular in time, peopling the mind with permanent and recognisable objects, and strengthening it with a synthetic, dramatic apprehension of itself and its own experience. Concretion in existence, on the contrary, yields essentially detached and empirical unities, foreign to mind in spite of their order, and unintelligible in spite of their clearness. Reason fails to assimilate in them precisely that which makes them real, namely, their presence here and now, in this order and number. The form and quality of them we can retain, domesticate, and weave into the texture of reflection, but their existence and individuality remain a datum of sense needing to be verified anew at every moment and actually receiving continual verification or disproof while we live in this world.

"This world" we call it, not without justifiable pathos, for many other worlds are conceivable and if discovered might prove more rational and intelligible and more akin to the soul than this strange universe which man has hitherto always looked upon with increasing astonishment. When an empirical philosophy, therefore, calls us back from the irresponsible flights of imagination to the shock of sense and tries to remind us that in this alone we touch existence and come upon fact, we feel dispossessed of our nature and cramped in our life. The dependence upon sense, which we are reduced to when we consider the world of existences, becomes a too plain hint of our essential impotence and mortality, while the play of logical fancy, though it remain inevitable, is saddened by a consciousness of its own insignificance.

That dignity, then, which inheres in logical ideas and their affinity to moral enthusiasm, springs from their congruity with the primary habits of intelligence and idealisation. The soul or self or personality, which in sophisticated social life is so much the centre of passion and concern, is itself an idea, a concretion in discourse; and the level at which it swims comes to be, by association and affinity, the region of all the more vivid and massive human interests. The pleasures which lie beneath it are despised, and the ideals which lie above it are not perceived. Aversion to an empirical or naturalistic philosophy accordingly expresses a sort of logical patriotism and attachment to homespun ideas. The actual is too remote and unfriendly to the dreamer; to understand it he has to learn a foreign tongue, which his native prejudice imagines to be unmeaning and unpoetical. The truth is, however, that nature's language is too rich for man; and the discomfort he feels when he is compelled to use it merely marks his lack of education. There is nothing cheaper than idealism. It can be had by merely not observing the ineptitude of our chance prejudices, and by declaring that the first rhymes that have struck our ear are the eternal and necessary harmonies of the world.

The thinker's bias is naturally favourable to logical ideas. The man of reflection will attribute, as far as possible, validity and reality to these alone. Platonism remains the classic instance of this way of thinking. Living in an age of rhetoric, with an education that dealt with nothing but ideal entities, verbal, moral, or mathematical, Plato saw in concretions in discourse the true elements of being. Definable meanings, being the terms of thought, must also, he fancied, be the constituents of reality. And with that directness and audacity which was possible to the ancient, and of which Pythagoreans and Eleatics had already given brilliant examples, he set up these terms of discourse, like the Pythagorean numbers, for absolute and eternal entities, existing before all things, revealed in all things, giving the cosmic artificer his models and the creature his goal. By some inexplicable necessity the creation had taken place. The ideas had multiplied themselves in a flux of innumerable images which could be recognised by their resemblance to their originals, but were at once canceled and expunged by virtue of their essential inadequacy. What sounds are to words and words to thoughts, that was a thing to its idea.

Plato, however, retained the moral and significant essence of his ideas, and while he made them ideal absolutes, fixed meanings antecedent to their changing expressions, never dreamed that they could be natural existences, or psychological beings. In an original thinker, in one who really thinks and does not merely argue, to call a thing supernatural, or spiritual, or intelligible is to declare that it is no *thing* at all, no existence actual or possible, but a value, a term of thought, a merely ideal principle; and the more its reality in such a sense is insisted on the more its incommensurability with brute existence is asserted. To express this ideal reality myth is the natural vehicle; a vehicle Plato could avail himself of all the more freely that he inherited a religion still plastic and conscious of its poetic essence, and did not have to struggle, like his modern disciples, with the arrested childishness of minds that for a hundred generations have learned their metaphysics in the cradle. His ideas, although their natural basis was ignored, were accordingly always ideal; they always represented meanings and functions and were never degraded from the moral to the physical sphere. The counterpart of this genuine ideality was that the theory retained its moral forces and did not degenerate into a bewildered and idolatrous pantheism. Plato conceived the soul's destiny to be her emancipation from those material things which in this illogical apparition were so alien to her essence. She should return, after her baffling and stupefying intercourse with the world of sense and accident, into the native heaven of her ideas. For animal desires were no less illusory, and yet no less significant, than sensuous perceptions. They engaged man in the pursuit of the good and taught him, through disappointment, to look for it only in those satisfactions which can be permanent and perfect. Love, like intelligence, must rise from appearance to reality, and rest in that divine world which is the fulfilment of the human.

A geometrician does a good service when he declares and explicates the nature of the triangle, an object suggested by many casual and recurring sensations. His service is not less real, even if less obvious, when he arrests some fundamental concretion in discourse, and formulates the first principles of logic. Mastering such definitions, sinking into the dry life of such forms, he may spin out and develop indefinitely, in the freedom of his irresponsible logic, their implications and congruous extensions, opening by his demonstration a depth of knowledge which we should otherwise never have discovered in ourselves. But if the geometer had a fanatical zeal and forbade us to consider space and the triangles it contains otherwise than as his own ideal science considers them: forbade us, for instance, to inquire how we came to perceive those triangles or that space; what organs and senses conspired in furnishing the idea of them; what material objects show that character, and how they came to offer themselves to our observation—then surely the geometer would qualify his service with a distinct injury and while he opened our eyes to one fascinating vista would tend to blind them to others no less tempting and beautiful. For the naturalist and psychologist have also their rights and can tell us things well worth knowing; nor will any theory they may possibly propose concerning the origin of spatial ideas and their material embodiments ever invalidate the demonstrations of geometry. These, in their hypothetical sphere, are perfectly autonomous and self-generating, and their applicability to experience will hold so long as the initial images they are applied to continue to abound in perception.

If we awoke to-morrow in a world containing nothing but music, geometry would indeed lose its relevance to our future experience; but it would keep its ideal cogency, and become again a living language if any spatial objects should ever reappear in sense.

The history of such reappearances—natural history—is meantime a good subject for observation and experiment. Chronicler and critic can always approach reality with a method complementary to the deductive methods pursued in mathematics and logic: instead of developing the import of a definition, the prophet develops the import of his trance, and the theologian the import of the prophecy: which prevents not the historian from coming later and showing the origin, the growth, and the possible function of that maniacal sort of wisdom. True, the theologian commonly dreads a critic more than does the geometer, but this happens only because the theologian has probably not developed the import of his facts with any austerity or clearness, but has distorted that ideal interpretation with all sorts of concessions and side-glances at other tenets to which he is already pledged, so that he justly fears, when his methods are exposed, that the religious heart will be alienated from him and his conclusions be left with no foothold in human nature. If he had not been guilty of such misrepresentation, no history or criticism that reviewed his construction would do anything but recommend it to all those who found in themselves the primary religious facts and religious faculties which that construction had faithfully interpreted in its ideal deductions and extensions. All who perceived the facts would thus learn their import; and theology would reveal to the soul her natural religion.

The most legitimate constructions of reason soon become merely speculative, soon pass, I mean, beyond the sphere of practical application; and the man of affairs, adjusting himself at every turn to the opaque brutality of fact, loses his respect for the higher reaches of logic and forgets that his recognition of facts themselves is an application of logical principles. In his youth, perhaps, he pursued metaphysics, which are the love-affairs of the understanding; now he is wedded to convention and seeks in the passion he calls business or in the habit he calls duty some substitute for natural happiness. He fears to question the value of his life, having found that such questioning adds nothing to his powers; and he thinks the mariner would die of old age in port who should wait for reason to justify his voyage. Reason is indeed like the sad Iphigenia whom her royal father, the Will, must sacrifice before any wind can fill his sails. The emanation of all things from the One involves not only the incarnation but the crucifixion of the Logos. Reason must be eclipsed by its supposed expressions, and can only shine in a darkness which does not comprehend it. For reason is essentially hypothetical and subsidiary, and can never constitute what it expresses in man, nor what it recognises in nature. The idea of nature remains true after psychology has analysed its origin, and not only true, but beautiful and beneficent. For unlike many negligible products of speculative fancy it is woven out of recurrent perceptions into a hypothetical cause from which further perceptions can be deduced as they are actually experienced.

Such a naturalism once discovered confirms itself at every breath we draw, and surrounds every object in history and nature with infinite and true suggestions, making it doubly interesting, fruitful, and potent over the mind. The naturalist accordingly welcomes criticism because his constructions, though no less hypothetical and speculative than the idealist's dreams, are such legitimate and fruitful fictions that they are obvious truths. For truth, at the intelligible level where it arises, means not sensible fact, but valid ideation, verified hypothesis, and inevitable, stable inference.

If idealism is intrenched in the very structure of human reason, empiricism represents all those energies of the external universe which, as Spinoza says, must infinitely exceed the energies of man. If meditation breeds science, wisdom comes by disillusion, even on the subject of science itself. Docility to the facts makes the sanity of science. Reason is only half grown and not really distinguishable from imagination so long as she cannot check and recast her own processes wherever they render the moulds of thought unfit for their subject-matter. Docility is, as we have seen, the deepest condition of reason's existence; for if a form of mental synthesis were by chance developed which was incapable of appropriating the data of sense, logical thoughts would play idly, like so many parasites in the mind, and ultimately languish and die of inanition. To be nourished and employed, intelligence must have developed such structure and habits as will enable it to assimilate what food comes in its way; so that the persistence of any intellectual habit is a proof that it has some applicability, however partial, to the facts of sentience. This applicability, the prerequisite of significant thought, is also its eventual test; and the gathering of new experiences, the consciousness of more and more facts crowding into the memory and demanding co-ordination, is at once the presentation to reason of her legitimate problem and a proof that she is already at work. It is a presentation of her problem, because reason is not a faculty of dreams but the art of living.

CHAPTER 8

THE MEASURE OF VALUES IN REFLECTION

To PUT value in pleasure and pain, regarding a given quantity of pain as balancing a given quantity of pleasure, is to bring to practical ethics a worthy intention to be clear and, what is more precious, an undoubted honesty not always found in those moralists who maintain the opposite opinion and care more for edification than for truth. For in spite of all logical and psychological scruples, conduct that should not justify itself somehow by the satisfactions secured and the pains avoided would not justify itself at all. The most instinctive and unavoidable desire is forthwith chilled if you discover that its ultimate end is to be a preponderance of suffering; and what arrests this desire is not fear or weakness but conscience in its most categorical and sacred guise. Who would not be ashamed to acknowledge or to propose so inhuman an action?

By sad experience rooted impulses may be transformed or even obliterated. And quite intelligibly: for the idea of pain is already the sign and the beginning of a certain stoppage. To imagine failure is to interpret ideally a felt inhibition. To prophesy a check would be impossible but for an incipient movement already meeting an incipient arrest. Intensified, this prophecy becomes its own fulfilment and totally inhibits the opposed tendency. Therefore a mind that foresees pain to be the ultimate result of action cannot continue unreservedly to act, seeing that its foresight is the conscious transcript of a recoil already occurring. Conversely, the mind that surrenders itself wholly to any impulse must think that its execution would be delightful. A perfectly wise and representative will, therefore, would aim only at what, in its attainment, could continue to be aimed at and approved; and this is another way of saying that its aim would secure the maximum of satisfaction eventually possible.

In spite, however, of this involution of pain and pleasure in all deliberate forecast and volition, pain and pleasure are not the ultimate sources of value. A correct psychology and logic cannot allow that an eventual and, in strictness, unpresentable feeling, can determine any act or volition, but must insist that, on the contrary, all

62

beliefs about future experience, with all premonition of its emotional quality, is based on actual impulse and feeling; so that the source of value is nothing but the inner fountain of life and imagination, and the object of pursuit nothing but the ideal object, counterpart of the present demand. Abstract satisfaction is not pursued, but, if the will and the environment are constant, satisfaction will necessarily be felt in achieving the object desired. A rejection of hedonistic psychology, therefore, by no means involves any opposition to eudaemonism in ethics. Eudaemonism is another name for wisdom: there is no other *moral* morality. Any system that, for some sinister reason, should absolve itself from good-will toward all creatures, and make it somehow a duty to secure their misery, would be clearly disloyal to reason, humanity, and justice. Nor would it be hard, in that case, to point out what superstition, what fantastic obsession, or what private fury, had made those persons blind to prudence and kindness in so plain a matter. Happiness is the only sanction of life; where happiness fails, existence remains a mad and lamentable experiment. The question, however, what happiness shall consist in, its complexion if it should once arise, can only be determined by reference to natural demands and capacities; so that while satisfaction by the attainment of ends can alone justify their pursuit, this pursuit itself must exist first and be spontaneous, thereby fixing the goals of endeavour and distinguishing the states in which satisfaction might be found. Natural disposition, therefore, is the principle of preference and makes morality and happiness possible.

The standard of value, like every standard, must be one. Pleasures and pains are not only infinitely diverse but, even if reduced to their total bulk and abstract opposition, they remain two. Their values must be compared, and obviously neither one can be the standard by which to judge the other. This standard is an ideal involved in the judgment passed, whatever that judgment may be. Thus when Petrarch says that a thousand pleasures are not worth one pain, he establishes an ideal of value deeper than either pleasure or pain, an ideal which makes a life of satisfaction marred by a single pang an offence and a horror to his soul. If our demand for rationality is less acute and the miscellaneous affirmations of the will carry us along with a well-fed indifference to some single tragedy within us, we may aver that a single pang is only the thousandth part of a thousand pleasures and that a life so balanced is nine hundred and ninety-nine times better than nothing. This judgment, for all its air of mathematical calculation, in truth expresses a choice as irrational as Petrarch's. It merely means that, as a matter of fact, the mixed prospect presented to us attracts our wills and attracts them vehemently. So that the only possible criterion for the relative values of pains and pleasures is the will that chooses among them or among combinations of them; nor can the intensity of pleasures and pains, apart from the physical violence of their expression, be judged by any other standard than by the power they have, when represented, to control the will's movement.

Here we come upon one of those initial irrationalities in the world which theories of all sorts, since they are attempts to find rationality in things, are in serious danger of overlooking. In estimating the value of any experience, our endeavour, our pretension, is to weigh the value which that experience possesses when it is actual. But to weigh is to compare, and to compare is to represent, since the transcendental isolation and self-sufficiency of actual experience precludes its lying side by side with another datum, like two objects given in a single consciousness. Successive values, to be compared, must be represented; but the conditions of representation are such that they rob objects of the values they had at their first appearance to substitute the values they possess at their recurrence. For representation mirrors consciousness only by mirroring its objects, and the emotional reaction upon those objects cannot be represented directly, but is approached by indirect methods, through an imitation or assimilation of will to will and emotion to emotion. Only by the instrumentality of signs, like gesture or language, can we bring ourselves to reproduce in some measure an absent experience and to feel some premonition of its absolute value. Apart from very elaborate and cumulative suggestions to the contrary, we should always attribute to an event in every other experience the value which its image now had in our own. But in that case the pathetic fallacy would be present; for a volitional reaction upon an idea in one vital context is no index to what the volitional reaction would be in another vital context upon the situation which that idea represents.

This divergence falsifies all representation of life and renders it initially cruel, sentimental, and mythical. We dislike to trample on a flower, because its form makes a kind of blossoming in our own fancy which we call beauty; but we laugh at pangs we endured in childhood and feel no tremor at the incalculable sufferings of all mankind beyond our horizon, because no imitable image is involved to start a contrite thrill in our own bosom. The same cruelty appears in aesthetic pleasures, in lust, war, and ambition; in the illusions of desire and memory; in the unsympathetic quality of theory everywhere, which regards the uniformities of cause and effect and the beauties of law as a justification for the inherent evils in the experience described; in the unjust judgments, finally, of mystical optimism, that sinks so completely into its subjective commotion as to mistake the suspension of all discriminating and representative faculties for a true union in things, and the blur of its own ecstasy for a universal glory. These pleasures are all on the sensuous plane, the plane of levity and unintentional wickedness; but in their own sphere they have their own value. Æsthetic and speculative emotions make an important contribution to the total worth of existence, but they do not abolish the evils of that experience on which they reflect with such ruthless satisfaction. The satisfaction is due to a private flood of emotion submerging the images present in fancy, or to the exercise of a new intellectual function, like that of abstraction, synthesis, or comparison. Such a faculty, when fully developed, is capable of yielding pleasures as intense and voluminous as those proper to rudimentary animal functions, wrongly supposed to be more vital. The acme of vitality lies in the most comprehensive and penetrating thought. The rhythms, the sweep, the impetuosity of impassioned contemplation not only contain in themselves a great vitality and potency, but they often succeed in engaging the lower functions in a sympathetic vibration, and we see the whole body and soul rapt, as we say, and borne along by the harmonies of imagination and thought. In these fugitive moments of intoxication the detail of truth is submerged and forgotten.

That luminous blindness which in these cases takes an extreme form is present in principle throughout all reflection. Something yet unrealised, irresistibly solicited the will and seemed to promise incomparable ecstasy; and perhaps it yields an indescribable moment of excitement and triumph—a moment only half-appropriated into waking experience, so fleeting is it, and so unfit the mind to possess or retain its tenser attitudes. The same situation, if revived in memory when the system is in an opposite and relaxed state, forfeits all power to attract and fills the mind rather with aversion and disgust. For all violent pleasures, as Shakespeare says, are cruel and not to be trusted.

> A bliss in proof and, proved, a very woe:
> Before, a joy proposed; behind, a dream . . .
> Enjoyed no sooner but despised straight;
> Past reason hunted and, no sooner had,
> Past reason hated.

Past reason, indeed. For although an impulsive injustice is inherent in the very nature of representation and cannot be overcome altogether, yet reason, by attending to all the evidences that can be gathered and by confronting the first pronouncement by others fetched from every quarter of experience, has power to minimise the error and reach a practically just estimate of absent values.

This projection of interest into excellence takes place mechanically and is in the first instance irrational. Did all glow die out from memory and expectation, the events represented remaining unchanged, we should be incapable of assigning any value to those events, just as, if eyes were lacking, we should be incapable of assigning colour to the world, which would, notwithstanding, remain as it is at present. So fame could never be regarded as a good if the idea of fame gave no pleasure; yet now, because the idea pleases, the reality is regarded as a good, absolute and intrinsic. This moral hypostasis involved in the love of fame could never be rationalised, but would subsist unmitigated or die out unobserved, were it not associated with other conceptions and other habits of estimating values. For the passions are humanised only by being juxtaposed and forced to live together. As fame is not man's only goal and the realisation of it comes into manifold relations with other interests no less vivid, we are able to criticise the impulse to pursue it.

Fame may be the consequence of benefits conferred upon mankind. In that case the abstract desire for fame would be reinforced and, as it were, justified by its congruity with the more voluminous and stable desire to benefit our fellow-men. Or, again, the achievements which insure fame and the genius that wins it probably involve a high degree of vitality and many profound inward satisfactions to the man of genius himself; so that again the abstract love of fame would be reinforced by the independent and more rational desire for a noble and comprehensive experience. On the other hand, the minds of posterity, whose homage is craved by the ambitious man, will probably have very false conceptions of his thoughts and purposes. What they will call by his name will be, in a great measure, a fiction of their own fancy and not his portrait at all. Would Cæsar recognise himself in the current notions of him, drawn from some school-history, or perhaps from Shakespeare's satirical portrait? Would Christ recognise himself upon our altars, or in the romances about him constructed by imaginative critics? And not only is remote experience thus hopelessly lost and misrepresented, but even this nominal memorial ultimately disappears.

The love of fame, if tempered by these and similar considerations, would tend to take a place in man's ideal such as its roots in human nature and its functions in human progress might seem to justify. It would be rationalised in the only sense in which any primary desire can be rationalised, namely, by being combined with all others in a consistent whole. How much of it would survive a thorough sifting and criticism, may well remain in doubt. The result would naturally differ for different temperaments and in different states of society.

The fact that value is attributed to absent experience according to the value experience has in representation appears again in one of the most curious anomalies in human life—the exorbitant interest which thought and reflection take in the form of experience and the slight account they make of its intensity or volume. Sea-sickness and child-birth when they are over, the pangs of despised love when that love is finally forgotten or requited, the travail of sin when once salvation is assured, all melt away and dissolve like a morning mist leaving a clear sky without a vestige of sorrow. So also with merely remembered and not reproducible pleasures; the buoyancy of youth, when absurdity is not yet tedious, the rapture of sport or passion, the immense peace found in a mystical surrender to the universal, all these generous ardours count for nothing when they are once gone. The memory of them cannot cure a fit of the blues nor raise an irritable mortal above some petty act of malice or vengeance, or reconcile him to foul weather. An Ode of Horace, on the other hand, a scientific monograph, or a well-written page of music is a better antidote to melancholy than thinking on all the happiness which one's own life or that of the universe may ever have contained. Why should overwhelming masses of suffering and joy affect imagination so little while it responds sympathetically to æsthetic and intellectual irritants of very slight intensity, objects that, it must be confessed, are of almost no importance to the welfare of mankind? Why should we be so easily awed by artistic genius and exalt men whose works we know only by name, perhaps, and whose influence upon society has been infinitesimal, like a Pindar or a Leonardo. There is a prodigious selfishness in dreams: they live perfectly deaf and invulnerable amid the cries of the real world.

Thus it appears that the great figures of art or religion, together with all historic and imaginative ideals, advance insensibly on the values they represent. The image has more lustre than the original, and is often the more important and influential fact. Things are esteemed as they weigh in representation. A *memorable thing*, people say in their eulogies, little thinking to touch the ground of their praise. For things are called great because they are memorable, they are not remembered because they were great. The deepest pangs, the highest joys, the widest influences are lost to apperception in its haste, and if in some rational moment reconstructed and acknowledged, are soon forgotten again and cut off from living consideration. But the emptiest experience, even the most pernicious tendency, if embodied in a picturesque image, if reverberating in the mind with a pleasant echo, is idolised and enshrined. Fortunate indeed was Achilles that Homer sang of him, and fortunate the poets that make a public titillation out of their sorrows and ignorance. This imputed and posthumous fortune is the only happiness they have. The favours of memory are extended to those feeble realities and denied to the massive substance of daily life. When life dies, when what was present becomes a memory, its ghost flits still among the living, feared or worshipped not for the experience it once possessed but for the aspect it now wears. Yet this injustice in representation, speculatively so offensive, is practically excusable; for it is in one sense right and useful that all things, whatever their original or inherent dignity, should be valued at each moment only by their present function and utility.

The error involved in attributing value to the past is naturally aggravated when values are to be assigned to the future. In the latter case imagination cannot be controlled by circumstantial evidence, and is consequently the only basis for judgment. But as the conception of a thing naturally evokes an emotion different from that involved in its presence, ideals of what is desirable for the future contain no warrant that the experience desired would, when actual, prove to be acceptable and good. An ideal carries no extrinsic assurance that its realisation would be a benefit. To convince ourselves that an ideal has rational authority and represents a better life than the actual one it is contrasted with, we must control the prophetic image by as many circumlocutions as possible.

As in the case of fame, we must buttress or modify our spontaneous judgment with all the other judgments that the object envisaged can prompt: we must make our ideal harmonise with all interests rather than with a part only. The possible error remains even then; but a prudent mind will always accept the risk of error when it has made every possible correction. A rational will is not a will that has reason for its basis or that possesses any better proof that it is well inspired than the oracle of a living will. The rationality possible to the will lies not in its source but in its method. An ideal cannot wait for its realisation to prove its validity. To deserve loyalty it needs only to be adequate as an ideal, that is, to express completely what the soul at present demands, and to do justice to all extant interests.

CHAPTER 9

SOME ABSTRACT CONDITIONS OF THE IDEAL

REASON'S FUNCTION is to embody the good, but the test of excellence is itself ideal; therefore before we can assure ourselves that reason has been manifested in any given case we must make out the reasonableness of the ideal that inspires us. And in general, before we can convince ourselves that a Life of Reason, or behaviour guided by science and directed toward spiritual goods, is at all worth having, we must make out the possibility and character of its ultimate end. Yet each ideal is its own justification; so that the only sense in which an ultimate end can be established and become a test of general progress is this: that a harmony and cooperation of impulses should be conceived, leading to the maximum satisfaction possible in the whole community of spirits affected by our action. Now, without considering for the present any concrete Utopia, such, for instance, as Plato's Republic or the heavenly beatitude described by theologians, we may inquire what formal qualities are imposed on the ideal by its nature and function and by the relation it bears to experience and to desire.

The rational ideal has the same relation to given demands that the reality has to given perceptions. In the face of the ideal, particular demands forfeit their authority and the goods to which a particular being may aspire cease to be absolute; nay, the satisfaction of desire comes to appear an indifferent or unholy thing when compared or opposed to the ideal to be realised. So, precisely, in perception, flying impressions come to be regarded as illusory when contrasted with a stable conception of reality. Yet of course flying impressions are the only material out of which that conception can be formed. Life itself is a flying impression, and had we no personal and instant experience, importuning us at each successive moment, we should have no occasion to ask for a reality at all, and no materials out of which to construct so gratuitous an idea. In the same way present demands are the only materials and occasions for any ideal: without demands the ideal would have no *locus standi* or foothold in the world, no power, no charm, and no prerogative.

If the ideal can confront particular desires and put them to shame, that happens only because the ideal is the object of a more profound and voluminous desire and embodies the good which they blindly and perhaps deviously pursue. Otherwise each demand would render its object a detached, absolute, and unimpeachable good. But when each desire in turn has singed its wings and retired before some disillusion, reflection may set in to suggest residual satisfactions that may still be possible, or some shifting of the ground by which much of what was hoped for may yet be attained.

The force for this new trial is but the old impulse renewed; this new hope is a justified remnant of the old optimism. Each passion, in this second campaign, takes the field conscious that it has indomitable enemies and ready to sign a reasonable peace, and even to capitulate before superior forces. Such tameness may be at first merely a consequence of exhaustion and prudence; but a mortal will, though absolute in its deliverances, is very far from constant, and its sacrifices soon constitute a habit, its exile a new home. The old ambition, now proved to be unrealisable, begins to seem capricious and extravagant; the circle of possible satisfactions becomes the field of conventional happiness. Experience, which brings about this humbler and more prosaic state of mind, has its own imaginative fruits. Among those forces which compelled each particular impulse to abate its pretensions, the most conspicuous were other impulses, other interests active in oneself and in one's neighbours. When the power of these alien demands is recognised they begin, in a physical way, to be respected; when an adjustment to them is sought they begin to be understood, for it is only by studying their expression and tendency that the degree of their hostility can be measured. But to understand is more than to forgive, it is almost to adopt; and the passion that thought merely to withdraw into a sullen and maimed self-indulgence can feel itself expanded by sympathies which in its primal vehemence it would have excluded. Experience, in bringing humility, brings intelligence also. Personal interests begin to seem relative, factors only in a general voluminous welfare secured by many common institutions and arts, moulds for whatever is communicable or rational in every passion. Each original impulse, when trimmed down more or less according to its degree of savageness, can then inhabit the state, and every good, when sufficiently transfigured, can be found again in the general ideal. The factors may indeed often be unrecognisable in the result, so much does the process of domestication transform them; but the interests that animated them survive this discipline and the new purpose is really esteemed; else the ideal would have no moral force. As an absolute reality would be indescribable and without a function in the elucidation of phenomena, so a supreme good which was good for nobody would be without conceivable value. Respect for such an idol is a dialectical superstition; and if zeal for that shibboleth should actually begin to inhibit the exercise of intelligent choice or the development of appreciation for natural pleasures, it would constitute a reversal of the Life of Reason.

No less important, however, than this basis which the ideal must have in extant demands, is the harmony with which reason must endow it. If without the one the ideal loses its value, without the other it loses its finality. Human nature is fluid and imperfect; its demands are based on incidental desires, elicited by a variety of objects which perhaps cannot coexist in the world. If we merely transcribe these miscellaneous demands or allow these floating desires to dictate to us the elements of the ideal, we shall never come to a Whole or to an End.

The picture of life as an eternal war for illusory ends was drawn at first by satirists, unhappily with too much justification in the facts. Some grosser minds, too undisciplined to have ever pursued a good either truly attainable or truly satisfactory, then proceeded to mistake that satire on human folly for a sober account of the whole universe; and finally others were not ashamed to represent it as the ideal itself—so soon is the dyer's hand subdued to what it works in. A barbarous mind cannot conceive life, like health, as a harmony continually preserved or restored, and containing those natural and ideal activities which disease merely interrupts. Such a mind, never having tasted order, cannot conceive it, and identifies progress with new conflicts and life with continual death. Its deification of unreason, instability, and strife comes partly from piety and partly from inexperience. There is piety in saluting nature in her perpetual flux and in thinking that since no equilibrium is maintained for ever none, perhaps, deserves to be. There is inexperience in not considering that wherever interests and judgments exist, the natural flux has fallen, so to speak, into a vortex, and created a natural good, a cumulative life, and an ideal purpose. Art, science, government, human nature itself, are self-defining and self-preserving: by partly fixing a structure they fix an ideal. But the barbarian can hardly regard such things, for to have distinguished and fostered them would be to have founded a civilisation.

The aim prescribed by reason differs from the prescription of conscience, in that conscience is often the spokesman of one interest or of a group of interests in opposition to other primary impulses which it would annul altogether; while reason and the ideal are not active forces nor embodiments of passion at all, but merely a method by which objects of desire are compared in reflection. The goodness of an end is felt inwardly by conscience; by reason it can be only taken upon trust and registered as a fact. For conscience the object of an opposed will is an evil, for reason it is a good on the same ground as any other good, because it is pursued by a natural impulse and can bring a real satisfaction. Conscience, in fine, is a party to moral strife, reason an observer of it who, however, plays the most important and beneficent part in the outcome by suggesting the terms of peace. This suggested peace, inspired by sympathy and by knowledge of the world, is the ideal, which borrows its value and practical force from the irrational impulses which it embodies, and borrows its final authority from the truth with which it recognises them all and the necessity by which it imposes on each such sacrifices as are requisite to a general harmony.

Reason as such represents or rather constitutes a single formal interest, the interest in harmony. When two interests are simultaneous and fall within one act of apprehension the desirability of harmonising them is involved in the very effort to realise them together. If attention and imagination are steady enough to face this implication and not to allow impulse to oscillate between irreconcilable tendencies, reason comes into being. Henceforth things actual and things desired are confronted by an ideal which has both pertinence and authority.

CHAPTER 10

FLUX AND CONSTANCY IN HUMAN NATURE

A CONCEPTION of something called human nature arises not un-
naturally on observing the passions of men, passions which under
various disguises seem to reappear in all ages and countries. The
tendency of Greek philosophy, with its insistence on general concepts, was to define this idea of human nature still further and to
encourage the belief that a single and identical essence, present in
all men, determined their powers and ideal destiny. Christianity,
while it transposed the human ideal and dwelt on the superhuman
affinities of man, did not abandon the notion of a specific humanity.
On the contrary, such a notion was implied in the Fall and Redemption, in the Sacraments, and in the universal validity of
Christian doctrine and precept. For if human nature were not one,
there would be no propriety in requiring all men to preserve
unanimity in faith or conformity in conduct. Human nature was
likewise the entity which the English psychologists set themselves
to describe; and Kant was so entirely dominated by the notion of
a fixed and universal human nature that its constancy, in his opinion,
was the source of all natural as well as moral laws. Had he doubted
for a moment the stability of human nature, the foundations of his
system would have fallen out; the forms of perception and thought
would at once have lost their boasted necessity, since to-morrow
might dawn upon new categories and a modified *a priori* intuition
of space or time; and the avenue would also have been closed by
which man was led, through his unalterable moral sentiments, to
assumptions about metaphysical truths.

The force of this long tradition has been broken, however, by
two influences of great weight in recent times, the theory of evolution and the revival of pantheism. The first has reintroduced flux
into the conception of existence and the second into the conception
of values. If natural species are fluid and pass into one another,
human nature is merely a name for a group of qualities found by
chance in certain tribes of animals, a group to which new qualities
are constantly tending to attach themselves while other faculties

become extinct, now in whole races, now in sporadic individuals. Human nature is therefore a variable, and its ideal cannot have a greater constancy than the demands to which it gives expression. Nor can the ideal of one man or one age have any authority over another, since the harmony existing in their nature and interests is accidental and each is a transitional phase in an indefinite evolution. The crystallisation of moral forces at any moment is consequently to be explained by universal, not by human, laws; the philosopher's interest cannot be to trace the implications of present and unstable desires, but rather to discover the mechanical law by which these desires have been generated and will be transformed, so that they will change irrevocably both their basis and their objects.

To this picture of physical instability furnished by popular science are to be added the mystical self-denials involved in pantheism. These come to reinforce the doctrine that human nature is a shifting thing with the sentiment that it is a finite and unworthy one: for every determination of being, it is said, has its significance as well as its origin in the infinite continuum of which it is a part. Forms are limitations, and limitations, according to this philosophy, would be defects, so that man's only goal would be to escape humanity and lose himself in the divine nebula that has produced and must invalidate each of his thoughts and ideals. As there would be but one spirit in the world, and that infinite, so there would be but one ideal and that omnivorous. The despair which the naturalist's view of human instability might tend to produce is turned by this mystical initiation into a sort of ecstasy; and the deluge of conformity suddenly submerges that Life of Reason which science seemed to condemn to gradual extinction.

Reason is a human function. Though the name of reason has been applied to various alleged principles of cosmic life, vital or dialectical, these principles all lack the essence of rationality, in that they are not conscious movements toward satisfaction, not, in other words, moral and beneficent principles at all. Be the instability of human nature what it may, therefore, the instability of reason is not less, since reason is but a function of human nature. However relative and subordinate, in a physical sense, human ideals may be, these ideals remain the only possible moral standards for man, the only tests which he can apply for value or authority in any other quarter. And among unstable and relative ideals none is more relative and unstable than that which transports all value to a universal law, itself indifferent to good and evil, and worships it as a deity. Such an idolatry would indeed be impossible if it were not partial and veiled, arrived at in following out some human interest and clung to by force of moral inertia and the ambiguity of words. In truth mystics do not practise so entire a renunciation of reason as they preach: eternal validity and the capacity to deal with absolute reality are still assumed by them to belong to thought or at least to feeling. Only they overlook in their description of human nature just that faculty which they exercise in their speculation; their map leaves out the ground on which they stand. The rest, which they are not identified with for the moment, they proceed to regard *de haut en bas* and to discredit as a momentary manifestation of universal laws, physical or divine. They forget that this faith in law, this absorption in the blank reality, this enthusiasm for the ultimate thought, are mere human passions like the rest; that they endure them as they might a fever and that the animal instincts are patent on which those spiritual yearnings repose.

This last fact would be nothing against the feelings in question, if they were not made vehicles for absolute revelations. On the contrary, such a relativity in instincts is the source of their importance. In virtue of this relativity they have some basis and function in the world; for did they not repose on human nature they could never express or transform it. Religion and philosophy are not always beneficent or important, but when they are it is precisely because they help to develop human faculty and to enrich human life. To imagine that by means of them we can escape from human nature and survey it from without is an ostrich-like illusion obvious to all but to the victim of it. Such a pretension may cause admiration in the schools, where self-hypnotisation is easy, but in the world it makes its professors ridiculous. For in their eagerness to empty their mind of human prejudices they reduce its rational burden to a minimum, and if they still continue to dogmatise, it is sport for the satirist to observe what forgotten accident of language or training has survived the crash of the universe and made the one demonstrable path to Absolute Truth.

Neither the path of abstraction followed by the mystics, nor that of direct and, as it avers, unbiassed observation followed by the naturalists, can lead beyond that region of common experience, traditional feeling, and conventional thought which all minds enter at birth and can elude only at the risk of inward collapse and extinction. The fact that observation involves the senses, and the senses their organs, is one which a naturalist can hardly overlook; and when we add that logical habits, sanctioned by utility, are needed to interpret the data of sense, the humanity of science and all its constructions becomes clearer than day. Superstition itself could not be more human. The path of unbiassed observation is not a path away from conventional life; it is a progress in conventions. It improves human belief by increasing the proportion of two of its ingredients, attentive perception and relevant calculus. The whole resulting vision, as it is sustained from moment to moment by present experience and instinct, has no value apart from actual ideals. And if it proves human nature to be unstable, it can build that proof on nothing more stable than human faculty as at the moment it happens to be.

Nor is abstraction a less human process, as if by becoming very abstruse indeed we could hope to become divine. Is it not a commonplace of the schools that to form abstract ideas is the prerogative of man's reason? Is not abstraction a method by which mortal intelligence makes haste? Is it not the makeshift of a mind overloaded with its experience, the trick of an eye that cannot master a profuse and ever-changing world? Shall these diagrams drawn in fancy, this system of signals in thought, be the Absolute Truth dwelling within us? Do we attain reality by making a silhouette of our dreams? If the scientific world be a product of human faculties, the metaphysical world must be doubly so; for the material there given to human understanding is here worked over again by human art. This constitutes the dignity and value of dialectic, that in spite of appearances it is so human; it bears to experience a relation similar to that which the arts bear to the same, where sensible images, selected by the artist's genius and already coloured by his æsthetic bias, are redyed in the process of reproduction whenever he has a great style, and saturated anew with his mind.

There can be no question, then, of eluding human nature or of conceiving it and its environment in such a way as to stop its operation. We may take up our position in one region of experience or in another, we may, in unconsciousness of the interests and assumptions that support us, criticise the truth or value of results obtained elsewhere. Our criticism will be solid in proportion to the solidity of the unnamed convictions that inspire it, that is, in proportion to the deep roots and fruitful ramifications which those convictions may have in human life. Ultimate truth and ultimate value will be reasonably attributed to those ideas and possessions which can give human nature, as it is, the highest satisfaction. We may admit that human nature is variable; but that admission, if justified, will be justified by the satisfaction which it gives human nature to make it. We might even admit that human ideals are vain but only if they were nothing worth for the attainment of the veritable human ideal.

The given constitution of reason, with whatever a dialectical philosophy might elicit from it, obviously determines nothing about the causes that may have brought reason to its present pass or the phases that may have preceded its appearance. Certain notions about physics might no doubt suggest themselves to the moralist, who never can be the whole man; he might suspect, for instance, that the transitive intent of intellect and will pointed to their vital basis. Transcendence in operation might seem appropriate only to a being with a history and with an organism subject to external influences, whose mind should thus come to represent not merely its momentary state but also its constitutive past and its eventual fortunes. Such suggestions, however, would be extraneous to dialectical self-knowledge. They would be tentative only, and human nature would be freely admitted to be as variable, as relative, and as transitory as the natural history of the universe might make it.

The error, however, would be profound and the contradiction hopeless if we should deny the ideal authority over ourselves of human nature because we had discovered its origin and conditions. Nature and evolution, let us say, have brought life to the present form; but this life lives, these organs have determinate functions, and human nature, here and now, in relation to the ideal energies it unfolds, is a fundamental source. As the structure of the steam-engine has varied greatly since its first invention, and its attributions have increased, so the structure of human nature has undoubtedly varied since man first appeared upon the earth; but as in each steam-engine at each moment there must be a limit of mobility, a unity of function and a clear determination of parts and tensions, so in human nature, as found at any time in any man, there is a definite scope by virtue of which alone he can have a reliable memory, a recognisable character, a faculty of connected thought and speech, a social utility, and a moral ideal.

Thinkers of different experience and organisation have *pro tanto* different logics and different moral laws. There are limits to communication even among beings of the same race, and the faculties and ideals of one intelligence are not transferable without change to any other. If this historic diversity in minds were complete, so that each lived in its own moral world, a science of each of these moral worlds would still be possible provided some inner fixity or constancy existed in its meaning. In every human thought together with an immortal intent there is a mortal and irrecoverable perception: something in it perishes instantly. Unanimity in thought involves identity of functions and similarity in organs. These conditions mark off the sphere of rational communication and society; where they fail altogether there is no mutual intelligence, no conversation, no moral solidarity.

The inner authority of reason, however is no more destroyed because it has limits in physical expression or because irrational things exist, than the grammar of a given language is invalidated because other languages do not share it, or because some people break its rules and others are dumb altogether. Innumerable madmen make no difference to the laws of thought, which borrow their authority from the inward intent and cogency of each rational mind. Reason, like beauty, is its own excuse for being.

The true philosopher, who is not one chiefly by profession, must be prepared to tread the winepress alone. He may indeed flourish like the baytree in a grateful environment, but more often he will rather resemble a reed shaken by the wind. Whether starved or fed by the accidents of fortune he must find his essential life in his own ideal. In spiritual life, heteronomy is suicide. That universal soul sometimes spoken of, which is to harmonise and correct individual demands, if it were a will and an intelligence in act, would itself be an individual like the others; while if it possessed no will and no intelligence, such as individuals may have, it would be a physical force or law, a dynamic system without moral authority and with a merely potential or represented existence. For to be actual and self-existent is to be individual. The living mind cannot surrender its rights to any physical power or subordinate itself to any figment of its own art without falling into manifest idolatry.

Human nature, in the sense in which it is the transcendental foundation of all science and morals, is a functional unity in each man; it is no general or abstract essence, the average of all men's characters, nor even the complex of the qualities common to all men. It is the entelechy of the living individual, be he typical or singular. That his type should be odd or common is merely a physical accident. If he can know himself by expressing the entelechy of his own nature in the form of a consistent ideal, he is a rational creature after his own kind, even if, like the angels of Saint Thomas, he be the only individual of his species. What the majority of human animals may tend to, or what the past or future variations of a race may be, has nothing to do with determining the ideal of human nature in a living man, or in an ideal society of men bound together by spiritual kinship. Otherwise Plato could not have reasoned well about the republic without adjusting himself to the politics of Buddha or Rousseau, and we should not be able to determine our own morality without making concessions to the cannibals or giving a vote to the ants. Within the field of an anthropology that tests humanity by the skull's shape, there might be room for any number of independent moralities, and although, as we shall see, there is actually a similar foundation in all human and even in all animal natures, which supports a rudimentary morality common to all, yet a perfect morality is not really common to any two men nor to any two phases of the same man's life.

The distribution of reason, though a subject irrelevant to pure logic or morals, is one naturally interesting to a rational man, for he is concerned to know how far beings exist with a congenial structure and an ideal akin to his own. That circumstance will largely influence his happiness if, being a man, he is a gregarious and sympathetic animal. His moral idealism itself will crave support from others, if not to give it direction, at least to give it warmth and courage. The best part of wealth is to have worthy heirs, and mind can be transmitted only to a kindred mind. Hostile natures cannot be brought together by mutual invective nor harmonised by the brute destruction and disappearance of either party. But when one or both parties have actually disappeared, and the combat has ceased for lack of combatants, natures not hostile to one another can fill the vacant places. In proportion to their inbred unanimity these will cultivate a similar ideal and rejoice together in its embodiment.

This has happened to some extent in the whole world, on account of natural conditions which limit the forms of life possible in one region; for nature is intolerant in her laxity and punishes too great originality and heresy with death. Such moral integration has occurred very markedly in every good race and society whose members, by adapting themselves to the same external forces, have created and discovered their common soul. Spiritual unity is a natural product. There are those who see a great mystery in the presence of eternal values and impersonal ideals in a moving and animal world, and think to solve that dualism, as they call it, by denying that nature can have spiritual functions or spirit a natural cause; but nothing can be simpler if we make, as we should, existence the test of possibility. *Ab esse ad posse valet illatio.* Nature is a perfect garden of ideals, and passion is the perpetual and fertile soil for poetry, myth, and speculation. Nor is this origin merely imputed to ideas by a late and cynical observer: it is manifest in the ideals themselves, by their subject matter and intent. For what are ideals about, what do they idealise, except natural existence and natural passions? That would be a miserable and superfluous ideal indeed that was nobody's ideal of nothing. The pertinence of ideals binds them to nature, and it is only the worst and flimsiest ideals, the ideals of a sick soul, that elude nature's limits and belie her potentialities. Ideals are forerunners or heralds of nature's successes, not always followed, indeed, by their fulfilment, for nature is but nature and has to feel her way; but they are an earnest, at least, of an achieved organisation, an incipient accomplishment, that tends to maintain and root itself in the world.

To speak of nature's successes is, of course, to impute success retroactively; but the expression may be allowed when we consider that the same functional equilibrium which is looked back upon as a good by the soul it serves, first creates individual being and with it creates the possibility of preference and the whole moral world; and it is more than a metaphor to call that achievement a success which has made a sense of success possible and actual. That nature cannot intend or previously esteem those formations which are the condition of value or intention existing at all, is a truth too obvious to demand repetition; but when those formations arise they determine estimation, and fix the direction of preference, so that the evolution which produced them, when looked back upon from the vantage-ground thus gained, cannot help seeming to have been directed toward the good now distinguished and partly attained. For this reason creation is regarded as a work of love, and the power that brought order out of chaos is called intelligence.

These natural formations, tending to generate and realise each its ideal, are, as it were, eddies in the universal flux, produced no less normally, doubtless, than the onward current, yet seeming to arrest or to reverse it. Inheritance arrests the flux by repeating a series of phases with a recognisable rhythm; memory reverses it by modifying this rhythm itself by the integration of earlier phases into those that supervene. Inheritance and memory make human stability. This stability is relative, being still a mode of flux, and consists fundamentally in repetition. Repetition marks some progress on mere continuity, since it preserves form and disregards time and matter. Inheritance is repetition on a larger scale, not excluding spontaneous variations; while habit and memory are a sort of heredity within the individual, since here an old perception reappears, by way of atavism, in the midst of a forward march. Life is thus enriched and reaction adapted to a wider field; much as a note is enriched by its overtones, and by the tensions, inherited from the preceding notes, which give it a new setting.

Progress, far from consisting in change, depends on retentiveness. When change is absolute there remains no being to improve and no direction is set for possible improvement: and when experience is not retained, as among savages, infancy is perpetual. Those who cannot remember the past are condemned to repeat it. In the first stage of life the mind is frivolous and easily distracted; it misses progress by failing in consecutiveness and persistence. This is the condition of children and barbarians, in whom instinct has learned nothing from experience. In a second stage men are docile to events, plastic to new habits and suggestions, yet able to graft them on original instincts, which they thus bring to fuller satisfaction. This is the plane of manhood and true progress. Last comes a stage when retentiveness is exhausted and all that happens is at once forgotten; a vain, because unpractical, repetition of the past takes the place of plasticity and fertile readaptation. In a moving world readaptation is the price of longevity. The hard shell, far from protecting the vital principle, condemns it to die down slowly and be gradually chilled; immortality in such a case must have been secured earlier, by giving birth to a generation plastic to the contemporary world and able to retain its lessons. Thus old age is as forgetful as youth, and more incorrigible; it displays the same inattentiveness to conditions; its memory becomes self-repeating and degenerates into an instinctive reaction, like a bird's chirp.

Not all readaptation, however, is progress, for ideal identity must not be lost. The Latin language did not progress when it passed into Italian. It died. Its amiable heirs may console us for its departure, but do not remove the fact that their parent is extinct. So every indivdual, nation, and religion has its limit of adaptation; so long as the increment it receives is digestible, so long as the organisation already attained is extended and elaborated without being surrendered, growth goes on; but when the foundation itself shifts, when what is gained at the periphery is lost at the centre, the flux appears again and progress is not real. Thus a succession of generations or languages or religions constitutes no progress unless some ideal present at the beginning is transmitted to the end and reaches a better expression there; without this stability at the core no common standard exists and all comparison of value with value must be external and arbitrary. Retentiveness, we must repeat, is the condition of progress.

The variation human nature is open to is not, then, variation in any direction. There are transformations that would destroy it. So long as it endures it must retain all that constitutes it now, all that it has so far gathered and worked into its substance. The genealogy of progress is like that of man, who can never repudiate a single ancestor. It starts, so to speak, from a single point, free as yet to take any direction. When once, however, evolution has taken a single step, say in the direction of vertebrates, that step cannot be retraced without extinction of the species. Such extinction may take place while progress in other lines is continued. All that preceded the forking of the dead and the living branch will be as well represented and as legitimately continued by the surviving radiates as it could have been by the vertebrates that are no more; but the vertebrate ideal is lost for ever, and no more progress is possible along that line.

The future of moral evolution is accordingly infinite, but its character is more and more determinate at every step. Mankind can never, without perishing, surrender its animal nature, its need to eat and drink, its sexual method of reproduction, its vision of nature, its faculty of speech, its arts of music, poetry, and building. Particular races cannot subsist if they renounce their savage instincts, but die, like wild animals, in captivity; and particular individuals die when not suffered any longer to retain their memories, their bodies, or even their master passions. Thus human nature survives amid a continual fluctuation of its embodiments. At every step twigs and leaves are thrown out that last but one season; but the underlying stem may have meantime grown stronger and more luxuriant. Whole branches sometimes wither, but others may continue to bloom. Spiritual unity runs, like sap, from the common root to every uttermost flower; but at each forking in the growth the branches part company, and what happens in one is no direct concern of the others. The products of one age and nation may well be unintelligible to another; the elements of humanity common to both may lie lower down. So that the highest things are communicable to the fewest persons, and yet, among these few, are the most perfectly communicable. The more elaborate and determinate a man's heritage and genius are, the more he has in common with his next of kin, and the more he can transmit and implant in his posterity for ever. Civilisation is cumulative. The farther it goes the intenser it is, substituting articulate interests for animal fumes and for enigmatic passions. Such articulate interests can be shared; and the infinite vistas they open up can be pursued for ever with the knowledge that a work long ago begun is being perfected and that an ideal is being embodied which need never be outworn.

So long as external conditions remain constant it is obvious that the greater organisation a being possesses the greater strength he will have. If indeed primary conditions varied, the finer creatures would die first; for their adaptation is more exquisite and the irreversible core of their being much larger relatively; but in a constant environment their equipment makes them irresistible and secures their permanence and multiplication. Now man is a part of nature and her organisation may be regarded as the foundation of his own; the word nature is therefore less equivocal than it seems, for every nature is Nature herself in one of her more specific and better articulated forms. Man therefore represents the universe that sustains him; his existence is a proof that the cosmic equilibrium that fostered his life is a natural equilibrium, capable of being long maintained. Some of the ancients thought it eternal; physics now suggests a different opinion. But even if this equilibrium, by which the stars are kept in their courses and human progress is allowed to proceed, is fundamentally unstable, it shows what relative stability nature may attain. Could this balance be preserved indefinitely, no one knows what wonderful adaptations might occur within it, and to what excellence human nature in particular might advance. Nor is it unlikely that before the cataclysm comes time will be afforded for more improvement than moral philosophy has ever dreamed of. For it is remarkable how inane and unimaginative Utopias have generally been. This possibility is not uninspiring and may help to console those who think the natural conditions of life are not conditions that a good life can be lived in. The possibility of essential progress is bound up with the tragic possibility that progress and human life should some day end together. If the present equilibrium of forces were eternal all adaptations to it would have already taken place and, while no essential catastrophe would need to be dreaded, no essential improvement could be hoped for in all eternity. I am not sure that a humanity such as we know, were it destined to exist for ever, would offer a more exhilarating prospect than a humanity having indefinite elasticity together with a precarious tenure of life. Mortality has its compensations: one is that all evils are transitory, another that better times may come.

Human nature, then, has for its core the substance of nature at large, and is one of its more complex formations. Its determination is progressive. It varies indefinitely in its historic manifestations and fades into what, as a matter of natural history, might no longer be termed human. At each moment it has its fixed and determinate entelechy, the ideal of that being's life, based on his instincts, summed up in his character, brought to a focus in his reflection, and shared by all who have attained or may inherit his organisation. His perceptive and reasoning faculties are parts of human nature, as embodied in him; all objects of belief or desire, with all standards of justice and duty which he can possibly acknowledge, are transcripts of it, conditioned by it, and justifiable only as expressions of its inherent tendencies.

This definition of human nature, clear as it may be in itself and true to the facts, will perhaps hardly make sufficiently plain how the Life of Reason, having a natural basis, has in the ideal world a creative and absolute authority. A more concrete description of human nature may accordingly not come amiss, especially as the important practical question touching the extension of a given moral authority over times and places depends on the degree of kinship found among the creatures inhabiting those regions. To give a general picture of human nature and its rational functions will be the task of the following pages. The truth of a description which must be largely historical may not be indifferent to the reader, and I shall study to avoid bias in the presentation, in so far as is compatible with frankness and brevity; yet even if some bias should manifest itself and if the picture were historically false, the rational principles we shall be trying to illustrate will not thereby be invalidated. Illustrations might have been sought in some fictitious world, if imagination had not seemed so much less interesting than reality, which besides enforces with unapproachable eloquence the main principle in view, namely, that nature carries its ideal with it and that the progressive organisation of irrational impulses makes a rational life.

I I

REASON IN SOCIETY

CHAPTER 1

LOVE

THE CONSCIOUS quality of this passion differs so much in various races and individuals, and at various points in the same life, that no account of it will ever satisfy everybody.* Poets and novelists never tire of depicting it anew; but although the experience they tell of is fresh and unparalleled in every individual, their rendering suffers, on the whole, from a great monotony. Love's gesture and symptoms are noted and unvarying; its vocabulary is poor and worn. Even a poet, therefore, can give of love but a meagre expression, while the philosopher, who renounces dramatic representation, is condemned to be avowedly inadequate. Love, to the lover, is a noble and immense inspiration; to the naturalist it is a thin veil and prelude to the self-assertion of lust. This opposition has prevented philosophers from doing justice to the subject. Two things need to be admitted by anyone who would not go wholly astray in such speculation: one, that love has an animal basis; the other, that it has an ideal object. Since these two propositions have usually been thought contradictory, no writer has ventured to present more than half the truth, and that half out of its true relations.

Plato, who gave eloquent expression to the ideal burden of the passion, and divined its political and cosmic message, passed over its natural history with a few mythical fancies; and Schopenhauer, into whose system a naturalistic treatment would have fitted so easily, allowed his metaphysics to carry him at this point into verbal inanities; while, of course, like all profane writers on the subject, he failed to appreciate the oracles which Plato had delivered. In popular feeling, where sentiment and observation must both make themselves felt somehow or other, the tendency is to imagine that

* The wide uses of the English word love add to the difficulty. I shall take the liberty of limiting the term here to imaginative passion, to being in love, excluding all other ways of loving.

love is an absolute, non-natural energy which, for some unknown reason, or for none at all, lights upon particular persons, and rests there eternally, as on its ultimate goal. In other words, it makes the origin of love divine and its object natural: which is the exact opposite of the truth. If it were once seen, however, that every ideal expresses some natural function, and that no natural function is incapable, in its free exercise, of evolving some ideal and finding justification in an inherent operation like life or thought, then the philosophy of love should not prove permanently barren. For love is a brilliant illustration of a principle everywhere discoverable: namely, that human reason lives by turning the friction of material forces into the light of ideal goods. There can be no philosophic interest in disguising the animal basis of love, or in denying its spiritual sublimations, since all life is animal in its origin and spiritual in its possible fruits.

Plastic matter, in transmitting its organisation, takes various courses which it is the part of natural history to describe. Even after reproduction has become sexual, it will offer no basis for love if it does not require a union of the two parent bodies. Did germinal substances, unconsciously diffused, meet by chance in the external medium and unite there, it is obvious that whatever obsessions or pleasures maturity might bring they would not have the quality which men call love. But when an individual of the opposite sex must be met with, recognised, and pursued, and must prove responsive, then each is haunted by the possible other. Each feels in a generic way the presence and attraction of his fellows; he vibrates to their touch, he dreams of their image, he is restless and wistful if alone. When the vague need that solicits him is met by the presence of a possible mate it is extraordinarily kindled. Then, if it reaches fruition, it subsides immediately, and after an interval, perhaps, of stupor and vital recuperation, the animal regains his independence, his peace, and his impartial curiosity. You might think him on the way to becoming intelligent; but the renewed nutrition and cravings of the sexual machinery soon engross his attention again; all his sprightly indifference vanishes before nature's categorical imperative. That fierce and turbid pleasure, by which his obedience is rewarded, hastens his dissolution; every day the ensuing lassitude and emptiness give him a clearer premonition of death. It is not figuratively only that his soul has passed into his offspring. The vocation to produce them was a chief part of his being, and when that function is sufficiently fulfilled he is superfluous in the world and becomes partly superfluous even to himself. The confines of his dream are narrowed. He moves apathetically and dies forlorn.

Some echo of the vital rhythm which pervades not merely the generations of animals, but the seasons and the stars, emerges sometimes in consciousness; on reaching the tropics in the mortal ecliptic, which the human individual may touch many times without much change in his outer fortunes, the soul may occasionally divine that it is passing through a supreme crisis. Passion, when vehement, may bring atavistic sentiments. When love is absolute it feels a profound impulse to welcome death, and even, by a transcendental confusion, to evoke the end of the universe.* The human soul reverts at such a moment to what an ephemeral insect might feel, buzzing till it finds its mate in the noon. Its whole destiny was wooing, and, that mission accomplished, it sings its *Nunc dimittis*, renouncing heartily all irrelevant things, now that the one fated and all-satisfying good has been achieved. Where parental instincts exist also, nature soon shifts her loom: a milder impulse succeeds, and a satisfaction of a gentler sort follows in the birth of children. The transcendental illusion is here corrected, and it is seen that the extinction the lovers had accepted needed not to be complete. The death they welcomed was not without its little resurrection. The feeble worm they had generated bore their immortality within it.

The varieties of sexual economy are many and to each may correspond, for all we know, a special sentiment. Sometimes the union established is intermittent; sometimes it crowns the end of life and dissolves it altogether; sometimes it remains, while it lasts, monogamous; sometimes the sexual and social alertness is constant in the male, only periodic in the female. Sometimes the group

* One example, among a thousand, is the cry of Siegfried and Brünhilde in Wagner:

Lachend lass' uns verderben
Lachend zu Grunde geh'n.
Fahr hin, Walhall's
Leuchtende Welt! . . .
Leb' wohl, pragende
Götter Pracht!
Ende in Wonne,
Du ewig Geschlecht!

established for procreation endures throughout the seasons, and from year to year; sometimes the males herd together, as if normally they preferred their own society, until the time of rut comes, when war arises between them for the possession of what they have just discovered to be the fair.

A naturalist not ashamed to indulge his poetic imagination might easily paint for us the drama of these diverse loves. It suffices for our purpose to observe that the varying passions and duties which life can contain depend upon the organic functions of the animal. A fish incapable of coition, absolved from all care for its young, which it never sees or never distinguishes from the casual swimmers darting across its path, such a fish, being without social faculties or calls to cooperation, cannot have the instincts, perceptions, or emotions which belong to social beings. A male of some higher species that feels only once a year the sudden solicitations of love cannot be sentimental in all the four seasons: his headlong passion, exhausted upon its present object and dismissed at once without remainder, leaves his senses perfectly free and colourless to scrutinise his residual world. Whatever further fears or desires may haunt him will have nothing mystical or sentimental about them. He will be a man of business all the year round, and a lover only on May-day. A female that does not suffice for the rearing of her young will expect and normally receive her mate's aid long after the pleasures of love are forgotten by him. Disinterested fidelity on his part will then be her right and his duty. But a female that, once pregnant, needs, like the hen, no further cooperation on the male's part will turn from him at once with absolute indifference to brood perpetually on her eggs, undisturbed by the least sense of solitude or jealousy. And the chicks that at first follow her and find shelter under her wings will soon be forgotten also and relegated to the mechanical landscape. There is no pain in the timely snapping of the dearest bonds where society has not become a permanent organism, and perpetual friendship is not one of its possible modes.

Transcendent and ideal passions may well judge themselves to have an incomparable dignity. Yet that dignity is hardly more than what every passion, were it articulate, would assign to itself and to its objects. The dumbness of a passion may accordingly, from one point of view, be called the index of its baseness; for if it cannot ally itself with ideas its affinities can hardly lie in the rational mind nor its advocates be among the poets. But if we listen to the master-passion itself rather than to the loquacious arts it may have enlisted in its service, we shall understand that it is not self-condemned because it is silent, nor an anomaly in nature because inharmonious with human life. The fish's heartlessness is his virtue; the male bee's lasciviousness is his vocation; and if these functions were retrenched or encumbered in order to assimilate them to human excellence they would be merely dislocated. We should not produce virtue where there was vice, but defeat a possible arrangement which would have had its own vitality and order.

Animal love is a marvellous force; and while it issues in acts that may be followed by a revulsion of feeling, it yet deserves a more sympathetic treatment than art and morals have known how to accord it. Erotic poets, to hide their want of ability to make the dumb passion speak, have played feebly with veiled insinuations and comic effects; while more serious sonneteers have harped exclusively on secondary and somewhat literary emotions, abstractly conjugating the verb to love. Lucretius, in spite of his didactic turns, has been on this subject, too, the most ingenuous and magnificent of poets, although he chose to confine his description to the external history of sexual desire. It is a pity that he did not turn, with his sublime sincerity, to the inner side of it also, and write the drama of the awakened senses, the poignant suasion of beauty, when it clouds the brain, and makes the conventional earth, seen through that bright haze, seem a sorry fable. Western poets should not have despised what the Orientals, in their fugitive stanzas, seem often to have sung most exquisitely: the joy of gazing on the beloved, of following or being followed, of tacit understandings and avowals, of flight together into some solitude to people it with those ineffable confidences which so naturally follow the outward proofs of love. All this makes the brightest page of many a life, the only bright page in the thin biography of many a human animal; while if the beasts could speak they would give us, no doubt, endless versions of the only joy in which, as we may fancy, the blood of the universe flows consciously through their hearts.

The darkness which conventionally covers this passion is one of the saddest consequences of Adam's fall. It was a terrible misfortune in man's development that he should not have been able to acquire the higher functions without deranging the lower. Why should the depths of his being be thus polluted and the most delightful of nature's mysteries be an occasion not for communion with her, as it should have remained, but for depravity and sorrow?

This question, asked in moral perplexity, admits of a scientific answer. Man, in becoming more complex, becomes less stably organised. His sexual instinct, instead of being intermittent, but violent and boldly declared, becomes practically constant, but is entangled in many cross-currents of desire, in many other equally imperfect adaptations of structure to various ends. Indulgence in any impulse can then easily become excessive and thwart the rest; for it may be aroused artificially and maintained from without, so that in turn it disturbs its neighbours. Sometimes the sexual instinct may be stimulated out of season by example, by a too wakeful fancy, by language, by pride—for all these forces are now working in the same field and intermingling their suggestions. At the same time the same instinct may derange others, and make them fail at their proper and pressing occasions.

In consequence of such derangements, reflection and public opinion will come to condemn what in itself was perfectly innocent. The corruption of a given instinct by others and of others by it, becomes the ground for long attempts to suppress or enslave it. With the haste and formalism natural to language and to law, external and arbitrary limits are set to its operation. As no inward adjustment can possibly correspond to these conventional barriers and compartments of life, a war between nature and morality breaks out both in society and in each particular bosom—a war in which every victory is a sorrow and every defeat a dishonour. As one instinct after another becomes furious or disorganised, cowardly or criminal, under these artificial restrictions, the public and private conscience turns against it all its forces, necessarily without much nice discrimination; the frank passions of youth are met with a grimace of horror on all sides, with *rumores senum severiorum*, with an insistence on reticence and hypocrisy. Such suppression is favourable to corruption: the fancy with a sort of idiotic ingenuity comes to supply the place of experience; and nature is rendered vicious and overlaid with pruriency, artifice, and the love of novelty. Hereupon the authorities that rule in such matters naturally redouble their vigilance and exaggerate their reasonable censure: chastity begins to seem essentially holy and perpetual virginity ends by becoming an absolute ideal. Thus the disorder in man's life and disposition, when grown intolerable, leads him to condemn the very elements out of which order might have been constituted, and to mistake his total confusion for his total depravity.

Banished from the open day, covered with mockery, and publicly ignored, this necessary pleasure flourishes none the less in dark places and in the secret soul. Its familiar presence there, its intimate habitation in what is most oneself, helps to cut the world in two and to separate the inner from the outer life. In that mysticism which cannot disguise its erotic affinities this disruption reaches an absolute and theoretic form; but in many a youth little suspected of mysticism it produces estrangement from the conventional moralising world, which he instinctively regards as artificial and alien. It prepares him for excursions into a private fairy-land in which unthought-of joys will blossom amid friendlier magic forces. The truly good then seems to be the fantastic, the sensuous, the prodigally unreal. He gladly forgets the dreary world he lives in to listen for a thousand and one nights to his dreams.

To brood on such an Elysium is a likely prelude and fertile preparation for romantic passion. When the passion takes form it calls fancy back from its loose reveries and fixes it upon a single object. Then the ideal seems at last to have been brought down to earth. Its embodiment has been discovered amongst the children of men. Imagination narrows her range. Instead of all sorts of flatteries to sense and improbable delicious adventures, the lover imagines but a single joy: to be master of his love in body and soul. Jealousy pursues him. Even if he dreads no physical betrayal, he suffers from terror and morbid sensitiveness at every hint of mental estrangement.

This attachment is often the more absorbing the more unaccountable it seems; and as in hypnotism the subject is dead to all influences but that of the operator, so in love the heart surrenders itself entirely to the one being that has known how to touch it. That being is not selected; it is recognised and obeyed. Pre-arranged reactions in the system respond to whatever stimulus, at a propitious moment, happens to break through and arouse them pervasively. Nature has opened various avenues to that passion in whose successful operation she has so much at stake. Sometimes the magic influence asserts itself suddenly, sometimes gently and unawares. One approach, which in poetry has usurped more than its share of attention, is through beauty; another, less glorious, but often more efficacious, through surprised sense and premonitions of pleasure; a third through social sympathy and moral affinities. Contemplation, sense, and association are none of them the essence nor even the seed of love; but any of them may be its soil and supply it with a propitious background. It would be mere sophistry to pretend, for instance, that love is or should be nothing but a moral bond, the sympathy of two kindred spirits or the union of two lives. For such an effect no passion would be needed, as none is needed to perceive beauty or to feel pleasure.

What Aristotle calls friendships of utility, pleasure, or virtue, all resting on common interests of some impersonal sort, are far from possessing the quality of love, its thrill, flutter, and absolute sway over happiness and misery. But it may well fall to such influences to awaken or feed the passion where it actually arises. Whatever circumstances pave the way, love does not itself appear until a sexual affinity is declared. When a woman, for instance, contemplating marriage, asks herself whether she really loves her suitor or merely accepts him, the test is the possibility of awakening a sexual affinity. For this reason women of the world often love their husbands more truly than they did their lovers, because marriage has evoked an elementary feeling which before lay smothered under a heap of coquetries, vanities, and conventions.

Man, on the contrary, is polygamous by instinct, although often kept faithful by habit no less than by duty. If his fancy is left free, it is apt to wander. We observe this in romantic passion no less than in a life of mere gallantry and pleasure. Sentimental illusions may become a habit, and the shorter the dream is the more often it is repeated, so that any susceptible poet may find that he, like Alfred de Musset, "must love incessantly, who once has loved." Love is indeed much less exacting than it thinks itself. Nine-tenths of its cause are in the lover, for one-tenth that may be in the object. Were the latter not accidentally at hand, an almost identical passion would probably have been felt for someone else; for although with acquaintance the quality of an attachment naturally adapts itself to the person loved, and makes that person its standard and ideal, the first assault and mysterious glow

of the passion is much the same for every object. What really
affects the character of love is the lover's temperament, age, and
experience. The objects that appeal to each man reveal his nature;
but those unparalleled virtues and that unique divinity which the
lover discovers there are reflections of his own adoration, things
that ecstasy is very cunning in. He loves what he imagines and
worships what he creates.

Those who do not consider these matters so curiously may feel
that to refer love in this way chiefly to inner processes is at once
ignominious and fantastic. But nothing could be more natural;
the soul accurately renders, in this experience, what is going on
in the body and in the race. Nature had a problem to solve in
sexual reproduction which would have daunted a less ruthless ex-
perimenter. She had to bring together automatically, and at the
dictation, as they felt, of their irresponsible wills, just the creatures that by uniting might reproduce the species. The complete
sexual reaction had to be woven together out of many incomplete
reactions to various stimuli, reactions not specifically sexual. The
outer senses had to be engaged, and many secondary characters
found in bodies had to be used to attract attention, until the deeper
instinctive response should have time to gather itself together and
assert itself openly. Many mechanical preformations and reflexes
must conspire to constitute a determinate instinct. We name this
instinct after its ultimate function, looking forward to the uses
we observe it to have; and it seems to us in consequence an inexplicable anomaly that many a time the instinct is set in motion
when its alleged purpose cannot be fulfilled; as when love appears
prematurely or too late, or fixes upon a creature of the wrong
age or sex. These anomalies show us how nature is built up and,
far from being inexplicable, are hints that tend to make everything
clear, when once a verbal and mythical philosophy has been
abandoned.

Responses which we may call sexual in view of results to which
they may ultimately lead are thus often quite independent, and
exist before they are drawn into the vortex of a complete and
actually generative act. External stimulus and present idea will
consequently be altogether inadequate to explain the profound
upheaval which may ensue, if, as we say, we actually fall in love.
That the senses should be played upon is nothing, if no deeper
reaction is aroused. All depends on the juncture at which, so to

speak, the sexual circuit is completed and the emotional currents begin to circulate. Whatever object, at such a critical moment, fills the field of consciousness becomes a signal and associate for the whole sexual mood. It is breathlessly devoured in that pause and concentration of attention, that rearrangement of the soul, which love is conceived in; and the whole new life which that image is engulfed in is foolishly supposed to be its effect. For the image is in consciousness, but not the profound predispositions which gave it place and power.

This association between passion and its signals may be merely momentary, or it may be perpetual: a Don Juan and a Dante are both genuine lovers. In a gay society the gallant addresses every woman as if she charmed him, and perhaps actually finds any kind of beauty, or mere femininity anywhere, a sufficient spur to his desire. These momentary fascinations are not necessarily false: they may for an instant be quite absorbing and irresistible; they may genuinely suffuse the whole mind. Such mercurial fire will indeed require a certain imaginative temperament; and there are many persons who, short of a life-long domestic attachment, can conceive of nothing but sordid vice. But even an inconstant flame may burn brightly, if the soul is naturally combustible. Indeed these sparks and glints of passion, just because they come and vary so quickly, offer admirable illustrations of it, in which it may be viewed, so to speak, under the microscope and in its formative stage.

Thus Plato did not hesitate to make the love of all wines, under whatever guise, excuse, or occasion, the test of a true taste for wine and an unfeigned adoration of Bacchus; and, like Lucretius after him, he wittily compiled a list of names, by which the lover will flatter the most opposite qualities, if they only succeed in arousing his inclination. To be omnivorous is one pole of true love: to be exclusive is the other. A man whose heart, if I may say so, lies deeper, hidden under a thicker coat of mail, will have less play of fancy, and will be far from finding every charm charming, or every sort of beauty a stimulus to love. Yet he may not be less prone to the tender passion, and when once smitten may be so penetrated by an unimagined tenderness and joy, that he will declare himself incapable of ever loving again, and may actually be so. Having no rivals and a deeper soil, love can ripen better in such a constant spirit; it will not waste itself in a continual patter of little pleasures and illusions. But unless the passion of it is to die down, it must somehow assert its universality: what it loses in diversity it must gain in applicability. It must become a principle of action and an influence colouring everything that is dreamt of; otherwise it would have lost its dignity and sunk into a dead memory or a domestic bond.

True love, it used to be said, is love at first sight. Manners have much to do with such incidents, and the race which happens to set, at a given time, the fashion in literature makes its temperament public and exercises a sort of contagion over all men's fancies. If women are rarely seen and ordinarily not to be spoken to; if all imagination has to build upon is a furtive glance or casual motion, people fall in love at first sight. For they must fall in love somehow, and any stimulus is enough if none more powerful is forthcoming. When society, on the contrary, allows constant and easy intercourse between the sexes, a first impression, if not reinforced, will soon be hidden and obliterated by others. Acquaintance becomes necessary for love when it is necessary for memory. But what makes true love is not the information conveyed by acquaintance, not any circumstantial charms that may be therein discovered: it is still a deep and dumb instinctive affinity, an inexplicable emotion seizing the heart, an influence organising the world, like a luminous crystal, about one magic point. So that although love seldom springs up suddenly in these days into anything like a full-blown passion, it is sight, it is presence, that makes in time a conquest over the heart; for all virtues, sympathies, confidences will fail to move a man to tenderness and to worship, unless a poignant effluence from the object envelop him, so that he begins to walk, as it were, in a dream.

Not to believe in love is a great sign of dulness. There are some people so indirect and lumbering that they think all real affection must rest on circumstantial evidence. But a finely constituted being is sensitive to its deepest affinities. This is precisely what refinement consists in, that we may feel in things immediate and infinitesimal a sure premonition of things ultimate and important. Fine senses vibrate at once to harmonies which it may take long to verify; so sight is finer than touch, and thought than sensation. Well-bred instinct meets reason half-way, and is prepared for the consonances that may follow. Beautiful things, when taste is formed, are obviously and unaccountably beautiful. The grounds we may bring ourselves to assign for our preferences are discovered by analysing those preferences, and articulate judgments follow upon emotions which they ought to express, but which they sometimes sophisticate. So, too, the reasons we give for love either express what it feels or else are insincere, attempting to justify at the bar of reason and convention something which is far more primitive than they and underlies them both. True instinct can dispense with such excuses. It appeals to the event and is justified by the response which nature makes to it. It is, of course, far from infallible; it cannot dominate circumstances, and has no discursive knowledge; but it is presumably true, and what it foreknows is always essentially possible. Unrealisable it may indeed be in the jumbled context of this world, where the Fates, like an absent-minded printer, seldom allow a single line to stand perfect and unmarred.

The profoundest affinities are those most readily felt, and though a thousand later considerations may overlay and override them, they remain a background and standard for all happiness. If we trace them out we succeed. If we put them by, although in other respects we may call ourselves happy, we inwardly know that we have dismissed the ideal, and all that was essentially possible has not been realised. Love in that case still owns a hidden and potential object, and we sanctify, perhaps, whatever kindnesses or partialities we indulge in by a secret loyalty to something impersonal and unseen. Such reserve, such religion, would not have been necessary had things responded to our first expectations. We might then have identified the ideal with the object that happened to call it forth. The Life of Reason might have been led instinctively, and we might have been guided by nature herself into the ways of peace.

As it is, circumstances, false steps, or the mere lapse of time, force us to shuffle our affections and take them as they come, or as we are suffered to indulge them. Every real object must cease to be what it seemed, and none could ever be what the whole soul desired. Yet what the soul desires is nothing arbitrary. Life is no objectless dream, but continually embodies, with varying success, the potentialities it contains and that prompt desire. Everything that satisfies at all, even if partially and for an instant, justifies aspiration and rewards it. Existence, however, cannot be arrested;

and only the transmissible forms of things can endure, to match the transmissible faculties which living beings hand down to one another. The ideal is accordingly significant, perpetual, and as constant as the nature it expresses; but it can never itself exist, nor can its particular embodiments endure.

Love is accordingly only half an illusion; the lover, but not his love, is deceived. His madness, as Plato taught, is divine; for though it be folly to identify the idol with the god, faith in the god is inwardly justified. That egregious idolatry may therefore be interpreted ideally and give a symbolic scope worthy of its natural causes and of the mystery it comes to celebrate. The lover knows much more about absolute good and universal beauty than any logician or theologian, unless the latter, too, be lovers in disguise. Logical universals are terms in discourse, without vital ideality, while traditional gods are at best natural existences, more or less indifferent facts. What the lover comes upon, on the contrary, is truly persuasive, and witnesses to itself, so that he worships from the heart and upholds what he worships. That the true object is no natural being, but an ideal form essentially eternal and capable of endless embodiments, is far from abolishing its worth; on the contrary, this fact makes love ideally relevant to generation, by which the human soul and body may be for ever renewed, and at the same time makes it a thing for large thoughts to be focussed upon, a thing representing all rational aims.

Whenever this ideality is absent and a lover sees nothing in his mistress but what everyone else may find in her, loving her honestly in her unvarnished and accidental person, there is a friendly and humorous affection, admirable in itself, but no passion or bewitchment of love; she is a member of his group, not a spirit in his pantheon. Such an affection may be altogether what it should be; it may bring a happiness all the more stable because the heart is quite whole, and no divine shaft has pierced it. It is hard to stanch wounds inflicted by a god. The glance of an ideal love is terrible and glorious, foreboding death and immortality together. Love is a true natural religion; it has a visible cult, it is kindled by natural beauties and bows to the best symbol it may find for its hope; it sanctifies a natural mystery; and, finally, when understood, it recognises that what it worshipped under a figure was truly the principle of all good.

The loftiest edifices need the deepest foundations. Love would never take so high a flight unless it sprung from something profound and elementary. It is accordingly most truly love when it is irresistible and fatal. The substance of all passion, if we could gather it together, would be the basis of all ideals, to which all goods would have to refer. Love actually accomplishes something of the sort; being primordial it underlies other demands, and can be wholly satisfied only by a happiness which is ultimate and comprehensive. Lovers are vividly aware of this fact: their ideal, aparently so inarticulate, seems to them to include everything. It shares the mystical quality of all primitive life. Sophisticated people can hardly understand how vague experience is at bottom, and how truly that vagueness supports whatever clearness is afterward attained. In truth, all spiritual interests are supported by animal life; in this the generative function is fundamental; and it is therefore no paradox, but something altogether fitting, that if that function realised all it comprises, nothing human would remain outside. Such an ultimate fulfilment would differ, of course, from a first satisfaction, just as all that reproduction reproduces differs from the reproductive function itself, and vastly exceeds it. All organs and activities which are inherited, in a sense, grow out of the reproductive process and serve to clothe it; so that when the generative energy is awakened all that can ever be is virtually called up and, so to speak, made consciously potential; and love yearns for the universe of values.

This secret is gradually revealed to those who are inwardly attentive and allow love to teach them something. A man who has truly loved, though he may come to recognise the thousand incidental illusions into which love may have led him, will not recant its essential faith. He will keep his sense for the ideal and his power to worship. In fortunate cases love may glide imperceptibly into settled domestic affections, giving them henceforth a touch of ideality; for when love dies in the odour of sanctity people venerate his relics. In other cases allegiance to the ideal may appear more sullenly, breaking out in whims, or in little sentimental practices which might seem half-conventional. Again it may inspire a religious conversion, charitable works, or even artistic labours. In all these ways people attempt more or less seriously to lead the Life of Reason, expressing outwardly allegiance to whatever in their minds has come to stand for the ideal. The machinery which serves reproduction thus finds kindred but higher uses, as every organ does in a liberal life; and what Plato called a desire for birth in beauty may be sublimated even more, until it yearns for an ideal immortality in a transfigured world, a world made worthy of that love which its children have so often lavished on it in their dreams.

CHAPTER 2

THE FAMILY

Love is but a prelude to life, an overture in which the theme of the impending work is exquisitely hinted at, but which remains nevertheless only a symbol and a promise. What is to follow, if all goes well, begins presently to appear. Passion settles down into possession, courtship into partnership, pleasure into habit. A child, half mystery and half plaything, comes to show us what we have done and to make its consequences perpetual. We see that by indulging our inclinations we have woven about us a net from which we cannot escape: our choices, bearing fruit, begin to manifest our destiny. That life which once seemed to spread out infinitely before us is narrowed to one mortal career. We learn that in morals the infinite is a chimera, and that in accomplishing anything definite a man renounces everything else. He sails henceforth for one point of the compass.

The family is one of nature's masterpieces. It would be hard to conceive a system of instincts more nicely adjusted, where the constituents should represent or support one another better. The husband has an interest in protecting the wife, she in serving the husband. The weaker gains in authority and safety, the wilder and more unconcerned finds a help-mate at home to take thought for his daily necessities. Parents lend children their experience and a vicarious memory; children endow their parents with a vicarious immortality.

The long childhood in the human race has made it possible and needful to transmit acquired experience: possible, because the child's brain, being immature, allows instincts and habits to be formed after birth, under the influence of that very environment in which they are to operate; and also needful, since children are long incapable of providing for themselves and compel their parents, if the race is not to die out, to continue their care, and to diversify it. To be born half-made is an immense advantage. Structure preformed is formed blindly; the *a priori* is as dangerous in life as in philosophy. Only the cruel workings of compulsion and extermination keep what is spontaneous in any creature harmonious with the world it is called upon to live in. Nothing but casual variations could permanently improve such a creature; and casual variations will seldom improve it. But if experience can co-operate in forming instincts, and if human nature can be partly a work of art, mastery can be carried quickly to much greater lengths. This is the secret of man's pre-eminence. His liquid brain is unfit for years to control action advantageously. He has an age of play which is his apprenticeship; and he is formed unawares by a series of selective experiments, of curious gropings, while he is still under tutelage and suffers little by his mistakes.

Had all intelligence been developed in the womb, as it might have been, nothing essential could have been learned afterward. Mankind would have contained nothing but doctrinaires, and the arts would have stood still for ever. Capacity to learn comes with dependence on education; and as that animal which at birth is most incapable and immature is the most teachable, so too those human races which are most precocious are most incorrigible, and while they seem the cleverest at first prove ultimately the least intelligent. They depend less on circumstances, but do not respond to them so well. In some nations everybody is by nature so astute, versatile, and sympathetic that education hardly makes any difference in manners or mind; and it is there that generation follows generation without essential progress, and no one ever remakes himself on a better plan. It is perhaps the duller races, with a long childhood and a brooding mind, that bear the hopes of the world within them, if only nature avails to execute what she has planned at such long range.

Generation answers no actual demand except that existing in the parents, and it establishes a new demand without guaranteeing its satisfaction. Birth is a benefit only problematically and by anticipation, on the presumption that the faculties newly embodied are to be exercised successfully. The second function of the family, to rear, is therefore higher than the first. To foster and perfect a life after it has been awakened, to co-operate with a will already launched into the world, is a positive good work. It has a moral quality and is not mere vegetation; for in expressing the agent and giving him ideal employment, it helps the creature affected to employ itself better, too, and to find expression. In propagating and sowing broadcast precarious beings there is fertility only, such

as plants and animals may have; but there is charity in furthering
what is already rooted in existence and is striving to live.

This principle is strikingly illustrated in religion. When the
Jews had become spiritual they gave the name of Father to
Jehovah, who had before been only the Lord of Armies or the
architect of the cosmos. A mere source of being would not deserve
to be called father, unless it shared its creatures' nature and therefore their interests. A deity not so much responsible for men's
existence or situation as solicitous for their welfare, who pitied a
weakness he could not have intended and was pleased by a love
he could not command, might appropriately be called a father. It
then becomes possible to conceive moral intercourse and mutual
loyalty between God and man, such as Hebrew religion so earnestly
insisted on; for both then have the same interests in the world
and look toward the same consummations. So the natural relations
subsisting between parents and children become moral when it is
not merely derivation that unites them, but community of purpose.
The father then represents his children while they are under his
tutelage, and afterward they represent him, carrying on his arts
and inheriting his mind.

These arts in some cases are little more than retarded instincts,
faculties that ripen late and that manifest themselves without
special instruction when the system is mature. So a bird feeds her
young until they are fledged and can provide for themselves.
Parental functions in such cases are limited to nursing the extremely young. This phase of the instinct, being the most primitive
and fundamental, is most to be relied upon even in man. Especially
in the mother, care for the children's physical well-being is un-
failing to the end. She understands the vegetative soul, and the
first lispings of sense and sentiment in the child have an absorbing
interest for her. In that region her skill and delights are miracles
of nature; but her insight and keenness gradually fade as the
children grow older. Seldom is the private and ideal life of a young
son or daughter a matter in which the mother shows particular
tact or for which she has instinctive respect. Even rarer is any
genuine community in life and feeling between parents and their
adult children. Often the parents' influence comes to be felt as a
dead constraint, the more cruel that it cannot be thrown off without unkindness; and what makes the parents' claim at once unjust
and pathetic is that it is founded on passionate love for a remem-

bered being, the child once wholly theirs, that no longer exists in the man.

To train character and mind would seem to be a father's natural office, but as a matter of fact he commonly delegates that task to society. The fledgling venturing for the first time into the air may learn of his father and imitate his style of flight; but once launched into the open it will find the whole sky full of possible masters. The one ultimately chosen will not necessarily be the nearest; in reason it should be the most congenial, from whom most can be learned. To choose an imitable hero is the boy's first act of freedom; his heart grows by finding its elective affinities, and it grows most away from home. It will grow also by returning there, when home has become a part of the world or a refuge from it; but even then the profoundest messages will come from religion and from solitary dreams. A consequence is that parental influence, to be permanent, requires that the family should be hedged about with high barriers and that the father be endowed with political and religious authority. He can then exercise the immense influence due to all tradition, which he represents, and all law, which he administers; but it is not his bare instincts as a father that give him this ascendency. It is a social system that has delegated to him most of its functions, so that all authority flows through him, and he retails justice and knowledge, besides holding all wealth in his hand. When the father, apart from these official prerogatives, is eager and able to mould his children's minds, a new relation half natural and half ideal, which is friendship, springs up between father and son. In this ties of blood merely furnish the opportunity, and what chiefly counts is a moral impulse, on the one side, to beget children in the spirit, and on the other a youthful hunger for experience and ideas.

If *Nunc dimittis* is a psalm for love to sing, it is even more appropriate for parental piety. On seeing heirs and representatives of ours already in the world, we are inclined to give them place and trust them to realise our foiled ambitions. They, we fancy, will be more fortunate than we; we shall have screened them from whatever has most maimed our own lives. Their purer souls, as we imagine, will reach better things than are now possible to ours, distracted and abused so long. We commit the blotted manuscript of our lives more willingly to the flames, when we find the immortal text already half engrossed in a fairer copy.

In all this there is undoubtedly a measure of illusion, since little clear improvement is ordinarily possible in the world, and while our children may improve upon us in some respects, the devil will catch them unprepared in another quarter. Yet the hope in question is a transcript of primary impersonal functions to which nature, at certain levels, limits the animal will. To keep life going was, in the beginning, the sole triumph of life. Even when nothing but reproduction was aimed at or attained, existence was made possible and ideally stable by securing so much; and when the ideal was enlarged so as to include training and rearing the new generation, life was even better intrenched and protected. Though further material progress may not be made easier by this development, since more dangers become fatal as beings grow complex and mutually dependent, a great step in moral progress has at any rate been taken.

In itself, a desire to see a child grow and prosper is just as irrational as any other absolute desire; but since the child also desires his own happiness, the child's will sanctions and supports the father's. Thus two irrationalities, when they conspire, make one rational life. The father's instinct and sense of duty are now vindicated experimentally in the child's progress, while the son, besides the joy of living, has the pious function of satisfying his parent's hopes. Even if life could achieve nothing more than this, it would have reached something profoundly natural and perfectly ideal. In patriarchal ages men feel it is enough to have inherited their human patrimony, to have enjoyed it, and to hand it down unimpaired. He who is not childless goes down to his grave in peace. Reason may afterward come to larger vistas and more spiritual aims, but the principle of love and responsibility will not be altered. It will demand that wills be made harmonious and satisfactions compatible.

Life is experimental, and whatever performs some necessary function, and cannot be discarded, is a safe nucleus for many a parasite, a starting-point for many new experiments. So the family, in serving to keep the race alive, become a point of departure for many institutions. It assumes offices which might have been allotted to some other agency, had not the family pre-empted them, profiting by its established authority and annexing them to its domain. In no civilised community, for instance, has the union of man and wife been limited to its barely necessary period.

It has continued after the family was reared and has remained life-long; it has commonly involved a common dwelling and religion and often common friends and property. Again, the children's emancipation has been put off indefinitely. The Roman father had a perpetual jurisdiction and such absolute authority that, in the palmy days of the Roman family, no other subsisted over it. He alone was a citizen and responsible to the state, while his household were subject to him in law, as well as in property and religion. In simple rural communities the family has often been also the chief industrial unit, almost all necessaries being produced under domestic economy.

Now the instincts and delights which nature associates with reproduction cannot stretch so far. Their magic fails, and the political and industrial family, which still thinks itself natural, is in truth casual and conventional. There is no real instinct to protect those who can already protect themselves; nor have they any profit in obeying nor, in the end, any duty to do so. A *patria potestas* much prolonged or extended is therefore an abuse and prolific in abuses. The government and supervision required by adults is what we call political; it should stretch over all families alike.

After all, the family is an early expedient and in many ways irrational. If the race had developed a special sexless class to be nurses, pedagogues, and slaves, like the workers among ants and bees, then the family would have been unnecessary. Such a division of labour would doubtless have involved evils of its own, but it would have obviated some drags and vexations proper to the family. For we pay a high price for our conquests in this quarter, and the sweets of home are balanced not only by its tenderer sorrows, but by a thousand artificial prejudices, enmities, and restrictions. It takes patience to appreciate domestic bliss; volatile spirits prefer unhappiness. Young men escape as soon as they can, at least in fancy, into the wide world; all prophets are homeless and all inspired artists; philosophers think out some communism or other, and monks put it in practice. There is indeed no more irrational ground for living together than that we have sprung from the same loins. They say blood is thicker than water; yet similar forces easily compete while dissimilar forces may perhaps co-operate. It is the end that is sacred, not the beginning. A common origin unites reasonable creatures only if it involves common thoughts and purposes; and these may bind together individuals of the most remote races and ages, when once they have discovered one another. It is difficulties of access, ignorance, and material confinement that shut in the heart to its narrow loyalties; and perhaps greater mobility, science, and the mingling of nations will one day reorganise the moral world. It was a pure spokesman of the spirit who said that whosoever should do the will of his *Father who was in heaven,* the same was his brother and sister and mother.

The family also perpetuates accidental social differences, ex- aggerating and making them hereditary; it thus defeats that just moiety of the democratic ideal which demands that all men should have equal opportunities. In human society chance only decides what education a man shall receive, what wealth and influence he shall enjoy, even what religion and profession he shall adopt. People shudder at the system of castes which prevails in India; but is not every family a little caste? Was a man assigned to his family because he belonged to it in spirit, or can he choose an- other? Half the potentialities in the human race are thus stifled, half its incapacities fostered and made inveterate. The family, too, is largely responsible for the fierce prejudices that prevail about women, about religion, about seemly occupations, about war, death, and honour. In all these matters men judge in a blind way, inspired by a feminine passion that has no mercy for anything that eludes the traditional household, not even for its members' souls.

At the same time there are insuperable difficulties in proposing any substitute for the family. In the first place, all society at present rests on this institution, so that we cannot easily discern which of our habits and sentiments are parcels of it, and which are attached to it adventitiously and have an independent basis. A reformer hewing so near to the tree's root never knows how much he may be felling. For instance, it is conceivable that a communist, abolishing the family in order to make opportunities equal and remove the more cruel injustices of fortune, might be drying up that milk of human kindness which had fed his own enthusiasm; for the found- lings which he decreed were to people the earth might at once dis- own all socialism and prove a brood of inhuman egoists.

On the other hand, an opposite danger is present in this sort of speculation. Things now associated with the family may not de- pend upon it, but might flourish equally well in a different soil. One of the great lessons, for example, which society has to teach its members is that society exists. The child, like the animal, is a colossal egoist, not from a want of sensibility, but through his deep transcendental isolation. The mind is naturally its own world and its solipsism needs to be broken down by social influence. The child must learn to sympathise intelligently, to be considerate, rather than instinctively to love and hate: his imagination must become cognitive and dramatically just, instead of remaining, as it naturally is, sensitively, selfishly fanciful.

To break down transcendental conceit is a function usually confided to the family, and yet the family is not well fitted to perform it. To mothers and nurses their darlings are always exceptional; even fathers and brothers teach a child that he is very different from other creatures and of infinitely greater consequence, since he lies closer to their hearts and may expect from them all sorts of favouring services. The whole household, in proportion as it spreads about the child a brooding and indulgent atmosphere, nurses wilfulness and illusion. For this reason the noblest and happiest children are those brought up, as in Greece or England, under simple general conventions by persons trained and hired for the purpose. The best training in character is found in very large families or in schools, where boys educate one another. Priceless in this regard is athletic exercise; for here the test of ability is visible, the comparison not odious, the need of co-operation clear, and the consciousness of power genuine and therefore ennobling. Socratic dialectic is not a better means of learning to know oneself. Such self-knowledge is objective and free from self-consciousness; it sees the self in a general medium and measures it by a general law.

Even the tenderer associations of home might, under other circumstances, attach to other objects. Consensus of opinion has a distorting effect, sometimes, on ideal values. So wealth, religion, military victory gain more rhetorical than efficacious worth. The family might well be, to some extent, a similar idol of the tribe. Everyone has had a father and a mother; but how many have had a friend? Everyone likes to remember many a joy and even sorrow of his youth which was linked with family occasions; but to name a man's more private memories, attached to special surroundings, would awaken no response in other minds. Yet these other surroundings may have been no less stimulating to emotion, and if familiar to all might be spoken of with as much conventional effect. This appears so soon as any experience is diffused enough to enable a tradition to arise, so that the sentiment involved can find a social echo. Thus there is a loyalty, very powerful in certain quarters, toward school, college, club, regiment, church, and country. Who shall say that such associations, had they sprung up earlier and been more zealously cultivated, or were they now reinforced by more general sympathy, would not breed all the tenderness and infuse all the moral force which most men now derive from the family?

While a desirable form of society entirely without the family is hard to conceive, yet the general tendency in historic times, and the marked tendency in periods of ripe development, has been toward individualism. Individualism is in one sense the only possible ideal; for whatever social order may be most valuable can be valuable only for its effect on conscious individuals. Man is of course a social animal and needs society first that he may come safely into being, and then that he may have something interesting to do. But society itself is no animal and has neither instincts, interests, nor ideals. To talk of such things is either to speak metaphorically or to think mythically; and myths, the more currency they acquire, pass the more easily into superstitions. It would be a gross and pedantic superstition to venerate any form of society in itself, apart from the safety, breadth, or sweetness which it lent to individual happiness. If the individual may be justly subordinated to the state, not merely for the sake of a future freer generation, but permanently and in the ideal society, the reason is simply that such subordination is a part of man's natural devotion to things rational and impersonal, in the presence of which alone he can be personally happy. Society, in its future and its past, is a natural object of interest like art or science; it exists, like them, because only when lost in such rational objects can a free soul be active and immortal. But all these ideals are terms in some actual life, not alien ends, important to nobody, to which, notwithstanding, everybody is to be sacrificed. Individualism is therefore the only ideal possible. The excellence of societies is measured by what they provide for their members.

The family in a barbarous age remains sacrosanct and traditional; nothing in its law, manners, or ritual is open to amendment. The unhappiness which may consequently overtake individuals is hushed up or positively blamed, with no thought of tinkering with the holy institutions which are its cause. Civilised men think more and cannot endure objectless tyrannies. It is inevitable, therefore, that as barbarism recedes the family should become more sensitive to its members' personal interests. Husband and wife, when they are happily matched, are in liberal communities more truly united than before, because such closer friendship expresses their personal inclination. Children are still cared for, because love of them is natural, but they are ruled less and sooner suffered to choose their own associations. They are more largely given in charge to persons not belonging to the family, especially fitted to supply their education. The whole, in a word, exists more and more for the sake of the parts, and the closeness, duration, and scope of family ties comes to vary greatly in different households. Barbaric custom, imposed in all cases alike without respect of persons, yields to a regimen that dares to be elastic and will take pains to be just.

How far these liberties should extend and where they would pass into license and undermine rational life, is another question. To what extent men and women, in a future age, may need to rely on ties of consanguinity or marriage in order not to grow solitary, purposeless, and depraved, is for prophets only to predict. If changes continue in the present direction much that is now in bad odour may come to be accepted as normal. It might happen, for instance, as a consequence of woman's independence, that mothers alone should be their children's guardians and sole mistresses in their houses; the husband, if he were acknowledged at all, having at most a pecuniary responsibility for his offspring. Such an arrangement would make a stable home for the children, while leaving marriage dissoluble at the will of either party.

It may well be doubted, however, whether women, if given every encouragement to establish and protect themselves, would not in the end fly again into man's arms and prefer to be drudges and mistresses at home to living disciplined and submerged in some larger community. Indeed, the effect of women's emancipation might well prove to be the opposite of what was intended. Really free and equal competition between men and women might reduce the weaker sex to such graceless inferiority that, deprived of the deference and favour they now enjoy, they should find themselves entirely without influence. In that case they would have to begin again at the bottom and appeal to arts of seduction to regain their lost social position.

For any functon to reach perfection it must fufil two conditions: it must be delightful in itself, endowing its occasions and results with ideal interest, and it must also co-operate harmoniously with all other functions so that life may be profitable and happy. In the matter of reproduction nature has already fulfilled the first of these conditions in its essentials. It has indeed superabundantly fulfilled them, and not only has love appeared in man's soul, the type and symbol of all vital perfection, but a tenderness and charm, a pathos passing into the frankest joy, has been spread over pregnancy, birth, and childhood. If many pangs and tears still prove how tentative and violent, even here, are nature's most brilliant feats, science and kindness may strive not unsuccessfully to diminish or abolish those profound traces of evil. But reproduction will not be perfectly organised until the second condition is fulfilled as well, and here nature has as yet been more remiss. Family life, as Western nations possess it, is still regulated in a very bungling, painful and unstable manner. Hence, in the first rank of evils, prostitution, adultery, divorce, improvident and unhappy marriages; and in the second rank, a morality compacted of three inharmonious parts, with incompatible ideals, each in its way legitimate: I mean the ideals of passion, of convention, and of reason; add, besides, genius and religion thwarted by family ties, single lives empty, wedded lives constrained, a shallow gallantry, and a dull virtue.

How to surround the natural sanctities of wedlock with wise custom and law, how to combine the maximum of spiritual freedom with the maximum of moral cohesion, is a problem for experiment to solve. It cannot be solved, even ideally, in a Utopia. For each interest in play has its rights and the prophet neither knows what interests may at a given future time subsist in the world, nor what relative force they may have, nor what mechanical conditions may control their expression. The statesman in his sphere and the individual in his must find, as they go, the best practical solutions. All that can be indicated beforehand is the principle which improvements in this institution would comply with if they were really improvements. They would reform and perfect the function of reproduction without discarding it; they would maintain the family unless they could devise some institution that combined intrinsic and representative values better than does that natural artifice, and they would recast either the instincts or the laws concerned, or both simultaneously, until the family ceased to clash seriously with any of these three things: natural affection, rational nurture, and moral freedom.

CHAPTER 3

INDUSTRY, GOVERNMENT, AND WAR

CIVILISATION SECURES three chief advantages: greater wealth, greater safety, and greater variety of experience. Whether, in spite of this, there is a real—that is, a moral—advance is a question impossible to answer offhand, because wealth, safety, and variety are not absolute goods, and their value is great or small according to the further values they may help to secure. This is obvious in the case of riches. But safety also is only good when there is something to preserve better than courage, and when the prolongation of life can serve to intensify its excellence. An animal's existence is not improved when made safe by imprisonment and domestication; it is only degraded and rendered passive and melancholy. The human savage likewise craves a freedom and many a danger inconsistent with civilisation, because independent of reason. He does not yet identify his interests with any persistent and ideal harmonies created by reflection. And when reflection is absent, length of life is no benefit: a quick succession of generations, with a small chance of reaching old age, is a beautiful thing in purely animal economy, where vigour is the greatest joy, propagation the highest function, and decrepitude the sorriest woe. The value of safety, accordingly, hangs on the question whether life has become reflective and rational. But the fact that a state arises does not in itself imply rationality. It makes rationality possible, but leaves it potential.

Similar considerations apply to variety. To increase the number of instincts and functions is probably to produce confusion and to augment that secondary and reverberating kind of evil which consists in expecting pain and regretting misfortune. On the other hand, a perfect life could never be accused of monotony. All desirable variety lies within the circle of perfection. Thus we do not tire of possessing two legs nor wish, for the sake of variety, to be occasionally lunatics. Accordingly, an increase in variety of function is a good only if a unity can still be secured embracing that variety; otherwise it would have been better that the irrelevant function should have been developed by independent individuals or should

115

not have arisen at all. The function of seeing double adds more to the variety than to the spice of life. Whether civilisation is a blessing depends, then, on its ulterior uses. Judged by those interests which already exist when it arises, it is very likely a burden and oppression. The birds' instinctive economy would not be benefited by a tax-gatherer, a recruiting-sergeant, a sect or two of theologians, and the other usual organs of human polity.

For the Life of Reason, however, civilisation is a necessary condition. Although animal life, within man and beyond him, has its wild beauty and mystic justifications, yet that specific form of life which we call rational, and which is no less natural than the rest, would never have arisen without an expansion of human faculty, an increase in mental scope, for which civilisation is necessary. Wealth, safety, variety of pursuits, are all requisite if memory and purpose are to be trained increasingly, and if a steadfast art of living is to supervene upon instinct and dream.

Wealth is itself expressive of reason for it arises whenever men, instead of doing nothing or beating about casually in the world, take to gathering fruits of nature which they may have uses for in future, or fostering their growth, or actually contriving their appearance. Such is man's first industrial habit, seen in grazing, agriculture, and mining. Among nature's products are also those of man's own purposeless and imitative activity, results of his idle ingenuity and restlessness. Some of these, like nature's other random creations, may chance to have some utility. They may then become conspicuous to reflection, be strengthened by the relations which they establish in life, and be henceforth called works of human art. They then constitute a second industrial habit and that other sort of riches which is supplied by manufacture.

The amount of wealth man can produce is apparently limited only by time, invention, and the material at hand. It can very easily exceed his capacity for enjoyment. As the habits which produce wealth were originally spontaneous and only crystallised into reasonable processes by mutual checks and the gradual settling down of the organism into harmonious action, so also the same habits may outrun their uses. The machinery to produce wealth, of which man's own energies have become a part, may well work on irrespective of happiness. Indeed, the industrial ideal would be an international community with universal free trade, extreme division of labour, and no unproductive consumption. Such an arrangement would un-

doubtedly produce a maximum of riches, and any objections made
to it, if intelligent, must be made on other than universal economic
grounds. Free trade may be opposed, for instance (while patriotism
takes the invidious form of jealousy and while peace is not secure),
on the ground that it interferes with vested interests and settled
populations or with national completeness and self-sufficiency, or
that absorption in a single industry is unfavourable to intellectual
life. The latter is also an obvious objection to any great division
of labour, even in liberal fields; while any man with a tender heart
and traditional prejudices might hesitate to condemn the irresponsible rich to extinction, together with all paupers, mystics, and old
maids living on annuities.

Such attacks on industrialism, however, are mere skirmishes
and express prejudices of one sort or another. The formidable
judgment industrialism has to face is that of reason, which demands
that the increase and specification of labour be justified by benefits
somewhere actually realised and integrated in individuals. Wealth
must justify itself in happiness. Someone must live better for having
produced or enjoyed these possessions. And he would not live better, even granting that the possessions were in themselves advantages, if these advantages were bought at too high a price and removed other greater opportunities or benefits. The belle must not
sit so long prinking before the glass as to miss the party, and man
must not work so hard and burden himself with so many cares as to
have no breath or interest left for things free and intellectual. Work
and life too often are contrasted and complementary things; but
they would not be contrasted nor even separable if work were not
servile, for of course man can have no life save in occupation, and in
the exercise of his faculties; contemplation itself can deal only with
what practice contains or discloses. But the pursuit of wealth is a
pursuit of instruments. The division of labour when extreme does
violence to natural genius and obliterates natural distinctions in
capacity. What is properly called industry is not art or self-justifying activity, but on the contrary a distinctly compulsory and merely
instrumental labour, which if justified at all must be justified by
some ulterior advantage which it secures. In regard to such instrumental activities the question is always pertinent whether they do
not produce more than is useful, or prevent the existence of something that is intrinsically good.

Occidental society has evidently run in this direction into great abuses, complicating life prodigiously without ennobling the mind. It has put into rich men's hands facilities and luxuries which they trifle with without achieving any dignity or true magnificence in living, while the poor, if physically more comfortable than formerly, are not meantime notably wiser or merrier. Ideal distinction has been sacrificed in the best men, to add material comforts to the worst. Things, as Emerson said, are in the saddle and ride mankind. The means crowd out the ends and civilisation reverts, when it least thinks it, to barbarism.

The acceptable side of industrialism, which is supposed to be inspired exclusively by utility, is not utility at all but pure achievement. If we wish to do such an age justice we must judge it as we should a child and praise its feats without inquiring after its purposes. That is its own spirit: a spirit dominant at the present time, particularly in America, where industrialism appears most free from alloy. There is a curious delight in turning things over, changing their shape, discovering their possibilities, making of them some new contrivance. Use, in these experimental minds, as in nature, is only incidental. There is an irrational creative impulse, a zest in novelty, in progression, in beating the other man, or, as they say, in breaking the record. There is also a fascination in seeing the world unbosom itself of ancient secrets, obey man's coaxing, and take on unheard-of shapes. The highest building, the largest steamer, the fastest train, the book reaching the widest circulation have, in America, a clear title to respect. When the just functions of things are as yet not discriminated, the superlative in any direction seems naturally admirable. Again, many possessions, if they do not make a man better, are at least expected to make his children happier; and this pathetic hope is behind many exertions. An experimental materialism, spontaneous and divorced from reason and from everything useful, is also confused in some minds with traditional duties; and a school of popular hierophants is not lacking that turns it into a sort of religion and perhaps calls it idealism. Impulse is more visible in all this than purpose, imagination more than judgment; but it is pleasant for the moment to abound in invention and effort and to let the future cash the account.

Wealth is excessive when it reduces a man to a middleman and a jobber, when it prevents him, in his preoccupation with material things, from making his spirit the measure of them. There are Nibelungen who toil underground over a gold they will never use, and in their obsession with production begrudge themselves all holidays, all concessions to inclination, to merriment, to fancy; nay, they would even curtail as much as possible the free years of their youth, when they might see the blue, before rendering up their souls to the Leviathan. Visible signs of such unreason soon appear in the relentless and hideous aspect which life puts on; for those instruments which somehow emancipate themselves from their uses soon become hateful. In nature irresponsible wildness can be turned to beauty, because every product can be recomposed into some abstract manifestation of force or form; but the monstrous in man himself and in his works immediately offends, for here everything is expected to symbolise its moral relations. The irrational in the human has something about it altogether repulsive and terrible, as we see in the maniac, the miser, the drunkard, or the ape. A barbaric civilisation, built on blind impulse and ambition, should fear to awaken a deeper detestation than could ever be aroused by those more beautiful tyrannies, chivalrous or religious, against which past revolutions have been directed.

Both the sordidness and the luxury which industrialism may involve, could be remedied, however, by a better distribution of the product. The riches now created by labour would probably not seriously debauch mankind if each man had only his share; and such a proportionate return would enable him to perceive directly how far his interests required him to employ himself in material production and how far he could allow himself leisure for spontaneous things—religion, play, art study, conversation. In a world composed entirely of philosophers an hour or two a day of manual labour—a very welcome quantity—would provide for material wants; the rest could then be all the more competently dedicated to a liberal life; for a healthy soul needs matter quite as much for an object of interest as for a means of sustenance. But philosophers do not yet people nor even govern the world, and so simple a Utopia which reason, if it had direct efficacy, would long ago have reduced to act, is made impossible by the cross-currents of instinct, tradition, and fancy which variously deflect affairs.

What are called the laws of nature are so many observations made by man on a way things have of repeating themselves by replying always to their old causes and never, as reason's prejudice would expect, to their new opportunities. This inertia, which physics registers in the first law of motion, natural history and psychology call habit. Habit is a physical law. It is the basis and force of all morality, but is not morality itself. In society it takes the form of custom which, when codified, is called law and when enforced is called government. Government is the political representative of a natural equilibrium, of custom, of inertia; it is by no means a representative of reason. But, like any inevitable complication, it may become rational, and many of its forms and operations may be defended on rational grounds. All natural organisms can exercise certain ideal functions and symbolise in their structure certain ideal relations. Protoplasm tends to propagate iself, and in so doing may turn into a conscious ideal the end it already tends to realise; but there could be no desire for self-preservation were there not already a self preserved. So government can by its existence define the commonwealth it tends to preserve, and its acts may be approved from the point of view of those eventual interests which they satisfy. But government neither subsists nor arises because it is good or useful, but solely because it is inevitable. It becomes good in so far as the inevitable adjustment of political forces which it embodies is also a just provision for all the human interests which it creates or affects.

Suppose a cold and hungry savage, failing to find berries and game enough in the woods, should descend into some meadow where a flock of sheep were grazing and pounce upon a lame lamb which could not run away with the others, tear its flesh, suck up its blood, and dress himself in its skin. All this could not be called an affair undertaken in the sheep's interest. And yet it might well conduce to their interest in the end. For the savage, finding himself soon hungry again, and insufficiently warm in that scanty garment, might attack the flock a second time, and thereby begin to accustom himself, and also his delighted family, to a new and more substantial sort of raiment and diet. Suppose, now, a pack of wolves, or a second savage, or a disease should attack those unhappy sheep. Would not their primeval enemy defend them? Would he not have identified himself with their interests to this extent, that their total extinction or discomfiture would alarm him also? And in so far as he provided for their well-being, would he not have become a good shepherd? If, now, some philosophic wether, a lover of his kind, reasoned with his fellows upon the change in their condition, he might shudder indeed at those early episodes and at the contribution of lambs and fleeces which would not cease to be levied by the new government; but he might also consider that such a contribution was nothing in comparison with what was formerly exacted by wolves, diseases, frosts, and casual robbers, when the flock was much smaller than it had now grown to be, and much less able to withstand decimation. And he might even have conceived an admiration for the remarkable wisdom and beauty of that great shepherd, dressed in such a wealth of wool; and he might remember pleasantly some occasional caress received from him and the daily trough filled with water by his providential hand. And he might not be far from maintaining not only the rational origin, but the divine right of shepherds.

Such a savage enemy, incidentally turned into a useful master, is called a conqueror or king. Only in human experience the case is not so simple and harmony is seldom established so quickly. The history of Asia is replete with examples of conquest and extortion in which a rural population living in comparative plenty is attacked by some more ferocious neighbour who, after a round of pillage, establishes a quite unnecessary government, raising taxes and soldiers for purposes absolutely remote from the conquered people's interests. Such a government is nothing but a chronic raid, mitigated by the desire to leave the inhabitants prosperous enough to be continually despoiled afresh. Even this modicum of protection, however, can establish a certain moral bond between ruler and subject; an intelligent government and an intelligent fealty become conceivable. Not only may the established régime be superior to any other that could be substituted for it at the time, but some security against total destruction, and a certain opportunity for the arts and for personal advancement may follow subjugation. A moderate decrease in personal independence may be compensated by a novel public grandeur; palace and temple may make amends for hovels somewhat more squalid than before. Hence, those who cannot conceive a rational polity, or a co-operative greatness in the state, especially if they have a luxurious fancy, can take pleasure in despotism; for it does not, after all, make so much difference to an ordinary fool whether what he suffers from is another's oppression or his own lazy improvidence; and he can console himself by saying with Goldsmith:

> How small, of all that human hearts endure,
> The part which laws or kings can cause or cure.

At the same time a court and a hierarchy, with their interesting pomp and historic continuity, with their combined appeal to greed and imagination, redeem human existence from pervasive vulgarity and allow somebody at least to strut proudly over the earth. Serfs are not in a worse material condition than savages, and their spiritual opportunities are infinitely greater; for their eye and fancy are fed with visions of human greatness, and even if they cannot improve their outward estate they can possess a poetry and a religion. The ideas evolved may be wild and futile and the emotions savagely sensuous, yet they constitute a fund of inner experience, a rich soil for better imaginative growths. To such Oriental cogitations, for instance, carried on under the shadow of uncontrollable despotisms, mankind owes all its greater religions.

A government's origin has nothing to do with its legitimacy; that is, with its representative operation. An absolutism based on conquest or on religious fraud may wholly lose its hostile function. It may become the nucleus of a national organization expressing justly enough the people's requirements. Such a representative character is harder to attain when the government is foreign, for diversity in race language and local ties makes the ruler less apt involuntarily to represent his subjects; his measures must subserve their interests intentionally, out of sympathy, policy, and a sense of duty, virtues which are seldom efficacious for any continuous period. A native government, even if based on initial outrage, can more easily drift into excellence; for when a great man mounts the throne he has only to read his own soul and follow his instinctive ambitions in order to make himself the leader and spokesman of his nation. An Alexander, an Alfred, a Peter the Great, are examples of persons who with varying degrees of virtue were representative rulers: their policy, however irrationally inspired, happened to serve their subjects and the world. Besides, a native government is less easily absolute. Many influences control the ruler in his aims and habits, such as religion, custom, and the very language he speaks, by which praise and blame are assigned automatically to the objects loved or hated by the people. He cannot, unless he be an intentional monster, oppose himself wholly to the common soul.

For this very reason, however, native governments are little fitted to redeem or transform a people, and all great upheavals and regenerations have been brought about by conquest, by the substitution of one race and spirit for another in the counsels of the world. What the Orient owes to Greece, the Occident to Rome, India to England, native America to Spain, is a civilisation incomparably better than that which the conquered people could ever have provided for themselves. Conquest is a good means of recasting those ideals, perhaps impracticable and ignorant, which a native government at its best would try to preserve. Such inapt ideals, it is true, would doubtless remodel themselves if they could be partly realised. Progress from within is possible, otherwise no progress would be possible for humanity at large. But conquest gives at once a freer field to those types of polity which, since they go with strength, presumably represent the better adjustment to natural conditions, and therefore the better ideal. Though the motive force of ideals is the will, their mould must be experience and a true discernment of opportunity; so that while all ideals, regarded *in vacuo*, are equal in ideality, they are under given circumstances, very diverse in worth.

When not founded on conquest, which is the usual source of despotism, government is ordinarily based on traditional authority vested in elders or patriarchal kings. This is the origin of the classic state, and of all aristocracy and freedom. The economic and political unit is a great household with its lord, his wife and children, clients and slaves. In the interstices of these households there may be a certain floating residuum—freedmen, artisans, merchants, strangers. These people, while free, are without such rights as even slaves possess; they have no share in the religion, education, and resources of any established family. For purposes of defence and religion the heads of houses gather together in assemblies, elect or recognise some chief, and agree upon laws, usually little more than extant customs regulated and formally sanctioned.

Such a state tends to expand in two directions. In the first place, it becomes more democratic; that is, it tends to recognise other influences than that which heads of families—*patres conscripti*—possess. The people without such fathers, those who are not patricians, also have children and come to imitate on a smaller scale the patriarchal economy. These plebeians are admitted to citizenship. But they have no such religious dignity and power in their little families as the patricians have in theirs; they are scarcely better than loose individuals, representing nothing but their own sweet wills. This individualism and levity is not, however; confined to the plebeians; it extends to the patrician houses. Individualism is the second direction in which a patriarchal society yields to innovation. As the state grows the family weakens; and while in early Rome, for instance, only the *pater familias* was responsible to the city, and his children and slaves only to him, in Greece we find from early times individuals called to account before public judges. A federation of households thus became a republic. The king, that chief who enjoyed a certain hereditary precedence in sacrifices or in war, yields to elected generals and magistrates whose power, while it lasts, is much greater; for no other comparable power now subsists in the levelled state.

Modern Europe has seen an almost parallel development of democracy and individualism, together with the establishment of great artificial governments. Though the feudal hierarchy was originally based on conquest or domestic subjection, it came to have a fanciful or chivalrous or political force. But gradually the plebeian classes—the burghers—grew in importance, and military allegiance was weakened by being divided between a number of superposed lords, up to the king, emperor, or pope. The stronger rulers grew into absolute monarchs, representatives of great states, and the people became, in a political sense, a comparatively level multitude. Where parliamentary government was established it became possible to subordinate or exclude the monarch and his court; but the government remains an involuntary institution, and the individual must adapt himself to its exigencies. The church which once overshadowed the state has now lost its coercive authority and the single man stands alone before an impersonal written law, a constitutional government, and a widely diffused and contagious public opinion, characterised by enormous inertia, incoherence, and blindness. Contemporary national units are strongly marked and stimulate on occasion a perfervid artificial patriotism; but they are strangely unrepresentative of either personal or universal interests and may yield in turn to new combinations, if the industrial and intellectual solidarity of mankind, every day more obvious, ever finds a fit organ to express and to defend it.

A despotic military government founded on alien force and aiming at its own magnificence is often more efficient in defending its subjects than is a government expressing only the people's energies, as the predatory shepherd and his dog prove better guardians for a flock than its own wethers. The robbers that at their first incursion brought terror to merchant and peasant may become almost immediately representative organs of society—an army and a judiciary.

Disputes between subjects are naturally submitted to the invader, under whose laws and good-will alone a practical settlement can now be effected; and this alien tribunal, being exempt from local prejudices and interested in peace that taxes may be undiminished, may administer a comparatively impartial justice, until corrupted by bribes. The constant compensation tyranny brings, which keeps it from at once exhausting its victims, is the silence it imposes on their private squabbles. One distant universal enemy is less oppressive than a thousand unchecked pilferers and plotters at home. For this reason the reader of ancient history so often has occasion to remark what immense prosperity Asiatic provinces enjoyed between the periods when their successive conquerors devastated them. They flourished exceedingly the moment peace and a certain order were established in them.

Tyranny not only protects the subject against his kinsmen, thus taking on the functions of law and police, but it also protects him against military invasion, and thus takes on the function of an army. An army, considered ideally, is an organ for the state's protection; but it is far from being such in its origin, since at first an army is nothing but a ravenous and lusty horde quartered in a conquered country; yet the cost of such an incubus may come to be regarded as an insurance against further attack, and so what is in its real basis an inevitable burden resulting from a chance balance of forces may be justified in afterthought as a rational device for defensive purposes. Such an ulterior justification has nothing to do, however, with the causes that maintain armies or military policies: and accordingly those virginal minds that think things originated in the uses they may have acquired, have frequent cause to be pained and perplexed at the abuses and over-development of militarism. An insurance capitalised may exceed the value of the property insured, and the drain caused by armies and navies may be much greater than the havoc they prevent. The evils against which they are supposed to be directed are often evils only in a cant and conventional sense, since the events deprecated (like absorption by a neighbouring state) might be in themselves no misfortune to the people, but perhaps a singular blessing. And those dreaded possibilities, even if really evil, may well be less so than is the hateful actuality of military taxes, military service, and military arrogance.

Nor is this all: the military classes, since they inherit the blood and habits of conquerors, naturally love war and their irrational

combativeness is reinforced by interest; for in war officers can shine
and rise, while the danger of death, to a brave man, is rather a spur
and a pleasing excitement than a terror. A military class is therefore
always recalling, foretelling, and meditating war; it fosters artificial
and senseless jealousies toward other governments that possess
armies; and finally, as often as not, it precipitates disaster by bringing about the objectless struggle on which it has set its heart.

These natural phenomena, unintelligently regarded as anomalies and abuses, are the appanage of war in its pristine and proper
form. To fight is a radical instinct; if men have nothing else to
fight over they will fight over words, fancies, or women, or they
will fight because they dislike each other's looks, or because they
have met walking in opposite directions. To knock a thing down,
especially if it is cocked at an arrogant angle, is a deep delight to
the blood. To fight for a reason and in a calculating spirit is something your true warrior despises; even a coward might screw his
courage up to such a reasonable conflict. The joy and glory of fighting lie in its pure spontaneity and consequent generosity; you are
not fighting for gain, but for sport and for victory. Victory, no
doubt, has its fruits for the victor. If fighting were not a possible
means of livelihood the bellicose instinct could never have established itself in any long-lived race. A few men can live on plunder,
just as there is room in the world for some beasts of prey; other
men are reduced to living on industry, just as there are diligent
bees, ants, and herbivorous kine. But victory need have no good
fruits for the people whose army is victorious. That it sometimes
does so is an ulterior and blessed circumstance hardly to be reckoned
upon.

Since barbarism has its pleasures it naturally has its apologists.
There are panegyrists of war who say that without a periodical
bleeding a race decays and loses its manhood. Experience is directly
opposed to this shameless assertion. It is war that wastes a nation's
wealth, chokes its industries, kills its flower, narrows its sympathies,
condemns it to be governed by adventurers, and leaves the puny,
deformed, and unmanly to breed the next generation. Internecine
war, foreign and civil, brought about the greatest set-back which the
Life of Reason has ever suffered; it exterminated the Greek and
Italian aristocracies. Instead of being descended from heroes, modern nations are descended from slaves; and it is not their bodies

only that show it. After a long peace, if the conditions of life are propitious, we observe a people's energies bursting their barriers; they become aggressive on the strength they have stored up in their remote and unchecked development. It is the unmutilated race, fresh from the struggle with nature (in which the best survive, while in war it is often the best that perish) that descends victoriously into the arena of nations and conquers disciplined armies at the first blow, becomes the military aristocracy of the next epoch and is itself ultimately sapped and decimated by luxury and battle, and merged at last into the ignoble conglomerate beneath. Then, perhaps, in some other virgin country a genuine humanity is again found, capable of victory because unbled by war. To call war the soil of courage and virtue is like calling debauchery the soil of love.

Military institutions, adventitious and ill-adapted excrescences as they usually are, can acquire rational values in various ways. Besides occasional defence, they furnish a profession congenial to many, and a spectacle and emotion interesting to all. Blind courage is an animal virtue indispensable in a world full of dangers and evils where a certain insensibility and dash are requisite to skirt the precipice without vertigo. Such animal courage seems therefore beautiful rather than desperate or cruel, and being the lowest and most instinctive of virtues it is the one most widely and sincerely admired. In the form of steadiness under risks rationally taken, and perseverance so long as there is a chance of success, courage is a true virtue; but it ceases to be one when the love of danger, a useful passion when danger is unavoidable, begins to lead men into evils which it was unnecessary to face. Bravado, provocativeness, and a gambler's instinct, with a love of hitting hard for the sake of exercise, is a temper which ought already to be counted among the vices rather than the virtues of man. To delight in war is a merit in the soldier, a dangerous quality in the captain, and a positive crime in the statesman.

Discipline, or the habit of obedience, is a better sort of courage which military life also requires. Discipline is the acquired faculty of surrendering an immediate personal good for the sake of a remote and impersonal one of greater value. This difficult wisdom is made easier by training in an army, because the great forces of habit, example and social suasion, are there enlisted in its service. But these natural aids make it lose its conscious rationality, so that it ceases to be a virtue except potentially; for to resist an impulse by force of habit or external command may or may not be to follow the better course.

Besides fostering these rudimentary virtues the army gives the nation's soul its most festive and flaunting embodiment. Popular heroes, stirring episodes, obvious turning-points in history, commonly belong to military life.

Nevertheless the panegyrist of war places himself on the lowest level on which a moralist or patriot can stand and shows as great a want of refined feeling as of right reason. For the glories of war are all bloodstained, delirious, and infected with crime; the combative instinct is a savage prompting by which one man's good is found in another's evil. The existence of such a contradiction in the moral world is the original sin of nature, whence flows every other wrong. He is a willing accomplice of that perversity in things who delights in another's discomfiture or in his own, and craves the blind tension of plunging into danger without reason, or the idiot's pleasure in facing a pure chance. To find joy in another's trouble is, as man is constituted, not unnatural, though it is wicked; and to find joy in one's own trouble, though it be madness, is not yet impossible for man. These are the chaotic depths of that dreaming nature out of which humanity has to grow.

If war could be abolished and the defence of all interests intrusted to courts of law, there would remain unsatisfied a primary and therefore ineradicable instinct—a love of conflict, of rivalry, and of victory. If we desire to abolish war because it tries to do good by doing harm, we must not ourselves do an injury to human nature while trying to smooth it out. Now the test and limit of all necessary reform is vital harmony. No impulse can be condemned arbitrarily or because some other impulse or group of interests is, in a Platonic way, out of sympathy with it. An instinct can be condemned only if it prevents the realisation of other instincts, and only in so far as it does so. War, which has instinctive warrant, must therefore be transformed only in so far as it does harm to other interests. The evils of war are obvious enough; could not the virtues of war, animal courage, discipline, and self-knowledge, together with gaiety and enthusiasm, find some harmless occasion for their development?

Such a harmless simulacrum of war is seen in sport. The arduous and competitive element in sport is not harmful, if the discipline involved brings no loss of faculty or of right sensitiveness, and the rivalry no rancour. In war states wish to be efficient in order to conquer, but in sport men wish to prove their excellence because they wish to have it. If this excellence does not exist, the aim is missed, and to discover that failure is no new misfortune. To have failed unwittingly would have been worse; and to recognise superiority in another is consistent with a relatively good and honourable performance, so that even nominal failure may be a substantial success. And merit in a rival should bring a friendly delight even to the vanquished if they are true lovers of sport and of excellence. Sport is a liberal form of war stripped of its compulsions and malignity; a rational art and the expression of a civilised instinct.

The abolition of war, like its inception, can only be brought about by a new collocation of material forces. As the suppression of some nest of piratical tribes by a great emperor substitutes judicial for military sanctions among them, so the conquest of all warring nations by some imperial people could alone establish general peace. The Romans approached this ideal because their vast military power stood behind their governors and praetors. Science and commerce might conceivably resume that lost imperial function. If at the present day two or three powerful governments could so far forget their irrational origin as to renounce the right to occasional piracy and could unite in enforcing the decisions of some international tribunal, they would therefore constitute that tribunal the organ of a universal government and render war impossible between responsible states. But on account of their irrational basis all governments largely misrepresent the true interests of those who live under them. They pursue conventional and captious ends to which alone public energies can as yet be efficiently directed.

CHAPTER 4

THE ARISTOCRATIC IDEAL

It is no loss of liberty to subordinate ourselves to a natural leader. On the contrary, we thereby seize an opportunity to exercise our freedom, availing ourselves of the best instrument obtainable to accomplish our ends. A man may be a natural leader either by his character or by his position. The advantages a man draws from that peculiar structure of his brain which renders him, for instance, a ready speaker or an ingenious mathematician, are by common consent regarded as legitimate advantages. The public will use and reward such ability without jealousy and with positive delight. In an unsophisticated age the same feeling prevails in regard to those advantages which a man may draw from more external circumstances. So long as by the operation of any causes whatever some real competence accrues to anyone, it is for the general interest that this competence should bear its natural fruits, diversifying the face of society and giving its possessor a corresponding distinction.

Variety in the world is an unmixed blessing so long as each distinct function can be exercised without hindrance to any other. There is no greater stupidity or meanness than to take uniformity for an ideal, as if it were not a benefit and a joy to a man, being what he is, to know that many are, have been, and will be better than he. Grant that no one is positively degraded by the great man's greatness and it follows that everyone is exalted by it. Beauty, genius, holiness, even power and extraordinary wealth, radiate their virtue and make the world in which they exist a better and a more joyful place to live in. Hence the insatiable vulgar curiosity about great people, and the strange way in which the desire for fame (by which the distinguished man sinks to the common level) is met and satisfied by the universal interest in whatever is extraordinary. This avidity not to miss knowledge of things notable, and to enact vicariously all singular rôles, shows the need men have of distinction and the advantage they find even in conceiving it. For it is the presence of variety and a nearer approach somewhere to just and ideal achievement that gives men perspective in their judgments and opens vistas from the dull foreground of their lives to sea, mountain, and stars.

No merely idle curiosity shows itself in this instinct; rather a mark of human potentiality that recognises in what is yet attained a sad caricature of what is essentially attainable. For man's spirit is intellectual and naturally demands light and science; it craves in all things friendliness and beauty. The least hint of attainment in these directions fills it with satisfaction and the sense of realised expectation. So much so that when no inkling of a supreme fulfilment is found in the world or in the heart, men still cling to the notion of it in God or the hope of it in heaven, and religion, when it entertains them with that ideal, seems to have reached its highest height. Love of uniformity would quench the thirst for new outlets, for perfect, even if alien, achievements, and this, so long as perfection had not been actually attained, would indicate a mind dead to the ideal.

For an ideal aristocracy we should not look to Plato's Republic, for that Utopia is avowedly the ideal only for fallen and corrupt states, since luxury and injustice, we are told, first necessitated war, and the guiding idea of all the Platonic regimen is military efficiency. Aristocracy finds a more ideal expression in theism; for theism imagines the values of existence to be divided into two unequal parts: on the one hand the infinite value of God's life, on the other the finite values of all the created hierarchy. According to theistic cosmology, there was a metaphysical necessity, if creatures were to exist at all, that they should be in some measure inferior to godhead; otherwise they would have been indistinguishable from the godhead itself according to the principle called the identity of indiscernibles. The propagation of life involved, then, declension from pure vitality, and to diffuse being meant to dilute it with nothingness. This declension might take place in infinite degrees, each retaining some vestige of perfection mixed, as it were, with a greater and greater proportion of impotence and nonentity. Below God stood the angels, below them man, and below man the brute and inanimate creation. Each sphere, as it receded, contained a paler adumbration of the central perfection; yet even at the last confines of existence some feeble echo of divinity would still resound. This inequality in dignity would be not only a beauty in the whole, to whose existence and order such inequalities would be essential, but also no evil to the creature and no injustice; for a modicum of good is not made evil simply because a greater good is elsewhere possible. On the contrary, by accepting that appointed place and that specific happiness, each servant of the universal harmony could feel its infinite value and could thrill the more profoundly to a music which he helped to intone.

Dante has expressed this thought with great simplicity and beauty. He asks a friend's spirit, which he finds lodged in the lowest circle of paradise, if a desire to mount higher does not sometimes visit her; and the spirit replies:

"Brother, the force of charity quiets our will, making us wish only for what we have and thirst for nothing more. If we desired to be in a sublimer sphere, our desires would be discordant with the will of him who here allots us our divers stations—a discord which you will see there is no room for in these circles, if to dwell in charity be needful here, and if you consider duly the nature of charity. For it belongs to the essence of that blessed state to keep within the divine purposes, that our own purposes may become one also. Thus, the manner in which we are ranged from step to step in this kingdom pleases the whole kingdom, as it does the king who gives us will to will with him. And his will is our peace; it is that sea toward which all things move that his will creates and that nature fashions." *

In realising his own will in his own way, each creature might be perfectly happy, without yearning or pathetic regrets for other forms of being. Such forms of being would all be unpalatable to him, even if conventionally called higher, because their body was larger, and their soul more complex. The overruling providence would then in truth be fatherly, by providing for each being that which it inwardly craved. Persons of one rank would not be improved by passing into the so-called higher sphere, any more than the ox would be improved by being transformed into a lark, or a king into a poet.

An aristocratic society might accordingly be a perfect heaven if the variety and superposition of functions in it expressed a corresponding diversity in its members' faculties and ideals. And, indeed, what aristocratic philosophers have always maintained is that men really differ so much in capacity that one is happier for being a slave, another for being a shopkeeper, and a third for being a king. All professions, they say, even the lowest, are or may be vocations.

* Paradiso. Canto III, 70–87.

Some men, Aristotle tells us, are slaves by nature; only physical functions are spontaneous in them. So long as they are humanely treated, it is, we may infer, a benefit for them to be commanded; and the contribution their labour makes toward rational life in their betters is the highest dignity they can attain, and should be prized by them as a sufficient privilege.

Such assertions, coming from lordly lips, have a suspicious optimism about them; yet the faithful slave, such as the nurse we find in the tragedies, may sometimes have corresponded to that description. In other regions it is surely true that to advance in conventional station would often entail a loss in true dignity and happiness. It would seldom benefit a musician to be appointed admiral or a housemaid to become a prima donna. Scientific breeding might conceivably develop much more sharply the various temperaments and faculties needed in the state; and then each caste or order of citizens would not be more commonly dissatisfied with its lot than men or women now are with their sex. One tribe would run errands as persistently as the ants; another would sing like the lark; a third would show a devil's innate fondness for stoking a fiery furnace.

Aristocracy logically involves castes. But such castes as exist in India, and the social classes we find in the western world, are not now based on any profound difference in race, capacity, or inclination. They are based probably on the chances of some early war, reinforced by custom and perpetuated by inheritance. A certain circulation, corresponding in part to proved ability or disability, takes place in the body politic, and, since the French Revolution, has taken place increasingly. Some, by energy and perseverance, rise from the bottom; some, by ill fortune or vice, fall from the top. But these readjustments are insignificant in comparison with the social inertia that perpetuates all the classes, and even such shifts as occur at once re-establish artificial conditions for the next generation. As a rule, men's station determines their occupation without their gifts determining their station. Thus stifled ability in the lower orders, and apathy or pampered incapacity in the higher, unite to deprive society of its natural leaders.

It would be easy, however, to exaggerate the havoc wrought by such artificial conditions. The monotony we observe in mankind must not be charged to the oppressive influence of circumstances crushing the individual soul. It is not society's fault that most men seem to miss their vocation. Most men have no vocation; and

society, in imposing on them some chance language, some chance
religion, and some chance career, first plants an ideal in their bosoms
and insinuates into them a sort of racial or professional soul. Their
only character is composed of the habits they have been led to acquire. Some little propensities betrayed in childhood may very
probably survive; one man may prove by his dying words that he
was congenitally witty, another tender, another brave. But these
native qualities will simply have added an ineffectual tint to some
typical existence or other; and the vast majority will remain, as
Schopenhauer said, *Fabrikwaaren der Natur.*

Variety in human dreams may indeed be inwardly very great,
but it is not efficacious. To be socially important and expressible in
some common medium, initial differences in temper must be organised into custom and become cumulative by being imitated and enforced. The only artists who can show great originality are those
trained in distinct and established schools; for originality and
genius must be largely fed and raised on the shoulders of some old
tradition. A rich organisation and heritage, while they predetermine
the core of all possible variations, increase their number, since every
advance opens up new vistas; and growth, in extending the periphery of the substance organised, multiplies the number of points
at which new growths may begin. Thus it is only in recent times
that discoveries in science have been frequent, because natural
science until lately possessed no settled method and no considerable fund of acquired truths. So, too, in political society, statesman-
ship is made possible by traditional policies, generalship by military
institutions, great financiers by established commerce.

If we ventured to generalise these observations we might say
that such an unequal distribution of capacity as might justify
aristocracy should be looked for only in civilised states. Savages are
born free and equal, but wherever a complex and highly specialised
environment limits the loose freedom of those born into it, it also
stimulates their capacity. Under forced culture remarkable growths
will appear, bringing to light possibilities in men which might, perhaps, not even have been possibilites had they been left to themselves; for mulberry leaves do not of themselves develop into
brocade. A certain personal idiosyncrasy must be assumed at bottom, else cotton damask would be as good as silk and all men having like opportunities would be equally great. This idiosyncrasy is
brought out by social pressure, while in a state of nature it might

have betrayed itself only in trivial and futile ways, as it does among
barbarians.

Distinction is thus in one sense artificial, since it cannot become
important or practical unless a certain environment gives play to
individual talent and preserves its originality; but distinction
nevertheless is perfectly real, and not merely imputed. In vain
does the man in the street declare that he, too, could have been a
king if he had been born in the purple; for that potentiality does
not belong to him as he is, but only as he might have been, if *per
impossibile* he had not been himself. There is a strange metaphysical
illusion in imagining that a man might change his parents, his body,
his early environment, and yet retain his personality. In its higher
faculties his personality is produced by his special relations. If
Shakespeare had been born in Italy he might, if you will, have been
a great poet, but Shakespeare he could never have been. Nor can it
be called an injustice to all of us who are not Englishmen of Queen
Elizabeth's time that Shakespeare had that advantage and was
thereby enabled to exist.

The sense of injustice at unequal opportunities arises only when
the two environments compared are really somewhat analogous,
so that the illusion of a change of rôles without a change of characters may retain some colour. It was a just insight, for instance, in
the Christian fable to make the first rebel against God the chief
among the angels, the spirit occupying the position nearest to that
which he tried to usurp. Lucifer's fallacy consisted in thinking
natural inequality artificial. His perversity lay in rebelling against
himself and rejecting the happiness proper to his nature. This was
the maddest possible way of rebelling against his true creator; for
it is our particular finitude that creates us and makes us be. The
penny that one man finds and another misses would not, had fortune been reversed, have transmuted each man into the other. So
adventitious a circumstance seems easily transferable without undermining that personal distinction which it had come to embitter. Yet
the incipient fallacy lurking even in such suppositions becomes obvious when we inquire whether so blind an accident, for instance, as
sex is also adventitious and ideally transferable and whether Jack
and Jill, remaining themselves, could have exchanged genders.

It is not mere inequality, therefore, that can be a reproach to the
aristocratic or theistic ideal. Could each person fulfil his own nature
the most striking differences in endowment and fortune would

trouble nobody's dreams. Injustice in this world is not something comparative; the wrong is deep, clear, and absolute in each private fate. A bruised child wailing in the street, his small world for the moment utterly black and cruel before him, does not fetch his unhappiness from sophisticated comparisons or irrational envy; nor can any compensations and celestial harmonies supervening later ever expunge or justify that moment's bitterness. The pain may be whistled away and forgotten; the mind may be rendered by it only a little harder, a little coarser, a little more secretive and sullen and familiar with unrightable wrong. But ignoring that pain will not prevent its having existed; it must remain for ever to trouble God's omniscience and be a part of that hell which the creation too truly involves.

Now nature, in her haste to be fertile, wants to produce everything at once, and her distracted industry has brought about terrible confusion and waste and terrible injustice. She has been led to punish her ministers for the services they render and her favourites for the honours they receive. She has imposed suffering on her creatures together with life; she has defeated her own objects and vitiated her bounty by letting every good do harm and bring evil in its train to some unsuspecting creature.

This oppression is the moral stain that sometimes attaches to aristocracy and makes it truly unjust. Every privilege that imposes suffering involves a wrong. Instead of the brutal but innocent injustice of nature, the lower classes then suffer from the sly injustice of men; and though the suffering be less—for the worst of men is human—the injury is more sensible. The inclemencies and dangers men must endure in a savage state, in scourging them, would not have profited by that cruelty. But suffering has an added sting when it enables others to be exempt from care and to live like the gods in irresponsible ease; the inequality which would have been innocent and even beautiful in a happy world becomes, in a painful world, a bitter wrong.

It would be a happy relief to the aristocrat's conscience, when he possesses one, could he learn from some yet bolder Descartes that common people were nothing but *bêtes-machines*, and that only a groundless prejudice had hitherto led us to suppose that life could exist where evidently nothing good could be attained by living. If all unfortunate people could be proved to be unconscious automata, what a brilliant justification that would be for the ways of both God and man! Philosophy would not lack arguments to support such an agreeable conclusion. Beginning with the axiom that whatever is is right, a metaphysician might adduce the truth that consciousness is something self-existent and indubitably real; therefore, he would contend, it must be self-justifying and indubitably good. And he might continue by saying that a slave's life was not its own excuse for being, nor were the labours of a million drudges otherwise justified than by the conveniences which they supplied their masters with. *Ergo*, those servile operations could come to consciousness only where they attained their end, and the world could contain nothing but perfect and universal happiness. A divine omniscience and joy, shared by finite minds in so far as they might attain perfection, would be the only life in existence, and the notion that such a thing as pain, sorrow, or hatred could exist at all would forthwith vanish like the hideous and ridiculous illusion that it was. This argument may be recommended to apologetic writers as no weaker than those they commonly rely on, and infinitely more consoling.

But so long as people remain on what such an invaluable optimist might call the low level of sensuous thought, and so long as we imagine that we exist and suffer, an aristocratic regimen can only be justified by radiating benefit and by proving that were less given to those above less would be attained by those beneath them. Such reversion of benefit might take a material form, as when, by commercial guidance and military protection, a greater net product is secured to labour, even after all needful taxes have been levied upon it to support greatness. An industrial and political oligarchy might defend itself on that ground. Or the return might take the less positive form of opportunity, as it does when an aristocratic society has a democratic government. Here the people neither accept guidance nor require protection; but the existence of a rich and irresponsible class offers them an ideal, such as it is, in their ambitious struggles. For they too may grow rich, exercise financial ascendancy, educate their sons like gentlemen, and launch their daughters into fashionable society. Finally, if the only aristocracy recognised were an aristocracy of achievement, and if public rewards followed personal merit, the reversion to the people might take the form of participation by them in the ideal interests of eminent men. Holiness, genius, and knowledge can reverberate through all society. The fruits of art and science are in themselves cheap and not to be monopolised or consumed in enjoyment. On the contrary, their wider diffusion stimulates their growth and makes their cultivation more intense and successful. When an ideal interest is general the share which falls to the private person is the more apt to be efficacious. The saints have usually had companions, and artists and philosophers have flourished in schools.

At the same time ideal goods cannot be assimilated without some training and leisure. Like education and religion they are degraded by popularity, and reduced from what the master intended to what the people are able and willing to receive. So pleasing an idea, then, as this of diffused ideal possessions has little application in a society aristocratically framed; for the greater eminence the few attain the less able are the many to follow them. Great thoughts require a great mind and pure beauties a profound sensibility. To attempt to give such things a wide currency is to be willing to denaturalise them in order to boast that they have been propagated. Culture is on the horns of this dilemma: if profound and noble it must remain rare, if common it must become mean. These alternatives can never be eluded until some purified and high-bred race succeeds the promiscuous bipeds that now blacken the planet.

Aristocracy, like everything else, has no practical force save that which natural causes endow it with. Its privileges are fruits of inevitable advantages. Its oppressions are simply new forms and vehicles for nature's primeval cruelty, while the benefits it may also confer are only further examples of her nice equilibrium and necessary harmony. For it lies in the essence of a mechanical world, where the interests of its products are concerned, to be fundamentally kind, since it has formed and on the whole maintains those products, and yet continually cruel, since it forms and maintains them blindly, without considering difficulties or probable failures. Now the most tyrannical government, like the best, is a natural product maintained by an equilibrium of natural forces. It is simply a new mode of energy to which the philosopher living under it must adjust himself as he would to the weather.

But when the vehicle of nature's inclemency is a heartless man, even if the harm done be less, it puts on a new and a moral aspect. The source of injury is then not only natural but criminal as well, and the result is a sense of wrong added to misfortune. It must needs be that offence come, but woe to him by whom the offence cometh. He justly arouses indignation and endures remorse.

Now civilisation cannot afford to entangle its ideals with the causes of remorse and of just indignation. In the first place nature in her slow and ponderous way levels her processes and rubs off her sharp edges by perpetual friction. Where there is maladjustment there is no permanent physical stability. Therefore the ideal of society can never involve the infliction of injury on anybody for any purpose. Such an ideal would propose for a goal something out of equilibrium, a society which even if established could not maintain itself; but an ideal life must not tend to destroy its ideal by abolishing its own existence. In the second place, it is impossible on moral grounds that injustice should subsist in the ideal. The ideal means the perfect, and a supposed ideal in which wrong still subsisted would be the denial of perfection. The ideal state and the ideal universe should be a family where all are not equal, but where all are happy. So that an aristocratic or theistic system in order to deserve respect must discard its sinister apologies for evil and clearly propose such an order of existences, one superposed upon the other, as should involve no suffering on any of its levels. The services required of each must involve no injury to any; to perform them should be made the servant's spontaneous and specific ideal. The privileges the system bestows on some must involve no outrage on the rest, and must not be paid for by mutilating other lives or thwarting their natural potentialities. For the humble to give their labour would then be blessed in reality, and not merely by imputation, while for the great to receive those benefits would be blessed also, not in fact only but in justice.

CHAPTER 5

DEMOCRACY

THE WORD democracy may stand for a natural social equality in the body politic or for a constitutional form of government in which power lies more or less directly in the people's hands. The former may be called social democracy and the latter democratic government. The two differ widely, both in origin and in moral principle. Genetically considered, social democracy is something primitive, unintended, proper to communities where there is general competence and no marked personal eminence. It is the democracy of Arcadia, Switzerland, and the American pioneers. Such a community might be said to have also a democratic government, for everything in it is naturally democratic. There will be no aristocracy, no prestige; but instead an intelligent readiness to lend a hand and to do in unison whatever is done, not so much under leaders as by a kind of conspiring instinct and contagious sympathy. In other words, there will be that most democratic of governments—no government at all. But when pressure of circumstances, danger, or inward strife makes recognised and prolonged guidance necessary to a social democracy, the form its government takes is that of a rudimentary monarchy, established by election or general consent. A natural leader presents himself and he is instinctively obeyed. He may indeed be freely criticised and will not be screened by any pomp or traditional mystery; he will be easy to replace and every citizen will feel himself radically his equal. Yet such a state is at the beginnings of monarchy and aristocracy, close to the stage depicted in Homer, where pre-eminences are still obviously natural, although already over-emphasised by the force of custom and wealth, and by the fission of society into divergent classes.

Political democracy, on the other hand, is a late and artificial product. It arises by a gradual extension of aristocratic privileges, through rebellion against abuses, and in answer to restlessness on the people's part. Its principle is not the absence of eminence, but the discovery that existing eminence is no longer genuine and representative. It is compatible with a very complex government, great empire, and an aristocratic society; it may retain, as notably in England and in all ancient republics, many vestiges of older and less democratic institutions. For under democratic governments the people have not created the state; they merely control it. Their suspicions and jealousies are quieted by assigning to them a voice, perhaps only a veto, in the administration; but the state administered is a prodigious self-created historical engine. Popular votes never established the family, private property, religious practices, or international frontiers. Institutions, ideals, and administrators may all be such as the popular classes could never have produced; but these products of natural aristocracy are suffered to subsist so long as no very urgent protest is raised against them. The people's liberty consists not in their original responsibility for what exists—for they are guiltless of it—but merely in the faculty they have acquired of abolishing any detail that may distress or wound them, and of imposing any new measure, which, seen against the background of existing laws, may commend itself from time to time to their instinct and mind.

If we turn from origins to ideals, the contrast between social and political democracy is no less marked. Social democracy is a general ethical ideal, looking to human equality and brotherhood, and inconsistent, in its radical form, with such institutions as the family and hereditary property. Democratic government, on the contrary, is merely a means to an end, an expedient for the better and smoother government of certain states at certain junctures. It involves no special ideals of life; it is a question of policy, namely, whether the general interest will be better served by granting all men (and perhaps all women) an equal voice in elections. For political democracy, arising in great and complex states, must necessarily be a government by deputy, and the questions actually submitted to the people can be only very large rough matters of general policy or of confidence in party leaders.

The possibility of intelligent selfishness and the prevalence of a selfishness far from intelligent unite to make men wary in intrusting their interests to one another's keeping. Yet if we assume a certain variety in endowments and functions among men, it would evidently conduce to the general convenience that each man should exercise his powers uncontrolled by the public voice. The government, having facilities for information and ready resources, might be left to determine all matters of policy; for its members' private

interests would coincide with those of the public, and even if prejudices and irrational habits prevented them from pursuing their own
advantage, they would surely not err more frequently or more
egregiously in that respect than would the private individual, to
whose ignorant fancy every decision would otherwise have to be
referred.

All just government pursues the general good; the choice between aristocratic and democratic forms touches only the means to
that end. One arrangement may well be better fitted to one place
and time, and another to another. Everything depends on the
existence or non-existence of available practical eminence. The
democratic theory is clearly wrong if it imagines that eminence is
not naturally representative. Eminence is synthetic and represents
what it synthesises. An eminence not representative would not constitute excellence, but merely extravagance or notoriety. Excellence
in anything, whether thought, action, or feeling, consists in representation, in standing for many diffuse constituents reduced to harmony, so that the upshot of the experience concerned is mirrored
and regarded with justice to all extant interests and speaking in
their total behalf. But anything approaching such true excellence
is as rare as it is great, and a democratic society, naturally jealous
of greatness, may be excused for not expecting true greatness and
for not even understanding what it is. A government is not made
representative or just by the mechanical expedient of electing its
members by universal suffrage. It becomes representative only by
embodying in its policy, whether by instinct or high intelligence,
the people's conscious and unconscious interests.

Democratic theory seems to be right, however, about the actual
failure of theocracies, monarchies, and oligarchies to secure the
general good. The true eminence which natural leaders may have
possessed in the beginning usually declines into a conventional and
baseless authority. The guiding powers which came to save and
express humanity fatten in office and end by reversing their function. The government reverts to the primeval robber; the church
stands in the way of all wisdom. Under such circumstances it is a
happy thing if the people possess enough initiative to assert themselves and, after clearing the ground in a more or less summary
fashion, allow some new organisation, more representative of actual
interests, to replace the old encumbrances and tyrannies.

In the heroic ages of Greece and Rome patriotism was stimulated in manifold ways. The city was a fatherland, a church, an army, and almost a family. It had its own school of art, its own dialect, its own feasts, its own fables. Every possible social interest was either involved in the love of country or, like friendship and fame, closely associated with it. Patriotism could then be expected to sway every mind at all capable of moral enthusiasm. Furthermore, only the flower of the population were citizens. In rural districts the farmer might be a freeman; but he probably had slaves whose work he merely superintended. The meaner and more debasing offices, mining, seafaring, domestic service, and the more laborious part of all industries, were relegated to slaves. The citizens were a privileged class. Military discipline and the street life natural in Mediterranean countries, kept public events and public men always under everybody's eyes: the state was a bodily presence. Democracy, when it arose in such communities, was still aristocratic; it imposed few new duties upon the common citizens, while it diffused many privileges and exemptions among them.

The social democracy which is the ideal of many in modern times, on the other hand, excludes slavery, unites whole nations and even all mankind into a society of equals, and admits no local or racial privileges by which the sense of fellowship may be stimulated. Public spirit could not be sustained in such a community by exemptions, rivalries, or ambitions. No one, indeed, would be a slave, everyone would have an elementary education and a chance to demonstrate his capacity; but he would be probably condemned to those occupations which in ancient republics were assigned to slaves. At least at the opening of his career he would find himself on the lowest subsisting plane of humanity, and he would probably remain on it throughout his life. In other words, the citizens of a social democracy would be all labourers; for even those who rose to be leaders would, in a genuine democracy, rise from the ranks and belong in education and habits to the same class as all the others.

Under such circumstances the first virtue which a democratic society would have to possess would be enthusiastic diligence. The motives for work which have hitherto prevailed in the world have been want, ambition, and love of occupation: in a social democracy, after the first was eliminated, the last alone would remain efficacious. Love of occupation, although it occasionally accompanies and cheers every sort of labour, could never induce men originally to undertake arduous and uninteresting tasks, nor to persevere in them if by chance or waywardness such tasks had been once undertaken. Inclination can never be the general motive for the work, now imposed on the masses. Before labour can be its own reward it must become less continuous, more varied, more responsive to individual temperament and capacity. Otherwise it would not cease to repress and warp human faculties.

A state composed exclusively of such workmen and peasants as make up the bulk of modern nations would be an utterly barbarous state. Every liberal tradition would perish in it; and the rational and historic essence of patriotism itself would be lost. The emotion of it, no doubt, would endure, for it is not generosity that the people lack. They possess every impulse; it is experience that they cannot gather, for in gathering it they would be constituting those higher organs that make up an aristocratic society. Civilisation has hitherto consisted in diffusion and dilution of habits arising in privileged centres. It has not sprung from the people; it has arisen in their midst by a variation from them, and it has afterward imposed itself on them from above. All its founders in antiquity passed for demi-gods or were at least inspired by an oracle or a nymph. The vital genius thus bursting forth and speaking with authority gained a certain ascendency in the world; it mitigated barbarism without removing it. This is one fault, among others, which current civilisation has; it is artificial. If social democracy could breed a new civilisation out of the people, this new civilisation would be profounder than ours and more pervasive. But it doubtless cannot. What we have rests on conquest and conversion, on leadership and imitation, on mastership and service. To abolish aristocracy, in the sense of social privilege and sanctified authority, would be to cut off the source from which all culture has hitherto flowed.

Civilisation, however, although we are wont to speak the word with a certain unction, is a thing whose value may be questioned. One way of defending the democratic ideal is to deny that civilisation is a good. In one sense, indeed, social democracy is essentially a reversion to a more simple life, more Arcadian and idyllic than that which aristocracy has fostered. Equality is more easily attained in a patriarchal age than in an age of concentrated and intense activities. Possessions, ideal and material, may be fewer in a simple community, but they are more easily shared and bind men together in moral and imaginative bonds instead of dividing them, as do all

highly elaborate ways of living or thinking. The necessaries of life
can be enjoyed by a rural people, living in a sparsely settled country, and among these necessaries might be counted not only bread
and rags, which everyone comes by in some fashion even in our
society, but that communal religion, poetry, and fellowship which
the civilised poor are so often without. If social democracy should
triumph and take this direction it would begin by greatly diminish-
ing the amount of labour performed in the world. All instruments
of luxury, many instruments of vain knowledge and art, would no
longer be produced. We might see the means of communication,
lately so marvelously developed, again disused; the hulks of great
steamers rusting in harbours, the railway bridges collapsing and the
tunnels choked; while a rural population, with a few necessary and
perfected manufactures, would spread over the land and abandon
the great cities to ruin, calling them seats of Babylonian servitude
and folly.

Such anticipations may seem fantastic, and of course there is no
probability that a reaction against material progress should set in in
the near future, since as yet the tide of commercialism and population continues everywhere to rise; but does any thoughtful man suppose that these tendencies will be eternal and that the present
experiment in civilisation is the last the world will see?

If social democracy, however, refused to diminish labour and
wealth and proposed rather to accelerate material progress and
keep every furnace at full blast, it would come face to face with a
serious problem. By whom would the product be enjoyed? By those
who created it? What sort of pleasures, arts, and sciences would
those grimy workmen have time and energy for after a day of hot
and unremitting exertion? What sort of religion would fill their
Sabbaths and their dreams? We see how they spend their leisure
to-day, when a strong aristocratic tradition and the presence of a
rich class still profoundly influence popular ideals. Imagine those
aristocratic influences removed, and would any head be lifted above
a dead level of infinite dulness and vulgarity? Would mankind be
anything but a trivial, sensuous, superstitious, custom-ridden herd?
There is no tyranny so hateful as a vulgar and anonymous tyranny
It is all-permeating, all-thwarting; it blasts every budding novelty
and sprig of genius with its omnipresent and fierce stupidity. Such
a headless people has the mind of a worm and the claws of a dragon.
Anyone would be a hero who should quell the monster. A foreign

invader or domestic despot would at least have steps to his throne, possible standing-places for art and intelligence; his supercilious in-difference would discountenance the popular gods, and allow some courageous hand at last to shatter them. Social democracy at high pressure would leave no room for liberty. The only freeman in it would be one whose whole ideal was to be an average man.

Perhaps, however, social democracy might take a more liberal form. It might allow the benefits of civilisation to be integrated in eminent men, whose influence in turn should direct and temper the general life. This would be timocracy—a government by men of merit. The same abilities which raised these men to eminence would enable them to apprehend ideal things and to employ material resources for the common advantage. They would formulate reli-gion, cultivate the arts and sciences, provide for government and all public conveniences, and inspire patriotism by their discourse and example. At the same time a new motive would be added to com-mon labour, I mean ambition. For there would be not only a pos-sibility of greater reward but a possibility of greater service. The competitive motive which socialism is supposed to destroy would be restored in timocracy, and an incentive offered to excellence and industry. The country's resources would increase for the very reason that somebody might conceivably profit by them; and every-one would have at least an ideal interest in ministering to that com-plete life which he or his children, or whoever was most capable of appreciation, was actually to enjoy.

Such a timocracy (of which the Roman Church is a good example) would differ from the social aristocracy that now exists only by the removal of hereditary advantages. People would be born equal, but they would grow unequal, and the only equality subsisting would be equality of opportunity. If power remained in the people's hands, the government would be democratic; but a full development of timocracy would allow the proved leader to gain great ascendancy. The better security the law offered that the men at the top should be excellent, the less restraint would it need to put upon them when once in their places. Their eminence would indeed have been factitious and their station undeserved if they were not able to see and do what was requisite better than the com-munity at large. An assembly has only the lights common to the majority of its members, far less, therefore, than its members have when added together and less even than the wiser part of them.

A timocracy would therefore seem to unite the advantages of all forms of government and to avoid their respective abuses. It would promote freedom scientifically. It might be a monarchy, if men existed fit to be kings; but they would have to give signs of their fitness and their honours would probably not be hereditary. Like aristocracy, it would display a great diversity of institutions and superposed classes, a stimulating variety in ways of living; it would be favourable to art and science and to noble idiosyncrasies. Among its activities the culminating and most conspicuous ones would be liberal. Yet there would be no isolation of the aristocratic body; its blood would be drawn from the people, and only its traditions from itself. Like social democracy, finally, it would be just and open to every man, but it would not depress humanity nor wish to cast everybody in a common mould.

What might happen if the human race were immensely improved and exalted there is as yet no saying; but experience has given no example of efficacious devotion to communal ideals except in small cities, held together by close military and religious bonds and having no important relations to anything external. Even this antique virtue was short-lived and sadly thwarted by private and party passion. We may say, therefore, that a zeal sufficient to destroy selfishness is, as men are now constituted, worse than selfishness itself. In pursuing prizes for themselves people benefit their fellows more than in pursuing such narrow and irrational ideals as alone seem to be powerful in the world. To ambition, to the love of wealth and honour, to love of a liberty which meant opportunity for experiment and adventure, we owe whatever benefits we have derived from Greece and Rome, from Italy and England. It is doubtful whether a society which offered no personal prizes would inspire effort; and it is still more doubtful whether that effort, if actually stimulated by education, would be beneficent. For an indoctrinated and collective virtue turns easily to fanaticism; it imposes irrational sacrifices prompted by some abstract principle or habit once, perhaps, heroic; but that convention soon becomes superstitious and ceases to represent general human excellence.

Now it is in the spirit of social democracy to offer no prizes. Office in it, being the reward of no great distinction, brings no great honour, and being meanly paid it brings no great profit, at least while honestly administered. All wealth in a true democracy would be the fruit of personal exertion and would come too late to be

nobly enjoyed or to teach the art of liberal living. It would be
either accumulated irrationally or given away outright. And if fortunes could not be transmitted or used to found a great family they
would lose their chief imaginative charm. The pleasures a democratic society affords are vulgar and not even by an amiable illusion
can they become an aim in life. A life of pleasure requires an aristocratic setting to make it interesting or really conceivable. Intellectual and artistic greatness does not need prizes, but it sorely needs
sympathy and a propitious environment. Genius, like goodness
(which can stand alone), would arise in a democratic society as frequently as elsewhere; but it might not be so well fed or so well
assimilated. There would at least be no artificial and simulated
merit; everybody would take his ease in his inn and sprawl un-
buttoned without respect for any finer judgment or performance
than that which he himself was inclined to. The only excellence subsisting would be spontaneous excellence, inwardly prompted, sure
of itself, and inwardly rewarded. For such excellence to grow general mankind must be notably transformed. If a noble and civilised
democracy is to subsist, the common citizen must be something of a
saint and something of a hero. We see therefore how justly flattering and profound, and at the same time how ominous, was Mon-
tesquieu's saying that the principle of democracy is virtue.

CHAPTER 6

FREE SOCIETY

NATURAL SOCIETY unites beings in time and space; it fixes affection on those creatures on which we depend and to which our action must be adapted. Natural society begins at home and radiates over the world, as more and more things become tributary to our personal being. In marriage and the family, in industry, government, and war, attention is riveted on temporal existences, on the fortunes of particular bodies, natural or corporate. There is then a primacy of nature over spirit in social life; and this primacy, in a certain sense, endures to the end, since all spirit must be the spirit of something, and reason could not exist or be conceived at all unless a material organism, personal or social, lay beneath to give thought an occasion and a point of view, and to give preference a direction. Things could not be near or far, worse or better, unless a definite life were taken as a standard, a life lodged somewhere in space and time. Reason is a principle of order appearing in a subject-matter which in its subsistence and quantity must be an irrational datum. Reason expresses purpose, purpose expresses impulse, and impulse expresses a natural body with self-equilibrating powers.

At the same time, natural growths may be called achievements only because, when formed, they support a joyful and liberal experience. Nature's works first acquire a meaning in the commentaries they provoke; material processes have interesting climaxes only from the point of view of the life that expresses them, in which their ebb and flow grows impassioned and vehement. Nature's values are imputed to her retroactively by spirit, which in its material dependence has a logical and moral primacy of its own. In themselves events are perfectly automatic, steady, and fluid, not stopping where we see a goal nor avoiding what we call failures. And so they would always have remained in crude experience, if no cumulative reflection, no art, and no science had come to dominate and foreshorten that equable flow of substance, arresting it ideally in behalf of some rational interest.

Thus it comes to pass that rational interests have a certain

149

ascendancy in the world, as well as an absolute authority over it; for they arise where an organic equilibrium has naturally established itself. Such an equilibrium maintains itself by virtue of the same necessity that produced it; without arresting the flux or introducing any miracle, it sustains in being an ideal form. This form is what consciousness corresponds to and raises to felt existence; so that significant thoughts are something which nature necessarily lingers upon and seems to serve. The being to whom they come is the most widely based and synthetic of her creatures. The mind spreads and soars in proportion as the body feeds on the surrounding world. Noble ideas, although rare and difficult to attain, are not naturally fugitive.

Consciousness is not ideal merely in its highest phases; it is ideal through and through. At one level as much as at another, it celebrates an attained balance in nature, or grieves at its collapse; it prophesies and remembers, it loves and dreams. It sees even nature from the point of view of ideal interests, and measures the flux of things by ideal standards. It registers its own movement, like that of its objects, entirely in ideal terms, looking to fixed goals of its own imagining, and using nothing in the operation but concretions in discourse. Primary mathematical notions, for instance, are evidences of a successful reactive method attained in the organism and translated in consciousness into a stable grammar which has wide applicability and great persistence, so that it has come to be elaborated ideally into prodigious abstract systems of thought. Every experience of victory, eloquence, or beauty is a momentary success of the same kind, and if repeated and sustained becomes a spiritual possession. Society also breeds its ideal harmonies. At first it establishes affections between beings naturally conjoined in the world; later it grows sensitive to free and spiritual affinities, to oneness of mind and sympathetic purposes. These ideal affinities, although grounded like the others on material relations (for sympathy presupposes communication), do not have those relations for their theme but rest on them merely as on a pedestal from which they look away to their own realm, as music, while sustained by vibrating instruments, looks away from them to its own universe of sound.

Ideal society is a drama enacted in the imagination. Its personages are mythical, beginning with that brave protagonist who calls himself I and speaks all the soliloquies. When most nearly mate-

rial these personages are human souls—the life of particular bodies
—or floating mortal reputations—echoes of those lives in one another. From this source in their bodies they evoke notions of country, posterity, humanity, and the gods. These figures all represent
some circle of events or forces in the real world; but such representation, besides being mythical, is usually most inadequate. The
boundaries of that province which each spirit presides over are
vaguely drawn, the spirit itself being correspondingly indefinite.
This ambiguity is most conspicuous, perhaps, in the most absorbing
of the personages which a man constructs in this imaginative fashion
—his idea of himself. "There is society where none intrudes"; and
for most men sympathy with their imaginary selves is a powerful
and dominant emotion. True memory offers but a meagre and interrupted vista of past experience, yet even that picture is far too rich
a term for mental discourse to bandy about; a name with a few
physical and social connotations is what must represent the man to
his own thinkings. Or rather it is no memory, however eviscerated,
that fulfils that office. A man's notion of himself is a concretion in
discourse for which his more constant somatic feelings, his ruling
interests, and his social relations furnish most of the substance.

The more reflective and self-conscious a man is the more completely will his experience be subsumed and absorbed in his perennial "I." If philosophy has come to reinforce this reflective egotism, he may even regard all nature as nothing but his half-volun-
tary dream and encourage himself thereby to give even to the
physical world a dramatic and sentimental colour. But the more
successful he is in stuffing everything into his self-consciousness, the
more desolate will the void become which surrounds him. For self
is, after all, but one term in a primitive dichotomy and would lose
its specific and intimate character were it no longer contrasted with
anything else. The egotist must therefore people the desert he has
spread about him, and he naturally peoples it with mythical counterparts of himself. Sometimes, if his imagination is sensuous, his
alter-egos are incarnate in the landscape, and he creates a poetic
mythology; sometimes, when the inner life predominates, they
are projected into his own forgotten past or infinite future. He will
then say that all experience is really his own and that some inexplicable illusion has momentarily raised opaque partitions in his
omniscient mind.

Philosophers less pretentious and more worldly than these have sometimes felt, in their way, the absorbing force of self-consciousness. La Rochefoucauld could describe *amour propre* as the spring of all human sentiments. *Amour propre* involves preoccupations not merely with the idea of self, but with that idea reproduced in other men's minds; the soliloquy has become a dialogue, or rather a solo with an echoing chorus. Interest in one's own social figure is to some extent a material interest, for other men's love or aversion is a principle read into their acts; and a social animal like man is dependent on other men's acts for his happiness. An individual's concern for the attitude society takes toward him is therefore in the first instance concern for his own welfare. But imagination here refines upon worldly interest. What others think of us would be of little moment did it not, when known, so deeply tinge what we think of ourselves. Nothing could better prove the mythical character of self-consciousness than this extreme sensitiveness to alien opinions; for if a man really knew himself he would utterly despise the ignorant notions others might form on a subject in which he had such matchless opportunities for observation. Indeed, those opinions would hardly seem to him directed upon the reality at all, and he would laugh at them as he might at the stock fortune-telling of some itinerant gypsy.

As it is, however, the least breath of irresponsible and anonymous censure lashes our self-esteem and sometimes quite transforms our plans and affections. The passions grafted on wounded pride are the most inveterate; they are green and vigorous in old age. We crave support in vanity, as we do in religion, and never forgive contradictions in that sphere; for however persistent and passionate such prejudices may be, we know too well that they are woven of thin air. A hostile word, by starting a contrary imaginative current, buffets them rudely and threatens to dissolve their being.

The highest form of vanity is love of fame. It is a passion easy to deride but hard to understand, and in men who live at all by imagination almost impossible to eradicate. The good opinion of posterity can have no possible effect on our fortunes, and the practical value which reputation may temporarily have is quite absent in posthumous fame. The direct object of this passion—that a name should survive in men's mouths to which no adequate idea of its original can be attached—seems a thin and fantastic satisfaction, especially when we consider how little we should probably sympathise with the creatures that are to remember us. What comfort would it be to Virgil that boys still read him at school, or to Pindar that he is sometimes mentioned in a world from which everything he loved has departed? Yet, beneath this desire for nominal longevity, apparently so inane, there may lurk an ideal ambition of which the ancients cannot have been unconscious when they set so high a value on fame. They often identified fame with immortality, a subject on which they had far more rational sentiments than have since prevailed.

Fame, as a noble mind conceives and desires it, is not embodied in a monument, a biography, or the repetition of a strange name by strangers; it consists in the immortality of a man's work, his spirit, his efficacy, in the perpetual rejuvenation of his soul in the world. When Horace—no model of magnanimity—wrote his *exegi monumentum*, he was not thinking that the pleasure he would continue to give would remind people of his trivial personality, which indeed he never particularly celebrated and which had much better lie buried with his bones. He was thinking, of course, of that pleasure itself; thinking that the delight, half lyric, half sarcastic, which those delicate cameos had given him to carve would be perennially renewed in all who retraced them. Nay, perhaps we may not go too far in saying that even that impersonal satisfaction was not the deepest he felt; the deepest, very likely, flowed from the immortality, not of his monument, but of the subject and passion it commemorated; that tenderness, I mean, and that disillusion with mortal life which rendered his verse immortal. He had expressed, and in expressing appropriated, some recurring human moods, some mocking renunciations; and he knew that his spirit was immortal, being linked and identified with that portion of the truth. He had become a little spokesman of humanity, uttering what all experience repeats more or less articulately; and even if he should cease to be honoured in men's memories, he would continue to be unwittingly honoured and justified in their lives.

What we may conceive to have come in this way even within a Horace's apprehension is undoubtedly what has attached many nobler souls to fame. With an inversion of moral derivations which all mythical expression involves we speak of fame as the reward of genius, whereas in truth genius, the imaginative dominion of experience, is its own reward and fame is but a foolish image by which its worth is symbolised. When the Virgin in the Magnificat says, "Behold, from henceforth all generations shall call me blessed," the psalmist surely means to express a spiritual exaltation exempt from vanity; he merely translates into a rhetorical figure the fact that what had been first revealed to Mary would also bless all generations. That the Church should in consequence deem and pronounce her blessed is an incident describing, but not creating, the unanimity in their religious joys. Fame is thus the outward sign or recognition of an inward representative authority residing in genius or good fortune, an authority in which lies the whole worth of fame. Those will substantially remember and honour us who keep our ideals, and we shall live on in those ages whose experience we have anticipated.

Free society differs from that which is natural and legal precisely in this, that it does not cultivate relations which in the last analysis are experienced and material, but turns exclusively to unanimities in meanings, to collaborations in an ideal world. The basis of free society is of course natural, as we said, but free society has ideal goals. Spirits cannot touch save by becoming unanimous. At the same time public opinion, reputation, and impersonal sympathy reinforce only very general feelings, and reinforce them vaguely; and as the inner play of sentiment becomes precise, it craves more specific points of support or comparison. It is in creatures of our own species that we chiefly scent the aroma of inward sympathy, because it is they that are visibly moved on the same occasions as ourselves; and it is to those among our fellow-men who share our special haunts and habits that we feel more precise affinities. Though the ground for such feeling is animal contact and contagion, its deliverance does not revert to those natural accidents, but concerns a represented sympathy in represented souls. Friendship, springing from accidental association, terminates in a consciousness of ideal and essential agreement.

Comradeship is a form of friendship still akin to general sociability and gregariousness. When men are "in the same boat together," when a common anxiety, occupation, or sport unites them, they feel their human kinship in an intensified form without any greater personal affinity subsisting between them. The same effect is produced by a common estrangement from the rest of society. For this reason comradeship lasts no longer than the circumstances that bring it about. Its constancy is proportionate to the monotony of people's lives and minds. There is a lasting bond among school-fellows because no one can become a boy again and have a new set of playmates. There is a persistent comradeship with one's country-men, especially abroad, because seldom is a man pliable and polyglot enough to be at home among foreigners, or really to understand them. There is an inevitable comradeship with men of the same breeding or profession, however bad these may be, because habits soon monopolise the man. Nevertheless a greater buoyancy, a longer youth, a richer experience, would break down all these limits of fellowship. Such clingings to the familiar are three parts dread of the unfamiliar and want of resource in its presence, for one part in them of genuine loyalty. Plasticity loves new moulds because it can fill them, but for a man of sluggish mind and bad manners there is decidedly no place like home.

Though comradeship is an accidental bond, it is the condition of ideal friendship, for the ideal, in all spheres, is nothing but the accidental confirming itself and generating its own standard. Men must meet to love, and many other accidents besides conjunction must conspire to make a true friendship possible. In order that friendship may fulfil the conditions even of comradeship, it is requisite that the friends have the same social status, so that they may live at ease together and have congenial tastes. They must further have enough community of occupation and gifts to give each an appreciation of the other's faculty; for qualities are not complementary unless they are qualities of the same substance. Nothing must be actual in either friend that is not potential in the other.

For this reason, among others, friends are generally of the same sex, for when men and women agree, it is only in their conclusions; their reasons are always different. So that while intellectual har-mony between men and women is easily possible, its delightful and magic quality lies precisely in the fact that it does not arise from mutual understanding, but is a conspiracy of alien essences and a kissing, as it were, in the dark. As man's body differs from woman's in sex and strength, so his mind differs from hers in quality and function: they can co-operate but can never fuse. The human race, in its intellectual life, is organised like the bees: the masculine soul is a worker, sexually atrophied, and essentially dedicated to im-personal and universal arts; the feminine is a queen, infinitely fertile, omnipresent in its brooding industry, but passive and abounding in intuitions without method and passions without justice.

Friendship with a woman is therefore apt to be more or less than friendship: less, because there is no intellectual parity; more, because (even when the relation remains wholly dispassionate, as in respect to old ladies) there is something mysterious and oracular about a woman's mind which inspires a certain instinctive deference and puts it out of the question to judge what she says by masculine standards. She has a kind of sibylline intuition and the right to be irrationally à propos. There is a gallantry of the mind which pervades all conversation with a lady, as there is a natural courtesy toward children and mystics; but such a habit of respectful concession, marking as it does an intellectual alienation as profound as that which separates us from the dumb animals, is radically incompatible with friendship.

Friends, moreover, should have been young together. Much difference in age defeats equality and forbids frankness on many a fundamental subject; it confronts two minds of unlike focus: one near-sighted and without perspective, the other seeing only the background of present things. While comparisons in these respects may be interesting and borrowings sometimes possible, lending the older mind life and the younger mind wisdom, such intercourse has hardly the value of spontaneous sympathy, in which the spark of mutual intelligence flies, as it should, almost without words. Contagion is the only source of valid mind-reading: you must imitate to understand, and where the plasticity of two minds is not similar their mutual interpretations are necessarily false. They idealise in their friends whatever they do not invent or ignore, and the friendship which should have lived on energies conspiring spontaneously together dies into conscious appreciation.

All these are merely permissive conditions for friendship; its positive essence is yet to find. How, we may ask, does the vision of the general socius, humanity, become specific in the vision of a particular friend without losing its ideality or reverting to practical values? Of course, individuals might be singled out for the special benefits they may have conferred; but a friend's only gift is himself, and friendship is not friendship, it is not a form of free or liberal society, if it does not terminate in an ideal possession, in an object loved for its own sake. Such objects can be ideas only, not forces, for forces are subterranean and instrumental things, having only such value as they borrow from their ulterior effects and manifestations. To praise the utility of friendship, as the ancients so often did, and to regard it as a political institution justified, like victory or government, by its material results, is to lose one's moral bearings. The value of victory or good government is rather to be found in the fact that, among other things, it might render friendship possible. We are not to look now for what makes friendship useful, but for whatever may be found in friendship that may lend utility to life.

The first note that gives sociability a personal quality and raises the comrade into an incipient friend is doubtless sensuous affinity. Whatever reaction we may eventually make on an impression, after it has had time to soak in and to merge in some practical or intellectual habit, its first assault is always on the senses, and no sense is an indifferent organ. Each has, so to speak, its congenial rate of vibration and gives its stimuli a varying welcome. Little as we may attend to these instinctive hospitalities of sense, they betray themselves in unjustified likes and dislikes felt for casual persons and things, in the *je ne sais quoi* that makes instinctive sympathy. Voice, manner, aspect, hints of congenial tastes and judgments, a jest in the right key, a gesture marking the right aversions, all these trifles leave behind a pervasive impression. We reject a vision we find indigestible and without congruity to our inner dream; we accept and incorporate another into our private pantheon, where it becomes a legitimate figure, however dumb and subsidiary it may remain.

In a refined nature these sensuous premonitions of sympathy are seldom misleading. Liking cannot, of course, grow into friendship over night as it might into love; the pleasing impression, even if retained, will lie perfectly passive and harmless in the mind, until new and different impressions follow to deepen the interest at first evoked and to remove its centre of gravity altogether from the senses. In love, if the field is clear, a single glimpse may, like Tristan's potion, produce a violent and irresistible passion; but in friendship the result remains more proportionate to the incidental causes, discrimination is preserved, jealousy and exclusiveness are avoided. That vigilant, besetting, insatiable affection, so full of doubts and torments, with which the lover follows his object, is out of place here; for the friend has no property in his friend's body or leisure or residual ties; he accepts what is offered and what is acceptable, and the rest he leaves in peace. He is distinctly not his brother's keeper, for the society of friends is free.

Friendship may indeed come to exist without sensuous liking or comradeship to pave the way; but unless intellectual sympathy and moral appreciation are powerful enough to react on natural instinct and to produce in the end the personal affection which at first was wanting, friendship does not arise. Recognition given to a man's talent or virtue is not properly friendship. Friends must desire to live as much as possible together and to share their work, thoughts, and pleasures. Good-fellowship and sensuous affinity are indispensable to give spiritual communion a personal accent; otherwise men would be indifferent vehicles for such thoughts and powers as emanated from them, and attention would not be in any way arrested or refracted by the human medium through which it beheld the good.

No natural vehicle, however, is indifferent; no natural organ is or should be transparent. Transparency is a virtue only in artificial instruments, organs in which no blood flows and whose intrinsic operation is not itself a portion of human life. In looking through a field-glass I do not wish to perceive the lenses nor to see rainbows about their rim; yet I should not wish the eye itself to lose its pigments and add no dyes to the bulks it discerns. The sense for colour is a vital endowment and an ingredient in human happiness; but no vitality is added by the intervention of further media which are not themselves living organs.

A man is sometimes a coloured and sometimes a clear medium for the energies he exerts. When a thought conveyed or a work done enters alone into the observer's experience, no friendship is possible. This is always the case when the master is dead; for if his reconstructed personality retains any charm, it is only as an explanation or conceived nexus for the work he performed. In a philosopher or artist, too, personality is merely instrumental, for, although in a sense pervasive, a creative personality evaporates into its expression, and whatever part of it may not have been translated into ideas is completely negligible from the public point of view. That portion of a man's soul which he has not alienated and objectified is open only to those who know him otherwise than by his works and do not estimate him by his public attributions. Such persons are his friends. Into their lives he has entered not merely through an idea with which his name may be associated, nor through the fame of some feat he may have performed, but by awakening an inexpressible animal sympathy, by the contagion of emotions felt before the same objects. Estimation has been partly arrested at its medium and personal relations have added their homely accent to universal discourse. Friendship might thus be called ideal sympathy refracted by a human medium, or comradeship and sensuous affinity colouring a spiritual light.

The tie that in contemporary society most nearly resembles the ancient ideal of friendship is a well-assorted marriage. In spite of intellectual disparity and of divergence in occupation, man and wife are bound together by a common dwelling, common friends, common affection for children, and, what is of great importance, common financial interests. These bonds often suffice for substantial and lasting unanimity, even when no ideal passion preceded; so that what is called a marriage of reason, if it is truly reasonable, may give a fair promise of happiness, since a normal married life can produce the sympathies it requires.

When the common ideal interests needed to give friendship a noble strain become altogether predominant, so that comradeship and personal liking may be dispensed with, friendship passes into more and more political fellowships. Discipleship is a union of this kind. Without claiming any share in the master's private life, perhaps without having ever seen him, we may enjoy communion with his mind and feel his support and guidance in following the ideal which links us together. Hero-worship is an imaginative passion in which latent ideals assume picturesque shapes and take actual persons for their symbols. Such companionship, perhaps wholly imaginary, is a very clear and simple example of ideal society. The unconscious hero, to be sure, happens to exist, but his existence is irrelevant to his function, provided only he be present to the idealising mind. There is or need be no comradeship, no actual force or influence transmitted from him. Certain capacities and tendencies in the worshipper are brought to a focus by the hero's image, who is thereby first discovered and deputed to be a hero. He is an unmoved mover, like Aristotle's God and like every ideal to which thought or action is directed.

The symbol, however, is ambiguous in hero-worship, being in one sense ideal, the representation of an inner demand, and in another sense a sensible experience, the representative of an external reality. Accordingly the symbol, when highly prized and long contemplated, may easily become an idol; that in it which is not ideal nor representative of the worshipper's demand may be imported confusedly into the total adored, and may thus receive a senseless worship. The devotion which was, in its origin, an ideal tendency grown conscious and expressed in fancy may thus become a mechanical force vitiating that ideal. For this reason it is very important that the first objects to fix the soul's admiration should be really admirable, for otherwise their accidental blemishes will corrupt the mind to which they appear *sub specie boni*.

Discipleship and hero-worship are not stable relations. Since the meaning they embody is ideal and radiates from within outward, and since the image to which that meaning is attributed is controlled by a real external object, meaning and image, as time goes on, will necessarily fall apart. The idol will be discredited. An ideal, ideally conceived and known to be an ideal, a spirit worshipped in spirit and in truth, will take the place of the pleasing phenomenon; and in regard to every actual being, however noble, discipleship will yield to emulation, and worship to an admiration more or less selective and critical.

A disembodied ideal, however, is unmanageable and vague; it cannot exercise the natural and material suasion proper to a model we are expected to imitate. The more fruitful procedure is accordingly to idealise some historical figure or natural force, to ignore or minimise in it what does not seem acceptable, and to retain at the same time all the unobjectionable personal colour and all the graphic traits that can help to give that model a persuasive vitality. This poetic process is all the more successful for being automatic. It is in this way that heroes and gods have been created. A legend or fable lying in the mind and continually repeated gained insensibly at each recurrence some new eloquence, some fresh congruity with the emotion it had already awakened, and was destined to awake again. To measure the importance of this truth the reader need only conceive the distance traversed from the Achilles that may have existed to the hero in Homer, or from Jesus as he might have been in real life, or even as he is in the gospels, to Christ in the Church.

CHAPTER 7

PATRIOTISM

THE MYTHICAL social idea most potent over practical minds is perhaps the idea of country. When a tribe, enlarged and domiciled, has become a state, each man remains no less dependent than formerly on his nation, although less swayed by its visible presence and example. If a sense for social relations is to endure, some symbol must take the place of the moving crowd, the visible stronghold, and the outspread fields and orchards that once made up his country; some intellectual figment must arise to focus political interests, no longer confined to the crops and the priest's medicinal auguries. It is altogether impossible that the individual should have a discursive and adequate knowledge of statecraft and economy. Whatever idea, then, he frames to represent his undistinguished political relations becomes the centre of his patriotism.

When intelligence is not keen this idea may remain sensuous. The visible instruments of social life—chieftains, armies, monuments, the dialect and dress of the district, with all customs and pleasures traditional there—these are what a sensuous man may understand by his country. Bereft of these sensations he would feel lost and incapable; the habits formed in that environment would be galled by any other. This fondness for home, this dread of change and exile, is all the love of country he knows. If by chance, without too much added thought, he could rise to a certain poetic sentiment, he might feel attachment also to the landscape, to the memorable spots and aspects of his native land. These objects, which rhetoric calls sacred, might really have a certain sanctity for him; a wave of pious emotion might run over him at the sight of them, a pang when in absence they were recalled. These very things, however, like the man who prizes them, are dependent on a much larger system; and if patriotism is to embrace ideally what really produces human well-being it should extend over a wider field and to less picturable objects.

To define one's country is not so simple a matter as it may seem. France, for instance, is an uncommonly distinct and self-

161

conscious nation, with a long historic identity and a compact territory. Yet what is the France a Frenchman is to think of and love?
Paris itself has various quarters and moral climates, one of which
may well be loved while another is detested. The provinces have
customs, temperaments, political ideals, and even languages of
their own. Is Alsace-Lorraine beyond the pale of French patriotism? And if not, why utterly exclude French-speaking Switzerland,
the Channel Islands, Belgium, or Quebec? Or is a Frenchman
rather to love the colonies by way of compensation? Is an Algerian
Moor or a native of Tonquin his true fellow-citizen? Is Tahiti a
part of his "country"? The truth is, if we look at the heart of the
matter, a Protestant born in Paris is less a Frenchman than is a
Catholic born in Geneva.

If we pass from geography to institutions the same vagueness
exists. France to one man represents the Revolution, to another the
Empire, to a third the Church, and the vestiges of the *ancien
régime*. Furthermore, how far into the past is patriotism to look?
Is Charlemagne one of the glories of French history? Is it Julius
Caesar or Vicingetorix that is to warm the patriotic heart? Want of
reflection and a blind subservience to the colours of the map has led
some historians to call Roman victories defeats suffered by their
country, even when that country is essentially so Roman, for instance, as Spain. With as good reason might a Sicilian or a Floren-
tine chafe under the Latin conquest, or an American blush at the
invasion of his country by the Pilgrim Fathers. Indeed, even
geographically, the limits and the very heart of a man's country are
often ambiguous. Was Alexander's country Macedon or Greece?
Was General Lee's the United States or Virginia? The ancients
defined their country from within outward; its heart was the city
and its limits those of that city's dominion or affinities. Moderns
generally define their country rather stupidly by its administrative
frontiers; and yet an Austrian * would have some difficulty in
applying even this conventional criterion.

The object of patriotism is in truth something ideal, a moral
entity definable only by the ties which a man's imagination and
reason can at any moment recognise. If he has insight and depth of
feeling he will perceive that what deserves his loyalty is the entire
civilisation to which he owes his spiritual life and into which that
life will presently flow back, with whatever new elements he may

* Written before 1914. Author's note.

have added. Patriotism accordingly has two aspects: it is partly sentiment, by which it looks back upon the sources of culture, and partly policy, or allegiance to those ideals which, being suggested by what has already been attained, animate the better organs of society and demand further embodiment. To love one's country, unless that love is quite blind and lazy, must involve a distinction between the country's actual condition and its inherent ideal; and this distinction in turn involves a demand for changes and for effort. Party allegiance is a true form of patriotism. For a party, at least in its intent, is an association of persons advocating the same policy. Every thoughtful man must advocate some policy, and unless he has the misfortune to stand quite alone in his conception of public welfare he will seek to carry out that policy by the aid of such other persons as advocate it also.

The springs of culture, which retrospective patriotism regards, go back in the last instance to cosmic forces. The necessity that marshals the stars makes possible the world men live in, and is the first general and law-giver to every nation. The earth's geography, its inexorable climates with their flora and fauna, make a play-ground for the human will which should be well surveyed by any statesman who wishes to judge and act, not fantastically, but with reference to the real situation. Geography is a most enlightening science. In describing the habitat of man it largely explains his history. Animal battles give the right and only key to human conflicts, for the superadded rational element in man is not partisan, but on the contrary insinuates into his economy the novel principle of justice and peace. As this leaven, however, can mingle only with elements predisposed to receive it, the basis of reason itself, in so far as it attains expression, must be sought in the natural world. The fortunes of the human family among the animals thus come to concern reason and to be the background of progress.

Within humanity the next sphere of interest for a patriot is the race from which he is descended, with its traditional languages and religions. Blood is the ground of character and intelligence. The fruits of civilisation may, indeed, be transmitted from one race to another and consequently a certain artificial homogeneity may be secured amongst different nations; yet unless continual intermarriage takes place each race will soon recast and vitiate the common inheritance. The fall of the Roman Empire offered such a spectacle, when various types of barbarism, with a more or less classic veneer,

re-established themselves everywhere. Perhaps modern cosmopolitanism, if not maintained by commerce or by permanent conquest, may break apart in the same way and yield to local civilisations no less diverse than Christendom and Islam.

Environment, education, fashion, may be all powerful while
they last and may make it seem a prejudice to insist on race, turning
its assumed efficacy into a sheer dogma, with fanatical impulses
behind it; yet in practice the question will soon recur: What shall
sustain that omnipotent fashion, education, or environment? Nothing is more treacherous than tradition, when insight and force are
lacking to keep it warm. Under Roman dominion, the inhabitants
of Sparta still submitted to the laws of Lycurgus and their life
continued to be a sort of ritualistic shadow of the past. Those en-
franchised helots thought they were maintaining a heroic state
when, in fact, they were only turning its forms into a retrospective
religion. The old race was practically extinct; ephors, gymnasia,
and common meals could do nothing to revive it. The ways of the
Roman world—a kindred promiscuous population—prevailed over
that local ritual and rendered it perfunctory, because there were
no longer any living souls to understand that a man might place
his happiness in his country's life and care nothing for Oriental
luxury or Oriental superstition, things coming to flatter his personal lusts and make him useless and unhappy.

Institutions without men are as futile as men without institutions. Before race can be a rational object for patriotism there must
exist a *traditional genius*, handed down by inheritance or else by
adoption, when the persons adopted can really appreciate the mysteries they are initiated into. Blood could be disregarded, if only
the political ideal remained constant and progress was sustained,
the laws being modified only to preserve their spirit. A state lives
in any case by exchanging persons, and all spiritual life is maintained by exchanging expressions. Life is a circulation; it can digest
whatever materials will assume a form already determined ideally
and enable that form to come forth more clearly and be determined
in more particulars. Stagnant matter necessarily decays and in effect
is false to the spirit no less than a spirit that changes is false to itself.

The spirit of a race is a mythical entity expressing the individual soul in its most constant and profound instincts and expanding it in the direction in which correct representation is most easily
possible, in the direction of ancestors, kinsmen, and descendants. In

ancient cities, where patriotism was intense, it was expressed in a tribal and civic religion. The lares, the local gods, the deified heroes associated with them, were either ancestors idealised or ideals of manhood taking the form of patrons and supernatural protectors. Jupiter Capitolinus and the Spirit of Rome were a single object. To worship Jupiter in that Capitol was to dedicate oneself to the service of Rome. A foreigner could no more share that devotion than a neighbour could share the religion of the hearth without sharing by adoption the life of the family. Paganism was the least artificial of religions and the most poetical; its myths were comparatively transparent and what they expressed was comparatively real. In that religion patriotism and family duties could take imaginable forms, and those forms, apart from the inevitable tinge of superstition which surrounded them, did not materially vitiate the allegiance due to the actual forces on which human happiness depends.

What has driven patriotism, as commonly felt and conceived, so far from rational courses and has attached it to vapid objects has been the initial illegitimacy of all governments. Under such circumstances, patriotism is merely a passion for ascendency. Properly it animates the army, the government, the aristocracy; from those circles it can percolate, not perhaps without the help of some sophistry and intimidation, into the mass of the people, who are told that their government's fortunes are their own. Now the rabble has a great propensity to take sides, promptly and passionately, in any spectacular contest; the least feeling of affinity, the slightest emotional consonance, will turn the balance and divert in one direction sympathetic forces which, for every practical purpose, might just as well have rushed the other way. Most governments are in truth private societies pitted against one another in the international arena and giving meantime at home exhibitions of eloquence and more rarely of enterprise; but the people's passions are easily enlisted in such a game, of course on the side of their own government, just as each college or region backs its own athletes, even to the extent of paying their bills. Nations give the same kind of support to their fighting governments, and the sporting passions and illusions concerned are what, in the national game, is called patriotism.

Where parties and governments are bad, as they are in most ages and countries, it makes practically no difference to a com munity, apart from local ravages, whether its own army or the enemy's is victorious in war, nor does it really affect any man's welfare whether the party he happens to belong to is in office or not. These issues concern, in such cases, only the army itself, whose lives and fortunes are at stake, or the official classes, who lose their places when their leaders fall from power. The private citizen in any event continues in such countries to pay a maximum of taxes and to suffer, in all his private interests, a maximum of vexation and neglect. Nevertheless, because he has some son at the front, some cousin in the government, or some historical sentiment for the flag and the nominal essence of his country, the oppressed subject will glow like the rest with patriotic ardour, and will decry as dead to duty and honour anyone who points out how perverse is this helpless allegiance to a government representing no public interest.

In proportion as governments become good and begin to operate for the general welfare, patriotism itself becomes representative and an expression of reason; but just in the same measure does hostility to that government on the part of foreigners become groundless and perverse. A competitive patriotism involves ill-will toward all other states and a secret and constant desire to see them thrashed and subordinated. But a good government is an international benefit, and the prosperity and true greatness of any country is a boon sooner or later to the whole world; it may eclipse alien governments and draw away local populations or industries, but it necessarily benefits alien individuals in so far as it is allowed to affect them at all.

Animosity against a well-governed country is therefore madness. A rational patriotism would rather take the form of imitating and supporting that so-called foreign country, and even, if practicable, of fusing with it. The invidious and aggressive form of patriotism, though inspired generally only by local conceit, would nevertheless be really justified if such conceit happened to be well grounded. A dream of universal predominance visiting a truly virtuous and intelligent people would be an aspiration toward universal beneficence. For every man who is governed at all must be governed by others; the point is, that the others, in ruling him, shall help him to be himself and give scope to his congenial activities. When coerced in that direction he obeys a force which, in the best sense of the word, *represents* him, and consequently he is truly free; nor could he be ruled by a more native and rightful authority than by one that divines and satisfies his true necessities.

A man's nature is not, however, a quantity or quality fixed unalterably and *a priori*. As breeding and selection improve a race, so every experience modifies the individual and offers a changed basis for future experience. The language, religion, education, and prejudices acquired in youth bias character and predetermine the directions in which development may go on. A child might possibly change his country; a man can only wish that he might change it. Therefore, among the true interests which a government should represent, nationality itself must be included.

Mechanical forces, we must not weary of repeating, do not come merely to vitiate the ideal; they come to create it. The historical background of life is a part of its substance and the ideal can never grow independently of its spreading roots. A sanctity hangs about the sources of our being, whether physical, social, or imaginative. The ancients who kissed the earth on returning to their native country expressed nobly and passionately what every man feels for those regions and those traditions whence the sap of his own life has been sucked in. There is a profound friendliness in whatever revives primordial habits, however they may have been overlaid with later sophistications. For this reason the homelier words of a mother tongue, the more familiar assurances of an ancestral religion, and the very savour of childhood's dishes, remain always a potent means to awaken emotion. Such ingrained influences, in their vague totality, make a man's true nationality. A government, in order to represent the general interests of its subjects, must move in sympathy with their habits and memories; it must respect their idiosyncrasy for the same reason that it protects their lives. If parting from a single object of love be, as it is, true dying, how much more would a shifting of all the affections be death to the soul.

Tenderness to such creative influences is a mark of profundity; it has the same relation to political life that transcendentalism has to science and morals; it shrinks back into radical facts, into centres of vital radiation, and quickens the sense for inner origins. Nationality is a natural force and a constituent in character which should be reckoned with and by no means be allowed to miss those fruits which it alone might bear; but, like the things it venerates, it is only a starting-point for liberal life. Just as to be always talking about transcendental points of reference, primordial reality, and

the self to which everything appears, though at first it might pass
for spiritual insight, is in the end nothing but pedantry and impotence, so to be always harping on nationality is to convert what
should be a recognition of natural conditions into a ridiculous pride
in one's own oddities. Nature has hidden the roots of things, and
though botany must now and then dig them up for the sake of comprehension, their place is still under ground, if flowers and fruits
are to be expected. The private loyalties which a man must have
toward his own people, grounding as they alone can his morality
and genius, need nevertheless to be seldom paraded. Attention,
when well directed, turns rather to making immanent racial forces
blossom out in the common medium and express themselves in
ways consonant with practical reason and universal progress. A
man's feet must be planted in his country, but his eyes should survey the world.

What a statesman might well aim at would be to give the special sentiments and gifts of his countrymen such a turn that, while
continuing all vital traditions, they might find less and less of what
is human alien to their genius. Differences in nationality, founded
on race and habitat, must always subsist; but what has been superadded artificially by ignorance and bigotry may be gradually
abolished in view of universal relations better understood. There
is a certain plane on which all races, if they reach it at all, must live
in common, the plane of morals and science; which is not to say
that even in those activities the mind betrays no racial accent. What
is excluded from science and morals is not variety, but contradiction.
Any community which had begun to cultivate the Life of Reason in
those highest fields would tend to live rationally on all subordinate
levels also; for with science and morality rationally applied the best
possible use would be made of every local and historical accident.
Where traditions had some virtue or necessity about them they
would be preserved; where they were remediable prejudices they
would be superseded.

The essence of patriotism may be annulled by a kind of sympathy which is merely vicarious or epidemic selfishness; patriotism
consists rather in being sensitive to a set of interests which no one
could have had if he had lived in isolation, but which accrue to
men conscious of living in society, and in a society having the scope
and history of a nation. It was the vice of liberalism to believe that
common interests covered nothing but the sum of those objects

which each individual might pursue alone; whereby science, religion, art, language, and nationality itself would cease to be matters of public concern and would appeal to the individual merely as instruments. The welfare of a flock of sheep is secured if each is well fed and watered, but the welfare of a human society involves the partial withdrawal of every member from such pursuits to attend instead to memory and to ideal possessions; these involve a certain conscious continuity and organisation in the state not necessary for animal existence. It is not for man's interest to live unless he can live in the spirit, because his spiritual capacity, when unused, will lacerate and derange even his physical life. The brutal individualist falls into the same error into which despots fall when they declare war out of personal pique or tax the people to build themselves a pyramid, not discerning their country's interests, which they might have appropriated, from interests of their own which no one else can share.

Democracies, too, are full of patriots of this lordly stripe, men whose patriotism consists in joy at their personal possessions and in desire to increase them. The resultant of general selfishness might conceivably be a general order; but though intelligent selfishness, if universal, might suffice for good government, it could not suffice for nationality. Patriotism is an imaginative passion, and imagination is ingenuous. The value of patriotism is not utilitarian, but ideal. It belongs to the free forms of society and ennobles a man not so much because it nerves him to work or to die, which the basest passions may also do, but because it associates him, in working or dying, with an immortal and friendly companion, the spirit of his race. This he received from his ancestors tempered by their achievements, and may transmit to posterity qualified by his own.

CHAPTER 8

IDEAL SOCIETY

IT IS an inspiring thought, and a true one, that in proportion as a man's interests become humane and his efforts rational, he appropriates and expands a communicable life, which reappears in all individuals who reach the same impersonal level of ideas. Patriotism envisages this ideal life in so far as it is locally coloured and grounded in certain racial aptitudes and traditions; but the community recognised in patriotism is imbedded in a larger one embracing all living creatures. While in some respects we find sympathy more complete the nearer home we remain, in another sense there is no true companionship except with the universe. Instinctive society, with its compulsory affections, is of course deeper and more elementary than any free or intellectual union. Love is at once more animal than friendship and more divine; and the same thing may be said of family affection when compared with patriotism. What lies nearer the roots of our being must needs enjoy a wider prevalence and engage the soul more completely, being able to touch its depths and hush its primordial murmurs.

On the other hand, the free spirit, the political and speculative genius in man, chafes under those blind involutions and material bonds. Natural, beneficent, sacred, as in a sense they may be, they somehow oppress the intellect and, like a brooding mother, half stifle what they feed. Something drives the youth afield, into solitude, into alien friendships; only in the face of nature and an indifferent world can he become himself. Such a flight from home and all its pieties grows more urgent when there is some real conflict of temper or conscience between the young man and what is established in his family; and this happens often because, after all, the most beneficent conventions are but mechanisms which must ignore the nicer sensibilities and divergences of living souls.

Common men accept these spiritual tyrannies, weak men repine at them, and great men break them down. But to defy the world is a serious business, and requires the greatest courage, even if the defiance touch in the first place only the world's ideals. Most men's conscience, habits, and opinions are borrowed from convention and gather continual comforting assurances from the same social consensus that originally suggested them. To reverse this process, to consult one's own experience and elicit one's own judgment, challenging those in vogue, seems too often audacious and futile; but there are impetuous minds born to disregard the chances against them, even to the extent of denying that they are taking chances at all. For in the first instance it never occurs to the inventor that he is the source of his new insight; he thinks he has merely opened his eyes and seen what, by an inconceivable folly, the whole world had grown blind to. Wise men in antiquity, he imagines, saw the facts as he sees them, as the gods see them now, and as all sane men shall see them henceforward.

Thus, if the innovator be a religious soul, grown conscious of some new spiritual principle, he will try to find support for his inspiration in some lost book of the law or in some early divine revelation corrupted, as he will assert, by wicked men, or even in some direct voice from heaven; no delusion will be too obvious, no re-interpretation too forced, if it can help him to find external support somewhere for his spontaneous conviction. To denounce one authority he needs to invoke another, and if no other be found, he will invent or, as they say, he will postulate one. His courage in facing the actual world is thus supported by his ability to expand the world in imagination. In separating himself from his fellow-men he has made a new companion out of his ideal. An impetuous spirit when betrayed by the world will cry, "I know that my redeemer liveth"; and the antiphonal response will come more wistfully after reflection:

> "It fortifies my soul to know
> That though I perish, Truth is so."

The deceptions which nature practises on men are not always cruel. These are also kindly deceptions which prompt him to pursue or expect his own good when, though not destined to come in the form he looks for, this good is really destined to come in some shape or other. Such, for instance, are the illusions of romantic love, which may really terminate in a family life practically better than the absolute and chimerical unions which that love had dreamed of. Such, again, are those illusions of conscience which attach unspeakable vague penalties and repugnances to acts which commonly have bad results, though these are impossible to forecast with precision. When disillusion comes, while it may bring a momentary shock, it ends by producing a settled satisfaction unknown before, a satisfaction which the coveted prize, could it have been attained, would hardly have secured. When on the day of judgment, or earlier, a man perceives that what he thought he was doing for the Lord's sake he was really doing for the benefit of the least, perhaps, of the Lord's creatures, his satisfaction, after a moment's surprise, will certainly be very genuine.

Ideal society belongs entirely to this realm of kindly illusion, for it is the society of symbols. Whenever religion, art, or science presents us with an image or a formula, involving no matter how momentous a truth, there is something delusive in the representation. And yet there is another aspect to the matter. Symbols are presences, and they are those particularly congenial presences which we have inwardly evoked and cast in a form intelligible and familiar to human thinking. Their function is to give flat experience a rational perspective, translating the general flux into stable objects and making it representable in human discourse. They are therefore precious, not only for their representative or practical value, implying useful adjustments to the environing world, but even more, sometimes, for their immediate or æsthetic power, for their kinship to the spirit they enlighten and exercise.

This is prevailingly true in the fine arts, which seem to express man even more than they express nature; although in art also the symbol would lose all its significance and much of its inward articulation if natural objects and eventual experience could be disregarded in constructing it. In music, indeed, this ulterior significance is reduced to a minimum; yet it persists, since music brings an ideal object before the mind which needs, to some extent, translation into terms no longer musical—terms, for instance, of skill, dramatic passion, or moral sentiment. But in music preeminently, and very largely in all the arts, external propriety is adventitious; so much can the mere presence and weight of a symbol fill the mind and constitute an absolute possession.

In religion and science the overt purpose of symbols is to represent external truths. The inventors of these symbols think they are merely uncovering a self-existent reality, having in itself the very form seen in their idea. They do not perceive that the society of God or Nature is an ideal society, nor that these phantoms, looming in their imagination, are but significant figments whose subjective basis is a minute and indefinite series of ordinary perceptions. They consequently attribute whatever value their genial syntheses may have to the object as they picture it. The gods have, they fancy, the aspect and passions, the history and influence which their myth unfolds; nature in its turn contains hypostatically just those laws and forces which are described by theory. Consequently the presence of God or Nature seems to the mythologist not an ideal, but a real and mutual society, as if collateral beings, endowed with the conceived characters, actually existed as men exist. But this opinion is untenable. As Hobbes said, in a phrase which ought to be inscribed in golden letters over the head of every talking philosopher: *No discourse whatsoever can end in absolute knowledge of fact.* Absolute knowledge of fact is immediate, it is experiential. We should have to come up against God or Nature as we imagine them, in order to know for a fact that they existed. Intellectual knowledge, on the other hand, where it relates to hidden existence, is faith only, a faith which in these matters means trust.

The divine and the material are contrasted points of reference required by the actual. Reason, working on the immediate flux of appearances, reaches these ideal realms and, resting in them, perforce calls them realities. One—the realm of causes—supplies appearances with a basis and calculable order; the other—the realm of truth and felicity—supplies them with a standard and justification. Natural society may accordingly be contrasted with ideal society, not because our idea of Nature is not, logically speaking, ideal too, but because in natural society we ally ourselves consciously with our origins and surroundings, in ideal society with our thoughts. There is an immense difference in spirituality, in ideality of the moral sort, between gathering or conciliating forces for action and fixing the ends which action should pursue. Both fields are ideal in the sense that intelligence alone could discover or exploit them; yet to call nature ideal is undoubtedly equivocal, since its ideal function is precisely to be the substance and cause of the given flux, a ground-work for experience which, while merely inferred and potential, is none the less dynamic and material. The significance of the word nature is indeed of such a sort as to be forfeited if the trusty instrument and true antecedent of human life were not found there. We should be frivolous and inconstant, taking our philosophy for a game and not for method in living, if having set out to look for the causes and practical order of things, and having found them, we should declare that they were not *really* casual or efficient, on the strange ground that our discovery of them had been a feat of intelligence and had proved a priceless boon. The absurdity could not be greater if in moral science, after the goal of all agitation had been determined and defined, we declared that this was not *really* the good.

Those who are shocked at the assertion that God and Nature are ideal, and that their contrasted prerogatives depend on that fact, may, of course, use the same words in a different way, making them synonymous, and may readily "prove" that God or Nature exists materially and has absolute being. We need but agree to designate by those terms the sum of existences, whatever they (or it) may be on their own account. Then the ontological proof asserts its rights unmistakably. Science and religion, however, are superfluous if what we wish to learn is that there is Something, and that All-there-is must assuredly be All-there-is. Ecstasies may doubtless ensue upon considering that Being is and Non-Being is not, as they are said to ensue upon long enough considering one's navel; but the Life of Reason is made of more variegated stuff. Science, when it is not dialectical, describes an ideal order of existences in space and time, such that all incidental facts, as they come, may fill it in and lend it body. Religion, when pure, contemplates some pertinent ideal of intelligence and goodness. Both religion and science live in imaginative discourse, one being an aspiration and the other a hypothesis. Both introduce into the mind an ideal society.

The Life of Reason is no fair reproduction of the universe, but the expression of man alone. A theory of nature is nothing but a mass of observations, made with a hunter's and an artist's eye. A mortal in order to live must devour one-half the world and disregard the other, so in order to think and practically to know he must deal summarily and selfishly with his materials; otherwise his intellect would melt again into endless and irrevocable dreams. The law of gravity, because it so notably unifies the motions of matter, is something which these motions themselves know nothing of; it is a description of them in terms of human discourse. Such discourse can never assure us absolutely that the motions it forecasts will occur; the sensible proof must ensue spontaneously in its own good time. In the interval our theory remains pure presumption and hypothesis. Reliable as it may be in that capacity, it is no replica of anything of its own character existing beyond. It creates, like all intelligence, a secondary and merely symbolic world.

When this diversity between the truest theory and the simplest fact, between potential generalities and actual particulars, has been thoroughly appreciated, it becomes clear that much of what is valued in science and religion is not lodged in the miscellany underlying these creations of reason, but is lodged rather in the rational activity itself, and in the intrinsic beauty of all symbols bred in a genial mind. Of course, if these symbols had no real points of reference, if they were symbols of nothing, they could have no great claim to consideration and no rational character; at most they would be agreeable sensations. They are, however, at their best good symbols for a diffused order and tendency in events; they render that reality with a difference, reducing it to a formula or a myth, in which its tortuous length and trivial detail can be surveyed to advantage without undue waste or fatigue. Symbols may thus become eloquent, vivid, important, being endowed with both poetic grandeur and practical truth.

The facts from which this truth is borrowed, if they were rehearsed unimaginatively, in their own flat infinity, would be far from arousing the same emotions. The human eye sees in perspective; its glory would vanish were it reduced to a crawling, exploring antenna. Not that it loves to falsify anything. That to the worm the landscape might possess no light and shade, that the mountain's atomic structure should be unpicturable, cannot distress the landscape gardener nor the poet; what concerns them is the effect such things may produce in the human fancy, so that the soul may live in a congenial world.

Naturalist and prophet are landscape painters on canvases of their own; each is interested in his own perception and perspective, which, if he takes the trouble to reflect, need not deceive him about what the world would be if not foreshortened in that particular manner. This special interpretation is nevertheless precious and shows up the world in that light in which it interests naturalists or prophets to see it. Their figments make their chosen world, as the painter's apperceptions are the life of his works.

While the symbol's applicability is essential to its worth—since otherwise science would be useless and religion demoralising—its power and fascination lie in its acquiring a more and more profound affinity to the human mind, so long as it can do so without surrendering its relevance to practice. Thus natural science is at its best when it is most thoroughly mathematical, since what can be expressed mathematically can speak a human language. In such science only the ultimate material elements remain surds; all their further movement and complication can be represented in that kind of thought which is most intimately satisfactory and perspicuous. And in like manner, religion is at its best when it is most anthropomorphic; indeed, the two most spiritual religions, Buddhism and Christianity, have actually raised a man, overflowing with utterly human tenderness and pathos, to the place usually occupied only by cosmic and thundering deities. The human heart is lifted above misfortune and encouraged to pursue unswervingly its inmost ideal when no compromise is any longer attempted with what is not moral or human, and Prometheus is honestly proclaimed to be holier than Zeus. At that moment religion ceases to be superstitious and becomes a rational discipline, an effort to perfect the spirit rather than to intimidate it.

We have seen that society has three stages—the natural, the free, and the ideal. In the natural stage its function is to produce the individual and equip him with the prerequisites of moral freedom. When this end is attained society can rise to friendship, to unanimity and disinterested sympathy, where the ground of association is some ideal interest, while this association constitutes at the same time a personal and emotional bond. Ideal society, on the contrary, transcends accidental conjunctions altogether. Here the ideal interests themselves take possession of the mind; its companions are the symbols it breeds and possesses for excellence, beauty, and truth. Religion, art, and science are the chief spheres in which ideal companionship is found. It remains for us to traverse these provinces in turn and see to what extent the Life of Reason may flourish there.

III

REASON IN RELIGION

CHAPTER 1

HOW RELIGION MAY BE AN EMBODIMENT OF REASON

EXPERIENCE HAS repeatedly confirmed that well-known maxim of Bacon's, that "a little philosophy inclineth man's mind to atheism, but depth in philosophy bringeth men's minds about to religion." Even the heretics and atheists, if they have profundity, turn out after a while to be forerunners of some new orthodoxy. What they rebel against is a religion alien to their nature; they are atheists only by accident, and relatively to a convention which inwardly offends them, but they yearn mightily in their own souls after the religious acceptance of a world interpreted in their own fashion. So it appears in the end that their atheism and loud protestation were in fact the hastier part of their thought, since what emboldened them to deny the poor world's faith was that they were too impatient to understand it. Indeed, the enlightenment common to young wits and worm-eaten old satirists, who plume themselves on detecting the scientific ineptitude of religion— something which the blindest half see—is not nearly enlightened enough: it points to notorious facts incompatible with religious tenets literally taken, but it leaves unexplored the habits of thought from which those tenets sprang, their original meaning, and their true function. Such studies would bring the sceptic face to face with the mystery and pathos of mortal existence. They would make him understand why religion is so profoundly moving and in a sense so profoundly just. If nothing, as Hooker said, is "so malapert as a splenetic religion," a sour irreligion is almost as perverse.

At the same time, when Bacon penned the sage epigram we have quoted he forgot to add that the God to whom depth in philosophy brings back men's minds is far from being the same from whom a little philosophy estranges them. Traditional conceptions, when they are felicitous, may be adopted by the poet, but they must be purified by the moralist and disintegrated by the philosopher. Each religion necessarily contradicts every other religion, and probably contradicts itself. What religion a man shall have is a historical accident, quite as much as what language he shall speak. In the rare circumstances where a choice is possible, he may, with some difficulty, make an exchange; but even then he is only adopting a new convention which may be more agreeable to his personal temper but which is essentially as arbitrary as the old.

The attempt to speak without speaking any particular language is not more hopeless than the attempt to have a religion that shall be no religion in particular. A courier's or a dragoman's speech may indeed be often unusual and drawn from disparate sources, not without some mixture of personal originality; but that private jargon will have a meaning only because of its analogy to one or more conventional languages and its obvious derivation from them. So travellers from one religion to another, people who have lost their spiritual nationality, may often retain a neutral and confused residuum of belief, which they may egregiously regard as the essence of all religion, so little may they remember the graciousness and naturalness of that ancestral accent which a perfect religion should have. Yet a moment's probing of the conceptions surviving in such minds will show them to be nothing but vestiges of old beliefs, creases which thought, even if emptied of all dogmatic tenets, has not been able to smooth away at its first unfolding. Later generations, if they have any religion at all, will be found either to revert to ancient authority, or to attach themselves spontaneously to something wholly novel and immensely positive, to some faith promulgated by a fresh genius and passionately embraced by a converted people. Thus every living and healthy religion has a marked idiosyncrasy. Its power consists in its special and surprising message and in the bias which that revelation gives to life. The vistas it opens and the mysteries it propounds are another world to live in; and another world to live in—whether we expect ever to pass wholly into it or no—is what we mean by having a religion.

What relation, then, does this great business of the soul, which we call religion, bear to the Life of Reason? For reason, the Life of Reason is an ideal to which everything in the world should be subordinated; it establishes lines of moral cleavage everywhere and makes right eternally different from wrong. Religion does the same thing. It makes absolute moral decisions. It sanctions, unifies, and transforms ethics. Religion thus exercises a function of the Life of Reason. And a further function which is common to both is that of emancipating man from his personal limitations. In different ways religions promise to transfer the soul to better conditions. A supernaturally favoured kingdom is to be established for posterity upon earth, or for all the faithful in heaven, or the soul is to be freed by repeated purgations from all taint and sorrow, or it is to be lost in the absolute, or it is to become an influence and an object of adoration in the places it once haunted or wherever the cult it once loved may be carried on by future generations of its kindred. Now reason in its way lays before us all these possibilities: it points to common objects, political and intellectual, in which an individual may lose what is mortal and accidental in himself and perpetuate what is rational and human; it teaches us how calm and fortunate death may be to those whose spirit can still live in their country and in their ideas; it reveals the radiating effects of action and the eternal objects of thought.

Yet the difference in tone and language must strike us, so soon as it is philosophy that speaks. Even if the function of religion and that of reason coincide, this function is performed in the two cases by very different organs. Religions are many, reason one. Religion consists of specific ideas, hopes, enthusiasms, and objects of worship; it operates by grace and flourishes by prayer. Reason, on the other hand, is a mere principle or potential order which we conform or do not conform to; it does not urge or chide us, nor call for any emotions on our part other than those naturally aroused by the various objects which it unfolds in their true nature and proportion. Religion brings some order into life by weighting it with new materials. Reason adds to the natural materials only the perfect order which it introduces into them. Rationality is nothing but a form, an ideal constitution which life may more or less embody. Religion is a second life in itself, a magic mass of sentiments and ideas. The one is an inviolate principle, the other a changing and struggling force. And yet this struggling and changing force of religion seems to direct man toward something eternal. It seems to make for an ultimate harmony within the soul and for an ultimate harmony between the soul and all the soul depends upon. So that religion, in its intent, is a more conscious and direct pursuit of the Life of Reason than is society, science, or art. For these approach and fill out the ideal life tentatively and piecemeal, hardly regarding the goal or caring for the ultimate justification of their instinctive aims. Religion also has an instinctive and blind side, and bubbles up in all manner of chance practices and intuitions; soon, however, it feels its way toward the heart of things, and, from whatever quarter it may come, veers in the direction of the ultimate.

Nevertheless, we must confess that this religious pursuit of the Life of Reason has been singularly abortive. Those within the pale of each religion may prevail upon themselves to express satisfaction with its results, thanks to a fond partiality in reading the past and generous draughts of hope for the future; but any one regarding the various religions at once and comparing their achievements with what reason requires, must feel how terrible is the disappointment which they have one and all prepared for mankind. Their chief anxiety has been to offer imaginary remedies for mortal ills, some of which are incurable essentially, while others might have been really cured by well-directed effort. The Greek oracles, for instance, pretended to heal our natural ignorance, which has its appropriate though difficult cure, while the Christian vision of heaven pretended to be an antidote to our natural death, the inevitable correlate of birth and of a changing and conditioned existence. By methods of this sort little can be done for the real betterment of life. To confuse intelligence and dislocate sentiment by gratuitous fictions is a short-sighted way of pursuing happiness. Nature is soon avenged. An unhealthy exaltation and a one-sided morality have to be followed by regrettable reactions. When these come, the real rewards of life may seem vain to a relaxed vitality, and the very name of virtue may irritate young spirits untrained in any natural excellence. Thus religion too often debauches the morality it comes to sanction, and impedes the science it ought to fulfil.

What is the secret of this ineptitude? Why does religion, so near to rationality in its purpose, fall so far short of it in its texture and in its results? The answer is easy: Religion pursues rationality through the imagination. When it explains events or assigns causes, it is an imaginative substitute for science. When it gives precepts, insinuates ideals, or remoulds aspiration, it is an imaginative substitute for wisdom—I mean for the deliberate and impartial pursuit of all good. The conditions and the aims of life are both represented in religion poetically, but this poetry tends to arrogate to itself literal truth and moral authority, neither of which it possesses. Hence the depth and importance of religion become intelligible no less than its contradictions and practical disasters. Its object is the same as that of reason, but its method is to proceed by intuition and by unchecked poetical conceits. These are repeated and vulgarised in proportion to their original fineness and significance, till they pass for reports of objective truth and come to constitute a world of faith, superposed upon the world of experience and regarded as materially enveloping it, if not in space at least in time and in profundity. The only truth of religion comes from its interpretation of life, from its symbolic rendering of that aspiration which it springs out of and which it seeks to elucidate. Its falsehood comes from the insidious misunderstanding which clings to it, to the effect that these poetic conceptions are not merely poetical, but are literal information about experience or reality elsewhere—an experience and reality which, strangely enough, supply just the defects betrayed by reality and experience here.

Thus religion has the same original relation to life that poetry has; only poetry, which never pretends to literal validity, adds a pure value to existence, the value of a liberal imaginative exercise. The poetic value of religion would initially be greater than that of poetry itself, because religion deals with higher and more vital themes, with sides of life which are in greater need of some imaginative touch and ideal interpretation than are those pleasant or pompous things which ordinary poetry dwells upon. But this initial advantage is neutralised in part by the abuse to which religion is subject, whenever its symbolic rightness is taken for scientific truth. Like poetry, it improves the world only by imagining it improved, but not content with making this addition to the mind's furniture—an addition which might be useful and ennobling—it thinks to confer a more radical benefit by persuading mankind that, in spite of appearances, the world is really such as that rather arbitrary idealisation has painted it. This spurious satisfaction is naturally the prelude to many a disappointment, and the soul has infinite trouble to emerge again from the artificial problems and sentiments into which it is thus plunged. The value of religion becomes equivocal. Religion remains an imaginative achievement, a symbolic representation of moral reality which may have a most important function in vitalising the mind and in transmitting, by way of parables, the lessons of experience. But it becomes at the same time a continuous incidental deception; and this deception, in proportion as it is strenuously denied to be such, can work indefinite harm in the world and in the conscience.

On the whole, however, religion should not be conceived as having taken the place of anything better, but rather as having come to relieve situations which, but for its presence, would have been infinitely worse. In the thick of active life, or in the monotony of practical slavery, there is more need to stimulate fancy than to control it. Natural instinct is not much disturbed in the human brain by what may happen in that thin superstratum of ideas which commonly overlays it. We must not blame religion for preventing the development of a moral and natural science which at any rate would seldom have appeared; we must rather thank it for the sensibility, the reverence, the speculative insight which it has introduced into the world.

If we hope to gain any understanding of these matters we must begin by taking them out of that heated and fanatical atmosphere in which the Hebrew tradition has enveloped them. The Jews had no philosophy, and when their national traditions came to be theoretically explicated and justified, they were made to issue in a puerile scholasticism and a rabid intolerance. The question of monotheism, for instance, was a terrible question to the Jews. Idolatry did not consist in worshipping a god who, not being ideal, might be unworthy of worship, but rather in recognising other gods than the one worshipped in Jerusalem. To the Greeks, on the contrary, whose philosophy was enlightened and ingenuous, monotheism and polytheism seemed perfectly innocent and compatible. To say God or the gods was only to use different expressions for the same influence, now viewed in its abstract unity and correlation with all existence, now viewed in its various manifestations in moral life, in nature, or in history. So that what in Plato, Aristotle, and the Stoics meets us at every step—the combination of monotheism with polytheism—is no contradiction, but merely an intelligent variation of phrase to indicate various aspects or functions in physical and moral things. When religion appears to us in this light its contradictions and controversies lose all their bitterness. Each doctrine will simply represent the moral plane on which they live who have devised or adopted it. Religions will thus be better or worse, never true or false. We shall be able to lend ourselves to each in turn, and seek to draw from it the secret of its inspiration.

CHAPTER 2

RATIONAL ELEMENTS IN SUPERSTITION

WE NEED not impose upon ourselves the endless and repulsive task of describing all the superstitions that have existed in the world. In his impotence and laziness the natural man unites any notion with any other in a loose causal relation. A single instance of juxtaposition, nay, the mere notion and dream of such a combination, will suffice to arouse fear or to prompt experimental action.

When philosophers have objected to Hume's account of causation that he gave no sufficient basis for the *necessary* influence of cause on effect, they have indulged in a highly artificial supposition. They have assumed that people actually regard causes as necessary. But a cause, in real life, means a justifying circumstance. We are absolutely without insight into the machinery of causation, notably in the commonest cases, like that of generation, nutrition, or the operation of mind on matter. But we are familiar with the more notable superficial conditions in each case, and the appearance in part of any usual phenomenon makes us look for the rest of it. We do not ordinarily expect virgins to bear children nor prophets to be fed by ravens nor prayers to move mountains; but we may believe any of these things at the merest suggestion of fancy or report, without any warrant from experience, so loose is the bond and so external the relation between the terms morally associated.* When we come to adopt scientific hypotheses, at least in certain provinces of our thought, we lose our primitive openness and simplicity of mind. With an unjustified haste, we assert that miracles are imposible, i.e., that nothing interesting and fundamentally natural can happen unless all the usual, though adventitious, *mise-en-scène* has been prepared behind the curtain.

The philosopher may eventually discover that such machinery is really needed and that even the actors themselves have a mecha-

* They form a dramatic event, single and acceptable to the spirit. Author's note, 1952.

nism within them, so that not only their smiles and magnificent gestures, but their heated fancy itself and their conception of their rôles are but outer effects and dramatic illusions produced by the natural stage-carpentry in their brains. Yet such eventual scientific conclusions have nothing to do with the tentative first notions of men when they begin to experiment in the art of living. As the seeds of lower animals have to be innumerable, so that in a chance environment a few may grow to maturity, so the seeds of rational thinking, the first categories of reflection, have to be multitudinous, in order that some lucky principle of synthesis may somewhere come to light and find successful application. Science, which thinks to make belief in miracles impossible, is itself belief in miracles—in the miracles best authenticated by history and by daily life.

When men begin to understand things, when they begin to reflect and to plan, they divide the world into the hateful and the delightful, the avoidable and the attainable. And in feeling their way toward what attracts them, or in escaping what they fear, they at first follow passively the lead of instinct, they watch themselves live, or rather sink without reserve into their living; their reactions are as little foreseen and as naturally accepted as their surroundings. Their ideas are incidents in their perpetual oscillation between apathy and passion. The stream of animal life leaves behind a little sediment of knowledge, the sand of that auriferous river; a few grains of experience remain to mark the path traversed by the flood. These residual ideas and premonitions, these first categories of thought, are of any and every sort. All the contents of the mind and all the threads of relation that weave its elements together are alike fitted, for all we can then see, to give the clue to the labyrinth in which we find ourselves wandering.

There is *prima facie* no ground for not trying to apply to experience such categories, for instance, as that of personal omnipotence, as if everything were necessarily arranged as we may command or require. On this principle children often seem to conceive an obedient world in which they are astonished not to find themselves living. Or we may try æsthetic categories and allow our reproductive imagination—by which memory is fed—to bring under the unity of apperception only what can fall within it harmoniously, completely, and delightfully. Such an understanding, impervious to anything but the beautiful, might be a fine thing in itself, but would not chronicle the fortunes of that organism to which it was attached. It would yield an experience—doubtless a highly interesting and elaborate experience—but one which could never serve as an index to successful action. It would totally fail to represent its conditions, and consequently would imply nothing about its continued existence. It would be an experience irrelevant to conduct, no part, therefore, of a Life of Reason, but a kind of lovely vapid music or parasitic dream.

Now such dreams are in fact among the first and most absorbing formations in the human mind. If we could penetrate into animal consciousness we should not improbably find that what there accompanies instinctive motions is a wholly irrelevant fancy, whose flaring up and subsidence no doubt coincide with the presence of objects interesting to the organism and causing marked reactions within it; yet this fancy may in no way represent the nature of surrounding objects nor the eventual results, for the animal's future, of its own present experience.

The unlimited number of possible categories, their arbitrariness and spontaneity, may, however, have this inconvenience, that the categories may be irrelevant to one another no less than to the natural life they ought to express. The experience they respectively synthesise may therefore be no consecutive experience. One pictured world may succeed another in the sphere of sensibility, while the body whose sensibility they compose moves in a single and constant physical cosmos. Each little mental universe may be intermittent, or, if any part of it endures while a new group of ideas comes upon the stage, there may arise contradictions, discords, and a sense of lurking absurdity which will tend to disrupt thought logically at the same time that the processes of nutrition and the oncoming of new dreams tend to supplant it mechanically. Such drifting categories have no mutual authority. They replace but do not dominate one another, and the general conditions of life—by conceiving which life itself might be surveyed—remain entirely unrepresented.

What we mean, indeed, by the natural world in which the conditions of consciousness are found and in reference to which mind and its purposes can attain moral relevance, is simply the world constructed by categories found to yield a constant, sufficient, and consistent object. Having attained this conception, we justly call it the truth and measure the intellectual value of all other constructions by their affinity to that rational vision.

Such a rational vision has not yet been attained by mankind, but it would be absurd to say that because we have not fully nor even proximately attained it, we have not gained any conception whatever of a reliable and intelligible world. The modicum of rationality achieved in the sciences gives us a hint of a perfect rationality which, if unattainable in practice, is not inconceivable in idea. So, in still more inchoate moments of reflection, our ancestors nursed even more isolated, less compatible, less adequate conceptions than those which leave our philosophers still unsatisfied. The categories they employed dominated smaller regions of experience than do the categories of history and natural science; they had far less applicability to the conduct of affairs and to the happy direction of life as a whole. Yet they did yield vision and flashes of insight. They lighted men a step ahead in the dark places of their careers, and gave them at certain junctures a sense of creative power and moral freedom. So that the necessity of abandoning one category in order to use a better one need not induce us to deny that the worse category could draw the outlines of a sort of world and furnish men with an approach to wisdom. If our ancestors, by such means, could not dominate life as a whole, neither can we, in spite of all progress. If literal truth or final applicability cannot be claimed for their thought, who knows how many and how profound the revolutions might be which our own thought would have to suffer if new fields of perception or new powers of snythesis were added to our endowment?

We sometimes speak as if superstition or belief in the miraculous was disbelief in law and was inspired by a desire to disorganise experience and defeat intelligence. No supposition could be more erroneous. Every superstition is a little science, inspired by the desire to understand, to foresee, or to control the real world. No doubt its hypothesis is chimerical, arbitrary, and founded on a confusion of efficient causes with ideal results. But the same is true of many a renowned philosophy. To appeal to what we call the supernatural is really to rest in the imaginatively obvious, in what we ought to call the natural, if natural

meant easy to conceive and originally plausible. Moral and individual forces are more easily intelligible than naturalistic universal laws. The former domesticate events in the mind more
readily and more completely than the latter. A miracle is so far
from being a contradiction to the causal principle which the mind
actually applies in its spontaneous observations that it is primarily
a better illustration of that principle than an event happening in
the ordinary course of nature. For the ground of the miracle is
immediately intelligible; we see the mercy or the desire to vindicate authority, or the intention of some other sort that inspired
it. A mechanical law, on the contrary, is only a record of the
customary but reasonless order of things. A merely inexplicable
event, manifesting no significant purpose, would be no miracle.
What surprises us in the miracle is that, contrary to what is usually
the case, we can see a real and just ground for it. Thus, if the
water of Lourdes, bottled and sold by chemists, cured all diseases, there would be no miracle, but only a new scientific discovery. In such a case, we should no more know why we were cured
than we now know why we were created. But if each believer
in taking the water thinks the effect morally conditioned, if he
interprets the result, should it be favourable, as an answer to his
faith and prayers, then the cure becomes miraculous because it
becomes intelligible and manifests the obedience of nature to the
exigencies of spirit.

What establishes superstitions is haste to understand, rash
confidence in the moral intelligibility of things. It turns out in the
end, as we have laboriously discovered, that understanding has to
be circuitous and cannot fulfil its function until it applies naturalistic categories to existence. A thorough philosophy will become aware that moral intelligibility can only be an incidental
ornament and partial harmony in the world. For moral significance is relative to particular interests and to natures having a
constitutional and definite bias, and having consequently special
preferences which it is chimerical to expect the rest of the world
to be determined by. The attempt to subsume the natural order
under the moral is like attempts to establish a government of the
parent by the child—something children are not averse to. But
such follies are the follies of an intelligent and eager creature,
restless in a world it cannot at once master and comprehend.
They are the errors of reason, wanderings in the by-paths of

philosophy, not due to lack of intelligence or of faith in law, but rather to a premature vivacity in catching at laws, a vivacity misled by inadequate information. The hunger for facile wisdom is the root of all false philosophy. The mind's reactions anticipate in such cases its sufficient nourishment; it has not yet matured under the rays of experience, so that both materials and guidance are lacking for its precocious organising force. Superstitious minds are penetrating and narrow, deep and ignorant. They apply the higher categories before the lower—an inversion which in all spheres produces the worst and most pathetic disorganisation, because the lower functions are then deranged and the higher contaminated. Poetry anticipates science, on which it ought to follow, and imagination rushes in to intercept memory, on which it ought to feed. Hence superstition and the magical function of religion; hence the deceptions men fall into by cogitating on things they are ignorant of and arrogating to themselves powers which they have never learned to exercise.

CHAPTER 3

MAGIC, SACRIFICE, AND PRAYER

THAT FEAR first created the gods is perhaps as true as anything so brief could be on so great a subject. To recognise an external power it is requisite that we should find the inner stream and tendency of life somehow checked or disturbed; if all went well and acceptably, we should attribute divinity only to ourselves. The external is therefore evil rather than good to early apprehension—a sentiment which still survives in respect to matter; for it takes reflection to conceive that external forces form a necessary environment, creating as well as limiting us, and offering us as many opportunities as rebuffs. The first things which a man learns to distinguish and respect are things with a will of their own, things which resist his casual demands; and so the first sentiment with which he confronts reality is a certain animosity, which becomes cruelty toward the weak and fear and fawning before the powerful. Toward men and animals and the docile parts of nature these sentiments soon become defined accurately, representing the exact degree of friendliness or use which we discover in these beings; and it is in practical terms, expressing this relation to our interests, that we define their characters. Much remains over, however, that we cannot easily define, indomitable, ambiguous regions of nature and of mind which we know not how to face; yet we cannot ignore them, since it is from them that comes what is most momentous in our fortunes—luck, disease, tempest, death, victory. Thence come also certain mysterious visitations to the inner mind—dreams, apparitions, warnings. To perceive these things is not always easy, nor is it easy to interpret them, while the great changes in nature which, perhaps, they forebode may indeed be watched but cannot be met intelligently, much less prevented. The feeling with which primitive man walks the earth must accordingly be, for the most part, apprehension; and what he meets, beyond the well-conned ways of his tribe and habitat, can be nothing but formidable spirits.

Impotence, however, has a more positive side. If the lightning and thunder, startling us in our peace, suddenly reveal unwelcome powers before which we must tremble, hunger, on the contrary, will torment us with floating ideas, intermittent impulses to act, suggesting things which would be wholly delightful if only we could find them, but which it becomes intolerable to remain without. In this case our fear, if we still choose to call it so, would be lest our cravings should remain unsatisfied, or rather fear has given place to need; we recognise our dependence on external powers not because they threaten but because they forsake us.

Obvious considerations like these furnish the proof of God's existence, not as philosophers have tried to express it after the fact and in relation to mythical conceptions of God already current, but as mankind originally perceived it, and (where religion is spontaneous) perceives it still. Whatever is serious in religion, whatever is bound up with morality and fate, is contained in those plain experiences of dependence and of affinity to that on which we depend. The rest is poetry, or mythical philosophy, in which definitions not warranted in the end by experience are given to that power which experience reveals. To reject such arbitrary definitions is called atheism by those who frame them; but a man who studies for himself the ominous and the friendly aspects of reality and gives them the truest and most adequate expression he can is repeating what the founders of religion did in the beginning. He is their companion and follower more truly than are the apologists for second-hand conceptions which these apologists themselves have never compared with the facts, and which they prize chiefly for misrepresenting actual experience and giving it imaginary extensions.

Religion is not essentially an imposture, though it might seem so if we consider it as its defenders present it to us rather than as its discoverers and original spokesmen uttered it in the presence of nature and face to face with unsophisticated men. Religion is an interpretation of the world, honestly made, and made in view of man's happiness and its empirical conditions. That this interpretation is poetical goes without saying, since natural and moral science, even to-day, are inadequate for the task. But the mythical form into which men cast their wisdom was not chosen by them because they preferred to be imaginative; it was not embraced, as its survivals are now defended, out of sentimental attachment to grandiloquent but inaccurate thoughts. Mythical forms were adopted because none other were available, nor could the primitive mind discriminate at all between the mythical and the scientific. Whether it is the myth or the wisdom it expresses that we call religion is a matter of words. Certain it is that the wisdom is alone what gives the myth its dignity, and what originally suggested it. A god's majesty lies in his power, not in his definition or his image.

The creation of a fabulous environment is not, however, the first or most pressing task employing the religious mind. Its first business is rather the work of propitiation; before we stop to contemplate the deity we hasten to appease it, to welcome it, or to get out of its way. Cult precedes fable and helps to frame it, because the feeling of need or fear is a practical feeling, and the ideas it may awaken are only incidental to the reactions its prompts. Worship is therefore earlier and nearer to the roots of religion than dogma is.

Religion arises under high pressure: in the last extremity, every one appeals to God. This appeal is necessarily made in the dark: it is the appeal of a conscious impotence, of an avowed perplexity. What a man in such a case may come to do to propitiate the deity, or to produce by magic a result he cannot produce by art, will obviously be some random action. He will be driven back to the place where instinct and reason begin. His movement will be absolutely experimental, altogether spontaneous. He will have no reason for what he does, save that he must do something.

It is pathetic, however, to observe how lowly the motives are that religion, even the highest, attributes to the deity, and from what a hard-pressed and bitter existence they have been drawn. To be given the best morsel, to be remembered, to be praised, to be obeyed blindly and punctiliously—these have been thought points of honour with the gods, for which they would dispense favours and punishments on the most exorbitant scale. Indeed, the widespread practice of sacrifice, like all mutilations and penances, suggests an even meaner jealousy and malice in the gods; for the disciplinary functions which these things may have were not aimed at in the beginning, and would not have associated them particularly with religion. In setting aside the fat for the gods' pleasure, in sacrificing the first-born, in a thousand other cruel ceremonies, the idea apparently was that an envious onlooker, lurking unseen, might poison the feast, or revenge himself for not having enjoyed it, unless a part—possibly sufficient for his hunger—were surrendered to him voluntarily. This onlooker was a veritable demon, treated as a man treats a robber to whom he yields his purse that his life may be spared.

To call the gods envious has a certain symbolic truth, in that earthly fortunes are actually precarious; and such an observation might inspire detachment from material things and a kind of philosophy. But what at first inspires sacrifice is a literal envy imputed to the gods, a spirit of vengeance and petty ill-will; so that they grudge a man even the good things which they cannot enjoy themselves. If the god is a tyrant, the votary will be a tax-payer surrendering his tithes to secure immunity from further levies or from attack by other potentates. God and man will be natural enemies, living in a sort of politic peace.

Sacrifices are far from having merely this sinister meaning. Once inaugurated they suggest further ideas, and from the beginning they had happier associations. The sacrifice was incidental to a feast, and the plenty it was to render safe existed already. What was a bribe, offered in the spirit of barter, to see if the envious power could not be mollified by something less than the total ruin of his victims, could easily become a genial distribution of what custom assigned to each: so much to the chief, so much to the god, so much to the husbandman. There is a certain openness, and as it were form of justice, in giving each what is conventionally his due, however little he may really deserve it. In religious observances this sentiment plays an important part, and men find satisfaction in fulfilling in a seemly manner what is prescribed; and since they know little about the ground or meaning of what they do, they feel content and safe if at least they have done it properly. Sacrifices are often performed in this spirit; and when a beautiful order and righteous calm have come to dignify the performance, the mind, having meantime very little to occupy it, may embroider on the given theme. It is then that fable, and new religious sentiments suggested by fable, appear prominently on the scene.

In agricultural rites, for instance, sacrifice will naturally be offered to the deity presiding over germination; that is the deity that might, perhaps, withdraw his favour with disastrous results. He commonly proves, however, a kindly and responsive being, and in offering to him a few sheaves of corn, some barley-cakes, or a libation from the vintage, the public is grateful rather than calculating; the sacrifice has become an act of thanksgiving. So in Christian devotion (which often follows primitive impulses and repeats the dialectic of paganism in a more speculative region) the redemption did not remain merely expiatory. It was not merely a debt to be paid off and a certain quantum of suffering to be endured which had induced the Son of God to become man and to take up his cross. It was, so the subtler theologians declared, an act of affection as much as of pity; and the spell of the doctrine over the human heart lay in feeling that God wished to assimilate himself to man, rather than simply from above to declare him forgiven; so that the incarnation was in effect a rehabilitation of man, a redemption in itself, and a forgiveness. Men like to think that God has sat at their table and walked among them in disguise. The idea is flattering; it suggests that the courtesy may some day be returned, and for those who can look so deep it expresses pointedly the philosophic truth of the matter. For are not the gods, too, in eternal travail after their ideal, and is not man a part of the world, and his art a portion of the divine wisdom? If the incarnation was a virtual redemption, the first incarnation was the laborious creation itself.

If sacrifice, in its more amiable aspect can become thanksgiving and an expression of profitable dependence, it can suffer an even nobler transformation while retaining all its austerity. Renunciation is the cornerstone of wisdom, the condition of all genuine achievement. The gods, in asking for a sacrifice, may invite us to give up not a part of our food or of our liberty but the foolish and inordinate part of our wills. The sacrifice may be dictated to us not by a jealous enemy needing to be pacified but by a far-seeing friend, wishing we may not be deceived. If what we are commanded to surrender is only what is doing us harm, the god demanding the sacrifice is our own ideal. He has no interests in the case other than our own; he is no part of the environment; he is the goal that determines for us how we should proceed in order to realise as far as possible our inmost aspirations. When religion reaches this phase it has become thoroughly moral. It has ceased to represent or misrepresent material conditions, and has learned to express spiritual goods.

Sacrifice is a rite, and rites can seldom be made to embody

ideas exclusively moral. Something dramatic or mystical will cling to the performance, and, even when the effect of it is to purify, it will bring about an emotional catharsis rather than a moral improvement. The mass is a ritual sacrifice, and the communion is a part of it, having the closest resemblance to what sacrifices have always been. Among the devout these ceremonies, and the lyric emotions they awaken, have a quite visible influence; but the spell is mystic, the god soon recedes, and it would be purely fanciful to maintain that any permanent moral effect comes from such an exercise. The Church has felt as much and introduced the confession, where a man may really be asked to consider what sacrifices he should make for his part, and in what practical direction he should imagine himself to be drawn by the vague Dionysiac influences to which the ritual subjects him.

As sacrifice expresses fear, prayer expresses need. Commonsense thinks of language as something meant to be understood by another and to produce changes in his disposition and behaviour, but language has pre-rational uses of which poetry and prayer are perhaps the chief. A man overcome by passion assumes dramatic attitudes surely not intended to be watched and interpreted; like tears, gestures may touch an observer's heart, but they do not come for that purpose. So the fund of words and phrases latent in the mind flow out under stress of emotion; they flow because they belong to the situation, because they fill out and complete a perception absorbing the mind; they do not flow primarily to be listened to. The instinct to pray is one of the chief avenues to the deity, and the form prayer takes helps immensely to define the power it is addressed to; indeed, it is in the act of praying that men formulate to themselves what God must be, and tell him at great length what they believe and what they expect of him. The initial forms of prayer are not so absurd as the somewhat rationalised forms of it. Unlike sacrifice, prayer seems to be justified by its essence and to be degraded by the transformations it suffers in reflection, when men try to find a place for it in their cosmic economy; for its essence is poetical, expressive, contemplative, and it grows more and more nonsensical the more people insist on making it a prosaic, commercial exchange of views between two interlocutors.

Prayer is a soliloquy; but being a soliloquy expressing need, and being furthermore, like sacrifice, a desperate expedient which men fly to in their impotence, it looks for an effect: to cry aloud, to make vows, to contrast eloquently the given with the ideal situation, is certainly as likely a way of bringing about a change for the better as it would be to chastise one's self severely, or to destroy what one loves best, or to perform acts altogether trivial and arbitrary. Prayer also is magic, and as such it is expected to do work. The answer looked for, or one which may be accepted instead, very often ensues; and it is then that mythology begins to enter in and seeks to explain by what machinery of divine passions and purposes that answering effect was produced.

Magic is in a certain sense the mother of art, art being the magic that succeeds and can establish itself. For this very reason mere magic is never appealed to when art has been found, and no unsophisticated man prays to have that done for him which he knows how to do for himself. When his art fails, if his necessity still presses, he appeals to magic, and he prays when he no longer can control the event, provided this event is momentous to him. Prayer is not a substitute for work; it is a desperate effort to work further and to be efficient beyond the range of one's powers. It is not the lazy who are most inclined to prayer; those pray most who care most, and, who, having worked hard, find it intolerable to be defeated.

What rational religion really should pass into is contemplation, ideality, poetry, in the sense in which poetry includes all imaginative moral life. That this is what religion looks to is very clear in prayer and in the efficacy which prayer consistently can have. In rational prayer the soul may be said to accomplish three things important to its welfare: it withdraws within itself and defines its good, it accommodates itself to destiny, and it grows like the ideal which it conceives.

If prayer springs from need it will naturally dwell on what would satisfy that necessity; sometimes, indeed, it does nothing else but articulate and eulogise what is most wanted and prized. This object will often be particular, and so it should be, since Socrates' prayer "for the best" would be perfunctory and vapid indeed in a man whose life had not been spent, like Socrates', in defining what the best was. Yet any particular good lies in a field of relations; it has associates and implications, so that the mind dwelling on it and invoking its presence will naturally be enticed also into its background, and will wander there, perhaps to come upon greater goods, or upon evils which the coveted good would make inevitable. An earnest consideration, therefore, of anything desired is apt to enlarge and generalise aspiration till it embraces an ideal life; for from almost any starting-point the limits and contours of mortal happiness are soon descried. Prayer, inspired by a pressing need, already relieves its importunity by merging it in the general need of the spirit and of mankind. It therefore calms the passions in expressing them, like all idealisation, and tends to make the will conformable with reason and justice.

A comprehensive ideal, however, is harder to realise than a particular one: the rain wished for may fall, the death feared may be averted, but the kingdom of heaven does not come. It is in the very essence of prayer to regard a denial as possible. There would be no sense in defining and begging for the better thing if that better thing had at any rate to be. The possibility of defeat is one of the circumstances with which meditation must square the ideal; seeing that my prayer may not be granted, what in that case should I pray for next? Now the order of nature is in many respects well known, and it is clear that all realisable ideals must not transgress certain bounds. The practical ideal, that which under the circumstances it is best to aim at and pray for, will not rebel against destiny. Conformity is an element in all religion and submission in all prayer; not because what must be is best, but because the best that may be pursued rationally lies within the possible, and can be hatched only in the general womb of being. The prayer, "Thy will be done," if it is to remain a prayer, must not be degraded from its original meaning, which was that an unfulfilled ideal should be fulfilled; it expressed aspiration after the best, not willingness to be satisfied with anything. Yet the inevitable must be accepted, and it is easier to change the human will than the laws of nature. To wean the mind from extravagant desires and teach it to find excellence in what life affords, when life is made as worthy as possible, is a part of wisdom and religion. Prayer, by confronting the ideal with experience and fate, tends to render that ideal humble, practical, and efficacious.

A sense for human limitations, however, has its foil in the ideal of deity, which is nothing but the ideal of man freed from those limitations which a humble and wise man accepts for himself, but which a spiritual man never ceases to feel as limitations. Man, for instance, is mortal, and his whole animal and social economy is built on that fact, so that his practical ideal must start on that basis, and make the best of it; but immortality is essentially better, and the eternal is in many ways constantly present to a noble mind; the gods therefore are immortal, and to speak their language in prayer is to learn to see all things as they do and as reason must, under the form of eternity. The gods are furthermore no respecters of persons; they are just, for it is man's ideal to be so. Prayer, since it addresses deity, will in the end blush to be selfish and partial; the majesty of the divine mind envisaged and consulted will tend to pass into the human mind.

This use of prayer has not been conspicuous in Christian times, because, instead of assimilating the temporal to the eternal, men have assimilated the eternal to the temporal, being perturbed fanatics in religion rather than poets and idealists. Pagan devotion, on the other hand, was full of this calmer spirit. The gods, being frankly natural, could be truly ideal. They embodied what was fairest in life and loved men who resembled them, so that it was delightful and ennobling to see their images everywhere, and to keep their names and story perpetually in mind. They did not by their influence alienate man from his appropriate happiness, but they perfected it by their presence. Peopling all places, changing their forms as all living things must according to place and circumstance, they showed how all kinds of being, if perfect in their kind, might be perfectly good. They asked for a reverence consistent with reason, and exercised prerogatives that left man free. Their worship was a perpetual lesson in humanity, moderation, and beauty. Something pre-rational and monstrous often peeped out behind their serenity, as it does beneath the human soul, and there was certainly no lack of wildness and mystic horror in their apparitions. The ideal must needs admit those elemental forces on which, after all, it rests; but reason exists to exorcise their madness and win them over to a steady expression of themselves and of the good.

Prayer, in fine, though it accomplishes nothing material, constitutes something spiritual. It will not bring rain, but until rain comes it may cultivate hope and resignation and may prepare the heart for any issue, opening up a vista in which human prosperity will appear in its conditioned existence and conditional value. A candle wasting itself before an image will prevent no misfortune, but it may bear witness to some silent hope or relieve some sorrow by expressing it; it may soften a little the bitter sense of impotence which would consume a mind aware of physical dependence but not of spiritual dominion. Worship, supplication, reliance on the gods, express both these things in an appropriate parable. Physical impotence is expressed by man's appeal for help; moral dominion by belief in God's omnipotence. This belief may afterwards seem to be contradicted by events. It would be so in truth if God's omnipotence stood for a material magical control of events by the values they were to generate. But the believer knows in his heart, in spite of the confused explanations he may give of his feelings, that a material efficacy is not the test of his faith. His faith will survive any outward disappointment. In fact, it will grow by that discipline and not become truly religious until it ceases to be a foolish expectation of improbable things and rises on stepping-stones of its material disappointments into a spiritual peace. What would sacrifice be but a risky investment if it did not redeem us from the love of those things which it asks us to surrender? What would be the miserable fruit of an appeal to God which, after bringing us face to face with him, left us still immersed in what we could have enjoyed without him? The real use and excuse for magic is this, that by enticing us, in the service of natural lusts, into a region above natural instrumentalities, it accustoms us to that rarer atmosphere, so that we may learn to breathe it for its own sake. By the time we discover the mechanical futility of religion we may have begun to blush at the thought of using religion mechanically; for what should be the end of life if friendship with the gods is a means only? When thaumaturgy is discredited, the childish desire to work miracles may itself have passed away. Before we weary of the attempt to hide and piece out our mortality, our concomitant immortality may have dawned upon us. While we are waiting for the command to take up our bed and walk we may hear a voice saying: Thy sins are forgiven thee.

CHAPTER 4

MYTHOLOGY

THE ILLUSION involved in fabulous thinking is not so complete and opaque as convention would represent it. In taking fable for fact, good sense and practice seldom keep pace with dogma. There is always a race of pedants whose function it is to materialise everything ideal,* but the great world, half shrewdly, half doggedly, manages to escape their contagion. Language may be entirely permeated with myth, since the affinities of language have much to do with men gliding into such thoughts; yet the difference between language itself and what it expresses is not so easily obliterated. In spite of verbal traditions, people seldom take a myth in the same sense in which they would take an empirical truth. All the doctrines that have flourished in the world about immortality have hardly affected men's natural sentiment in the face of death, a sentiment which those doctrines, if taken seriously, ought wholly to reverse. Men almost universally have acknowledged a Providence, but that fact has had no force to destroy natural aversions and fears in the presence of events; and yet, if Providence had ever been really trusted, those preferences would all have lapsed, being seen to be blind, rebellious, and blasphemous. Prayer, among sane people, has never superseded practical efforts to secure the desired end; a proof that the sphere of expression was never really confused with that of reality. Indeed, such a confusion, if it had passed from theory to practice, would have changed mythology into madness. With rare exceptions this declension has not occurred and myths have been taken with a grain of salt which not only made them digestible, but heightened their savour.

It is always by its applicability to things known, not by its revelation of things unknown and irrelevant, that a myth at its birth appeals to mankind. When it has lost its symbolic value and sunk to the level of merely false information, only an inert and stupid

* Or idealise everything material. Author's note, 1952.

202

tradition can keep it above water. Yet if the myth was originally accepted it could not be for this falsity plainly written on its face; it was accepted because it was understood, because it was seen to express reality in an eloquent metaphor. Its function was to show up some phase of experience in its totality and moral issue, as in a map we reduce everything geographically in order to overlook it better in its true relations. Had those symbols for a moment descended to the plane of reality they would have lost their meaning and dignity; they would tell us merely that they themselves existed bodily, which would be false, while about the real configuration of life they would no longer tell us anything.

The true function of mythical ideas is to present and interpret events in terms relative to spirit. Things have uses in respect to the will which are direct and obvious, while the inner machinery of these same things is intricate and obscure. We therefore conceive things roughly and superficially by their eventual practical functions and assign to them, in our poetry, some counterpart of the emotion they arouse in us. This counterpart, to our thinking, constitutes their inward character and soul. So conceived, soul and character are purely mythical, being arrived at by dramatising events according to our own fancy and interest. Such ideas may be adequate in their way if they cover all the uses we may eventually find in the objects they transcribe for us dramatically. But the most adequate mythology is expression, it is not prophecy. For this reason myth is something on which the mind rests; it is an ideal interpretation in which the phenomena are digested and transmuted into human energy, into imaginative harmonies. Scientific formulas, on the contrary, cry aloud for retranslation into perceptual terms; they are like tight-ropes, on which a man may walk but on which he cannot stand still. These unstable symbols lead, however, to real facts and define their experimental relations; while the mind reposing contentedly in a myth needs to have all observation and experience behind it, for it will not be driven to gather more. The perfect and stable myth would rest on a complete survey and steady focussing of all interests really affecting the thinker. This symbol would render the diffuse natural existences which it represented in an eloquent figure; and since this figure would not mislead practically it might be called true. But truth, in a myth, means a sterling quality and standard excellence, not a literal or logical truth. It will not, save by a singular accident, represent their proper internal being, as a forthright unselfish intellect would wish to know it. It will translate into the language of a private passion the smiles and frowns which that passion meets with in the world.

There are accordingly two factors in mythology, a moral consciousness and a corresponding poetic conception of things. Both factors are variable, and variations in the first, if more hidden, are no less important than variations in the second. Had fable started with a clear perception of human values, it would have gained immensely in significance, because its pictures, however wrong the external notions they built upon, would have shown what, in the world so conceived, would have been the ideals and prizes of life. Thus Dante's bad cosmography and worse history do not detract from the spiritual penetration of his thought, though they detract from its direct applicability. Had nature and destiny been what Dante imagined, his conception of the values involved would have been perfect, for the moral philosophy he brought into play was Aristotelian and rational. So his poem contains a false instance or imaginary rehearsal of true wisdom. It describes the Life of Reason in a fantastic world. We need only change man's situation to that in which he actually finds himself, and let the soul, fathomed and chastened as Dante left it, ask questions and draw answers from this steadier dream.

Myth travels among the people, and in their hands its poetic factor tends to predominate. It is easier to carry on the dialectic or drama proper to a fable than to confront it again with the facts and give them a fresh and more genial interpretation. The poet makes the fable; the sophist carries it on. Therefore historians and theologians discuss chiefly the various forms which mythical beings have received, and the internal logical or moral implications of those hypostases. They would do better to attend instead to the moral factor. However interesting a fable may be in itself, its religious value lies wholly in its revealing some function which nature has in human life. Not the beauty of the god makes him adorable, but his dispensing benefits and graces. Side by side with Apollo (a god having moral functions and consequently inspiring a fervent cult and tending himself to assume a moral character) there may be a Helios or a Phaëton, poetic figures expressing just as well the sun's physical operation, and no less capable, if the theologian took hold of them, of suggesting psychological problems. The moral factor, however, was not found in these minor deities. Only a verbal and sensuous poetry had been employed in defining them; the needs and hopes of mankind had been ignored. Apollo, on the contrary, in personifying the sun, had embodied also the sun's relations to human welfare. The vitality, the healing, the enlightenment, the lyric joy flowing into man's heart from that highest source of his physical being are all beautifully represented in the god's figure and fable. The religion of Apollo is therefore a true religion, as religions may be true: the mythology which created the god rested on a deep, observant sense for moral values, and drew a vivid, if partial, picture of the ideal, attaching it significantly to its natural ground.

The first function of mythology was to justify magic. But when mythology first appears in western literature it already possesses a highly articulate form. The gods are distinct personalities, with attributes and histories which it is hard to divine the source of and which suggest no obvious rational interpretation. The historian is therefore in the same position as a child who inherits a great religion. The gods and their doings are *prima facie* facts in his world like any other facts, objective beings that convention puts him in the presence of and with which he begins by having social relations. He envisages them with respect and obedience, or with careless defiance, long before he thinks of questioning or proving their existence. The attitude he assumes towards them makes them in the first instance factors in his moral world. Much subsequent scepticism and rationalising philosophy will not avail to efface the vestiges of that early communion with familiar gods. It is hard to reduce to objects of science what are essentially factors in moral intercourse. All thoughts on religion remain accordingly coloured with passion, and are felt to be, above all, a test of loyalty and an index to virtue. The more derivative, unfathomable, and opaque is the prevalent idea of the gods, the harder it is for a rational feeling to establish itself in their regard. Sometimes the most complete historical enlightenment will not suffice to dispel the shadow which their moral influence casts over the mind. In vain do we discard their fable and the thin proofs of their existence when, in spite of ourselves, we still live in their presence.

This pathetic phenomenon is characteristic of religious minds that have outgrown their traditional faith without being able to restate the natural grounds and moral values of that somehow precious system in which they no longer believe. The dead gods, in such cases, leave ghosts behind them, because the moral forces which the gods once expressed, and which, of course, remain, remain inarticulate; and therefore, in their dumbness, these moral forces persistently suggest their only known but now discredited symbols. To regain moral freedom—without which knowledge cannot be put to its rational use in the government of life—we must rediscover the origin of the gods, reduce them analytically to their natural and moral constituents, and then proceed to rearrange those materials, without any quantitative loss, in forms appropriate to a maturer reflection.

Of the innumerable and rather monotonous mythologies that have flourished in the world, only the Graeco-Roman and the Christian need concern us here, since they are by far the best known to us and the best defined in themselves, as well as the only two likely to have any continued influence on the western mind. Both these systems presuppose a long prior development. The gods of Greece and of Israel have a full-blown character when we first meet them in literature. In both cases, however, we are fortunate in being able to trace somewhat further back the history of mythology, and do not depend merely on philosophic analysis to reach the elements which we seek.

In the Vedic hymns there survives the record of a religion remarkably like the Greek in spirit, but less dramatic and articulate in form. The gods of the Vedas are unmistakably natural elements. Vulcan is there nothing but fire, Jupiter nothing but the sky. This patriarchal people, fresh from the highlands, had not yet been infected with the manias and diseases of the jungle. It lived simply, rationally, piously, loving all natural joys and delighted with all the instruments of a rude but pure civilisation. It saluted without servility the forces of nature which ministered to its needs. It burst into song in the presence of the magnificent panorama spread out before it—day-sky and night-sky, dawn and gloaming, clouds, thunder and rain, rivers, cattle and horses, grain, fruit, fire, and wine. Nor were the social sanctities neglected. Commemoration was made of the stages of mortal life, of the bonds of love and kinship, of peace, of battle, and of mourning for the dead. By a very intelligible figure and analogy the winds became shepherds, the clouds flocks, the day a conqueror, the dawn a maid, the night a wise sibyl and mysterious consort of heaven. These personifications were tentative and vague, and the consequent mythology was a system of rhetoric rather than of theology. The various gods had interchangeable attributes, and, by a voluntary confusion, quite in the manner of later Hindu poetry, each became on occasion any or all of the others.

Here the Indian pantheistic vertigo begins to appear. Many dark superstitions, no doubt, bubbled up in the torrent of that plastic reverie; for this people, clean and natural as on the whole it appears, cannot have been without a long and ignoble ancestry. The Greeks themselves, heirs to kindred general traditions, retained some childish and obscene practices in their worship. But such hobgoblins naturally vanish under a clear and beneficent sun and are scattered by healthy mountain breezes. A cheerful people knows how to take them lightly, play with them, laugh at them, and turn them again into figures of speech. Among the early speakers of Sanskrit, even more than among the Greeks, the national religion seems to have been nothing but a poetic naturalism.

Such a mythology, however, is exceedingly plastic and unstable. If the poet is observant and renews his impressions, his myths will become more and more accurate descriptions of the facts, and his hypotheses about phenomena will tend to be expressed more and more in terms of the phenomena themselves; that is, will tend to become scientific. If, on the contrary and as usually happens, the inner suggestions and fertility of his fables absorb his interest, and he neglects to consult his external perceptions any further, or even forgets that any such perceptions originally inspired the myth, he will tend to become a dramatic poet, guided henceforth in his fictions only by his knowledge and love of human life.

When we transport ourselves in fancy to patriarchal epochs and Arcadian scenes, we can well feel the inevitable tendency of the mind to mythologise and give its myths a more and more dramatic character. The phenomena of nature, unintelligible rationally but immensely impressive, must somehow be described and digested. But while they compel attention they do not, after a while, enlarge understanding. Husbandmen's lore is profound, practical, poetic, superstitious, but it is singularly stagnant. The cycle of natural changes goes its perpetual round and the ploughman's mind, caught in that narrow vortex, plods and plods after the seasons. Apart from an occasional flood, drought, or pestilence, nothing breaks his laborious torpor. The most cursory inspection of field and sky yields him information enough for his needs. Practical knowledge with him is all instinct and tradition. His mythology can for that very reason ride on nature with a looser rein. If at the same time, however, his circumstances are auspicious and he feels practically secure, he will have much leisure to ripen inwardly and to think. He will hasten to unfold in meditation the abstract potentialities of his mind. His social and ideal passions, his aptitude for art and fancy, will arouse within him a far keener and more varied experience than his outer life can supply. Yet all his fortunes continue to be determined by external circumstances and to have for their theatre this given and uncontrollable world. Some conception of nature and the gods—that is, in his case, some mythology—must therefore remain before him always and stand in his mind for the real forces controlling experience.

His moral powers and interests have meantime notably developed. His sense for social relations has grown clear and full in proportion as his observation of nature has sunk into dull routine. Consequently, the myths by which reality is represented lose, so to speak, their birthright and first nationality. They pass under the empire of abstract cogitation and spontaneous fancy. They become naturalised in the mind. The poet cuts loose from nature and works out instead whatever hints of human character or romantic story the myth already supplies. Analogies drawn from moral and passionate experience replace the further portraiture of outer facts. Human tastes, habits, and dreams enter the fable, expanding it into some little drama, or some mystic anagram of mortal life. While in the beginning the sacred poet had transcribed nothing but joyous perceptions and familiar industrial or martial actions, he now introduces intrigue, ingenious adventures, and heroic passions.

When we turn from the theology of the Vedas to that of Homer we see this revolution already accomplished. The new significance of mythology has obscured the old, and what was a symbol for material facts has become a drama, an apologue, and an ideal. Thus one function of mythology has been nothing less than to carry religion over from superstition into wisdom, from an excuse and apology for magic into an ideal representation of moral goods. In his impotence and sore need a man appeals to magic; this appeal he justifies by imagining a purpose and a god behind the natural agency. But after his accounts with the phenomena are settled by his own labour and patience, he continues to be fascinated by the invisible spirit he has evoked. He cherishes this image; it becomes his companion, his plastic and unaccountable witness and refuge in all the exigencies of life. Dwelling in the mind continually, the deity becomes acclimated there; the worship it receives endows it with whatever powers and ideal faculties are most feared or honoured by its votary. Now the thunder and the pestilence which were once its essence come to be regarded as its disguises and its foils. Faith comes to consist in disregarding what it was once religion to regard, namely, the ways of fortune and the conditions of earthly happiness. Thus the imagination sets up its ideals over against the world that occasioned them, and mythology, instead of cheating men with false and magic aids to action, moralises them by presenting an ideal standard for action and a perfect object for contemplation.

CHAPTER 5

THE HEBRAIC TRADITION

As THE Vedas offer a glimpse into the antecedents of Greek mythology, so Hebrew studies open up vistas into the antecedents of Christian dogma. Christianity in its Patristic form was an adaptation of Hebrew religion to the Græco-Roman world, and later, in the Protestant movement, a readaptation of the same to what we may call the Teutonic spirit. In the first adaptation, Hebrew positivism was wonderfully refined, transformed into a religion of redemption, and endowed with a semi-pagan mythology, a pseudo-Platonic metaphysics, and a quasi-Roman organisation. In the second adaptation, Christianity received a new basis and standard in the spontaneous faith of the individual; and, as the traditions thus undermined in principle gradually dropped away, it was reduced by the German theologians to a romantic and mystical pantheism. Throughout its transformations, however, Christianity remains indebted to the Jews not only for its founder, but for the nucleus of its dogma, cult, and ethical doctrine. If the religion of the Jews, therefore, should disclose its origin, the origin of Christianity would also be manifest.

Now the Bible, when critically studied, clearly reveals the source, if not of the earliest religion of Israel, at least of those elements in later Jewish faith which have descended to us and formed the kernel of Christian revelation. The earlier Hebrews, as their own records depict them, had a mythology and cultus extremely like that of other Semitic peoples. It was natural religion—I mean that religion which naturally expresses the imaginative life of a nation according to the conceptions there current about the natural world and to the interest then uppermost in men's hearts. It was a religion without a creed or scripture or founder or clergy. It consisted in local rites, in lunar feasts, in soothsayings and oracles, in legends about divine apparitions commemorated in the spots they had made holy. These spots, as in all the rest of the world, were tombs, wells, great trees, and, above all, the tops of mountains.

A wandering tribe, at once oppressed and aggressive, as Israel evidently was from the beginning, is conscious of nothing so much as of its tribal unity. To protect the tribe is accordingly the chief function of its god. Whatever character Jehovah may originally have had, whether a storm-god of Sinai or of Ararat, or a sacred bull, or each of these by affinity and confusion with the other, when the Israelites had once adopted him as their god they could see nothing essential in him but his power to protect them in the lands they had conquered. To this exclusive devotion of Jehovah to Israel, Israel responded by a devotion to Jehovah no less exclusive. They neglected, when at home, the worship of every other divinity, and later even while travelling abroad; and they tended to deny altogether, first the comparable power and finally even the existence of other gods.

Israel was a small people overshadowed by great empires, and its political situation was always highly precarious. After a brief period of comparative vigour under David and Solomon (a period afterward idealised with that oriental imagination which, creating so few glories, dreams of so many) they declined visibly toward an inevitable absorption by their neighbours. But, according to the significance which religion then had in Israel, the ruin of the state would have put Jehovah's honour and power in jeopardy. The nation and its god were like body and soul; it occurred to no one as yet to imagine that the one could survive the other. A few sceptical and unpatriotic minds, despairing of the republic, might turn to the worship of Baal or of the stars invoked by the Assyrians, hoping thus to save themselves and their private fortunes by a timely change of allegiance. But the true Jew had a vehement and unshakable spirit. He could not allow the waywardness of events to upset his convictions or the cherished habits of his soul. Accordingly he bethought himself of a new way of explaining and meeting the imminent catastrophe.

The prophets, for to them the revolution in question was due, conceived that the cause of Israel's misfortunes might be not Jehovah's weakness but his wrath—a wrath kindled against the immorality, lukewarmness, and infidelity of the people. Repentance and a change of life, together with a purification of the cultus, would bring back prosperity. It was too late, perhaps, to rescue the whole state. But a remnant might be saved like a brand from the burning, to be the nucleus of a great restoration, the seed of a mighty people that should live for ever in godliness and plenty. Jehovah's power would thus be vindicated, even if Israel were ruined; nay, his power would be magnified beyond anything formerly conceived, since now the great powers of Asia would be represented as his instruments in the chastisement of his people.

These views, if we regarded them from the standpoint common in theology as attempts to reexpress the primitive faith, would have to be condemned as absolutely heretical and spurious. But the prophets were not interpreting documents or traditions; they were publishing their own political insight. They were themselves inspired. They saw the identity of virtue and happiness, the dependence of success upon conduct. This new truth they announced in traditional language by saying that Jehovah's favour was to be won only by righteousness and that vice and folly alienated his goodwill. Their moral insight was genuine; yet by virtue of the mythical expression they could not well avoid and in respect to the old orthodoxy, their doctrine was a subterfuge, the first of those afterthoughts and ingenious reinterpretations by which faith is continually forced to cover up its initial blunders. For the Jews had believed that with such a God they were safe in any case; but now they were told that, to retain his protection, they must practice just those virtues by which the heathen also might have been made prosperous and great. It was a true doctrine, and highly salutary, but we need not wonder that before being venerated the prophets were stoned.

The ideal of this new prophetic religion was still wholly material and political. The virtues, emphasised and made the chief mark of a religious life, were recommended merely as magic means to propitiate the deity, and consequently to insure public prosperity. The thought that virtue is a natural excellence, the ideal expression of human life, could not be expected to impress those vehement barbarians any more than it has impressed their myriad descendants and disciples, Jewish, Christian, or Moslem. Yet superstitious as the new faith still remained, and magical as was the efficacy it attributed to virtue, the fact that virtue rather than burnt offerings was now endowed with miraculous influence and declared to win the favour of heaven, proved two things most creditable to the prophets: in the first place, they themselves loved virtue, else they would hardly have imagined that Jehovah loved it, or have believed it to be the only path to happiness; and in the second place, they saw that public events depend on men's character and conduct, not on omens, sacrifices, or intercessions. There was accordingly a sense for both moral and political philosophy in these inspired orators. By assigning a magic value to morality they gave a moral value to religion. The immediate aim of this morality—to propitiate Jehovah—was indeed imaginary, and its ultimate aim—to restore the kingdom of Israel—was worldly; yet that imaginary aim covered, in the form of a myth, a sincere consecration to the ideal, while the worldly purpose led to an almost scientific conception of the principles and movement of earthly things.

To this transformation in the spirit of the law, another almost as important corresponded in the letter. Scripture was codified, proclaimed, and given out formally to be inspired by Jehovah and written by Moses. That all traditions, legends, and rites were inspired and sacred was a matter of course in antiquity. Nature was full of gods, and the mind, with its unaccountable dreams and powers, could not be without them. Its inventions could not be less oracular than the thunder or the flight of birds. Israel, like every other nation, thought its traditions divine. These traditions, however, had always been living and elastic; the prophets themselves gave proof that inspiration was still a vital and human thing. It is all the more remarkable, therefore, that while the prophets were preparing their campaign, under pressure of the same threatened annihilation, the same puritanical party should have edited a new code of laws and attributed it retroactively to Moses. While the prophet's lips were being touched by the coal of fire, the priests and king in their conclave were establishing the Bible and the Church. It is easy to suspect, from the accounts we have, that a pious fraud was perpetrated on this occasion; but perhaps the finding of a forgotten book of the Law and its proclamation by Josiah, after consulting a certain prophetess, were not so remote in essence from prophetic sincerity. In an age when every prophet, seeing what was needful politically, could cry, "So saith the Lord," it could hardly be illegitimate for the priests, seeing what was expedient legally, to declare, "So said Moses." Conscience, in a primitive and impetuous people, may express itself in an apocryphal manner which in a critical age conscience would altogether exclude. It would have been hardly conceivable that what was obviously right and necessary should not be the will of Jehovah, manifested of old to the fathers in the desert and now again whispered in their children's hearts. To contrive a stricter observance was an act at once of experimental prudence—a means of making destiny, perhaps, less unfavourable—and an act of more fervent worship—a renewal of faith in Jehovah, to whose hands the nation was intrusted more solemnly and irrevocably than ever.

This pious experiment failed most signally. Jerusalem was taken, the Temple destroyed, and the flower of the people carried into exile. The effect of failure, however, was not to discredit the Law and the Covenant, now once for all adopted by the unshakable Jews. On the contrary, when they returned from exile they re-established the theocracy with greater rigour than ever, adding all the minute observances, ritualistic and social, enshrined in Leviticus. Israel became an ecclesiastical community. The Temple, half fortress, half sanctuary, resounded with perpetual psalms. Piety was fed on a sense at once of consecration and of guidance. All was prescribed, and to fulfil the Law, precisely because it involved so complete and, as the world might say, so arbitrary a regimen, became a precious sacrifice, a continual act of religion.

Dogmas are at their best when nobody denies them, for then their falsehood sleeps, like that of an unconscious metaphor, and their moral function is discharged instinctively. They count and are not defined, and the side of them that is not deceptive is the one that comes forward. What was condemnable in the Jews was not that they asserted the divinity of their law, for that they did with substantial sincerity and truth. Their crime is to have denied the equal prerogative of other nations' laws and deities, for this they did, not from critical insight or intellectual scruples, but out of pure bigotry, conceit, and stupidity. They did not want other nations also to have a god. The moral government of the world, which the Jews are praised for having first asserted, did not mean for them that nature shows a generic benevolence toward life and reason wherever these arise. Such a moral government might have been conceived by a pagan philosopher and was not taught in Israel until, selfishness having been outgrown, the birds and the heathen were also placed under divine protection. What the moral government of things meant when it was first asserted was that Jehovah expressly directed the destinies of heathen nations and the course of nature itself for the final glorification of the Jews.

No civilised people had ever had such pretensions before. They all recognised one another's religions, if not as literally true (for some familiarity is needed to foster that illusion), certainly as more or less sacred and significant. Had the Jews not rendered themselves odious to mankind by this arrogance, and taught Christians and Moslems the same fanaticism, the nature of religion would not have been falsified among us and we should not now have so much to apologise for and to retract.

Israel's calamities, of which the prophets saw only the beginning, worked a notable spiritualisation in its religion. The happy thought of attributing misfortune to wickedness remained a permanent element in the creed; but as no scrupulous administration of rites, no puritanism, no good conscience, could avail to improve the political situation, it became needful for the faithful to reconsider their idea of happiness. Since holiness must win divine favour, and Israel was undoubtedly holy, the marks of divine favour must be looked for in Israel's history. To have been brought in legendary antiquity out of Egypt was something; to have been delivered from captivity in Babylon was more; yet these signs of favour could not suffice unless they were at the same time emblems of hope. But Jewish life had meantime passed into a new phase: it had become pietistic, priestly, almost ascetic. Such is the might of suffering, that a race whose nature and traditions were alike positivistic could for the time being find it sweet to wash its hands among the innocent, to love the beauty of the Lord's house, and to praise him for ever and ever. It was agreed and settled beyond cavil that God loved his people and continually blessed them, and yet in the world of men tribulation after tribulation did not cease to fall upon them. There was no issue but to assert (what so chastened a spirit could now understand) that tribulation endured for the Lord was itself blessedness, and the sign of some mystical election. Whom the Lord loveth he chasteneth; so the chosen children of God were, without paradox, to be looked for among the most unfortunate of earth's children.

The prophets and psalmists had already shown some beginnings of this asceticism or inverted worldliness. The Essenes and the early Christians made an explicit reversal of ancient Jewish conceptions on this point the corner-stone of their morality. True, the old positivism remained in the background. Tribulation was to be shortlived. Very soon the kingdom of God would be established and a dramatic exchange of places would ensue between the proud and the humble. The mighty would be hurled from their seat, the lowly filled with good things. Yet insensibly the conception of a kingdom of God, of a theocracy, receded or became spiritualised. The joys of it were finally conceived as immaterial altogether, contemplative, and reserved for a life after death. Although the official and literal creed still spoke of a day of judgment, a resurrection of the body, and a New Jerusalem, these things were instinctively taken by Christian piety in a more or less symbolic sense. A longing for gross spectacular greatness, prolonged life, and many children, after the good old Hebraic fashion, had really nothing to do with the Christian notion of salvation. Salvation consisted rather in having surrendered all desire for such things, and all expectation of happiness to be derived from them. Thus the prophet's doctrine that not prosperity absolutely and unconditionally, but prosperity merited by virtue, was the portion of God's people changed by insensible gradations to an ascetic belief that prosperity was altogether alien to virtue and that a believer's true happiness would be such as Saint Francis paints it: upon some blustering winter's night, after a long journey, to have the convent door shut in one's face with many muttered threats and curses.

In the history of Jewish and Christian ethics the pendulum has swung between irrational extremes, without ever stopping at that point of equilibrium at which alone rest is possible. Yet this point was sometimes traversed and included in the gyrations of our tormented ancestral conscience. It was passed, for example, at the moment when the prophets saw that it was human interest that governed right and wrong and conduct that created destiny. But the mythical form in which this novel principle naturally presented itself to the prophets' minds, and the mixture of superstition and national bigotry which remained in their philosophy, contaminated its truth and were more prolific and contagious than its rational elements. Hence the incapacity of so much subsequent thinking to reach clear ideas, and the failure of Christianity, with its prolonged discipline and opportunities, to establish a serious moral education. The perpetual painful readjustments of the last twenty centuries have been adjustments to false facts and imaginary laws; so that neither could a worthy conception of prosperity and of the good be substituted for heathen and Hebrew crudities on that subject, nor could the natural goals of human endeavour come to be recognised and formulated, but all was left to blind impulse or chance tradition.

These defeats of reason are not to be wondered at, if we may indeed speak of the defeat of what never has led an army. The primitive naturalism of the Hebrews was not yet superseded by prophetic doctrines when a new form of materialism arose to stifle and denaturalise what was rational in those doctrines. Even before hope of earthly empire to be secured by Jehovah's favour had quite vanished, claims had arisen to supernatural knowledge founded on revelation. Mythology took a wholly new shape and alliance with God acquired a new meaning and implication. For mythology grew, so to speak, double; moral or naturalistic myths were now reinforced by others of a historical character, to the effect that the former myths had been revealed supernaturally. At the same time the sign of divine protection and favour ceased to be primarily political. Religion now chiefly boasted to possess the Truth, and with the Truth to possess the secret of a perfectly metaphysical and posthumous happiness. Revelation, enigmatically contained in Scripture, found its necessary explication in theology, while the priests, now guardians of the keys of heaven, naturally enlarged their authority over the earth. In fine, the poetic legends and patriarchal worship that had formerly made up the religion of Israel were transformed into two concrete and formidable engines —the Bible and the Church.

CHAPTER 6

REVOLUTIONS ARE ambiguous things. Their success is generally proportionate to their power of adaptation and to the reabsorption within them of what they rebelled against. A thousand reforms have left the world as corrupt as ever, for each successful reform has founded a new institution, and this institution has bred its new and congenial abuses. What is capable of truly purifying the world is not the mere agitation of its elements, but their organisation into a natural body that shall exude what redounds and absorb or generate what is lacking to the perfect expression of its soul.

Whence fetch this seminal force and creative ideal? It must evidently lie already in the matter it is to organise; otherwise it would have no affinity to that matter, no power over it, and no ideality or value in respect to the existences whose standard and goal it was to be. There can be no goods antecedent to the natures they benefit, no ideals prior to the wills they define. A revolution must find its strength and legitimacy not in the reformer's conscience and dream but in the temper of that society which he would transform; for no transformation is either permanent or desirable which does not forward the spontaneous life of the world, advancing those issues toward which it is already inwardly directed. How should a gospel bring glad tidings, save by announcing what was from the beginning native to the heart?

No judgment could well be shallower, therefore, than that which condemns a great religion for not being faithful to that local and partial impulse which may first have launched it into the world. A great religion has something better to consider: the conscience and imagination of those it ministers to. The prophet who announced it first was a prophet only because he had a keener sense and clearer premonition than other men of their common necessities; and he loses his function and is a prophet no longer when the public need begins to outrun his intuitions. Could Hebraism spread over the Roman Empire and take the name of Christianity

218

without adding anything to its native inspiration? Is it to be lamented that we are not all Jews? Yet what makes the difference is not the teaching of Jesus—which is pure Hebraism reduced to its spiritual essence—but the worship of Christ—something perfectly Greek. Christianity would have remained a Jewish sect had it not been made at once speculative, universal, and ideal by the infusion of Greek thought, and at the same time plastic and devotional by the adoption of pagan habits. The incarnation of God in man, and the divinisation of man in God are pagan conceptions, expressions of pagan religious sentiment and philosophy. Yet what would Christianity be without them? It would have lost not only its theology, which might be spared, but its spiritual aspiration, its artistic affinities, and the secret of its metaphysical charity and joy. It would have remained unconscious, as the Gospel is, that the hand or the mind of man can ever construct anything. Among the Jews there were no liberal interests for the ideal to express. They had only elementary human experience—the perpetual Oriental round of piety and servitude in the bosom of a scorched, exhausted country. A disillusioned eye, surveying such a world, could find nothing there to detain it; religion, when wholly spiritual, could do nothing but succour the afflicted, understand and forgive the sinful, and pass through the sad pageant of life unspotted and resigned. Its pity for human ills would go hand in hand with a mystic plebeian insensibility to natural excellence. It would breathe what Tacitus, thinking of the liberal life, could call *odium generis humani*; it would be inimical to human genius.

There were, we may say, two things in Apostolic teaching which rendered it capable of converting the world. One was the later Jewish morality and mysticism, beautifully expressed in Christ's parables and maxims, and illustrated by his miracles, those cures and absolutions which he was ready to dispense, whatever their sins, to such as called upon his name. This democratic and untrammelled charity could powerfully appeal to an age disenchanted with the world, and especially to those lower classes which pagan polity had covered with scorn and condemned to hopeless misery. The other point of contact which early Christianity had with the public need was the theme it offered to contemplation, the philosophy of history which it introduced into the western world, and the delicious unfathomable mysteries into which it launched the fancy. Here, too, the figure of Christ was the centre for all eyes.

Its lowliness, its simplicity, its humanity were indeed, for a while, obstacles to its acceptance; they did not really lend themselves to the metaphysical interpretation which was required. Yet even Greek fable was not without its Apollo tending flocks and its Demeter mourning for her lost child and serving in meek disguise the child of another. Feeling was ripe for a mythology loaded with pathos. The humble life, the homilies, the sufferings of Jesus could be felt in all their incomparable beauty all the more when the tenderness and tragedy of them, otherwise too poignant, were relieved by the story of his miraculous birth, his glorious resurrection, and his restored divinity.

The gospel, thus grown acceptable to the pagan mind, was, however, but a grain of mustard-seed destined to branch and flower in its new soil in a miraculous manner. Not only was the Greek and Roman to refresh himself under its shade, but birds of other climates were to build their nests, at least for a season, in its branches. Hebraism, when thus expanded and paganised, showed many new characteristics native to the minds which had now adopted and transformed it. The Jews, for instance, like other Orientals, had a figurative way of speaking and thinking; their poetry and religion were full of the most violent metaphors. Now to the classic mind violent and improper metaphors were abhorrent. Uniting, as it did, clear reason with lively fancy, it could not conceive one thing to *be* another, nor relish the figure of speech that so described it, hoping by that unthinkable phrase to suggest its affinities. But the classic mind could well conceive transformation, of which indeed nature is full; and in Greek fables anything might change its form, become something else, and display its plasticity, not by imperfectly being many things at once, but by being the perfection of many things in succession. While metaphor was thus unintelligible and confusing to the Greek, metamorphosis was perfectly familiar to him. Wherever Hebrew tradition, accordingly, used violent metaphors, puzzling to the Greek Christian, he rationalised them by imagining a metamorphosis instead; thus, for instance, the metaphors of the Last Supper, so harmless and vaguely satisfying to an Oriental audience, became the doctrine of transubstantiation—a doctrine where images are indeed lacking to illustrate the concepts, but where the concepts themselves are not confused. For that bread should *become* flesh and wine blood is not impossible, seeing that the chance occurs daily in digestion; what the assertion in this case contradicts is merely the evidence of sense.

Thus at many a turn in Christian tradition a metaphysical mystery takes the place of a poetic figure; the former now expressing by a little miraculous drama the emotion which the latter expressed by a tentative phrase. And the emotion is thereby immensely clarified and strengthened; it is, in fact, for the first time really expressed. For the idea that Christ stands upon the altar and mingles still with our human flesh is an explicit assertion that his influence and love are perpetual; whereas the original parable revealed at most the wish and aspiration, contrary to fact, that they might have been so. By substituting embodiment for allegory, the Greek mind thus achieved something very congenial to its habits: it imagined the full and adequate expression, not in words but in existences, of the emotion to be conveyed. The Eucharist is to the Last Supper what a centaur is to a horseman or a tragedy to a song. Similarly a Dantesque conception of hell and paradise embodies in living detail the innocent apologue in the gospel about a separation of the sheep fom the goats. The result is a chimerical metaphysics, containing much which, in reference to existing facts, is absurd; but that metaphysics, when taken for what it truly is, a new mythology, utters the subtler secrets of the new religion not less ingeniously and poetically than pagan mythology reflected the daily shifts in nature and in human life.

Metaphysics became not only a substitute for allegory but at the same time a background for history. Neo-Platonism had enlarged, in a way suited to the speculative demands of the time, the cosmos conceived by Greek science. In an intelligible region, unknown to cosmography and peopled at first by the Platonic ideas and afterward by Aristotle's solitary God, there was now the Absolute One, too exalted for any predicates, but manifesting its essence in the first place in a supreme Intelligence, the second hypostasis of a Trinity; and in the second place in the Soul of the World, the third hypostasis, already relative to natural existence. Now the Platonists conceived these entities to be permanent and immutable; the physical world itself had a meaning and an expressive value, like a statue, but no significant history. When the Jewish notion of creation and divine government of the world presented itself to the Greeks, they hastened to assimilate it to their familiar notions of imitation, expression, finality, and significance. And when the Christians spoke of Christ as the Son of God, who now sat at his right hand in the heavens, their Platonic disciples immediately thought of the Nous or Logos, the divine Intelligence, incarnate as they had always believed in the whole world, and yet truly the substance and essence of divinity. To say that this incarnation had taken place pre-eminently, or even exclusively, in Christ was not an impossible concession to make to pious enthusiasm, at least if the philosophy involved in the old conception could be retained and embodied in the new orthodoxy. Sacred history could thus be interpreted as a temporal execution of eternal decrees, and the plan of salvation as an ideal necessity. Cosmic scope and metaphysical meaning were given to Hebrew tenets, so unspeculative in their original intention, and it became possible even for a Platonic philosopher to declare himself a Christian.

The eclectic Christian philosophy thus engendered constitutes one of the most complete, elaborate, and impressive products of the human mind. The ruins of more than one civilisation and of more than one philosophy were ransacked to furnish materials for this heavenly Byzantium. It was a myth circumstantial and sober enough in tone to pass for an account of facts, and yet loaded with enough miracle, poetry, and submerged wisdom to take the place of a moral philosophy and present what seemed at the time an adequate ideal to the heart. Many a mortal, in all subsequent ages, perplexed and abandoned in this ungovernable world, has set sail resolutely for that enchanted island and found there a semblance of happiness, its narrow limits give so much room for the soul and its penitential soil breeds so many consolations. True, the brief time and narrow argument into which Christian imagination squeezes the world must seem to a speculative pantheist childish and poor, involving, as it does, a fatuous perversion of nature and history and a ridiculous emphasis laid on local events and partial interests. Yet just this violent reduction of things to a human stature, this half-innocent, half-arrogant assumption that what is important for a man must control the whole universe, is what made Christian philosophy originally appealing and what still arouses, in certain quarters, enthusiastic belief in its beneficence and finality.

Nor should we wonder at this enduring illusion. Man is still in his childhood; for he cannot respect an ideal which is not imposed on him against his will, nor can he find satisfaction in a good created by his own action. He is afraid of a universe that leaves him alone. Freedom appals him; he can apprehend in it nothing but tedium and desolation, so immature is he and so barren does he think himself to be. He has to imagine what the angels would say, so that his own good impulses (which create those angels) may gain in authority, and none of the dangers that surround his poor life make the least impression upon him until he hears that there are hobgoblins hiding in the wood. His moral life, to take shape at all, must appear to him in fantastic symbols. The history of these symbols is therefore the history of his soul.

There was in the beginning, so runs the Christian story, a great celestial King, wise and good, surrounded by a court of winged musicians and messengers. He had existed from all eternity, but had always intended, when the right moment should come, to create temporal beings, imperfect copies of himself in various degrees. These, of which man was the chief, began their career in the year 4004 B.C., and they would live on an indefinite time, possibly, that chronological symmetry might not be violated, until A.D. 4004. The opening and close of this drama were marked by two magnificent tableaux. In the first, in obedience to the word of God, sun, moon, and stars, and earth with all her plants and animals, assumed their appropriate places, and nature sprang into being with all her laws. The first man was made out of clay, by a special act of God, and the first woman was fashioned from one of his ribs, extracted while he lay in a deep sleep. They were placed in an orchard where they often could see God, its owner, walking in the cool of the evening. He suffered them to range at will and eat of all the fruits he had planted save that of one tree only. But they, incited by a devil, transgressed this single prohibition, and were banished from that paradise with a curse upon their head, the man to live by the sweat of his brow and the woman to bear children in labour. These children possessed from the moment of conception the inordinate natures which their parents had acquired. They were born to sin and to find disorder and death everywhere within and without them.

At the same time God, lest the work of his hands should wholly perish, promised to redeem in his good season some of Adam's children and restore them to a natural life. This redemption was to come ultimately through a descendant of Eve, whose foot should bruise the head of the serpent. But it was to be pre-figured by many partial and special redemptions. Thus, Noah was to be saved from the deluge, Lot from Sodom, Isaac from the sacrifice, Moses from Egypt, the captive Jews from Babylon, and all faithful souls from heathen forgetfulness and idolatry. For a certain tribe had been set apart from the beginning to keep alive the memory of God's judgments and promises, while the rest of mankind, abandoned to its natural depravity, sank deeper and deeper into crimes and vanities. The deluge that came to punish these evils did not avail to cure them. "The world was renewed * and the earth rose again above the bosom of the waters, but in this renovation there remained eternally some trace of divine venge-ance. Until the deluge all nature had been exceedingly hardy and vigorous, but by that vast flood of water which God had spread out over the earth, and by its long abiding there, all saps were diluted; the air, charged with too dense and heavy a moisture, bred ranker principles of corruption. The early constitution of the universe was weakened, and human life, from stretching as it had formerly done to near a thousand years, grew gradually briefer. Herbs and roots lost their primitive potency and stronger food had to be fur-nished to man by the flesh of other animals. . . . Death gained upon life and men felt themselves overtaken by a speedier chastise-ment. As day by day they sank deeper in their wickedness, it was but right they should daily, as it were, stick faster in their woe. The very change in nourishment made manifest their decline and degradation, since as they became feebler they became also more voracious and blood-thirsty."

Henceforth there were two spirits, two parties, or, as Saint Augustine called them, two cities in the world. The City of Satan, whatever its artifices in art, war, or philosophy, was essentially cor-rupt and impious. Its joy was but a comic mask and its beauty the whitening of a sepulchre. It stood condemned before God and before man's better conscience by its vanity, cruelty, and secret misery, by its ignorance of all that it truly behoved a man to know who was destined to immortality. Lost, as it seemed, within this Babylon, or visible only in its obscure and forgotten purlieus, lived on at the same time the City of God, the society of all the souls God predestined to salvation; a city which, however humble and inconspicuous it might seem on earth, counted its myriad trans-

* Bossuet: Discours sur l'histoire universelle, Part II, Chap. 1.

figured citizens in heaven, and had its destinies, like its foundations, in eternity. To this City of God belonged, in the first place, the patriarchs and the prophets who, throughout their plaintive and ardent lives, were faithful to what echoes still remained of a primeval revelation, and waited patiently for the greater revelation to come. To the same city belonged the magi who followed a star till it halted over the stable in Bethlehem; Simeon, who divined the present salvation of Israel; John the Baptist, who bore witness to the same and made straight its path; and Peter, to whom not flesh and blood, but the spirit of the Father in heaven, revealed the Lord's divinity. For salvation had indeed come with the fulness of time, not, as the carnal Jews had imagined it, in the form of an earthly restoration, but through the incarnation of the Son of God in the Virgin Mary, his death upon a cross, his descent into hell, and his resurrection at the third day according to the Scriptures. To the same city belonged finally all those who, believing in the reality and efficacy of Christ's mission, relied on his merits and followed his commandment of unearthly love.

All history was henceforth essentially nothing but the conflict between these two cities; two moralities, one natural, the other supernatural; two philosophies, one rational, the other revealed; two beauties, one corporeal, the other spiritual; two glories, one temporal, the other eternal; two institutions, one the world, the other the Church. These, whatever their momentary alliances or compromises, were radically opposed and fundamentally alien to one another. Their conflict was to fill the ages until, when wheat and tares had long flourished together and exhausted between them the earth for whose substance they struggled, the harvest should come; the terrible day of reckoning when those who had believed the things of religion to be imaginary would behold with dismay the Lord visibly coming down through the clouds of heaven, the angels blowing their alarming trumpets, all generations of the dead rising from their graves, and judgment without appeal passed on every man, to the edification of the universal company and his own unspeakable joy or confusion. Whereupon the blessed would enter eternal bliss with God their master and the wicked everlasting torments with the devil whom they served.

The drama of history was thus to close upon a second tableau: long-robed and beatified cohorts passing above, amid various psalmodies, into an infinite luminous space, while below the damned, howling, writhing, and half transformed into loathsome beasts, should be engulfed in a fiery furnace. The two cities, always opposite in essence, should thus be finally divided in existence, each bearing its natural fruits and manifesting its true nature.

Let the reader fill out this outline for himself with its thousand details; let him remember the endless mysteries, arguments, martyrdoms, consecrations that carried out the sense and made vital the beauty of the whole. Let him pause before the phenomenon; he can ill afford, if he wishes to understand history or the human mind, to let the apparition float by unchallenged without delivering up its secret. What shall we say of this Christian dream?

Those who are still troubled by the fact that this dream is by many taken for a reality, and who are consequently obliged to defend themselves against it, as against some dangerous error in science or in philosophy, may be allowed to marshal arguments in its disproof. Such, however, is not my intention. Do we marshal arguments against the miraculous birth of Buddha, or the story of Cronos devouring his children? We seek rather to honour the piety and to understand the poetry embodied in those fables. If it be said that those fables are believed by no one, I reply that those fables are or have been believed just as unhesitatingly as the Christian theology, and by men no less reasonable or learned than the persistent apologists of our own ancestral creeds. Matters of religion should never be matters of controversy. We neither argue with a lover about his taste, nor condemn him, if we are just, for knowing so human a passion. That he harbours it is no indication of a want of sanity on his part in other matters. But while we acquiesce in his satisfaction, and are glad he has it, we need no arguments to dissuade us from sharing it. Each man may have his own loves, but the object in each case is different. And so it is, or should be, in religion. Before the rise of those strange and fraudulent Hebraic pretensions there was no question among men about the national, personal, and poetic character of religious allegiance. It could never have been a duty to adopt a religion not one's own any more than a language, a coinage, or a costume not current in one's own country. The idea that religion contains a literal, not a symbolic, representation of truth and life is simply an impossible idea. Whoever entertains it has not come within the region of profitable philosophising on that subject. His science is not wide enough to cover all existence. He has not discovered that there can be no moral allegiance except to the ideal. His certitude and his arguments are no more pertinent to the religious question than would be the insults, blows, and murders to which, if he could, he would appeal in the next instance. Philosophy may describe unreason, as it may describe force; it cannot hope to refute them.

CHAPTER 7

PAGAN CUSTOM AND BARBARIAN GENIUS INFUSED
INTO CHRISTIANITY

THE WESTERN intellect, in order to accept the gospel, had to sublimate it into a neo-Platonic system of metaphysics. In like manner the western heart had to render Christianity congenial and adequate by a rich infusion of pagan custom and sentiment. This adaptation was more gentle and facile than might be supposed. We are too much inclined to impute an abstract and ideal Christianity to the polyglot souls of early Christians, and to ignore that mysterious and miraculous side of antique religions from which Christian cultus and ritual are chiefly derived. In the third century Christianity and devout paganism were, in a religious sense, closely akin; each differed much less from the other than from that religion which at other epochs had borne or should bear its own name. Had Julian the Apostate succeeded in his enterprise he would not have rescued anything which the admirers of classic paganism could at all rejoice in; a disciple of Iamblichus could not but plunge headlong into the same sea of superstition and dialectic which had submerged Christianity. In both parties ethics were irrational and morals corrupt. The political and humane religion of Hellenism had disappeared, and the question between Christians and pagans amounted simply to a choice of fanaticisms. Reason had suffered a general eclipse, but civilisation, although decayed, still subsisted, and a certain scholastic discipline, a certain speculative habit, and many an ancient religious usage remained in the world. The people could change their gods, but not the spirit in which they worshipped them. Christianity had insinuated itself almost unobserved into a society full of rooted traditions. The first disciples had been disinherited Jews, with religious habits which men of other races and interests could never have adopted intelligently; the Church was accordingly wise enough to perpetuate in its practice at least an indispensable minimum of popular paganism. How considerable this minimum was a glance at Catholic piety will suffice to convince us.

The Græco-Jewish system of theology constructed by the Fathers had its liturgical counterpart in the sacraments and in a devout eloquence which may be represented to us fairly enough by the Roman missal and breviary. This liturgy, transfused as it is with pagan philosophy and removed thereby from the Oriental directness and formlessness of the Bible, keeps for the most part its theological and patristic tone. Psalms abound, Virgin and saints are barely mentioned, a certain universalism and concentration of thought upon the Redemption and its speculative meaning pervades the Latin ritual sung behind the altar-rails. But any one who enters a Catholic church with an intelligent interpreter will at once perceive the immense distance which separates that official and impersonal ritual from the daily prayers and practices of Catholic people. The latter refer to the real exigencies of daily life and serve to express or reorganise personal passions. While mass is being celebrated the old woman will tell her beads, lost in a vague rumination over her own troubles; while the priests chant something unintelligible about Abraham or Nebuchadnezzar, the housewife will light her wax-candles, duly blessed for the occasion, before Saint Barbara, to be protected thereby from the lightning; and while the preacher is repeating, by rote, dialectical subtleties about the union of the two natures in Christ's person, a listener's fancy may float sadly over the mystery of love and of life, and (being himself without resources in the premises) he may order a mass to be said for the repose of some departed soul.

In a Catholic country, every spot and every man has a particular patron. These patrons are sometimes local worthies, canonised by tradition or by the Roman see, but no less often they are simply local appellations of Christ or the Virgin, appellations which are known theoretically to refer all to the same *numen*, but which practically possess diverse religious values; for the miracles and intercessions attributed to the Virgin under one title are far from being miracles and intercessions attributable to her under another. He who has been all his life devout to Loreto will not place any special reliance on the Pillar at Saragossa. A bereaved mother will not fly to the Immaculate Conception for comfort, but of course to Our Lady of the Seven Sorrows. Each religious order and all the laity more or less affiliated to it will cultivate special saints and special mysteries. There are also particular places and days on which graces are granted, as not on others, and the quantity of such graces is measurable by canonic standards. So many days of re-mitted penance correspond to a work of a certain merit, for there is a celestial currency in which mulcts and remissions may be accu-rately summed and subtracted by angelic recorders. One man's spiritual earnings may by gift be attributed and imputed to an-other, a belief which may seem arbitrary and superstitious but which is really a natural corollary to fundamental doctrines like the atonement, the communion of saints, and intercession for the dead and living.

Another phase of the same natural religion is seen in frequent festivals, in the consecration of buildings, ships, fields, labours, and seasons; in intercessions by the greater dead for the living and by the living for the lesser dead—a perfect survival of heroes and penates on the one hand and of pagan funeral rites and commemo-rations on the other. Add Lent with its carnival, ember-days, all saints' and all souls', Christmas with its magi or its Saint Nicholas, Saint Agnes's and Saint Valentine's days with their profane associa-tions, a saint for finding lost objects and another for prospering amourettes, since all great and tragic loves have their inevitable patrons in Christ and the Virgin, in Mary Magdalene, and in the mystics innumerable. This, with what more could easily be re-hearsed, makes a complete paganism within Christian tradition, a paganism for which little basis can be found in the gospel, the mass, the breviary, or the theologians.

Yet these accretions were as well authenticated as the sub-structure, for they rested on human nature. To feel, for instance, the special efficacy of your village Virgin or of the miraculous Christ whose hermitage is perched on the overhanging hill, is a genuine experience. The principle of it is clear and simple. Those shrines, those images, the festivals associated with them, have entered your mind together with your earliest feelings. Your first glimpses of mortal vicissitudes have coincided with the awe and glitter of sacramental moments in which those *numina* were in-voked; and on that deeper level of experience, in those lower reaches of irrationalism in which such impressions lie, they con-stitute a mystic resource subsisting beneath all conventions and overt knowledge. When the doctors blunder—as they commonly

do—the saints may find a cure; after all, the saints' success in medicine seems to a crude empiricism almost as probable as the physi-
cians'. Special and local patrons are the original gods, and whatever
religious value speculative and cosmic deities retain they retain
surreptitiously, by virtue of those very bonds with human interests
and passionate desires which ancestral demons once borrowed from
the hearth they guarded, the mountain they haunted, or the sacrifice they inhaled with pleasure, until their hearts softened toward
their worshippers. In itself, and as a minimised and retreating
theology represents it, a universal power has no specific energy,
no determinate interest at heart; there is nothing friendly about
it nor allied to your private necessities; no links of place and time
fortify and define its influence. Nor is it rational to appeal for a
mitigation of evils or for assistance against them to the very being
that has decreed and is inflicting them for some fixed purpose of
its own.

Paganism or natural religion was at first, like so many crude
religious notions, optimistic and material; the worshipper expected
his piety to make his pot boil, to cure his disease, to prosper his
battles, and to render harmless his ignorance of the world in which
he lived. But such faith ran up immediately against the facts; it
was discountenanced at every turn by experience and reflection.
The whole of nature and life, when they are understood at all,
have to be understood on an opposite principle, on the principle
that fate, having naturally furnished us with a determinate will and
a determinate endowment, gives us a free field and no favour in a
natural world. Hence the retreat of religion to the supernatural,
a region to which in its cruder forms it was far from belonging. Now
this retreat, in the case of classic paganism, took place with the
decay of military and political life and would have produced an
ascetic popular system, some compound of Oriental and Greek
traditions, even if Christianity had not intervened at that juncture
and opportunely pre-empted the ground.

Christianity, as we have seen, had elements in it which gave
it a decisive advantage; its outlook was historical, not cosmic, and
consequently admitted a non-natural future for the individual and
for the Church; it was anti-political and looked for progress only
in that region in which progress was at that time possible, in the
private soul; it was democratic, feminine, and unworldly; its Oriental deity and prophets had a primitive simplicity and pathos not

found in pagan heroes or polite metaphysical entities; its obscure Hebrew poetry opened, like music, an infinite field for brooding fancy and presumption. The consequence was a doubling of the world, so that every Christian led a dual existence, one full of trouble and vanity on earth, which it was piety in him to despise and neglect, another full of hope and consolation in a region parallel to earth and directly above it, every part of which corresponded to something in earthly life and could be reached, so to speak, by a Jacob's ladder upon which aspiration and grace ascended and descended continually. Birth had its sacramental consecration to the supernatural in baptism, growth in confirmation, self-consciousness in confession, puberty in communion, effort in prayer, defeat in sacrifice, sin in penance, speculation in revealed wisdom, art in worship, natural kindness in charity, poverty in humility, death in self-surrender and resurrection. When the mind grew tired of contemplation the lips could still echo some pious petition, keeping the body's attitude and habit expressive of humility and propitious to receiving grace; and when the knees and lips were themselves weary, a candle might be left burning before the altar, to witness that the desire momentarily forgotten was not extinguished in the heart. Through prayer and religious works the absent could be reached and the dead helped on their journey, and amid earthly estrangements and injustices there always remained the church open to all and the society of heaven.

Nothing is accordingly more patent than that Christianity was paganised by the early Church; indeed, the creation of the Church was itself what to a Hebraising mind must seem a corruption, namely, a mixing of pagan philosophy and ritual with the Gospel. But this sort of constitutive corruption would more properly be called an adaptation, an absorption, or even a civilisation of Hebraism; for by this marriage with paganism Christianity fitted itself to live and work in the civilised world. By this corruption it was completed and immensely improved, like Anglo-Saxon by its corruption through French and Latin; for it is always an improvement in religion, whose business is to express and inspire spiritual sentiment, that it should learn to express and inspire that sentiment more generously. Paganism was nearer than Hebraism to the Life of Reason because its myths were more transparent and its temper less fanatical; and so a paganised Christianity approached more closely that ideality which constitutes religious truth than a bare and intense Hebraism, in its hostility to human genius, could ever have done if isolated and unqualified.

The Christianity which the pagans adopted, in becoming itself pagan, remained a religion natural to their country and their heart. It constituted a paganism expressive of their later and calamitous experience, a paganism acquainted with sorrow, a religion that had passed through both civilisation and despair, and had been reduced to translating the eclipsed values of life into supernatural symbols. It became a post-rational religion. Of course, to understand such a system it is necessary to possess the faculties it exercises and the experience it represents. Where life has not reached the level of reflection, religion and philosophy must both be prerational; they must remain crudely experimental, unconscious of the limits of excellence and life. Under such circumstances it is obviously impossible that religion should be reconstituted on a supernatural plane, or should learn to express experience rather than impulse. Now the Christianity of the gospels was itself postrational; it had turned its back on the world. In this respect the mixture with paganism altered nothing; it merely reinforced the spiritualised and lyric despair of the Hebrews with the personal and metaphysical despair of the Romans and Greeks. For all the later classic philosophy—Stoic, Sceptic, or Epicurean—was founded on despair and was post-rational. Pagan Christianity, or Catholicism, may accordingly be said to consist of two elements: first, the genius of paganism, the faculty of expressing spiritual experience in myth and external symbol, and, second, the experience of disillusion, forcing that pagan imagination to take wing from earth and to decorate no longer the political and material circumstances of life, but rather to remove beyond the clouds and constitute its realm of spirit beyond the veil of time and nature, in a posthumous and metaphysical sphere. A mythical economy abounding in points of attachment to human experience and in genial interpretations of life, yet lifted beyond visible nature and filling a reported world, a world believed in on hearsay or, as it is called, on faith—that is Catholicism.

When this religion was established in the Roman Empire, that empire was itself threatened by the barbarians who soon permeated and occupied it and made a new and unhappy beginning to European history. They adopted Christianity, not because it represented their religious needs or inspiration, but because it formed part of a culture and a social organisation the influence of which they had not, in their simplicity, the means to withstand. During several ages they could only modify by their misunderstandings and inertia arts wholly new to their lives.

What sort of religion these barbarians may previously have had is beyond our accurate knowledge. They handed down a mythology not radically different from the Græco-Roman, though more vaguely and grotesquely conceived; and they recognised tribal duties and glories from which religious sanctions could hardly have been absent. But a barbarian mind, like a child's, is easy to convert and to people with what stories you will. The Northmen drank in with pleased astonishment what the monks told them about hell and heaven, God the Father and God the Son, the Virgin and the beautiful angels; they accepted the sacraments with vague docility; they showed a qualified respect, often broken upon, it is true, by instinctive rebellions, for a clergy which after all represented whatever vestiges of learning, benevolence, or art still lingered in the world. But this easy and boasted conversion was fanciful only and skin-deep. A non-Christian ethics of valour and honour, a non-Christian fund of superstition, legend, and sentiment, subsisted always among mediæval peoples. Their soul, so largely inarticulate, might be overlaid with churchly habits and imprisoned for the moment in the panoply of patristic dogma; but pagan Christianity always remained a religion foreign to them, accepted only while their minds continued in a state of helpless tutelage. It was thus that the Roman Church hatched the duck's egg of Protestantism.

In its native seats the Catholic system prompts among those who inwardly reject it satire and indifference rather than heresy, because on the whole it expresses well enough the religious instincts of the people. Only those strenuously oppose it who hate religion itself. But among converted barbarians the case was naturally different, and opposition to the Church came most vehemently from certain religious natures whose instincts it outraged or left unsatisfied. Even before heresy burst forth this religious restlessness found vent in many directions. It endowed Christianity with several beautiful but insidious gifts, several incongruous though well-meant forms of expression. Among these we may count Gothic art, chivalrous sentiment, and even scholastic philosophy. These things came, as we know, ostensibly to serve Christianity, which has learned to regard them as its own emanations. But in truth they barbarised Christianity just as Greek philosophy and worship and Roman habits of administration had paganised it in the beginning. And barbarised Christianity, even before it became heretical, was something new, something very different in temper and beauty from the pagan Christianity of the South and East.

In the Catholicism of the Middle Ages, as it flourished in the North, the barbarian soul, apprenticed to monkish masters, appeared in all its childlike trust, originality, and humour. The tragic meaning of the Christian faith, its immense renunciation of all things earthly and the merely metaphysical glory of its transfigured life, commonly escaped apprehension, as it still continues to do. People listened open-mouthed to the missionary and accepted his asseverations with unsuspecting emotion. A seed planted in such a virgin and uncultivated soil must needs bring forth fruit of a new savour.

In northern Christianity a fresh quality of brooding tenderness prevailed over the tragic passion elsewhere characteristic of Catholic devotion. Intricacy was substituted for dignity and poetry for rhetoric; the basilica became an abbey and the hermitage a school. The feudal ages were a wonderful seed-time in a world all gaunt with ruins. Horrors were there mingled with delicacies and confusion with idyllic peace. It was here a poet's childhood passed amid the crash of war, there an alchemist's old age flickering away amid cobwebs and gibberish. Something jocund and mischievous peeped out even in the cloister; gargoyles leered from the belfry, while ivy and holly grew about the cross. The Middle Ages were the true renaissance. Their Christianity was the theme, the occasion, the excuse for their art and jollity, their curiosity and tenderness; it was far from being the source of those delightful inventions. The Crusades were not inspired by the Prince of Peace, to whose honour they were fancifully and passionately dedicated; so chivalry, Gothic architecture, and scholastic philosophy were profane expressions of a self-discovering genius in a people incidentally Christian. The barbarians had indeed been indoctrinated, they had been introduced into an alien spiritual and historic medium, but they had not been made over or inwardly tamed. It had perhaps been rendered easier for them, by contact with an existing or remembered civilisation, to mature their own genius, even in the act of confusing its expression through foreign accretions. They had been thereby stimulated to civilise themselves and encouraged also to believe themselves civilised somewhat prematurely.

The process of finding their own art and polity was bound on the whole to diverge more and more from its Latin model. It consisted now of imitation, now of revulsion and fanciful originality; never was a race so much under the sway of fashions. Fashion is something barbarous, for it produces innovation without reason and imitation without benefit. It marks very clearly that margin of irresponsible variation in manners and thoughts which among a people artificially civilised may so easily be larger than the solid core. It is characteristic of occidental society in mediæval and modern times, because this society is led by people who, being educated in a foreign culture, remain barbarians at heart. Some educated persons, accordingly, are merely students and imbibers; they sit at the feet of a past which, not being really theirs, can produce no fruit in them but sentimentality. Others are merely *protestants*; they are active in the moral sphere only by virtue of an inward rebellion against something greater and overshadowing, yet repulsive and alien. They are conscious truants from a foreign school of life.

In the Protestant religion it is necessary to distinguish inner inspiration from historical entanglements. Unfortunately, as the whole doctrinal form of this religion is irrelevant to its spirit and imposed from without, being due to the step-motherly nurture it received from the Church, we can reach a conception of its inner spirit only by studying its tendency and laws of change or its incidental expression in literature and custom. Yet these indirect symptoms are so striking that even an outsider, if at all observant, need not fear to misinterpret them. Taken externally, Protestantism is, of course, a form of Christianity; it retains the Bible and a more or less copious selection of patristic doctrines. But in its spirit and inward inspiration it is something quite as independent of Judea as of Rome. It is simply the natural religion of the Teutons raising its head above the flood of Roman and Judean influences. Its character may be indicated by saying that it is a religion of pure spontaneity, of emotional freedom, deeply respecting itself but scarcely deciphering its purposes. It is the self-consciousness of a spirit in process of incubation, jealous of its potentialities, averse to definitions and finalities of any kind because it can itself discern nothing fixed or final. It is adventurous and puzzled by the world, full of rudimentary virtues and clear fire, energetic, faithful, and rebellious to tradition. It accordingly mistakes vitality, both in itself and in the universe, for spiritual life.

This underlying Teutonic religion, which we must call Protestantism for lack of a better name, is anterior to Christianity and can survive it. To identify it with the Gospel may have seemed possible so long as, in opposition to pagan Christianity, the Teutonic spirit could appeal to the Gospel for support. The Gospel has indeed nothing pagan about it, but it has also nothing Teutonic; and the momentary alliance of two such disparate forces must naturally cease with the removal of the common enemy which alone united them. The Gospel is unworldly, disenchanted, ascetic; it treats ecclesiastical establishments with tolerant contempt, conforming to them with indifference; it regards prosperity as a danger, earthly ties as a burden, Sabbaths as a superstition; it revels in miracles; it is democratic and antinomian; it loves contemplation, poverty and solitude; it meets sinners with sympathy and heartfelt forgiveness, but Pharisees and Puritans with biting scorn. In a word, it is a product of the Orient, where all things are old and equal and a profound indifference to the business of earth breeds a silent dignity and high sadness in the spirit. Protestantism is the exact opposite of all this. It is convinced of the importance of success and prosperity; it abominates what is disreputable; contemplation seems to it idleness, solitude selfishness, and poverty a sort of dishonourable punishment. It is constrained and punctilious in righteousness; it regards a married and industrious life as typically godly, and there is a sacredness to it, as of a vacant Sabbath, in the unoccupied higher spaces which such an existence leaves for the soul. It is sentimental, its ritual is meagre and unctuous, it expects no miracles, it thinks optimism akin to piety, and regards profitable enterprise and practical ambition as a sort of moral vocation. Its benevolence is optimistic and aims at raising men to a conventional well-being; it thus misses the inner appeal of Christian charity which, being merely remedial in physical matters, begins by renunciation and looks to spiritual freedom and peace.

Protestantism was therefore attached from the first to the Old Testament, in which Hebrew fervour appears in its worldly and pre-rational form. It is not democratic in the same sense as post-rational religions, which see in the soul an exile from some other sphere wearing for the moment, perhaps, a beggar's disguise: it is democratic only in the sense of having a popular origin and bending easily to popular forces. Swayed as it is by public opinion, it is necessarily conventional in its conception of duty and earnestly materialistic; for the meaning of the word vanity never crosses the vulgar heart. In fine, it is the religion of a race young, wistful, and adventurous, feeling its latent potentialities, vaguely assured of an earthly vocation, and possessing, like the barbarian and the healthy child, pure but unchastened energies. Thus in the Protestant religion the faith natural to barbarism appears clothed, by force of historical accident, in the language of an adapted Christianity.

As the Middle Ages advanced the new-born human genius which constituted their culture grew daily more playful, curious, and ornate. It was naturally in the countries formerly pagan that this new paganism principally flourished. Religion began in certain quarters to be taken philosophically; its relation to life began to be understood, that it was a poetic expression of need, hope, and ignorance. Here prodigious vested interests and vested illusions of every sort made dangerous the path of sincerity. Genuine moral and religious impulses could not be easily dissociated from a system of thought and discipline with which for a thousand years they had been intimately interwoven. Scepticism, instead of seeming, what it naturally is, a moral force, a tendency to sincerity, economy, and fine adjustment of life and mind to reality—scepticism seemed a temptation and a danger. This situation, which still prevails in a certain measure, strikingly shows into how artificial a posture Christianity has thrown the mind. If scepticism, under such circumstances, by chance penetrated among the clergy, it was not favourable to consistency of life, and it was the more certain to penetrate among them in that their ranks, in a fat and unscrupulous age, would naturally be largely recruited from men without ideal ambitions. It became accordingly necessary to reform something; either the gay world to suit the Church's primitive austerity and asceticism, or the Church to suit the world's profane and general interests. The latter task was more or less consciously undertaken by the humanists who would have abated the clergy's wealth and irrational authority, advanced polite learning, and, while of course retaining Christianity—for why should an ancestral religion be changed?— would have retained it as a form of paganism, as an ornament and poetic expression of human life. This movement, had it not been

overwhelmed by the fanatical Reformation and the fanatical reaction against it, would doubtless have met with many a check
from the Church's sincere zealots; but it could have overcome them
and, had it been allowed to fight reason's battle with reason's
weapons, would ultimately have led to general enlightenment
without dividing Christendom, kindling venomous religious and
national passions, or vitiating philosophy.

It was not humanism, however, that was destined to restrain
and soften the Church, completing by critical reflection that pagan-
isation of Christianity which had taken place at the beginning
instinctively and of necessity. There was now another force in the
field, the virgin conscience and wilfulness of the Teutonic races,
sincerely attached to what they had assimilated in Christianity and
now awakening to the fact that they inwardly abhorred and rejected the rest. This situation, in so uncritical an age, could be
interpreted as a return to primitive Christianity.

In thus meeting the world the soul without experience shows
a fine courage proportionate to its own vigour. We may well imagine that lions and porpoises have a more masculine assurance
that God is on their side than ever visits the breast of antelope or
jellyfish. This assurance, when put to the test in adventurous living,
becomes in a strong and high-bred creature a refusal to be defeated,
a gallant determination to hold the last ditch and hope for the best
in spite of appearances. It is a part of Protestantism to be austere,
energetic, unwearied in some laborious task. The end and profit are
not so much regarded as the mere habit of self-control and practical
devotion and steadiness. The only evils recognised seem so many
challenges to action, so many conditions for some glorious unthought-of victory. Such a religion is indeed profoundly ignorant,
it is the religion of inexperience, yet it has, at its core, the very
spirit of life. Its error is only to consider the will omnipotent and
sacred and not to distinguish the field of inevitable failure from
that of possible success. Success, however, would never be possible
without that fund of energy and that latent resolve and determination which bring also faith in success. Animal optimism is a great
renovator and disinfectant in the world.

In the end, with the complete crumbling away of Christian
dogma and tradition, Absolute Egotism appeared openly on the
surface in the shape of German speculative philosophy. This form,
which Protestantism assumed at a moment of high tension and

reckless self-sufficiency, it will doubtless shed in turn and take on
new expressions; but that declaration of independence on the part
of the Teutonic spirit marks emphatically its exit from Christianity
and the end of that series of transformations in which it took the
Bible and patristic dogma for its materials. It now bids fair to
apply itself instead to social life and natural science and to attempt
to feed its Protean hunger directly from these more homely
sources.

CHAPTER 8

CONFLICT OF MYTHOLOGY WITH MORAL TRUTH

MYTHICAL THINKING has its roots in reality, but, like a plant, touches the ground only at one end. It stands unmoved and flowers wantonly into the air, transmuting into unexpected and richer forms the substances it sucks from the soil. It is therefore a fruit of experience, an ornament, a proof of organic vitality; but it is no *vehicle* for knowledge; it cannot serve the purposes of transitive thought or action. Science, on the other hand, is constituted by those fancies which, arising like myths out of perception, retain a sensuous language and point to further perceptions of the same kind; so that the suggestions drawn from one object perceived are only ideas of other objects similarly perceptible. A scientific hypothesis is one which represents something continuous with the observed facts and conceivably existent in the same medium. Science is a bridge touching experience at both ends, over which practical thought may travel from act to act, from perception to perception.

Were mythology merely a poetic substitute for natural science the advance of science would sufficiently dispose of it. What remained over would, like the myths in Plato, be at least better than total silence on a subject that interests us and makes us think, although we have no means of testing our thoughts in regard to it. But the chief source of perplexity and confusion in mythology is its kinship with moral truth. The myth which originally was but a symbol for facts becomes in the sequel an idol substituted for ideal values. This complication, from which half the troubles of philosophy arise, deserves our careful attention.

European history has now come twice upon the dissolution of mythologies, first among the Stoics and then among the Protestants. The circumstances in the two cases were very unlike; so were the mythical systems that were discarded; and yet the issue was in both instances similar. Greek and Christian mythology have alike ended in pantheism. So soon as the constructions of the poets and the Fathers were seen to be ingenious fictions, criticism was con-

241

fronted with an obvious duty: to break up the mythical compound furnished by tradition into its elements, putting on one side what natural observation or actual history had supplied, and on the other what dramatic imagination had added. For a cool and disinterested observer the task, where evidence and records were not wanting, would be simple enough. But the critic in this case would not usually be cool or disinterested. His religion was concerned; he had no other object to hang his faith and happiness upon than just this traditional hybrid which his own enlightenment was now dissolving. To which part should he turn for support? In which quarter should he continue to place the object of his worship?

From the age of the Sophists to the final disappearance of paganism nearly a thousand years elapsed. Religions do not disappear when they are discredited; it is requisite that they should be replaced. For a thousand years the augurs may have laughed, they were bound nevertheless to stand at their posts until the monks came to relieve them. During this prolonged decrepitude paganism lived on inertia, by accretions from the Orient, and by philosophic reinterpretations. Of these reinterpretations the first was that attempted by Plato and afterward carried out by the neo-Platonists and Christians into the notion of a supernatural spiritual hierarchy; above, a dialectical deity, the hypostasis of intellect and its ontological phases; below, a host of angels and demons, hypostases of faculties, moral influences, and evil promptings. In other words, in the diremption of myths which yielded here a natural phenomenon to be explained and there a moral value to be discerned, Platonism attached divinity exclusively to the moral element. The ideas, which were essentially moral functions, were many and eternal; their physical embodiments were adventitious to them and constituted a lapse, a misfortune to be wiped out by an eventual reunion of the alienated nature with its own model. Religion in such a system necessarily meant redemption. In this movement paganism turned toward the future, toward supernatural and revealed religion, and away from its own naturalistic principle. Revelation, as Plato himself had said, was needed to guide a mind which distrusted phenomena and recoiled from earthly pursuits.

This divorce of neo-Platonic ideas from the functions they originally represented in human life and discourse was found in the end to defeat the very interest that had prompted it—enthusiasm for the ideal. Enthusiasm for the ideal had led Plato to treat all beauties as stepping-stones toward a perfect beauty in which all their charms might be present together, eternally and without alloy. Enthusiasm for the ideal had persuaded him that mortal life was only an impeded effort to fall back into eternity. These inspired but strictly unthinkable suggestions fell from his lips in his zeal to express how much the burden and import of experience exceeded its sensuous vehicle in permanence and value. A thousand triangles revealed one pregnant proportion of lines and areas; a thousand beds and bridles served one perpetual purpose in human life, and found in fulfilling it their essence and standard of excellence; a thousand fascinations taught the same lesson and coalesced into one reverent devotion to beauty and nobility wherever they might bloom. It was accordingly a poignant sense for the excellence of real things that made Plato wish to transcend them; his metaphysics was nothing but a visionary intuition of values, an idealism in the proper sense of the word. But when the momentum of such enthusiasm remained without its motive power, and its transcendence without its inspiration in real experience, idealism ceased to be an idealisation, an interpretation of reality reaching prophetically to its goals. It became a supernumerary second physics, a world to which an existence was attributed which could be hardly conceived and was certainly supported by no evidence; and, worst of all, it robbed the ideal of its ideality by tearing it up from its roots in natural will and in experienced earthly benefits. For an ideal is not ideal if it is the ideal of nothing.

Meantime, a second reinterpretation of mythology was attempted by the Stoics. Instead of moving forward, like Plato, toward the supernaturalism that was for so many ages to dominate the world, the Stoics, with greater loyalty to pagan principles, reverted to the natural forces that had been the chief basis for the traditional deities. The progress of philosophy had given the Stoics a notion of the cosmos such as the early Aryan could not have possessed when he recorded and took to heart his scattered observations in the form of divine influences. To the Stoics the world was evidently one dynamic system. The power that animated it was therefore one God. Accordingly, after explaining away the popular myths by turning them somewhat ruthlessly into moral apologues, they proceeded to identify Zeus with the order of nature. This identification was supported by many traditional tendencies and philosophic hints. The resulting concept, though still mythical, was perhaps as rationalistic as the state of science at the time could allow. Zeus had been from the beginning a natural force, at once serene and formidable, the thunderer no less than the spirit of the blue. He was the ruler of gods and men; he was, under limitations, a sort of general providence. Anaxagoras, too, in proclaiming the cosmic function of reason, had prepared the way for the Stoics in another direction. This "reason," which in Socrates and Plato was already a deity, meant an order, an order making for the good. It was the name for a principle much like that which Aristotle called Nature, an indwelling prophetic instinct by which things strive after their perfection and happiness. Now Aristotle observed this instinct, as behoved a disciple of Socrates, in its specific cases, in which the good secured could be discriminated and visibly attained. There were many souls, each with its provident function and immutable guiding ideal, one for each man and animal, one for each heavenly sphere, and one, the prime mover, for the highest sphere of all. But the Stoics, not trained in the same humane and critical school, had felt the unity of things more dramatically and vaguely in the realm of physics. Like Xenophanes of old, they gazed at the broad sky and exclaimed, "The All is One." Uniting these various influences, they found it easy to frame a conception of Zeus, or the world, or the universal justice and law, so as to combine in it a dynamic unity with a provident reason. A world conceived to be material and fatally determined was endowed with foresight of its own changes, perfect internal harmony, and absolute moral dignity. Thus mythology, with the Stoics, ended in pantheism.

On the other hand, mythology had not been a mere poetic physics; it had formulated the object of religion; it had embodied for mankind its highest ideals in worshipful forms. It was when this religious function was transferred to the god of pantheism that the paradox and impossibility of the reform became evident. Nature neither is nor can be man's ideal. The substitution of nature for the traditional and ideal object of religion involves giving nature moral authority over man; it involves that element of Stoicism which is the synonym of inhumanity. Life and death, good and ill fortune, happiness and misery, since they flow equally from the universal order, shall be declared, in spite of reason, to be equally good. True virtue shall be reduced to conformity. He who has no ideal but that nature should possess her actual constitution will be wise and superior to all flattery and calamity; he will be equal in dignity to Zeus. He who has any less conformable and more determinate interests will be a fool.

The wise man will, meantime, perform all the offices of nature; he will lend his body and his mind to her predestined labours. For pantheistic morals, though post-rational, are not ascetic. In dislodging the natural ideal from the mind, they put in its place not its supernatural exaggeration but a curtailment of it inspired by despair. The passions are not renounced on the ground that they impede salvation or some visionary ecstasy; they are merely chilled by the sense that their defeat, when it occurs, is also desirable. As all the gods have been reduced to one substance or law, so all human treasures are reduced to one privilege—that of fortitude. You can always consent, and by a forced and perpetual conformity to nature lift yourself above all vicissitudes. Those tender and tentative ideals which nature really breeds, and which fill her with imperfect but genuine excellences, you will be too stolid to perceive or too proud to share.

The horror which pantheism has always inspired in the Church is like that which materialism inspires in sentimental idealists; they attack it continually, not so much because anybody else defends it as because they feel it to be implied unmistakably in half their own tenets. The non-Platonic half of Christian theology, the Mosaic half, is bound to become pantheism in the hands of a philosopher. The Jews were not pantheists themselves, because they never speculated on the relation which omnipotence stood in to natural forces and human acts. They conceived Jehovah's omnipotence dramatically, as they conceived everything. He might pounce upon anything and anybody; he might subvert or play with the laws of nature; he might laugh at men's devices, and turn them to his own ends; his craft and energy could not but succeed in every instance; but that was not to say that men and nature had no will of their own, and did not proceed naturally on their respective ways when Jehovah happened to be busy elsewhere. So soon, however, as this dramatic sort of omnipotence was made systematic by dialectic, so soon as the doctrines of creation, omniscience, and providential government were taken absolutely, pantheism was clearly involved. The consequences to moral philosophy were truly appalling, for then the sins God punished so signally were due to his own contrivance. The fervours of his saints, the fate of his chosen people and holy temples, became nothing but a puppet-show in his ironical possession.

The strangest part of this system in recent times is that it is only half-conscious of its physical temper, and in calling itself an idealism (because it makes perception and will the substance of their objects), thinks itself an expression of human aspirations. This illusion has deep historical roots. It is the last stage of a mythical philosophy which has been earnestly criticising its metaphors, on the assumption that they were not metaphorical; whereby it has stripped them of all significance and reduced them at last to the bare principle of inversion. Nothing is any longer idealised, yet all is still called an idealism. A myth is an inverted image of things, wherein their moral effects are turned into their dramatic antecedents—as when the wind's rudeness is turned into his anger. When the natural basis of moral life is not understood, myth is the only way of expressing it theoretically, as eyes too weak to see the sun face to face may, as Plato says, for a time study its image mirrored in pools, and, as we may add, inverted there. So the good, which in itself is spiritual only, is transposed into a natural power. At first this amounts to an amiable misrepresentation of natural things; the gods inhabit Mount Olympus and the Elysian Fields are not far west of Cadiz. With the advance of geography the mythical facts recede, and in a cosmography like Hegel's, for instance, they have disappeared altogether; but there remain the mythical values once ascribed to those ideal objects but now transferred and fettered to the sad realities that have appeared in their place. The titles of honour once bestowed on a fabled world are thus applied to the real world by right of inheritance.

Nothing could be clearer than the grounds on which pious men in the beginning recognise divine agencies. We see, they say, the hand of God in our lives. He has saved us from dangers, he has comforted us in sorrow. He has blessed us with the treasures of life, of intelligence, of affection. He has set around us a beautiful world, and one still more beautiful within us. Pondering all these blessings, we are convinced that he is mighty in the world and will know how to make all things good to those who trust in him. In other words, pious men discern God in the excellence of things. If all were well, as they hope it may some day be, God would henceforth be present in everything. While good is mixed with evil, he is active in the good alone. The pleasantness of life, the preciousness of human possessions, the beauty and promise of the world, are proof of God's power; so is the stilling of tempests and the forgiveness of sins. But the sin itself and the tempest, which optimistic theology has to attribute just as much to God's purposes, are not attributed to him at all by pious feeling, but rather to his enemies. In spite of centuries wasted in preaching God's omnipotence, his omnipotence is contradicted by every Christian judgment and every Christian prayer. If the most pious of nations is engaged in war, and suffers a great accidental disaster, such as it might expect to be safe from. *Te deums* are sung for those that were saved and *Requiems* for those that perished. God's office, in both cases, is to save only.

The criterion of divine activity could not be placed more squarely and unequivocally in the good. Plato and Aristotle are not in this respect better moralists than is an unsophisticated piety. God is the ideal, and what manifests the ideal manifests God. The proof and measure of rationality in the world, and of God's power over it, is the extent of human satisfactions. The existence of any evil—and if evil is felt it exists, for experience is its locus—is a proof that some accident has intruded into God's works. If that loyalty to the good, which is the prerequisite of rationality, is to remain standing, we must admit into the world, while it contains anything practically evil, a principle, however minimised, which is not rational. This irrational principle may be inertia in matter, accidental perversity in the will, or ultimate conflict of interests. Somehow an element of resistance to the rational order must be introduced somewhere. And immediately, in order to distinguish the part furnished by reason from its irrational alloy, we must find some practical test; for if we are to show that there is a great and triumphant rationality in the world, in spite of irrational accidents and brute opposition, we must frame an idea of rationality different from that of being. It will no longer do to say, with the optimists, the rational is the real, the real is the rational. For we wish to make a distinction, in order to maintain our loyalty to the good, and not to eviscerate the idea of reason by emptying it of its essential meaning, which is action addressed to the good and thought envisaging the ideal. To pious feeling, the free-will of creatures, their power, active or passive, of independent origination, is the explanation of all defects; and everything which is not helpful to men's purposes must be assigned to their own irrationality as its cause. Herein lies the explanation of that paradox in religious feeling which attributes sin to the free will, but repentance and every good work to divine grace. Physically considered—as theology must consider the matter—both acts and both volitions are equally necessary and involved in the universal order; but practical religion calls divine only what makes for the good. Whence it follows at once that, both within and without us, what is done well is God's doing, and what is done ill is not.

Thus what we may call the practical or Hebrew theory of cosmic rationality betrays in the plainest possible manner that reason is primarily a function of human nature. Reason dwells in the world in so far as the world is good, and the world is good in so far as it supports the wills it generates—the excellence of each creature, the value of its life, and the satisfaction of its ultimate desires.

CHAPTER 9

THE CHRISTIAN COMPROMISE

THE HUMAN spirit has not passed in historical times through a more critical situation or a greater revulsion than that involved in accepting Christianity. Was this event favourable to the Life of Reason? Was it a progress in competence, understanding, and happiness? Any absolute answer would be misleading. Christianity did not come to destroy; the ancient springs were dry already, and for two or three centuries unmistakable signs of decadence had appeared in every sphere, not least in that of religion and philosophy. Christianity was a reconstruction out of ruins. In the new world competence could only be indirect, understanding mythical, happiness surreptitious; but all three subsisted, and it was Christianity that gave them their necessary disguises.

The young West had failed in its first great experiment, for, though classic virtue and beauty and a great classic state subsisted, the force that had created them was spent. Was it possible to try again? Was it necessary to sit down, like the Orient, in perpetual flux and eternal apathy? This question was answered by Christianity in a way, under the circumstances, extremely propitious. The Gospel had drawn a very sharp contrast between this world and the kingdom of heaven—a phrase admitting many interpretations. From the Jewish millennium or a celestial paradise it could shift its sense to mean the invisible Church, or even the inner life of each mystical spirit. Platonic philosophy, to which patristic theology was allied, had made a contrast not less extreme between sense and spirit, between life in time and absorption in eternity. Armed with this double dualism, Christianity could preach both renunciation and hope, both asceticism and action, both the misery of life and the blessing of creation. It even enshrined the two attitudes in its dogma, uniting the Jewish doctrine of a divine Creator and Governor of this world with that of a divine Redeemer to lead us into another. Persons were not lacking to perceive the contradiction inherent in such an eclecticism; and it was the Gnostic

249

or neo-Platonic party, which denied creation and taught a pure asceticism, that had the best of the argument. The West, however, would not yield to their logic. It might, in an hour of trouble and weakness, make concessions to quietism and accept the cross, but it would not suffer the naturalistic note to die out altogether. It preferred an inconsistency, which it hardly perceived, to a complete surrender of its instincts. It settled down to the conviction that God created the world *and* redeemed it; that the soul is naturally good *and* needs salvation.

This contradiction can be explained exoterically by saying that time and changed circumstances separate the two situations: having made the world perfect, God redeems it after it has become corrupt; and whereas all things are naturally good, they may by accident lose their excellence, and need to have it restored. There is, however, an esoteric side to the matter. A soul that may be redeemed, a will that may look forward to a situation in which its action will not be vain or sinful, is one that in truth has never sinned; it has merely been thwarted. Its ambition is rational, and what its heart desires is essentially good and ideal. So that the whole classic attitude, the faith in action, art, and intellect, is preserved under this protecting cuticle of dogma; nothing was needed but a little courage, and circumstances somewhat more favourable, for the natural man to assert himself again. A people believing in the resurrection of the flesh in heaven will not be averse to a reawakening of the mind on earth.

Another pitfall, however, opens here. These contrasted doctrines may change rôles. So long as by redemption we understand, in the mystic way, exaltation above finitude and existence, because all particularity is sin, to be redeemed is to abandon the Life of Reason; but redemption might mean extrication from untoward accidents, so that a rational life might be led under right conditions. Instead of being like Buddha, the redeemer might be like Prometheus. In that case, however, the creator would become like Zeus—a tyrant will responsible for our conditions rather than expressive of our ideal. The doctrine of creation would become pantheism and that of redemption, formerly ascetic, would represent struggling humanity.

The seething of these potent and ambiguous elements can be studied nowhere better than in Saint Augustine. He is a more genial and complete representative of Christianity than any of the Greek

Fathers, in whom the Hebraic and Roman vitality was comparatively absent. Philosophy was only one phase of Augustine's
genius; with him it was an instrument of zeal and a stepping-stone
to salvation. Scarcely had it been born out of rhetoric when it was
smothered in authority. Yet even in that precarious and episodic
form it acquired a wonderful sweep, depth, and technical elaboration. He stands at the watershed of history, looking over either
land; his invectives teach us almost as much of paganism and
heresy as his exhortations do of Catholicism. To Greek subtlety he
joins Hebrew fervour and monkish intolerance; he has a Latin
amplitude and (it must be confessed) coarseness of feeling; but
above all he is the illumined, enraptured, forgiven saint. In him
theology, however speculative, remains a vehicle for living piety;
and while he has, perhaps, done more than any other man to materialise Christianity, no one was ever more truly filled with its spirit.

Saint Augustine's way of conceiving God is an excellent illustration of the power, inherent in his religious genius and sincerity,
of giving life and validity to ideas which he was obliged to borrow
in part from a fabulous tradition and in part from a petrified metaphysics. God, to him, was simply the ideal eternal object of human
thought and love. All ideation on an intellectual plane was a vague
perception of the divine essence. "The rational soul understands
God, for it understands what exists always unchanged." . . .
"God is happiness; and in him and from him and through him all
things are happy which are happy at all. God is the good and the
beautiful." He was never tired of telling us that God is not true
but the truth (*i.e.*, the ideal object of thought in any sphere), not
good but the good (*i.e.*, the ideal object of will in all its rational
manifestations). In other words, whenever a man, reflecting on his
experience, conceived the better or the best, the perfect and the
eternal, he conceived God, inadequately, of course, yet essentially,
because God signified the comprehensive ideal of all the perfections
which the human spirit could behold in itself or in its objects. Of
this divine essence, accordingly, every interesting thing was a
manifestation; all virtue and beauty were parcels of it, tokens of
its superabundant grace. Hence the inexhaustible passion of Saint
Augustine toward his God; hence the sweetness of that endless
colloquy in prayer into which he was continually relapsing, a passion and a sweetness which no one will understand to whom God is
primarily a natural power and only accidentally a moral ideal.

Herein lies the chief difference between those in whom religion is spontaneous and primary—a very few—and those in whom it is imitative and secondary. To the former, divine things are inward values, projected by chance into images furnished by poetic tradition or by external nature, while to the latter, divine things are in the first instance objective factors of nature or of social tradition. Theology, for those whose religion is secondary, is simply a false physics, a doctrine about eventual experience not founded on the experience of the past. Such a false physics, however, is soon discredited by events; it does not require much experience or much shrewdness to discover that supernatural beings and laws are without the empirical efficacy which was attributed to them. True physics and true history must always tend, in enlightened minds, to supplant those misinterpreted religious traditions. Therefore, those whose reflection or sentiment does not furnish them with a key to the moral symbolism and poetic validity underlying theological ideas, if they apply their intelligence to the subject at all, and care to be sincere, will very soon come to regard religion as a delusion. Where religion is primary, however, all that worldly dread of fraud and illusion becomes irrelevant, as it would be irrelevant to a mathematician's reasoning to suspect that Pythagoras was a myth and his supposed philosophy an abracadabra. To the religious man religion is inwardly justified. God has no need of natural or logical witnesses, but speaks himself within the heart, being indeed that ineffable attraction which dwells in whatever is good and beautiful, and that persuasive visitation of the soul by the eternal and incorruptible by which she feels herself purified, rescued from mortality, and given an inheritance in the truth. This is precisely what Saint Augustine knew and felt with remarkable clearness and persistence, and what he expressed unmistakably by saying that every intellectual perception is knowledge of God or has God's nature for its object.

The horror with which an idealistic youth at first views the truculence of nature and the turpitude of worldly life is capable of being softened by experience. Time subdues our initial preferences by showing us the complexity of moral relations in this world, and by extending our imaginative sympathy to forms of existence and passion at first repulsive, which from new and ultra-personal points of view may have their natural sweetness and value. In this way, Saint Augustine was ultimately brought to appreciate the catholicity and scope of those Greek sages who had taught that all being was to itself good, that evil was but the impediment of natural function, and that therefore the conception of anything totally or essentially evil was only a petulance or exaggeration in moral judgment that turned an incidental conflict of interests into a metaphysical opposition of natures. All definite being is in itself congruous with the true and the good, since its constitution is intelligible and its operation is creative of values. Were it not for the limitations of matter and the accidental crowding and conflict of life, all existing natures might subsist and prosper in peace and concord, just as their various ideas live without contradiction in the realm of conceptual truth. We may say of all things, in the words of the Gospel, that their angels see the face of God. Their ideals are no less cases of the good, no less instances of perfection, than is the ideal locked in our private bosom. It is the part of justice and charity to recognise this situation, in view of which we may justly say that evil is always relative and subordinate to some constituted nature in itself a standard of worth, a point of departure for the moral valuation of eventual changes and of surrounding things. Evil is accordingly accidental and unnatural; it follows upon the maladaptation of actions to natures and of natures to one another. It can be no just ground for the condemnation of any of those natural essences which only give rise to it by their imperfect realisation.

The Semitic idea of creation could now receive that philosophical interpretation which it so sadly needed. Primordially, and in respect to what was positive in them, all things might be instances of the good; in their essence and ideal state they might be said to be created by God. What was evil must, therefore, be carried up into another concept, must be referred, if you will, to another mythical agent; and this mythical agent in Saint Augustine's theology was named sin.

Everything in the world which obscured the image of the creator or rebelled against his commandments (everything, that is, which prevented in things the expression of their natural ideals) was due to sin. Sin was responsible for disease of mind and body, for all suffering, for death, for ignorance, perversity, and dulness. Sin was responsible—so truly *original* was it—for what was painful and wrong even in the animal kingdom, and sin was responsible for sin itself. The insoluble problems of the origin of evil and of freedom, in a world produced in its every fibre by omnipotent goodness, can never be understood until we remember their origin. They are artificial problems, unknown to philosophy before it betook itself to the literal justification of fables in which the objects of rational endeavour were represented as causes of natural existence. The former are internal products of life, the latter its external conditions. The cause of everything must have been the cause of sin, yet the principle of good could not be the principle of evil. Both propositions were obviously true, and they were contradictory only after the mythical identification of the God which meant the ideal of life with the God which meant the forces of nature.

The sad effects of this degradation of God into a physical power are not hard to trace in Augustine's own doctrine and feeling. He became a champion of arbitrary grace and arbitrary predestination to perdition. The eternal damnation of innocents gave him no qualms; and in this we must admire the strength of his logic, since if it is right that there should be wrong at all, there is no particular reason for stickling at the quantity or the enormity of it. And yet there are sentences which for their brutality and sycophancy cannot be read without pain—sentences inspired by this misguided desire to apologise for the crimes of the universe. "Why should God not create beings that he foreknew were to sin, when indeed in their persons and by their fates he could manifest both what punishment their guilt deserved and what free gifts he might bestow on them by his favour?" "Thinking it more lordly and better to do well even in the presence of evil than not to allow evil to exist at all." Here the pitiful maxim of doing evil that good may come is robbed of the excuse it finds in human limitations and is made the first principle of divine morality. Repellent and contorted as these ultimate metaphysical theories may seem, we must not suppose that they destroyed in Saint Augustine that practical and devotional idealism which they contradicted: the region of Christian charity is fortunately far wider and far nearer home than that of Christian apologetics. The work of practical redemption went on, while the dialectics about the perfection of the universe were forgotten; and Saint Augustine never ceased, by a happy inconsistency, to bewail the sins and to combat the heresies which his God was stealthily nursing, so that in their melodramatic punishment his glory might be more beautifully manifested.

It was Saint Augustine, as we know, who, in spite of his fervid Catholicism, was the favourite master of both Luther and Calvin. They emphasized, however, his more fanatical side, and this very predestinarian and absolutist doctrine which he had prevailed on himself to accept. Here was the pantheistic leaven doing its work; and concentration of attention on the Old Testament, given the reformers' controversial and metaphysical habit of thought, could only precipitate the inevitable. While popular piety bubbled up into all sorts of emotional and captious sects, each with its pathetic insistence on some text or on some whimsey, but all inwardly inspired by an earnest religious hunger, academic and cultivated Protestantism became every day more pale and rationalistic. Mediocre natures continued to rehearse the old platitudes and tread the slippery middle courses of one orthodoxy or another; but distinguished minds could no longer treat such survivals as more than allegories, historic or mythical illustrations of general spiritual truths. So Lessing, Goethe, and the idealists in Germany, and after them such lay prophets as Carlyle and Emerson, had for Christianity only an inessential respect. They drank their genuine inspiration directly from nature, from history, from the total personal apprehension they might have of life. In them speculative theology rediscovered its affinity to neo-Platonism; in other words, Christian philosophy was washed clean of its legendary alloy to become a pure cosmic speculation. It was Gnosticism come again in a very different age to men in an opposite phase of culture, but with its logic unchanged. The creation was the self-diremption of the infinite into finite expression, the fall was the self-discovery of this finitude, the incarnation was the awakening of the finite to its essential infinity; and here the matter generally hastened to a conclusion; for the redemption with its means of application, once the central point in Christianity, was less pliable to the new pantheistic interpretation.

The world of German absolutism, like the Stoic world, was not fallen. On the contrary, it was divinely inspired and altogether authoritative; he alone who did not find his place and function in it was unholy and perverse. This world-worship gives to impulse and fact, whatever they may be, liberty to flourish under a divine warrant. Were the people accepting such a system corrupt, it would sanction their corruption, and thereby, most probably, lead to its own abandonment, for it would bring on an ascetic and supernaturalistic reaction by which its convenient sycophancy would be repudiated. But reflection and piety, even if their object be material and their worship idolatrous, exalt the mind and raise it above vulgar impulse. If you fetch from contemplation a theoretic license to be base, your contemplative habit itself will have purified you more than your doctrine will have power to degrade you afresh, for training affects instinct much more than opinion can. Antinomian theory can flourish blamelessly in a puritan soil, for there it instinctively remains theoretical. And the Teutonic pantheists are for the most part uncontaminated souls, puritan by training, and only interested in furthering the political and intellectual efficiency of the society in which they live. Their pantheism under these circumstances makes them the more energetic and turns them into practical positivists, docile to their social medium and apologists for all its conventions. So that, while they write books to disprove naturalism in natural philosophy where it belongs, in morals where naturalism is treason they are themselves naturalists of the most uncritical description, forgetting that only the interests of the finite soul introduce such a thing as good and evil into the world, and that nature and society are so far from being authoritative and divine that they have no value whatever save by the services they may render to each spirit in its specific and genuine ambitions.

Indeed, this pantheistic subordination of conscience to what happens to exist, betrays its immoral tendency very clearly so soon as it descends from theological seminaries into the lay world. Poets at first begin to justify, on its authority, their favourite passions and to sing the picturesqueness of a blood-stained world. "Practical" men follow, deprecating any reflection which may cast a doubt on the providential justification of their chosen activities, and on the invisible value of the same, however sordid, brutal, or inane they may visibly be. Finally, politicians learn to invoke destiny and the movement of the age to save themselves the trouble of discerning rational ends and to colour their secret indifference to the world's happiness. The follies thus sanctioned theoretically, because they are involved in a perfect world, would doubtless be perpetrated none the less by the same persons had they absorbed in youth a different religion; for conduct is rooted in deep instincts which affect opinion more than opinion can avail to affect them in turn. Yet there is an added indignity in not preserving a clear and honest mind, and in quitting the world without having in some measure understood and appreciated it.

Pantheism is mythical and has all the subversive powers of ordinary superstition. It turns the natural world, man's stamping-ground and system of opportunities, into a self-justifying and sacred life. By this idealisation the affinity which natural conditions often have to man's interests may be brought out in a striking manner; but their total and real mechanism is no better represented than that of animals in Aesop's fables. To detect the divergence it suffices to open the eyes; and while nature may be rationally admired and cherished for so supporting the soul, it is her eventual ministry to man that makes her admirable, not her independent magnitude or antiquity. To worship nature as she really is, with all her innocent crimes made intentional by our mythology and her unfathomable constitution turned into a caricature of barbarian passions, is to subvert the order of values and to falsify natural philosophy. Yet this dislocation of reason, both in its conceptions and in its allegiance, is the natural outcome of thinking on mythical lines. A myth, by turning phenomena into expressions of thought and passion, teaches man to look for models and goals of action in that external world where reason can find nothing but instruments and materials.

CHAPTER 10

PIETY

HEBRAISM IS a striking example of a religion tending to discard mythology and magic. It was a Hebraising apostle who said that true religion and undefiled was to visit the fatherless and the widow, and do other works of mercy. Although a complete religion can hardly remain without theoretic and ritual expression, we must remember that after all religion has other aspects less conspicuous, perhaps, than its mythology, but often more worthy of respect. If religion be, as we have assumed, an imaginative symbol for the Life of Reason, it should contain not only symbolic ideas and rites, but also symbolic sentiments and duties. It is therefore time to turn from religious ideas to religious emotions, from imaginative history and science to imaginative morals.

Piety, in its nobler and Roman sense, may be said to mean man's reverent attachment to the sources of his being and the steadying of his life by that attachment. If we wish to live associated with permanent racial interests we must plant ourselves on a broad historic and human foundation, we must absorb and interpret the past which has made us, so that we may hand down its heritage reinforced, if possible, and in no way undermined or denaturalised. This consciousness that the human spirit is derived and responsible, that all its functions are heritages and trusts, involves a sentiment of gratitude and duty which we may call piety.

The true objects of piety are, of course, those on which life and its interests really depend: parents first, then family, ancestors, and country; finally, humanity at large and the whole natural cosmos. But had a lay sentiment toward these forces been fostered by clear knowledge of their nature and relation to ourselves, the dutifulness or cosmic emotion thereby aroused would have remained purely moral and historical. As science would not in the end admit any myth which was not avowed poetry, so it would not admit any piety which was not plain reason and duty. But man, in his perplexities and pressing needs, has plunged, once for all, into imaginative courses through which it is our business to follow him, to see if he

258

may not eventually reach his goal even by those by-paths and dark circumlocutions.

What makes piety an integral part of traditional religions is the fact that moral realities are represented in the popular mind by poetic symbols. The awe inspired by principles so abstract and consequences so remote and general is arrested at their conventional name. We have all read in boyhood, perhaps with derision, about the pious Æneas. His piety may have seemed to us nothing but a feminine sensibility, a faculty of shedding tears on slight provocation. But in truth Æneas's piety, as Virgil or any Roman would have conceived it, lay less in his feelings than in his function and vocation. He was bearing the Palladium of his country to a new land, to found another Troy, so that the blood and traditions of his ancestors might not perish. His emotions were only the appropriate expression of his priestly office. The hero might have been stern and stolid enough on his own martial ground, but since he bore the old Anchises from the ruins of Ilium he had assumed a sacred mission. Henceforth a sacerdotal unction and lyric pathos belonged rightfully to his person. If those embers, so religiously guarded, should by chance have been extinguished, there could never have been a Vestal fire nor any Rome. So that all that Virgil and his readers, if they had any piety, revered in the world had been hazarded in those legendary adventures. It was not Æneas's own life or private ambition that was at stake to justify his emotion. His tenderness, like Virgil's own, was ennobled and made heroic by its magnificent and impersonal object. It was truly an epic destiny that inspired both poet and hero.

If we look closer, however, we shall see that mythical and magic elements were requisite to lend this loftiness to the argument. Had Æneas not been Venus's son, had no prophetic instinct animated him, had no Juno been planning the rise of Carthage, how could the future destinies of this expedition have been imported into it, to lift it above some piratical or desperate venture?

Now, what supernatural machinery and heroic figures do for an epic poet piety does for a race. It endows it, through mythical and magic symbols, with something like a vision of its past and future. Religion is normally the most traditional and national of things. It embodies and localises the racial heritage. Commandments of the law, feasts and fasts, temples and the tombs associated with them, are so many foci of communal life, so many points for the dissemination of custom. The Sabbath, which a critical age might justify on hygienic grounds, is inconceivable without a religious sanction. The craving for rest and emotion expressed itself spontaneously in a practice which, as it established itself, had to be sanctioned by fables till the recurrent holiday, with all its humane and chastening influences, came to be established on supernatural authority. It was now piety to observe it and to commemorate in it the sacred duties and traditions of the race. In this function, of course, lay its true justification, but the mythical one had to be assigned, since the diffused prosaic advantages of such a practice would never avail to impose it on irrational wills. Indeed, had Æneas foreseen in detail the whole history of Rome, would not his faith in his divine mission have been considerably dashed? That celestial mission, those heavenly apparitions, those incalculable treasures carried through many a storm, abused Æneas's mind but served to nerve him for his real destiny. Yet his illusion was merely intellectual. The mission undertaken was truly worth carrying out. Piety thus came to bear the fruits of a good instinct.

Philosophers who harbour illusions about the status of intellect in nature may feel that this leadership of instinct in moral life is a sort of indignity, and that to dwell on it so insistently is to prolong satire without wit. But the leadership of instinct, the conscious expression of automatism, is not merely a necessity in the Life of Reason, it is a safeguard. Piety, in spite of its allegories, contains a much greater wisdom than a half-enlightened and pert intellect can attain. Natural beings have natural obligations, and the value of things for them is qualified by distance and by accidental material connections. Intellect would tend to gauge things impersonally by their intrinsic values, since intellect is itself a sort of disembodied and universal function; it would tend to disregard material conditions and that irrational substratum of reason without which reason would have no organs and no points of application. Piety, on the contrary, esteems things apart from their intrinsic worth, on account of their relation to the agent's person and fortune. Yet such esteem is perfectly rational, partiality in man's affections and allegiance being justified by the partial nature and local status of his life. Piety is the spirit's acknowledgment of its incarnation. So, in filial and parental affection, which is piety in an elementary form, there is a moulding of will and emotion, a check to irresponsible initiative, in harmony with the facts of animal reproduction. Every living creature has an intrinsic and ideal worth; he is the centre of actual and yet more of potential interests. But this moral value, which even the remotest observer must recognise in both parent and child, is not the ground of their specific affection for each other, which no other mortal is called to feel in their regard. This affection is based on the incidental and irrational fact that the one has this particular man for a father, and the other that particular man for a son. Yet, considering the animal basis of human life, an attachment resting on that circumstance is a necessary and rational attachment.

Piety is in a sense pathetic because it involves subordination to physical accident and acceptance of finitude. But it is also noble and eminently fruitful because, in subsuming a life under the general laws of relativity, it meets fate with simple sincerity and labours in accordance with the conditions imposed. It exercises the eminently sane function of calling thought home. It saves speculative and emotional life from hurtful extravagance by keeping it traditional and social.

Patriotism is another form of piety in which its natural basis and rational function may be clearly seen. It is normal to prefer our own country to all others, because we are children and citizens before we can be travellers or philosophers. Specific character is a necessary point of origin for universal relations: a pure nothing can have no radiation or scope. It is no accident for the soul to be embodied; her very essence is to express and bring to fruition the body's functions and resources. Its instincts make her ideals and its relations her world. A native country is a sort of second body, another enveloping organism to give the will definition. A specific inheritance strengthens the soul. Cosmopolitanism has doubtless its place, because a man may well cultivate in himself, and represent in his nation, affinities to other peoples, and such assimilation to them as is compatible with personal integrity and clearness of purpose. Plasticity to things foreign need not be inconsistent with happiness and utility at home. But happiness and utility are possible nowhere to a man who represents nothing and who looks out on the world without a plot of his own to stand on, either on earth or in heaven. He wanders from place to place, a voluntary exile, always querulous, always uneasy, always alone. His very criticisms express no ideal. His experience is without sweetness, without cumulative fruits, and his children, if he has them, are without morality. For reason and happiness are like other flowers—they wither when plucked.

The object most commonly associated with piety is the gods. Popular philosophy, inverting the natural order of ideas, thinks piety to the gods the source of morality. But piety, when genuine, is rather an incidental expression of morality. Its sources are perfectly natural. Mankind at large is also, to some minds, an object of piety. But this religion of humanity is rather a desideratum than a fact: humanity does not actually appear to anybody in a religious light. The *nihil homine homini utilius* remains a signal truth, but the collective influence of men and their average nature are far too mixed and ambiguous to fill the soul with veneration. Piety to mankind must be three-fourths pity. There are indeed specific human virtues, but they are those necessary to existence, like patience and courage. Supported on these indispensable habits, mankind always carries an indefinite load of misery and vice. Life spreads rankly in every wrong and impracticable direction as well as in profitable paths, and the slow and groping struggle with its own ignorance, inertia, and folly, leaves it covered in every age of history with filth and blood. It would hardly be possible to exaggerate man's wretchedness if it were not so easy to overestimate his sensibility. There is a *fond* of unhappiness in every bosom, but the depths are seldom probed; and there is no doubt that sometimes frivolity and sometimes sturdy habit helps to keep attention on the surface and to cover up the inner void. Certain moralists, without meaning to be satirical, often say that the sovereign cure for unhappiness is work. Unhappily, the work they recommend is better fitted to dull pain than to remove its cause. It occupies the faculties without rationalising the life. Before mankind could inspire even moderate satisfaction, not to speak of worship, its whole economy would have to be reformed, its reproduction regulated, its thoughts cleared up, its affections equalised and refined.

To worship mankind as it is would be to deprive it of what alone makes it akin to the divine—its aspiration. For this human dust lives; this misery and crime are dark in contrast to an imagined excellence; they are lighted up by a prospect of good. Man is not adorable, but he adores, and the object of his adoration may be discovered within him and elicited from his own soul. In this sense the religion of humanity is the only religion, all others being sparks and abstracts of the same. The indwelling ideal lends all the gods their divinity. No power, either physical or psychical, has the least moral prerogative nor any just place in religion at all unless it supports and advances the ideal native to the worshipper's soul.

There is, finally, a philosophic piety which has the universe for its object. This feeling, common to ancient and modern Stoics, has an obvious justification in man's dependence upon the natural world and in its service to many sides of the mind. Such justification of cosmic piety is rather obscured than supported by the euphemisms and ambiguities in which these philosophers usually indulge in their attempt to preserve the customary religious unction. For the more they personify the universe and give it the name of God the more they turn it into a devil. The universe, so far as we can observe it, is a wonderful and immense engine; its extent, its order, its beauty, its cruelty, makes it alike impressive. If we dramatise its life and conceive its spirit, we are filled with wonder, terror, and amusement, so magnificent is that spirit, so prolific, inexorable, grammatical, and dull. Like all animals and plants, the cosmos has its own way of doing things, not wholly rational nor ideally best, but patient, fatal, and fruitful. Great is this organism of mud and fire, terrible this vast, painful, glorious experiment. Why should we not look on the universe with piety? Is it not our substance? Are we made of other clay? All our possibilities lie from eternity hidden in its bosom. It is the dispenser of all our joys. We may address it without superstitious terrors; it is not wicked. It follows its own habits abstractedly; it can be trusted to be true to its word. Society is not impossible between it and us, and since it is the source of all our energies, the home of all our happiness, shall we not cling to it and praise it, seeing that it vegetates so grandly and so sadly, and that it is not for us to blame it for what, doubtless, it never knew that it did? Where there is such infinite and laborious potency there is room for every hope. If we should abstain from judging a father's errors or a mother's foibles, why should we pronounce sentence on the ignorant crimes of the universe, which have passed into our own blood? The universe is the true Adam, the creation the true fall; and as we have never blamed our mythical first parent very much, in spite of the disproportionate consequences of his sin, because we felt that he was but human and that we, in his place, might have sinned too, so we may easily forgive our real ancestor, whose connatural sin we are from moment to moment committing, since it is only the necessary rashness of venturing to be without foreknowing the price of the fruits of existence.

CHAPTER 11

SPIRITUALITY AND ITS CORRUPTIONS

IN HONOURING the sources of life, piety is retrospective. It collects, as it were, food for morality, and fortifies it with natural and historic nutriment. But a digestive and formative principle must exist to assimilate this nutriment; a direction and an ideal have to be imposed on these gathered forces. So that religion has a second and a higher side, which looks to the end toward which we move as piety looks to the conditions and to the sources of life. This aspiring side of religion may be called Spirituality. Spirituality is nobler than piety, because what would fulfil our being and make it worth having is what alone lends value to that being's source. Nothing can be lower or more wholly instrumental than the substance and cause of all things. The gift of existence would be worthless unless existence was good and supported at least a possible perfection. A man is spiritual when he lives in the presence of the ideal, and whether he eat or drink does so for the sake of a true and ultimate good.

There is no need that this ideal should be pompously or mystically described. A simple life is its own reward, and continually realises its function. Though a spiritual man may perfectly well go through intricate processes of thought and attend to very complex affairs, his single eye, fixed on a rational purpose, will simplify morally the natural chaos it looks upon and will remain free. This spiritual mastery is, of course, no slashing and forced synthesis of things into a system of philosophy which, even if it were thinkable, would leave the conceived logical machine without ideality and without responsiveness to actual interests; it is rather an inward aim and fixity in affection that knows what to take and what to leave in a world over which it diffuses something of its own peace. It threads its way through the landscape with so little temptation to distraction that it can salute every irrelevant thing, as Saint Francis did the sun and moon, with courtesy and a certain affectionate independence.

Spirituality likes to say, Behold the lilies of the field! For its secret has the same simplicity as their vegetative art; only spirituality has succeeded in adding consciousness without confusing instinct. This success, unfortunately so rare in man's life as to seem paradoxical, is its whole achievement. Spirituality ought to have been a matter of course, since conscious existence has inherent value and there is no intrinsic ground why it should smother that value in alien ambitions and servitudes. But spirituality, though so natural and obvious a thing, is subject, like the lilies' beauty, to corruption.

None the less, spirituality, or life in the ideal, must be regarded as the fundamental and native type of all life; what deviates from it is disease and incipient dissolution, and is itself what might plausibly demand explanation and evoke surprise. The spiritual man should be quite at home in a world made to be used; the firmament is spread over him like a tent for habitation, and sublunary furniture is even more obviously to be taken as a convenience. He cannot, indeed, remove mountains, but neither does he wish to do so. He comes to endow the mountains with a function, and takes them at that, as a painter might take his brushes and canvas. Their beauty, their metals, their pasturage, their defence—this is what he observes in them and celebrates in his addresses to them. The spiritual man, though not ashamed to be a beggar, is cognisant of what wealth can do and of what it cannot. His unworldliness is true knowledge of the world, not so much a gaping and busy acquaintance as a quiet comprehension and estimation which, while it cannot come without intercourse, can very well lay intercourse aside.

The spirit's foe in man has not been simplicity, but sophistication. His instincts, in becoming many, became confused, and in growing permanent, grew feeble and subject to arrest and deviation. Every peeping impulse would drop its dark hint and hide its head in confusion, while some pedantic and unjust law would be passed in its absence and without its vote. Means would be pursued as if they were ends, and ends, under the illusion that they were forces, would be expected to further some activity, itself without justification. So pedantry might be substituted for wisdom, tyranny for government, superstition for piety, rhetoric for reason.

This sophistication is what renders the pursuit of reason so perplexing and prolonged a problem. Half-formed adjustments in the brain and in the body politic are represented in consciousness by what are called passions, prejudices, motives, animosities. None of these felt ebullitions in the least understands its own causes, effects, or relations, but is hatched, so to speak, on the wing and flutters along in the direction of its momentary preference until it lapses, it knows not why, or is crossed and overwhelmed by some contrary power. Thus the vital elements, which in their comparative isolation in the lower animals might have yielded simple little dramas, each with its obvious ideal, its achievement, and its quietus, when mixed in the barbarous human will make a boisterous medley. For they are linked enough together to feel a strain, but not knit enough to form a harmony. In this way the unity of apperception seems to light up at first nothing but disunion. The first dawn of that rational principle which brings victory breaks upon a discovery of death. The consequence is that ideality seems to man something supernatural and almost impossible. He finds himself at his awakening so confused that he puts chaos at the origin of the world. But only order can beget a world or evoke a sensation. Chaos is something secondary, composed of conflicting organisations interfering with one another. It is compounded like a common noise out of jumbled vibrations, each of which has its period and would in itself be musical. The problem is to arrange these sounds, naturally so tuneful, into concerted music. So long as total discord endures human life remains spasmodic and irresolute; it can find no ideal and admit no total representation of nature. Only when the disordered impulses and perceptions settle down into a trained instinct, a steady, vital response and adequate preparation for the world, do clear ideas and successful purposes arise in the mind. The Life of Reason, with all the arts, then begins its career.

Must unworldliness be either fanatical or mystical? That is a question of supreme importance to the moral philosopher. On the answer to it hangs the rationality of a spiritual life; nay, the existence of spirituality itself among the types of human activity. For the fanatic and mystic are only spiritual in appearance because they separate themselves from the prevalent interests of the world, the one by a special persistent aggression, the other by a general passivity and unearthly calm. The fanatic is, notwithstanding, nothing but a worldling too narrow and violent to understand the world, while the mystic is a sensualist too rapt and voluptuous to rationalise his sensations. Both represent arrested forms of common-sense, partial developments of a perfectly usual sensibility. There is no divine inspiration in having only one passion left, nor in dreamfully accepting or renouncing all the passions together. Spirituality, if identified with such types, might justly be called primitive. There is an innocent and incredulous childishness, with its useless eyes wide open, just as there is a malevolent and peevish childishness, eaten up with some mischievous whim. The man of experience and affairs can very quickly form an opinion on such phenomena. He has no reason to expect superior wisdom in those quarters. On the contrary, his own customary political and humane stand-point gives him the only authoritative measure of their merits and possible uses. "These sectaries and dreamers," he will say to himself, "cannot understand one another nor the rôle they themselves play in society. It is for us to make the best of them we can, taking such prudent measures as are possible to enlist the forces they represent in works of common utility."

The philosopher's task, in these premises, is to discover an escape from wordliness which shall offer a rational advance over it, such as fanaticism and mysticism cannot afford. Does the Life of Reason differ from that of convention? Is there a spirituality really wiser than common-sense? That there is appears in many directions. Worldliness is arrest and absorption in the instrumentalities of life; but instrumentalities cannot exist without ultimate purposes, and it suffices to lift the eyes to those purposes and to question the will sincerely about its essential preferences, to institute a catalogue of rational goods, by pursuing any of which we escape worldliness. Sense itself is one of these goods. The sensualist at least is not worldly, and though his nature be atrophied in all its higher part, there is not lacking a certain internal and abstract spirituality in his experience. He is a sort of sprightly and incidental mystic, treating his varied succession of little worlds as the mystic does his monotonous universe. Sense, moreover, is capable of many refinements, by which physical existence becomes its own reward. In the disciplined play of fancy which the fine arts afford, the mind's free action justifies itself and becomes intrinsically delightful. Science not only exercises in itself the intellectual powers, but assimilates nature to the mind, so that all things may nourish it. In love and friendship the liberal life extends also to the heart. All these interests, which justify themselves by their intrinsic fruits, make so many rational episodes and patches in conventional life; but it must be confessed in all candour that these are but oases in the desert, and that as the springs of life are irrational, so its most vehement and prevalent interests remain irrational to the end. When the pleasures of sense and art, of knowledge and sympathy, are stretched to the utmost, what part will they cover and justify of our passions, our industry, our governments, our religion?

It was a signal error in those rationalists who attributed their ideal retrospectively to nature that they grotesquely imagined that people were hungry so that they might enjoy eating, or curious in order to delight in discovering the truth, or in love the better to live in conscious harmony. Such a view forgets that all the forces of life work originally and fundamentally *a tergo*, that experience and reason are not the ground of preference but its result. In order to live men will work disproportionately and eat all manner of filth without pleasure; curiosity as often as not leads to illusion, and argument serves to foster hatred of the truth; finally, love is notoriously a great fountain of bitterness and frequently a prelude to crime and death. When we have skimmed from life its incidental successes, when we have harvested the moments in which existence justifies itself, its profound depths remain below in their obscure commotion, depths that breed indeed a rational efflorescence, but which are far from exhausted in producing it, and continually threaten, on the contrary, to engulf it.

The spiritual man needs, therefore, something more than a cultivated sympathy with the brighter scintillation of things. He needs to refer that scintillation to some essential light, so that in reviewing the motley aspects of experience he may not be reduced to culling superciliously the flowers that please him, but may view in them all only images and varied symbols of some eternal good. That happy constitution which human life has at its best moments—that, says Aristotle, the divine life has continually. The philosopher thus expressed with absolute clearness the principle which the poets had been clumsily trying to embody from the beginning. Burdened as traditional faiths might be with cosmological and fanciful matter, they still presented in a conspicuous and permanent image that which made all good things good, the ideal and standard of all excellence. By the help of such symbols the spiritual man could steer and steady his judgment; he could say, according to the form religion had taken in his country, that the truly good was what God commanded, or what made man akin to the divine, or what led the soul to heaven. Such expressions, though taken more or less literally by a metaphysical intellect, did not wholly forfeit their practical and moral meaning. God, for a long time, was understood to command what in fact was truly important, the divine was long the truly noble and beautiful, heaven hardly ever ceased to respond to impersonal and ideal aspirations. Under those figures, therefore, the ideals of life could confront life with clearness and authority. The spiritual man, fixing his eyes on them, could live in the presence of ultimate purposes and ideal issues. Before each immediate task, each incidental pleasure, each casual success, he could retain his sweetness and constancy, accepting what good these moments brought and laying it on the altar of what they ought to bring.

CHAPTER 12

CHARITY

THOSE whom a genuine spirituality has freed from the foolish enchantment of words and conventions and brought back to a natural ideal, have still another illusion to vanquish, one into which the very concentration and deepening of their life might lead them. This illusion is that they and their chosen interests alone are important or have a legitimate place in the moral world. Having discovered what is really good for themselves, they assume that the like is good for everybody. Having made a tolerable synthesis and purification of their own natures, they require every other nature to be composed of the same elements similarly combined. What they have vanquished in themselves they disregard in others; and the consequence sometimes is that an impossibly simplified and inconsiderate regimen is proposed to mankind, altogether unrepresentative of their total interests. Spiritual men, in a word, may fall into the aristocrat's fallacy; they may forget the infinite animal and vulgar life which remains quite disjointed, impulsive, and short-winded, but which nevertheless palpitates with joys and sorrows, and makes after all the bulk of moral values in this democratic world.

After adopting an ideal it is necessary, therefore, without abandoning it, to recognise its relativity. The right path is in such a matter rather difficult to keep to. On the one hand lies fanatical insistence on an ideal once arrived at, no matter how many instincts and interests (the basis of all ideals) are thereby outraged in others and ultimately also in one's self. On the other hand lies mystical disintegration, which leads men to feel so keenly the rights of everything in particular and of the All in general, that they retain no hearty allegiance to any human interest. Between these two abysses winds the narrow path of charity and valour. The ultimate ideal is absolutely authoritative, because if any ground were found to relax allegiance to it in any degree or for any consideration, that ground would itself be the ideal, found to be more nearly absolute and ultimate than the one, hastily so called, which it corrected. The ultimate ideal, in order to maintain its finality and preclude the possibility of an appeal which should dislodge it from its place of authority, must have taken all interests into consideration; it must be universally representative. Now, to take an interest into consideration and represent it means to intend, as far as possible, to secure the particular good which that particular interest looks to, and never, whatever measures may be adopted, to cease to look back on the elementary impulse as upon something which ought, if possible, to have been satisfied, and which we should still go back and satisfy now, if circumstances and the claims of rival interests permitted.

Justice and charity are identical. To deny the initial right of any impulse is not morality but fanaticism. However determined may be the prohibition which reason opposes to some wild instinct, that prohibition is never reckless; it is never inconsiderate of the very impulse which it suppresses. It suppresses that impulse unwillingly, pitifully, under stress of compulsion and *force majeure;* for reason, in representing this impulse in the context of life and in relation to every other impulse which, in its operation, it would effect mechanically, rejects and condemns it; but it condemns it not by antecedent hate but by supervising wisdom. The texture of the natural world, the conflict of interests in the soul and in society, all of which cannot be satisfied together, is accordingly the ground for moral restrictions and compromises. Whatever the upshot of the struggle may be, whatever the verdict pronounced by reason, the parties to the suit must in justice all be heard, and heard sympathetically.

Herein lies the great difference between first-hand and second-hand morality. The retailers of moral truth, the town-criers that go shouting in the streets some sentence passed long ago in reason's court against some inadmissible desire, know nothing of justice or mercy or reason—three principles essentially identical. They thunder conclusions without remembering the premises, and expose their precepts to the aversion and neglect of all who genuinely love what is good. The masters of life, on the contrary, the first framers and discoverers of moral ideals, are persons who disregard those worn conventions and their professional interpreters: they are persons who have a fresh sense for the universal need and cry of human souls, and reconstruct the world of duty to make it fit better with the world of desire and of possible happiness. Primary morality inspired by love of something naturally good, is accordingly charitable and ready to forgive; while secondary morality, founded on prejudice, is fanatical and ruthless.

As virtue carries with it a pleasure which perfects it and without which virtue would evidently be spurious and merely compulsory, so justice carries with it a charity which is its highest expression, without which justice remains only an organised wrong. Of justice without charity we have a classic illustration in Plato's Republic and in general in the pagan world. An end is assumed, in this case an end which involves radical injustice toward every interest not included in it; and then an organism is developed or conceived that shall subserve that end, and political justice is defined as the harmonious adjustment of powers and functions within that organism. Reason and art suffice to discover the right methods for reaching the chosen end, and the polity thus established, with all its severities and sacrifices of personal will, is rationally grounded. The chosen end, however, is arbitrary, and, in fact, perverse; for to maintain a conventional city with stable institutions and perpetual military efficiency would not secure human happiness; nor (to pass to the individual virtue symbolised by such a state) would the corresponding discipline of personal habits, in the service of vested interests and bodily life, truly unfold the potentialities of the human spirit.

There is accordingly a justice deeper and milder than that of pagan states, a universal justice called charity, a kind of all-penetrating courtesy, by which the limits of personal or corporate interests are transgressed in imagination. Value is attributed to rival forms of life; something of the intensity and narrowness inherent in the private will is surrendered to admiration and solicitude for what is most alien and hostile to one's self. When this imaginative expansion ends in neutralising the will altogether, we have mysticism; but when it serves merely to co-ordinate felt interests with other actual interests conceived sympathetically, and to make them converge, we have justice and charity. Charity is nothing but a radical and imaginative justice. So the Buddhist stretches his sympathy to all real beings and to many imaginary monsters; so the Christian chooses for his love the diseased, the sinful, the unlovely. His own salvation does not seem to either complete unless every other creature also is redeemed and forgiven.

Such universal solicitude is rational, however, only when the beings to which it extends are in practical efficient relations with the life that would co-operate with theirs. In other words, charity extends only to physical and discoverable creatures, whose destiny is interwoven dynamically with our own. Absolute and irresponsible fancy can be the basis of no duty. If not to take other real forces and interests into account made classic states unstable and unjust, to take into consideration purely imaginary forces yields a polity founded on superstition, one unjust to those who live under it. A compromise made with non-existent or irrelevant interests is a wrong to the real interests on which that sacrifice is imposed gratuitously. All sacrifices exacted by mere religion have accordingly been inhuman; at best they have unintentionally made some amends by favouring abstract discipline or artistic forms of expression. The sacrifice must be fruitful in the end and bring happiness to somebody: otherwise it cannot long remain tender or beautiful.

Charity is seldom found uncoloured by fables which illustrate it and lend it a motive by which it can justify itself verbally. Metempsychosis, heaven and hell, Christ's suffering for every sinner, are notions by which charity has often been guided and warmed. Like myth everywhere, these notions express judgments which they do not originate, although they may strengthen or distort them in giving them expression. The same myths, in cruel hands, become goads to fanaticism. That natural sensitiveness in which charity consists has many degrees and many inequalities; the spirit bloweth where it listeth. Incidental circumstances determine its phases and attachments in life. Christian charity, for instance, has two chief parts: first, it hastens to relieve the body; then, forgetting physical economy altogether, it proceeds to redeem the soul. The bodily works of mercy which Christians perform with so much tact and devotion are not such as philanthropy alone would inspire; they are more and less than that. They are more, because they are done with a certain disproportionate and absolute solicitude, quite apart from ultimate benefit or a thought of the best distribution of energies; they are also less, because they stop at healing, and cannot pass beyond the remedial and incidental phase without ceasing to be Christian. The poor, says Christian charity, we have always with us; every man must be a sinner—else what obligation should he have to repent?—and, in fine, this world is essentially the kingdom of Satan. Charity comes only to relieve the most urgent bodily needs, and then to wean the heart altogether from mortal interests. Thus Christianity covers the world with hospitals and orphanages; but its only positive labours go on in churches and convents, nor will it found schools, if left to itself, to teach anything except religion. These offices may be performed with more or less success, with more or less appeal to the miraculous; but, with whatever mixture of magic and policy, Christian charity has never aimed at anything but healing the body and saving the soul.

Christ himself, we may well feel, did not affect publicans and sinners, ignorant people and children, in order to save them in the regimental and prescriptive fashion adopted by the Church. He commanded those he forgave to sin no more and those he healed to go, as custom would have it, to the priest. He understood the bright good that each sinner was following when he stumbled into the pit. For this insight he was loved. To be rebuked in that sympathetic spirit was to be comforted; to be punished by such a hand was to be made whole. The Magdalene was forgiven because she had loved much; an absolution which rehabilitates the primary longing that had driven her on, a longing not insulted but comprehended in such an absolution, and purified by that comprehension. It is a charitable salvation which enables the newly revealed deity to be absolutely loved. Charity has this art of making men abandon their errors without asking them to forget their ideals.

In Buddhism the same charity wears a more speculative form. All beings are to be redeemed from the illusion which is the fountain of their troubles. None is to be compelled to assume irrationally an alien set of duties or other functions than his own. Spirit is not to be incarcerated perpetually in grotesque and accidental monsters, but to be freed from all fatality and compulsion. The goal is not some more flattering incarnation, but escape from incarnation altogether. Ignorance must be enlightened, passion calmed, mistaken vocations revoked; only what the inmost being desiderates, only what can really quiet the longings of any particular will, is to occupy the redeemed mind. Here, though charity is truly understood, reason is wholly wanting; for it avails little to make of kindness a vicarious selfishness and to use neighbourly offices to plunge our neighbour deeper into his favourite follies. Such servile sympathy would make men one another's accomplices rather than friends. It would treat them with a weak promiscuous favour, not with true mercy and justice. In charity there can be nothing to repent of, as there so often is in natural love and in partisan propaganda. Christians have sometimes interpreted charity as zeal to bring men into their particular fold; or, at other times, when enthusiasm for doctrine and institutes has cooled, they have interpreted charity to be mere blind co-operation, no matter in what.

The Buddhists seem to have shown a finer sense in their ministry, knowing how to combine universal sympathy with perfect spirituality. There was no brow-beating in their call to conversion, no new tyranny imposed or sanctioned by their promised deliverance. If they could not rise to a positive conception of natural life, this inability but marks the well-known limitations of Oriental fancy, which has never been able to distinguish steadily that imagination which rests on and expresses material life from that which, in its import, breaks loose from the given conditions of life altogether, and is therefore monstrous and dreamful. But at least Buddhism knew how to sound the heart and pierce to the genuine principles of happiness and misery. If it did not venture to interpret reason positively, it at least forbore to usurp its inward and autonomous authority, and did not set up, in the name of salvation, some new partiality, some new principle of folly and illusion. In destroying worldliness this religion avoided imposture. The clearing it made in the soul was soon overgrown again by the inexorable Indian jungle; but had a virile intellect been at hand, it would have been free to raise something solid and rational in the space so happily swept clean of all accumulated rubbish.

Against avarice, lust, and rancour, against cruel and vain national ambitions, tenderer and more recollected minds have always sought some asylum; but they have seldom possessed enough knowledge of nature and of human life to distinguish clearly the genuine and innocent goods which they longed for, and their protest against "the world" has too often taken on a mystical and irrational accent. Charity, for instance, in its profounder deliverances, has become a protest against the illusion of personality; whereby existence and action seem to be wholly condemned after their principle has been identified with selfishness. An artificial puzzle is thus created, the same concept, selfishness or an irrational partiality and injustice in the will, being applied to two principles of action, the one wrong and the other necessary. Every man is necessarily the seat of his own desires, which, if truly fulfilled, would bring him satisfaction; but the objects in which that satisfaction may be found, and the forces that must co-operate to secure it, lie far afield, and his life will remain cramped and self-destructive so long as he does not envisage its whole basis and co-operate with all his potential allies.

The rationality which would then be attained is so immensely exalted above the microscopic vision and punctiform sensibility of those who think themselves practical, that speculative natures seem to be proclaiming another set of interests, another and quite miraculous life, when they attempt to thaw out and vivify the vulgar mechanism; and the sense of estrangement and contradiction often comes over the spiritually minded themselves, making them confess sadly that the kingdom of heaven is not of this world. As common morality itself falls easily into mythical expressions and speaks of a fight between conscience and nature, reason and the passions, as if these were independent in their origin or could be divided in their operation, so spiritual life even more readily opposes the ideal to the real, the revealed and heavenly truth to the extant reality, as if the one could be anything but an expression and fulfillment of the other. Being equally convinced that spiritual life is authoritative and possible, and that it is opposed to all that earthly experience has as yet supplied, the prophet almost inevitably speaks of another world above the clouds and another existence beyond the grave; he thus seeks to clothe in concrete and imaginable form the ideal to which natural existence seems to him wholly rebellious. Spiritual life comes to mean life abstracted from politics, from art, from sense, even in the end from morality. Natural motives and natural virtues are contrasted with those which are henceforth called supernatural, and all the grounds and sanctions of right living are transferred to another life. A doctrine of immortality thus becomes the favourite expression of religion. By its variations and greater or less transparency and ideality we can measure the degree of spiritual insight which has been reached at any moment.

CHAPTER 13

THE BELIEF IN A FUTURE LIFE

At no point are the two ingredients of religion, superstition and moral truth, more often confused than in the doctrine of immortality, yet in none are they more clearly distinguishable. Ideal immortality is a principle revealed to insight; it is seen by observing the eternal quality of ideas and validities, and the affinity to them native to reason or the cognitive energy of mind. A future life, on the contrary, is a matter for faith or presumption; it is a prophetic hypothesis regarding occult existences. This latter question is scientific and empirical, and should be treated as such. A man is, forensically speaking, the same man after the nightly break in his consciousness. After many changes in his body and after long oblivion, parcels of his youth may be revived and may come to figure again among the factors in his action. Similarly, if evidence to that effect were available, we might establish the resurrection of a given soul in new bodies or its activity in remote places and times. Evidence of this sort has in fact always been offered copiously by rumour and superstition. The operation of departed spirits, like that of the gods, has been recognised in many a dream, or message, or opportune succour. The Dioscuri and Saint James the Apostle have appeared—preferably on white horses—in sundry battles. Spirits duly invoked have repeated forgotten gossip and revealed the places where crimes had been committed or treasure buried. More often, perhaps, ghosts have walked the night without any ostensible or useful purpose, apparently in obedience to some ghastly compulsion that crept over them in death, as if a hesitating sickle had left them still hanging to life by one attenuated fibre.

The mass of this evidence, ancient and modern, traditional and statistical, is beneath consideration; the palpating mood in which it is gathered and received, even when ostensibly scientific, is such that gullibility and fiction play a very large part in it. When due allowance has been made, however, for legend and fraud, there remains a certain residuum of clairvoyance and telepathy, and an occasional abnormal obedience of matter to mind which might pass for magic. There are unmistakable indications that in these regions we touch lower and more rudimentary faculties. There seems to be, as is quite natural, a sub-human sensibility in man, wherein ideas are connected together by bonds so irrational and tenacious that they seem miraculous to a mind already trained in practical and relevant thinking.

Among the blind, the retina having lost its function, the rest of the skin is said to recover its primordial sensitiveness to distance and light, so that the sightless have a clearer premonition of objects about them than seeing people could have in the dark. So when reason and the ordinary processes of sense are in abeyance a certain universal sensibility seems to return to the soul; influences at other times not appreciable make then a sensible impression, and automatic reactions may be run through in response to a stimulus normally quite insufficient. Now the complexity of nature is prodigious; everything that happens leaves, like buried cities, almost indelible traces which an eye, by chance attentive and duly prepared, can manage to read, recovering for a moment the image of an extinct life. Symbols, illegible to reason, can thus sometimes read themselves out in trance and madness. Faint vestiges may be found in matter of forms which it once wore, or which, like a perfume, impregnated and got lodgment within it. Slight echoes may suddenly reconstitute themselves in the mind's silence; and a half-stunned consciousness may catch brief glimpses of long-lost and irrelevant things. Real ghosts are such reverberations of the past, exceeding ordinary imagination and discernment both in vividness and in fidelity; they may not be explicable without appealing to material influences subtler than those ordinarily recognised, as they are obviously not discoverable without some derangement and hypertrophy of the senses.

That such subtler influences should exist is entirely consonant with reason and experience; and while a new survey of the facts, in the light of natural science and psychology, is certainly not superfluous, it can be expected to lead to nothing but a more detailed and conscientious description of natural processes. The thought of employing such investigations to save at the last moment religious doctrines founded on moral ideas is a pathetic blunder; the obscene supernatural has nothing to do with rational religion. If it were discovered that wretched echoes of a past life could be actually heard by putting one's ear long enough to a tomb, and if (*per impossibile*) those echoes could be legitimately attributed to another mind, and to the very mind, indeed, whose former body was interred there, a melancholy chapter would indeed be added to man's earthly fortunes, since it would appear that even after death he retained, under certain conditions, a fatal attachment to his dead body and to the other material instruments of his earthly life. Obviously such a discovery would teach us more about dying than about immortality; the truths disclosed, since they would be disclosed by experiment and observation, would be psycho-physical truths, implying nothing about what a truly disembodied life might be, if one were attainable; for a disembodied life could by no possibility betray itself in spectres, rumblings, and spasms. Actual thunders from Sinai and an actual discovery of two stone tables would have been utterly irrelevant to the moral authority of the ten commandments or to the existence of a truly supreme being. No less irrelevant to a supramundane immortality is the length of time during which human spirits may be condemned to operate on earth after their bodies are quiet. In other words, spectral survivals would at most enlarge our conception of the soul's physical basis, spreading out the area of its manifestations; they could not possibly, seeing the survivals are physical, reveal the disembodied existence of the soul.

Such a disembodied existence, removed by its nature from the sphere of empirical evidence, might nevertheless be actual, and grounds of a moral or metaphysical type might be sought for postulating its reality. Life and the will to live are at bottom identical. Experience itself is transitive and can hardly arise apart from a forward effort and prophetic apprehension by which adjustments are made to a future confidently foreseen. A postulate acted on is an act of genuine and dogmatic faith. I not only postulate a morrow when I prepare for it, but ingenuously and heartily believe that the morrow will come. This faith does not amount to certitude; I may confess, if challenged, that before to-morrow I and the world and time itself might conceivably come to an end together; but that idle possibility, so long as it does not slacken action, will not disturb belief. Every moment of life accordingly trusts in life's continuance; and this prophetic interpretation of action, so long as action lasts, amounts to continual faith in futurity.

A sophist might easily transform this psychological necessity into a dazzling proof of immortality. To believe anything, he might say, is to be active; but action involves faith in a future and in the fruits of action; and as no living moment can be without this confidence, belief in extinction would be self-contradictory and at no moment a possible belief. The question, however, is not whether every given moment has or has not a specious future before it to which it looks forward, but whether the realisation of such foresight is incapable of failing. Now expectation, never without its requisite antecedents and natural necessity, often lacks fulfilment, and never anticipates its fulfilment entire; so that the necessity of a postulate gives no warrant for its prophetic authority. Expectation and action are constantly suspended together; and what happens whenever thought loses itself or stumbles might well happen at crucial times to that train of intentions which we call a particular life or the life of humanity. The prophecy involved in action is not insignificant, but it is notoriously fallible and depends for its fulfilment on physical conditions. The question accordingly really is whether a man expecting to live for ever or one expecting to die in his time has the more representative and trustworthy notion of the future. The question, so stated, cannot be solved by an appeal to evidence, which is necessarily all on one side, but only by criticising the value of evidence as against instinct and hope, and by ascertaining the relative status which assumption and observation have in experience.

The transcendental compulsion under which action labours of envisaging a future, and the animal instinct that clings to life and flees from death as the most dreadful of evils are the real grounds why immortality seems initially natural and good. Confidence in living for ever is anterior to the discovery that all men are mortals and to the discovery that the thinker is himself a man. These discoveries flatly contradict that confidence, in the form in which it originally presents itself, and all doctrines of immortality which adult philosophy can entertain are more or less subterfuges and after-thoughts by which the observed fact of mortality and the transcendental ignorance of death are more or less clumsily reconciled.

Many a man dies too soon and some are born in the wrong age or station. Could these persons drink at the fountain of youth at least once more they might do themselves fuller justice and cut a better figure at last in the universe. Most people think they have stuff in them for greater things than time suffers them to perform. To imagine a second career is a pleasing antidote for ill-fortune; the poor soul wants another chance. But how should a future life be constituted if it is to satisfy this demand, and how long need it last? It would evidently have to go on in an environment closely analogous to earth; I could not, for instance, write in another world the epics which the necessity of earning my living may have stifled here, did that other world contain no time, no heroic struggles, or no metrical language. Nor is it clear that my epics, to be perfect, would need to be quite endless. If what is foiled in me is really poetic genius and not simply a tendency toward perpetual motion, it would not help me if in heaven, in lieu of my dreamt-of epics, I were allowed to beget several robust children. In a word, if hereafter I am to be the same man improved I must find myself in the same world corrected. Were I transformed into a cherub or transported into a timeless ecstasy, it is hard to see in what sense I should continue to exist. Those results might be interesting in themselves and might enrich the universe; they would not prolong my life nor retrieve my disasters.

For this reason a future life is after all best represented by those frankly material ideals which most Christians—being Platonists—are wont to despise. It would be genuine happiness for a Jew to rise again in the flesh and live for ever in Ezekiel's New Jerusalem, with its ceremonial glories and civic order. It would be truly agreeable for any man to sit in well-watered gardens with Mohammed, clad in green silks, drinking delicious sherbets, and transfixed by the gazelle-like glance of some young girl, all innocence and fire. Amid such scenes a man might remain himself and might fulfil hopes that he had actually cherished on earth. He might also find his friends again, which in somewhat generous minds is perhaps the thought that chiefly sustains interest in a posthumous existence. But to recognise his friends a man must find them in their bodies, with their familiar habits, voices, and interests; for it is surely an insult to affection to say that he could find them in an eternal formula expressing their idiosyncrasy. When, however, it is clearly seen that another life, to supplement this one, must closely resemble it, does not the magic of immortality altogether vanish? Is such a reduplication of earthly society at all credible? And the prospect of awakening again among houses and trees, among children and dotards, among wars and rumours of wars, still fettered to one personality and one accidental past, still uncertain of the future, is not this prospect wearisome and deeply repulsive? Having passed through these things once and bequeathed them to posterity, is it not time for each soul to rest? The universe doubtless contains all sorts of experiences, better and worse than the human; but it is idle to attribute to a particular man a life divorced from his circumstances and from his body.

Dogmas about such a posthumous experience find some shadowy support in various illusions and superstitions that surround death, but they are developed into articulate prophecies chiefly by certain moral demands. One of these requires rewards and punishments more emphatic and sure than those which conduct meets with in this world. Another requires merely a more favourable and complete opportunity for the soul's development. Considerations like these are pertinent to moral philosophy. It touches the notion of duty whether an exact hedonistic retribution is to be demanded for what is termed merit and guilt: so that without such supernatural remuneration virtue, perhaps, would be discredited and deprived of a motive. It likewise touches the ideality and nobleness of life whether human aims can be realised satisfactorily only in the agent's singular person, so that the fruits of effort would be forthwith missed if the labourer himself should disappear.

To establish justice in the world and furnish an adequate incentive to virtue was once thought the chief business of a future life. The Hebraic religions somewhat overreached themselves on these points: for the grotesque alternative between hell and heaven in the end only aggravated the injustice it was meant to remedy. Life is unjust in that it subordinates individuals to a general impersonal law, and the deeper and longer hold fate has on the soul, the greater that injustice. A perpetual life would be a perpetual subjection to arbitrary power, while a last judgment would be but a last fatality. That hell may have frightened a few villains into omitting a crime is perhaps credible; but the embarrassed silence which the churches, in a more sensitive age, prefer to maintain on that wholesome doctrine—once, as they taught, the only rational basis for virtue—shows how their teaching has to follow the independent progress of morals. Nevertheless, persons are not wanting, apparently free from ecclesiastical constraint, who still maintain that the value of life depends on its indefinite prolongation. By an artifice of reflection they substitute vanity for reason, and selfish for ingenuous instincts in man. Being apparently interested in nothing but their own careers, they forget that a man may remember how little he counts in the world and suffer that rational knowledge to inspire his purposes. Intense morality has always envisaged earthly goods and evils, and even when a future life has been accepted vaguely, it has never given direction to human will or aims, which at best it could only proclaim more emphatically. It may indeed be said that no man of any depth of soul has made his prolonged existence the touchstone of his enthusiasms. Such an instinct is carnal, and if immortality is to add a higher inspiration to life it must not be an immortality of selfishness. What a despicable creature must a man be, and how sunk below the level of the most barbaric virtue, if he cannot bear to live for his children, for his art, or for country!

To turn these moral questions, however, into arguments for a physical speculation, like that about human longevity, resurrection, or metempsychosis, a hybrid principle is required: thus, even if we have answered those moral questions in the conventional way and satisfied ourselves that personal immortality is a postulate of ethics, we cannot infer that immortality therefore exists unless we import into the argument a tremendous optimistic postulate, to the effect that what is requisite for moral rationality must in every instance be realised in experience.

Such an optimistic postulate is made not only despite all experience but in ignorance of the conditions under which alone ideals are framed and retain their significance. Every ideal expresses individual and specific tendencies, proper at some moment to some natural creature; every ideal therefore has for its basis a part only of the dynamic world, so that its fulfilment is problematical and altogether adventitious to its existence and authority. To decide whether an ideal can be or will be fulfilled we must examine the physical relation between such organic forces as that ideal expresses and the environment in which those forces operate; we may then perceive how far a realisation of the given aims is possible, how far it must fail, and how far the aims in question, by a shift in their natural basis, will lapse and yield to others, possibly more capable of execution and more stable in the world. The question of success is a question of physics. To say that an ideal will be inevitably fulfilled simply because it is an ideal is to say something gratuitous and foolish. Pretence cannot in the end avail against experience.

Human life, lying as it does in the midst of a larger process, will surely not be without some congruity with the universe. Every creature lends potential values to a world in which it can satisfy some at least of its demands and learn, perhaps, to modify the others. Happiness is always a natural and an essentially possible thing, and a total despair, since it ignores those goods which are attainable, can express only a partial experience. But before considering what ways a disciplined soul might make its peace with reality, we may consider what an undisciplined soul in the first instance desires; and from this starting-point we may trace her chastening and education, observing the ideal compensations which may console her for lost illusions.

CHAPTER 14

IDEAL IMMORTALITY

IN ORDER to give the will to live frank and direct satisfaction, it would have been necessary to solve the problem of perpetual motion in the animal body, as nature has approximately solved it in the solar system. Nutrition should have continually repaired all waste, so that the cycle of youth and age might have repeated itself yearly * in every individual, like summer and winter on the earth. Nor are some hints of such an equilibrium altogether wanting. Convalescence, sudden good fortune, a belated love, and even the April sunshine or morning air, bring about a certain rejuvenescence in man prophetic of what is not ideally impossible—perpetuity and constant reinforcement in his vital powers. Had nature furnished the elixir of life, or could art have discovered it, the whole face of human society would have been changed. The earth once full, no more children would have been begotten and parental instincts would have been atrophied for want of function. All men would have been contemporaries and, having all time before them for travel and experiment, would have allied themselves eventually with what was most congenial to them and would have come to be bound only by free and friendly ties. They would all have been well known and would have acted perpetually in their ultimate and true character, like the immortal gods. One might have loved fixity, like Hestia, and another motion, like Hermes; a third might have been untiring in the plastic arts, like Hephæstus, or, like Apollo, in music; while the infinite realms of mathematics and academic philosophy would have lain open to spirits of a quality not represented in Homer's pantheon.

That man's primary and most satisfying ideal is something of this sort is clear in itself, and attested by mythology; for the great use of the gods is that they interpret the human heart to us, and help us, while we conceive them, to discover our inmost ambition and, while we emulate them, to pursue it. Christian fancy, because

* Or once in every century. Author's note, 1952.

of its ascetic meagreness and fear of life, has not known how to fill out the picture of heaven and has left it mystical and vague; but whatever paradise it has ventured to imagine has been modelled on the same primary ideal. It has represented a society of immortal beings among which there was no marriage nor giving in marriage and where each found his congenial mansion and that perfected activity which brings inward peace.

After this easy fashion were death and birth conquered in the myths, which truly interpreted the will to live according to its primary intention, but in reality such direct satisfaction was impossible. A total defeat, on the other hand, might have extinguished the will itself and obliterated every human impulse seeking expression. Man's existence is proof enough that nature was not altogether unpropitious, but offered, in an unlooked-for direction, some thoroughfare to the soul. Roundabout imperfect methods were discovered by which something at least of what was craved might be secured. The individual perished, yet not without having segregated and detached a certain portion of himself capable of developing a second body and mind. The potentialities of this seminal portion, having been liberated long after the parent body had begun to feel the shock of the world, could reach full expression after the parent body had begun to decay; and the offspring needed not itself to succumb before it had launched a third generation. A cyclical life or arrested death, a continual motion by little successive explosions, could thus establish itself and could repeat from generation to generation a process not unlike nutrition; only that, while in nutrition the individual form remains and the inner substance is renewed insensibly, in reproduction the form is renewed openly and the inner substance is insensibly continuous.

Reproduction seems, from the will's point of view, a marvellous expedient involving a curious mixture of failure and success. The individual, who alone is the seat and principle of will, is thereby sacrificed, so that reproduction is no response to his original hopes and aspirations; yet in a double way he is enticed and persuaded to be almost satisfied: first, in that so like a counterfeit of himself actually survives, a creature to which all his ideal interests may be transmitted; and secondly, because a new and as it were a rival aim is now insinuated into his spirit. For the impulse toward reproduction has now become no less powerful, even if less constant, than the impulse toward nutrition; in other words, the will to live finds itself in the uncongenial yet inevitable company of the will to have an heir. Reproduction thus partly entertains the desire to be immortal by giving it a vicarious fulfilment, and partly cancels it by adding an impulse and joy which, when you think of it, accepts mortality. For love, whether sexual, parental, or fraternal, is essentially sacrificial, and prompts a man to give his life for his friends. In thus losing his life gladly he in a sense finds it anew, since it has now become a part of his function and ideal to yield his place to others and to live afterwards only in them. While the primitive and animal side of him may continue to cling to existence at all hazards and to find the thought of extinction intolerable, his reason and finer imagination will build a new ideal on reality better understood, and be content that the future he looks to should be enjoyed by others. When we consider such a natural transformation and discipline of the will, when we catch even a slight glimpse of nature's resources and mysteries, how thin and verbal those belated hopes must seem which would elude death and abolish sacrifice! Such puerile dreams not only miss the whole pathos of human life, but ignore those specifically moral virtues which might console us for not being so radiantly divine as we may at first have thought ourselves. Nature, in denying us perennial youth, has at least invited us to become unselfish and noble.

A first shift in aspiration, a capacity for radical altruism, thus supervenes upon the lust to live and accompanies parental and social interests. The new ideal, however, can never entirely obliterate the old and primary one, because the initial functions which the old Adam exclusively represented remain imbedded in the new life, and are its physical basis. If the nutritive soul ceased to operate, the reproductive soul could never arise; to be altruistic we must first be, and spiritual interests can never abolish or cancel the material existence on which they are grafted. The consequence is that death, even when circumvented by reproduction and relieved by surviving impersonal interests, remains an essential evil. It may be accepted as inevitable, and the goods its intrusion leaves standing may be heartily appreciated and pursued; but something pathetic and incomplete will always attach to a life that looks to its own termination.

The effort of physical existence is not to accomplish anything definite but merely to persist for ever. The will has its first law of motion, corresponding to that of matter; its initial tendency is to continue to operate in the given direction and in the given manner. Inertia is, in this sense, the essence of vitality. To be driven from that perpetual course is somehow to be checked, and an external and hostile force is required to change a habit or an instinct as much as to deflect a star. Indeed, nutrition itself, hunting, feeding, and digestion, are forced activities, and the basis of passions not altogether congenial nor ideal. Hunger is an incipient faintness and agony, and an animal that needs to hunt, gnaw, and digest is no immortal, free, or essentially victorious creature. His will is already driven into by-paths and expedients; his primitive beatific vision has to be interrupted by remedial action to restore it for a while, since otherwise it would obviously degenerate rapidly through all stages of distress until its total extinction.

The tasks thus imposed upon the protoplasmic will raise it, we may say, to a higher level; to hunt is better sport, and more enlightening, than to lie imbibing sunshine and air; and to eat is, we may well think, a more positive and specific pleasure than merely to be. Such judgments, however, show a human bias. They arise from incapacity to throw off acquired organs. Those necessities which have led to the forms of life which we happen to exemplify, and in terms of which our virtues are necessarily expressed, seem to us, in retrospect, happy necessities, since without them our conventional goods would not have come to appeal to us. These conventional goods, however, are only compromises with evil, and the will would never have taken to pursuing them if it had not been dislodged and beaten back from its primary aims. Even food is, for this reason, no absolute blessing; it is only the first and most necessary of comforts, of restorations, of truces and reprieves in that battle with death in which an ultimate defeat is too plainly inevitable; for the pitcher that goes often to the well is at last broken, and a creature that is forced to resist his inward collapse by adventitious aids will some day find that these aids have failed him, and that inward dissolution has become, for some mechanical reason, quite irresistible. It is therefore not only the lazy or mystical will that chafes at the need of material supports and deprecates anxieties about the morrow; the most conventional and passionate mind, when it attains any refinement, confesses the essential servitude involved in such preoccupations by concealing or ignoring them as much as may be. We study to eat as if we were not ravenous, to win as if we were willing to lose, and to treat personal wants in general as merely compulsory and uninteresting matters. Why dwell, we say to ourselves, on our stammerings and failures? The intent is all, and the bungling circumlocutions we may be driven to should be courteously ignored, like a stammerer's troubles, when once our meaning has been conveyed.

Even animal passions are, in this way, afterthoughts and expedients, and although in a brutal age they seem to make up the whole of life, later it appears that they would be gladly enough outgrown, did the material situation permit it. Intellectual life returns, in its freedom, to the attitude proper to primitive will, except that through the new machinery underlying reason a more stable equilibrium has been established with external forces, and the freedom originally absolute has become relative to certain underlying adjustments, adjustments which may be ignored but cannot be abandoned with impunity. Original action, as seen in the vegetable, is purely spontaneous. On the animal level instrumental action is added and chiefly attended to, so that the creature, without knowing what it lives for, finds attractive tasks and a sort of glory in the chase, in love, and in labour. In the Life of Reason this instrumental activity is retained, for it is a necessary basis for human prosperity and power, but the value of life is again sought in the supervening free activity which that adjustment to physical forces, or dominion over them, has made possible on a larger scale. Every free activity would gladly persist for ever; and if any be found that involves and aims at its own arrest or transformation, that activity is thereby proved to be instrumental and servile, imposed from without and not ideal.

Not only is man's original effort aimed at living for ever in his own person, but, even if he could renounce that desire, the dream of being represented perpetually by posterity is no less doomed. Reproduction, like nutrition, is a device not ultimately successful. If extinction does not defeat it, evolution will. Doubtless the fertility of whatever substance may have produced us will not be exhausted in this single effort; a potentiality that has once proved efficacious and been actualised in life, though it should sleep, will in time revive again. In some form and after no matter what intervals, nature may be expected always to restore consciousness. But beyond this planet and apart from the human race, experience is too little imaginable to be interesting. No definite plan or ideal of ours can find its realisation except in ourselves. Accordingly, a vicarious physical immortality always remains an unsatisfactory issue; what is thus to be preserved is but a counterfeit of our being, and even that counterfeit is confronted by omens of a total extinction more or less remote. A note of failure and melancholy must always dominate in the struggle against natural death.

This defeat is not really problematical, or to be eluded by reviving ill-digested hopes resting entirely on ignorance, an ignorance which these hopes will wish to make eternal. We need not wait for our total death to experience dying; we need not borrow from observation of others' demise a prophecy of our own extinction. Every moment celebrates obsequies over the virtues of its predecessor; and the possession of memory, by which we somehow survive in representation, is the most unmistakable proof that we are perishing in reality. In endowing us with memory, nature has revealed to us a truth utterly unimaginable to the unreflective creation, the truth of mortality. Everything moves in the midst of death, because it indeed *moves*; but it falls into the pit unawares and by its own action unmakes and disestablishes itself, until a wonderful visionary faculty is added, so that a ghost remains of what has perished to reveal that lapse and at the same time in a certain sense to neutralise it. The more we reflect, the more we live in memory and idea, the more convinced and penetrated we shall be by the experience of death; yet, without our knowing it, perhaps, this very conviction and experience will have raised us, in a way, above mortality. That was a heroic and divine oracle which, in informing us of our decay, made us partners of the gods' eternity, and by giving us knowledge poured into us, to that extent, the serenity and balm of truth. As it is memory that enables us to feel that we are dying and to know that everything actual is in flux, so it is memory that opens to us an ideal immortality, unacceptable and meaningless to the old Adam, but genuine in its own way and undeniably true. It is an immortality in representation—a representation which envisages things in their truth as they have in their own day possessed themselves in reality. This is no subterfuge or superstitious effrontery, called to disguise or throw off the lessons of experience; on the contrary, it is experience itself, reflection itself, and knowledge of mortality. Memory does not reprieve or postpone the changes which it registers, nor does it itself possess a permanent duration; it is, if possible, less stable and more mobile than primary sensation. It is, in point of existence, only an internal and complex kind of sensibility. But in intent and by its significance it plunges to the depths of time; it looks still on the departed and bears witness to the truth that, though absent from this period of time, and incapable of returning to life, they nevertheless existed once in their own right, were as living and actual as existence is to-day, and still help to make up, in company with all past, present, and future mortals, the filling and value of the world.

As the pathos and heroism of life consists in accepting as an opportunity the fate that makes our own death, partial or total, serviceable to others, so the glory of life consists in accepting the knowledge of natural death as an opportunity to live in the spirit. The sacrifice, the self-surrender, remains real; for, though the compensation is real, too, and at moments, perhaps, apparently overwhelming, it is always incomplete and leaves beneath an incurable sorrow. Yet life can never contradict its basis or reach satisfactions essentially excluded by its own conditions. Progress lies in moving forward from the given situation, and satisfying as well as may be the interests that exist. And if some initial demand has proved hopeless, there is the greater reason for cultivating other sources of satisfaction, possibly more abundant and lasting. Now, reflection is a vital function; memory and imagination have to the full the rhythm and force of life. But these faculties, in envisaging the past or the ideal, envisage the eternal, and the man in whose mind they predominate is to that extent detached in his affections from the world of flux, from himself, and from his personal destiny. This detachment will not make him infinitely long-lived, nor absolutely happy, but it may render him intelligent and just, and may open to him all intellectual pleasures and all human sympathies.

There is accordingly an escape from death open to man; one not found by circumventing nature, but by making use of her own expedients in circumventing her imperfections. Memory, nay, perception itself, is a first stage in this escape, which coincides with the acquisition and possession of reason. When the meaning of successive perceptions is recovered with the last of them, when a survey is made of objects whose constitutive sensations first arose independently, this synthetic moment contains an object raised above time on a pedestal of reflection, a thought indefeasibly true in its ideal deliverance, though of course fleeting in its psychic existence. Existence is essentially temporal and life foredoomed to be mortal, since its basis is a process and an opposition; it floats in the stream of time, never to return, never to be recovered or repossessed. But ever since substance became at some sensitive point intelligent and reflective, ever since time made room and pause for memory, for history, for the consciousness of time, a god, as it were, became incarnate in mortality and some vision of truth, some self-forgetful satisfaction, became a heritage that moment could transmit to moment and man to man. This heritage is humanity itself, the presence of immortal reason in creatures that perish. Apprehension, which makes man so like a god, makes him in one respect immortal; it quickens his numbered moments with a vision of what never dies, the truth of those moments and their inalienable values.

To participate in this vision is to participate at once in humanity and in divinity, since all other bonds are material and perishable, but the bond between two thoughts that have grasped the same truth, of two instants that have caught the same beauty, is a spiritual and imperishable bond. It is imperishable simply because it is ideal and resident merely in import and intent. The two thoughts, the two instants, remain existentially different; were they not two they could not come from different quarters to unite in one meaning and to behold one object in distinct and conspiring acts of apprehension. Being independent in existence, they can be united by the identity of their burden, by the common worship, so to speak, of the same god. Were this ideal goal itself an existence, it would be incapable of uniting anything; for the same gulf which separated the two original minds would open between them and their common object. But being, as it is, purely ideal, it can become the meeting-ground of intelligences and render their union ideally eternal. Among the physical instruments of thought there may be rivalry and impact—the two thinkers may compete and clash—but this is because each seeks his own physical survival and does not love the truth stripped of its accidental associations and provincial accent. Doctors disagree in so far as they are not truly doctors, but, as Plato would say, seek, like sophists and wage-earners, to circumvent and defeat one another. The conflict is physical and can extend to the subject-matter only in so far as this is tainted by individual prejudice and not wholly lifted from the sensuous to the intellectual plane. In the ether there are no winds of doctrine. The intellect, being the organ and source of the divine, is divine and single; if there were many sorts of intellect, many principles of perspective, they would fix and create incomparable and irrelevant worlds. Reason is one in that it gravitates toward an object, called truth, which could not have the function it has, of being a focus for mental activities, if it were not one in reference to the operations which converge upon it.

This unity in truth, as in reason, is of course functional only, not physical or existential. The beats of thought and the thinkers are innumerable; indefinite, too, the variations to which their endowment and habits may be subjected. But the condition of spiritual communion or ideal relevance in these intelligences is their possession of a method and grammar essentially identical. Language, for example, is significant in proportion to the constancy in meaning which words and locutions preserve in a speaker's mind at various times, or in the minds of various persons. This constancy is never absolute. Therefore language is never wholly significant, never exhaustively intelligible. There is always mud in the well, if we have drawn up enough water. Yet in peaceful rivers, though they flow, there is an appreciable degree of translucency. So, from moment to moment, and from man to man, there is an appreciable element of unanimity, of constancy and congruity of intent. On this abstract and perfectly identical function science rests together with every rational formation.

The same function is the seat of human immortality. Reason lifts a larger or smaller element in each man to the plane of ideality according as reason more or less thoroughly leavens and permeates the lump. No man is wholly immortal, as no philosophy is wholly true and no language wholly intelligible; but only in so far as intelligible is a language a language rather than a noise, only in so far as true is a philosophy more than a vent for cerebral humours, and only in so far as a man is rational and lives in the eternal is he a mind and not a sensorium.

It is hard to convince people that they have such a gift as intelligence. If they perceive its animal basis they cannot conceive its ideal affinities or understand what is meant by calling it divine;

if they perceive its ideality and see the immortal essences that swim into its ken, they hotly deny that it is an animal faculty, and invent ultramundane places and bodiless persons in which it is to reside; as if those celestial substances could be, in respect to thought, any less material than matter or, in repect to vision and life, any less instrumental than bodily organs. It never occurs to them that if nature has added intelligence to animal life it is because they belong together. Intelligence is a natural emanation of vitality. If eternity could exist otherwise than as a vision in time, eternity would have no meaning for men in the world, while the world, men, and time would have no status in eternity.

By having a status in eternity is not meant being parts of an eternal existence, petrified or congealed into something real but motionless. What is meant is only that whatever exists in time, when bathed in the light of reflection, reveals an indelible character and discloses irreversible relations; every fact, in being recognised, takes its place in the universe of discourse, in that ideal sphere of truth which is the common and unchanging standard for all assertions. Language, science, art, religion, and all ambitious dreams are compacted of ideas. Life is as much a mosaic of notions as the firmament is of stars; and these ideal and transpersonal objects, bridging time, fixing standards, establishing values, constituting the true history of all living, are the very furniture of eternity, the goals and playthings of that reason which is an instinct in the heart as vital and spontaneous as any other. Or rather, perhaps, reason satisfies a supervening instinct by which all other instincts are interpreted, just as the *sensus communis* or transcendental unity of apperception is a faculty by which all perceptions are brought face to face and compared. So that immortality is not a privilege reserved for a part only of existence, but rather a relation pervading every part. We may, in leaving the subject, mark the phases of this ideal status of all events.

Animal sensation is related to eternity only by the truth that it has taken place. The fact, fleeting as it is, is registered in ideal history, and no inventory of the world's riches, no true confession of its crimes, would ever be complete that ignored that incident. This indefeasible character in experience makes a first sort of ideal immortality. It was a consolation to the Epicurean to remember that, however brief and uncertain might be his tenure of delight, the past was safe and the present sure. "He lives happy," says Horace, "and master over himself, who can say daily, I have lived. To-morrow let Jove cover the sky with black clouds or flood it with sunshine; he shall not thereby render vain what lies behind, he shall not delete and make never to have existed what once the hour has brought in its flight." Such self-concentration and hugging of the facts has no power to improve them; it gives to pleasure and pain an impartial eternity, and rather tends to intrench in sensuous and selfish satisfactions a mind that has lost faith in reason and that deliberately ignores the difference in scope and dignity which exists among various pursuits. Yet the reflection is staunch and in its way heroic; it meets a vague and feeble aspiration, that looks to the infinite, with a just rebuke; it points to real satisfaction, experienced successes, and asks us to be content with the fulfilment of our own wills. If you have seen the world, if you have played your game and won it, what more would you ask for? If you have tasted the sweets of existence, you should be satisfied; if the experience has been bitter, you should be glad that it comes to an end.

Of course, as we have seen, there is a primary demand in man which death and mutation contradict flatly, so that no summons to cease can ever be obeyed with complete willingness. Even the suicide trembles and the ascetic feels the stings of the flesh. It is the part of philosophy, however, to pass over those natural repugnances and overlay them with as much countervailing rationality as can find lodgment in a particular mind. The Epicurean, having abandoned politics and religion and being afraid of any far-reaching ambition, applied philosophy honestly enough to what remained. Simple and healthy pleasures are the reward of simple and healthy pursuits; to chafe against them because they are limited is to import a foreign and disruptive element into the case; a healthy hunger has its limit, and its satisfaction reaches a natural term. Philosophy, far from alienating us from those values, should teach us to see their perfection and to maintain them in our ideal. In other words, the happy filling of a single hour is so much gained for the universe at large, and to find joy and sufficiency in the flying moment is perhaps the only means open to us for increasing the glory of eternity.

Moving events, while remaining enshrined in this fashion in their permanent setting, may contain other and less external relations to the immutable. They may represent it. If the pleasures of sense are not cancelled when they cease, but continue to satisfy reason in that they once satisfied natural desires, much more will the pleasures of reflection retain their worth, when we consider that what they aspired to and reached was no momentary physical equilibrium but a permanent truth. As Archimedes, measuring the hypothenuse, was lost to events, being engaged in an event of much greater transcendence, so art and science interrupt the sense for change by engrossing attention in its issues and its laws. Old age often turns pious to look away from ruins to some other age where what ought to have been is not overtaken by decay before it has quite come to maturity. Lost in such self-transcending contemplations, the mind is weaned from mortal concerns. It forgets for a few moments a world in which it has so little more to do and so much, perhaps, still to suffer. As a sensation of pure light would not be distinguishable from light itself, so a contemplation of things not implicating earthly dates or places becomes, so far as its own deliverance goes, a timeless idea. Unconsciousness of temporal conditions and of the very flight of time makes the thinker sink for a moment into identity with timeless objects. And so immortality, in a second ideal sense, touches the mind.

The transitive phases of consciousness, however, have themselves a reference to eternal things. They yield a generous enthusiasm and love of good which is richer in consolation than either Epicurean self-concentration or mathematical ecstasy. Events are more interesting than the terms we abstract from them, and the forward movement of the will is something more intimately real than is the catalogue of our past experiences. Now the forward movement of the will is an avenue to the eternal. What would you have? What is the goal of your endeavour? It must be some success, the establishment of some order, the expression of some principle. Every attainment of perfection in an art—as for instance in government—makes a return to perfection easier for posterity, since there remains an enlightening precedent, together with faculties predisposed by discipline to recover their virtue.

Since the ideal has this perpetual pertinence to mortal struggles, he who lives in the ideal and leaves it expressed in society or in art enjoys a double immortality. The eternal has absorbed him while he lived, and when he is dead his influence brings others to the same absorption, making them, through that ideal identity with the best in him, reincarnations and perennial seats of all in him which he could rationally hope to rescue from destruction. He can say, without any subterfuge or desire to delude himself, that he shall not wholly die; for he will have a better notion than the vulgar of what constitutes his being. By becoming the spectator and confessor of his own death and of universal mutation, he will have identified himself with what is spiritual in all spirits and masterful in all apprehension; and so conceiving himself, he may truly feel and know that he is eternal.

IV

REASON IN ART

CHAPTER 1

THE BASIS OF ART

MAN EXISTS amid a universal ferment of being, and not only needs plasticity in his habits and pursuits but finds plasticity also in the surrounding world. Life is an equilibrium which is maintained now by accepting modification and now by imposing it. Since the organ for all activity is a body in relation to other material objects, objects which the creature's instincts often compel him to appropriate or transform, changes in his habits and pursuits leave their mark on whatever he touches. His habitat must needs bear many a trace of his presence, from which intelligent observers might infer something about his life and action. These vestiges of action are for the most part imprinted unconsciously and aimlessly on the world. They are in themselves generally useless, like footprints; and yet almost any sign of man's passage might, under certain conditions, interest a man. A footprint could fill Robinson Crusoe with emotion, the devastation wrought by an army's march might prove many things to a historian, and even the disorder in which a room is casually left may express very vividly the owner's ways and character.

Sometimes, however, man's traces are traces of useful action which has so changed natural objects as to make them congenial to his mind. Instead of a footprint we might find an arrow; instead of a disordered room, a well-planted orchard—things which would not only have betrayed the agent's habits, but would have served and expressed his intent. Such propitious forms given by man to matter are no less instrumental in the Life of Reason than are propitious forms assumed by man's own habit or fancy. Any operation which thus humanises and rationalises objects is called art.

Of all reason's embodiments art is therefore the most splendid and complete. Merely to attain categories by which inner experience may be articulated, or to feign analogies by which a universe may be conceived, would be but a visionary triumph if it remained ineffectual and went with no actual remodelling of the outer world, to render man's dwelling more appropriate and his mind better fed and more largely transmissible. Mind grows self-perpetuating only by its expression in matter. What makes progress possible is that rational action may leave traces in nature, such that nature in consequence furnishes a better basis for the Life of Reason; in other words progress is art bettering the conditions of existence. Until art arises, all achievement is internal to the brain, dies with the individual, and even in him spends itself without recovery, like music heard in a dream. Art, in establishing instruments for human life beyond the human body, and moulding outer things into sympathy with inner values, establishes a ground whence values may continually spring up; the thatch that protects from to-day's rain will last and keep out to-morrow's rain also; the sign that once expresses an idea will serve to recall it in future.

Not only does the work of art thus perpetuate its own function, but the process of art is teachable. Every animal learns something by living; but if his offspring inherit only what he possessed at birth, they have to learn life's lessons over again from the beginning, with at best some vague help given by their parents' example. But when the fruits of experience exist in the common environment, when new instruments, unknown to nature, are offered to each individual for his better equipment, although he must still learn for himself how to live, he may learn in a humaner school, where artificial occasions are constantly open to him for expanding his powers. Wherever there is art there is a possibility of training. A father who calls his idle sons from the jungle to help him hold the plough, not only inures them to labour but compels them to observe the earth upturned and refreshed, and to watch the germination there; their wandering thought, their incipient rebellions, will be met by the hope of harvest; and it will not be impossible for them, when their father is dead, to follow the plough of their own initiative and for their own children's sake. So great is the sustained advance in rationality made possible by art which, being embodied in matter, is teachable and transmissible by training; for in art the values secured are recognised the more easily for having been first enjoyed when other people furnished the means to them; while the maintenance of these values is facilitated by an external tradition imposing itself contagiously or by force on each new generation.

Art is action which transcending the body makes the world a more congenial stimulus to the soul. All art is therefore useful and practical, and the notable aesthetic value which some works of art possess, for reasons flowing for the most part out of their moral significance, is itself one of the satisfactions which art offers to human nature as a whole. Between sensation and abstract discourse lies a region of deployed sensibility or synthetic representation. This region, called imagination, has pleasures more airy and luminous than those of sense, more massive and rapturous than those of intelligence. The values inherent in imagination, in instant intuition, in sense endowed with form, are called aesthetic values; they are found mainly in nature and living beings, but often also in man's artificial works, in images evoked by language, and in the realm of sound.

Productions in which an aesthetic value is or is supposed to be prominent take the name of fine art; but the work of fine art so defined is almost always an abstraction from the actual object, which has many non-aesthetic functions and values. To separate the aesthetic element is more misleading than helpful; for neither in the history of art nor in a rational estimate of its value can the aesthetic function of things be divorced from the practical and moral. What had to be done was, by imaginative races, done imaginatively; what had to be spoken or made, was spoken or made fitly, lovingly, beautifully. Or, to take the matter up on its psychological side, the ceaseless experimentation and ferment of ideas, in breeding what it had a propensity to breed, came sometimes on figments that gave it delightful pause; these beauties were the first knowledges and these arrests the first hints of real and useful things. The rose's grace could more easily be plucked from its petals than the beauty of art from its subject, occasion, and use. An aesthetic fragrance, indeed, all things may have, if in soliciting man's senses or reason they can awaken his imagination as well; but this middle zone is so mixed and nebulous, and its limits are so vague, that it cannot well be treated in theory otherwise than as it exists in fact—as a phase of man's sympathy with the world he moves in. If art is that element in the Life of Reason which consists in modifying its environment the better to attain its end, art may be expected to subserve all parts of the human ideal, to increase man's comfort, knowledge, and delight. And as nature, in her measure, is wont to satisfy these interests together, so art, in seeking to increase that satisfaction, will work simultaneously in every ideal direction. Nor will any of these directions be on the whole good, or tempt a well-trained will, if it leads to estrangement from all other interests. The aesthetic good will be accordingly hatched in the same nest with the others, and incapable of flying far in a different air.

CHAPTER 2

RATIONALITY OF INDUSTRIAL ART

WHAT ANTECEDENT interest does mechanical art subserve? What is the initial and commanding ideal of life by which all industrial developments are to be proved rational or condemned as vain? If we look to the most sordid and instrumental of industries we see that their purpose is to produce a foreordained result with the minimum of effort. They serve, in a word, to cheapen commodities. But the value of such an achievement is clearly not final; it hangs on two underlying ideals, one demanding abundance in the things produced and the other diminution in the toil required to produce them. At least the latter interest may in turn be analysed further, for to diminish toil is itself no absolute good; it is a good only when such diminution in one sphere liberates energies which may be employed in other fields, so that the total human accomplishment may be greater. Doubtless useful labour has its natural limits, for if overdone any activity may impair the power of enjoying both its fruits and its operation. Yet in so far as labour can become spontaneous and in itself delightful it is a positive benefit; and to its intrinsic value must be added all those possessions or useful dispositions which it may secure. Thus one ideal—to diminish labour—falls back into the other—to diffuse occasions for enjoyment. The aim is not to curtail occupation but rather to render occupation liberal by supplying it with more appropriate objects.

It is then liberal life, fostered by industry and commerce or involved in them, that alone can justify these instrumental pursuits. Those philosophers whose ethics is nothing but sentimental physics like to point out that happiness arises out of work and that compulsory activities, dutifully performed, underlie freedom. Of course matter or force underlies everything; but rationality does not accrue to spirit because mechanism supports it; it accrues to mechanism in so far as spirit is thereby called into free existence; so that while values derive existence only from their causes, causes derive value only from their results. Functions cannot be exercised

305

until their organs exist and are in operation, so that what is primary in the order of genesis is always last and most dependent in the order of worth. Where reason exists life cannot, indeed, be altogether slavish; for any operation, however menial and fragmentary, when it is accompanied by ideal representation of the ends pursued and by felt success in attaining them, becomes a sample and anagram of all freedom. Neverthelss to arrest attention on a means is really illiberal, though not so much by what such an interest contains as by what it ignores. Happiness in a treadmill is far from inconceivable; but for that happiness to be rational the wheel should be nothing less than the whole sky from which influences can descend upon us. There would be meanness of soul in being content with a smaller sphere, so that not everything that was relevant to our welfare should be envisaged in our thoughts and purposes. To be absorbed by the incidental is the animal's portion; to be confined to the instrumental is the slave's. For though within such activity there may be a rational movement, the activity ends in a fog and in mere physical drifting. Happiness has to be begged of fortune or found in mystical indifference: it is not yet subtended by rational art.

The Aristotelian theory of slavery, in making servile action wholly subservient, sins indeed against persons, but not against arts. It sins against persons because there is inconsiderate haste in asserting that whole classes of men are capable of no activities, except the physical, which justify themselves inherently. The lower animals also have physical interests and natural emotions. A man, if he deserves the name, must be credited with some rational capacity: prospect and retrospect, hope and the ideal portraiture of things, must to some extent employ him. Freedom to cultivate these interests is then his inherent right. As the lion vindicates his prerogative to ferocity and dignity, so every rational creature vindicates his prerogative to spiritual freedom. But a too summary classification of individuals covers, in Aristotle, a just discrimination among the arts. In so far as a man's occupation is merely instrumental and justified only externally, he is obviously a slave and his art at best an evil necessity. For the operation is by hypothesis not its own end; and if the product, needful for some ulterior purpose, had been found ready made in nature, the other and self-justifying activities could have gone on unimpeded, without the arrest or dislocation which is involved in first establishing the needful conditions for right action. If air had to be manufactured, as dwellings must be, or breathing to be learned like speech, mankind would start with an even greater handicap and would never have come within sight of such goals as it can now pursue. Thus all instrumental and remedial arts, however indispensable, are pure burdens; and progress consists in abridging them as much as is possible without contracting the basis for moral life.

The action to which industry should minister is accordingly liberal or spontaneous action; and this is one condition of rationality in the arts. But a second condition is implicit in the first: freedom means freedom in some operation, ideality means the ideality of something vital and natural. Activity, achievement, a passage from prospect to realisation, is evidently essential to life. If all ends were already reached, and no art were requisite, life could not exist at all, much less a Life of Reason. No politics, no morals, no thought would be possible, for all these move towards some ideal and envisage a goal to which they presently pass. The transition is the activity, without which achievement would lose its zest and indeed its meaning; for a situation could never be achieved which had been given from all eternity. The ideal is a concomitant emanation from the natural and has no other possible status.

A creature like man, whose mode of being is a life of experience and not a congealed ideality, such as eternal truth might show, must accordingly find something to do; he must operate in an environment in which everything is not already what he is presently to make it. In the actual world this first condition of life is only too amply fulfilled; the real difficulty in man's estate, the true danger to his vitality, lies not in want of work but in so colossal a disproportion between demand and opportunity that the ideal is stunned out of existence and perishes for want of hope. The Life of Reason is continually beaten back upon its animal sources, and nations are submerged in deluge after deluge of barbarism. Impressed as we may well be by this ancient experience, we should not overlook the complementary truth which under more favourable circumstances would be as plain as the other: namely, that our deepest interest is after all to live, and we could not live if all acquisition, assimilation, government, and creation had been made impossible for us by their foregone realisation. All objects envisaged either in vulgar action or in the airiest cognition must be at first ideal and distinct from the given facts, otherwise action would have

lost its function at the same moment that thought lost its significance. All life would have collapsed into a purposeless trance.

The ideal requires, then, that opportunities should be offered for
realising it through action, and that transition should be possible
to it from a given state of things. One form of such transition is
art, where the ideal is a possible and more excellent form to be
given to some external substance or medium. Art needs to find a
material relatively formless which its business is to shape; and
this initial formlessness in matter is essential to art's existence. Were
there no stone not yet sculptured and built into walls, no sentiment
not yet perfectly uttered in poetry, no distance or oblivion yet to be
abolished by motion or inferential thought, activity of all sorts
would have lost its occasion. Matter, or actuality in what is only
potentially ideal, is therefore a necessary condition for realising an
ideal at all.

Art, in calling for materials, calls for materials plastic to its
influence and definitely predisposed to its ends. Unsuitableness in
the data far from grounding action renders it abortive, and no expedient could be more sophistical than that into which theodicy, in
its desperate straits, has sometimes been driven, of trying to justify
as conditions for ideal achievement the very conditions which make
ideal achievement impossible. The given state from which transition is to take place to the ideal must support that transition; so
that the desirable want of ideality which plastic matter should possess is merely relative and strictly determined. Art and reason find
in nature the background they require; but nature, to be wholly
justified by its ideal functions, would have to subserve them perfectly. It would have to offer to reason and art a sufficient and favourable basis; it would have to feed sense with the right stimuli
at the right intervals, so that art and reason might continually
flourish and be always moving to some new success. A poet needs
emotions and perceptions to translate into language, since these are
his subject-matter and his inspiration; but starvation, physical or
moral, will not help him to sing. One thing is to meet with the
conditions inherently necessary for a given action; another thing
is to meet with obstacles fatal to the same.

Out of this appears, with sufficient clearness, the rational function which the arts possess. They give, as nature does, a form to
matter, but they give it a form humanly more propitious. Such
success in art is possible only when the materials and organs at

hand are in a large measure already well disposed; for it can as little exist with a dull organ as with no organ at all, while there are winds in which every sail must be furled. Art depends upon profiting by a bonanza and learning to sail in a good breeze, strong enough for speed and conscious power but placable enough for dominion and liberty of soul. Then perfection in action can be attained and a self-justifying energy can emerge out of apathy on the one hand and out of servile and wasteful work on the other. Art has accordingly two stages: one mechanical or industrial, in which untoward matter is better prepared, or impeding media are overcome; the other liberal, in which perfectly fit matter is appropriated to ideal uses and endowed with a direct spiritual function. A premonition or rehearsal of these two stages may be seen in nature, where nutrition and reproduction fit the body for its ideal functions, whereupon sensation and cerebration make it a direct organ of mind. Industry merely gives nature that form which, if more thoroughly humane, she might have originally possessed for our benefit; liberal arts bring to spiritual fruition the matter which either nature or industry has prepared and rendered propitious. This spiritual fruition consists in the activity of turning an apt material into an expressive and delightful form, thus filling the world with objects which by symbolising ideal energies tend to strengthen and refine them.

CHAPTER 3

EMERGENCE OF FINE ARTS

ART LIES between two extremes. On the one side is purely spontaneous fancy, which would never foresee its own works and scarcely recognise or value them after they had been created; and on the other side is pure utility, which would deprive the work of all inherent ideality, and render it inexpressive of anything in man save his necessities. War, for instance, is an art when, having set itself an ideal end, it devises means of attaining it; but this ideal end has for its chief basis some failure in politics and morals. War marks a weakness and disease in human society, and its best triumphs are glorious evils—cruel and treacherous remedies, big with new germs of disease. War is accordingly a servile art and not essentially liberal; whatever inherent values its exercise may have would better be realised in another medium. Yet out of the pomp and circumstance of war fine arts may arise—music, armoury, heraldry, and eloquence. So utility leads to art when its vehicle acquires intrinsic value and becomes expressive. On the other hand, spontaneous action leads to art when it acquires a rational function. Thus utterance, which is primarily automatic, becomes the art of speech when it serves to mark crises in experience, making them more memorable and influential through their artificial expression; but expression is never art while it remains expressive to no purpose.

A good way of understanding the fine arts would be to study how they grow, now out of utility, now out of automatism. We should thus see more clearly how they approach their goal, which can be nothing but the complete superposition of these two characters. If all practice were art and all art perfect, no action would remain compulsory and not justified inherently, while no creative impulse would any longer be wasteful or, like the impulse to thrum, symptomatic merely and irrelevant to progress. The meanest arts are those which lie near the limit either of utility or of automatic self-expression. They become nobler and more rational as their utility is rendered spontaneous or their spontaneity beneficent.

310

The spontaneous arts are older than the useful, since man must live and act before he can devise instruments for living and acting better. Both the power to construct machines and the end which, to be useful, they would have to serve, need to be given an initial impulse. There is accordingly a vast amount of irresponsible play and loose experiment in art, as in imagination, before these gropings acquire a settled habit and function, and rationality begins. The farther back we go into barbarism the more we find life and mind busied with futilities; and though these indulgences may repel a cultivated taste and seem in the end cruel and monotonous, their status is really nearer to that of religion and spontaneous art than to that of useful art or of science. Ceremony, for instance, is compulsory in society and sometimes truly oppressive, yet its root lies in self-expression and in a certain ascendency of play which drags all life along into conventional channels originally dug out in irresponsible bursts of action. This occurs inevitably and according to physical analogies. Bodily organs grow automatically and become necessary moulds of life. We must either find a use for them or bear as best we may the idle burden they impose. Of such burdens the barbarian carries the greatest possible sum; and while he paints the heavens with his grotesque mythologies, he encumbers earth with inventions and prescriptions almost as gratuitous. The fiendish dances and shouts, the cruel initiations, mutilations, and sacrifices in which savages indulge, are not planned by them deliberately nor justified in reflection. Men find themselves falling into these practices, driven by a tradition hardly distinguishable from instinct. In its periodic fury the spirit hurries them into wars and orgies, quite as it kindles sudden flaming visions in their brains, habitually so torpid. The spontaneous is the worst of tyrants, for it exercises a needless and fruitless tyranny in the guise of duty and inspiration. Without mitigating in the least the subjection to external forces under which man necessarily labours, it adds a new artificial subjection to his own false steps and childish errors.

This mental vegetation, this fitful nervous groping, is nevertheless a sign of life, out of which art emerges by discipline and by a gradual application to real issues. An artist is a dreamer consenting to dream of the actual world; he is a highly suggestible mind hypnotised by reality. Even barbaric genius may find points of application in the world. These points will be more numerous the more open the eyes have been, the more docile and intelligent the mind is that gathers and renders back its impressions in a synthetic and ideal form. Intuition will then represent, at least symbolically, an actual situation. Grimace and gesture and ceremony will be modified by a sense of their effect; they will become artful and will transform their automatic expressiveness into ideal expression. They will become significant of what it is intended to communicate and important to know; they will have ceased to be irresponsible exercises and vents for passing feeling, by which feeling is dissipated, as in tears, without being made concrete and intellectual, as in a work of art.

The dance is an early practice that passes after this fashion into an art. A prancing stallion may transfigure his movements more beautifully than man is capable of doing; for the springs and limits of effect are throughout organic, and man, in more than one respect, would have to become a centaur before he could rival the horse's prowess. Human instinct is very imperfect in this direction, and grows less happy the more artificial society becomes; most dances, even the savage ones, are somewhat ridiculous. A rudimentary instinct none the less remains, which not only involves a sense of heightened and rhythmic motion, but also assures a direct appreciation of such motion when seen in others. The conscious agility, *fougue*, and precision which fill the performer become contagious and delight the spectator as well. There are indeed dances so ugly that, like those of contemporary society, they cannot be enjoyed unless they are shared; they yield pleasures of exercise only, or at best of movement in unison. But when man was nearer to the animal and his body and soul were in happier conjunction, when society, too, was more compulsive over the individual, he could lend himself more willingly and gracefully to being a figure in the general pageant of the world. The dance could then detach itself from its early association with war and courtship and ally itself rather to religion and art. From being a spontaneous vent for excitement, or a blind means of producing it, the dance became a form of discipline and conscious social control—a cathartic for the soul; and this by a quite intelligible transition. Gesture, of which the dance is merely a pervasive use, is an incipient action. It is conduct in the groping stage, before it has lit on its purpose, as can be seen unmistakably in all the gesticulation of love and defiance. In this way the dance is attached to life initially by its physiological origin. Being an incipient act, it naturally leads to its own completion and may arouse in others the beginnings of an appropriate response. Gesture is only less catching and less eloquent than action itself. But gesture, while it has this power of suggesting action and stimulating the response which would be appropriate if the action took place, may be arrested in the process of execution, since it is incipient only; it will then have revealed an intention and betrayed a state of mind. Thus it will have found a function which action itself can seldom fulfil. When an act is done, indications of what it was to be are superfluous; but indications of possible acts are in the highest degree useful and interesting. In this way gesture assumes the rôle of language and becomes a means of rational expression. It remains suggestive and imitable enough to convey an idea, but not enough to precipitate a full reaction; it feeds that sphere of merely potential action which we call thought; it becomes a vehicle for intuition.

Under these circumstances, to tread the measures of a sacred dance, to march with an army, to bear one's share in any universal act, fills the heart with a voluminous silent emotion. The massive suggestion, the pressure of the ambient will, is out of all proportion to the present call for action. Infinite resources and definite premonitions are thus stored up in the soul; and merely to have moved solemnly together is the best possible preparation for living afterwards, even if apart, in the consciousness of a general monition and authority.

Parallel to this is the genesis and destiny of music, an art originally closely intertwined with the dance. The same explosive forces that agitate the limbs loosen the voice; hand, foot, and throat mark their wild rhythm together. Birds probably enjoy the pulsation of their singing rather than its sound. Even human music is performed long before it is listened to, and is at first no more an art than sighing. The original emotions connected with it are felt by participation in the performance—a participation which can become ideal only because, at bottom, it is always actual. The need of exercise and self-expression, the force of contagion and unison, bears the soul along before an artistic appreciation of music arises; and we may still observe among civilised races how music asserts itself without any aesthetic intent, as when the pious sing hymns in common, or the sentimental, at sea, cannot refrain from whining their whole homely repertory in the moonlight. Here as elsewhere, instinct and habit are phases of the same inner disposition. What has once occurred automatically on a given occasion will be repeated in much the same form when a similar occasion recurs. Thus impulse, reinforced by its own remembered expression, passes into convention. Savages have a music singularly monotonous, automatic, and impersonal; they cannot resist the indulgence, though they probably have little pleasure in it. The same thing happens with customary sounds as with other prescribed ceremonies; to omit them would be shocking and well-nigh impossible, yet to repeat them serves no end further than to avoid a sense of strangeness or inhibition. These automatisms, however, in working themselves out, are not without certain retroactive effects: they leave the system exhausted or relieved, and they have meantime played more or less agreeably on the senses. The music we make automatically we cannot help hearing incidentally; the sensation may even modify the expression, since sensation too has its physical side. The expression is reined in and kept from becoming vagrant, in proportion as its form and occasion are remembered. The automatic performer, being henceforth controlled more or less by reflection and criticism, becomes something of an artist: he trains himself to be consecutive, impressive, agreeable; he begins to compare his improvisation with its subject and function, and thus he develops what is called style and taste.

CHAPTER 4

MUSIC

SOUND READILY acquires ideal values. It has power in itself to engross attention and at the same time may be easily diversified, so
as to become a symbol for other things. Its direct empire is to be
compared with that of stimulants and opiates, yet it presents to the
mind, as these do not, a perception that corresponds, part by part,
with the external stimulus. To hear is almost to understand. The
process we undergo in mathematical or dialectical thinking is called
understanding, because a natural sequence is there adequately translated into ideal terms. Logical connections are seen to be internally
justified, while only the fact that we perceive them here and now,
with more or less facility, is attributed to brute causes. Sound approaches this sort of ideality; it presents to sense something like
the efficacious structure of the object. It is almost mathematical;
but like mathematics it is adequate only by being abstract; and
while it discloses point by point one strain in existence, it leaves
many other strains, which in fact are interwoven with it, wholly
out of account. Music is accordingly, like mathematics, very nearly
a world by itself; it contains a whole gamut of experience, from
sensuous elements to ultimate intellectual harmonies. Yet this second existence, this life in music, is no mere ghost of the other; it
has its own excitements, its quivering alternatives, its surprising
turns; the abstract energy of it takes on so much body, that in progression or declension it seems quite as impassioned as any animal
triumph or any moral drama.

That a pattering of sounds on the ear should have such moment
is a fact calculated to give pause to those philosophers who attempt
to explain consciousness by its utility, or who wish to make physical
and moral processes march side by side from all eternity. Music is
essentially useless, as life is: but both have an ideal extension which
lends utility to its conditions. That the way in which idle sounds
run together should matter so much is a mystery of the same order
as the spirit's concern to keep a particular body alive, or to propa-

315

gate its life. Such an interest is, from an absolute point of view, wholly gratuitous; and so long as the natural basis and expressive function of spirit are not perceived, this mystery is baffling. Delight in music is liberal; it makes useful the organs and processes that subserve it. These agencies, when they support a conscious interest in their operation, give that operation its first glimmering justification, and admit it to the rational sphere. Just so when organic bodies generate a will bent on their preservation, they add a value and a moral function to their equilibrium. In vain should we ask for what purpose existences arise, or become important; that purpose, to be such, must already have been important to some existence; and the only question that can be asked or answered is what recognised importance, what ideal values, actual existences involve.

We happen to breathe, and on that account are interested in breathing; and it is no greater marvel that, happening to be subject to intricate musical sensations, we should be in earnest about these too. The human ear discriminates sounds with ease; what it hears is so diversified that its elements can be massed without being confused, or can form a sequence having a character of its own, to be appreciated and remembered. The eye too has a field in which clear distinctions and relations appear, and for that reason is an organ favourable to intelligence; but what gives music its superior emotional power is its rhythmic advance. Time is a medium which appeals more than space to emotion. Since life is itself a flux, and thought an operation, there is naturally something immediate and breathless about whatever flows and expands. The visible world offers itself to our regard with a certain lazy indifference. "Peruse me," it seems to say, "if you will. I am here; and even if you pass me by now and later find it to your advantage to resurvey me, I may still be here." The world of sound speaks a more urgent language. It insinuates itself into our very substance, and it is not so much the music that moves us as we that move with it. Its rhythms seize upon our bodily life, to accelerate or to deepen it; and we must either become inattentive altogether or remain enslaved.

The musical quality of sounds has a simple physical measure for its basis; and the rate of vibration is complicated by its sweep or loudness, and by concomitant sounds. What a rich note is to a pure and thin one, that a chord is to a note; nor is melody wholly different in principle, for it is a chord rendered piecemeal. Time inter-

REASON IN ART   317

venes, and the harmony is deployed; so that in melody rhythm is added, with its immense appeal, to the cumulative effect already secured by rendering many notes together. The heightened effect which a note gets by figuring in a phrase, or a phrase in a longer passage, comes of course from the tensions established and surviving in the sensorium—a case, differently shaded, of chords and overtones. The difference is only that the more emphatic parts of the melody survive clearly to the end, while the detail, which if perceived might now clash, is largely lost, and out of the preceding parts perhaps nothing but a certain swing and potency is present at the close. The mind has been raked and set vibrating in an unusual fashion, so that the *finale* comes like a fulfilment after much premonition and desire, whereas the same event, unprepared for, might hardly have been observed. The whole technique of music is but an immense elaboration of this principle. It deploys a sensuous harmony by a sort of dialectic, suspending and revolving it, so that the parts become distinct and their relation vital.

Such elaboration often exceeds the synthetic power of all but the best trained minds. Both in scope and in articulation musical appreciation varies prodigiously. There is no fixed limit to the power of sustaining a given conscious process while new features appear in the same field; nor is there any fixed limit to the power of recovering, in a changed context, a process that was formerly suspended. A whole symphony might be felt at once, if the musician's power of sustained or cumulative hearing could stretch so far. What is tedious and formless to the inattentive may seem a perfect whole to one who, as they say, takes it all in; and similarly what is a frightful deafening discord to a sense incapable of discrimination, for one who can hear the parts may break into a celestial chorus. A musical education is necessary for musical judgment. What most people relish is hardly music; it is rather a drowsy revery relieved by nervous thrills.

Beneath its hypnotic power music, for the musician, has an intellectual essence. Out of simple chords and melodies, which at first catch only the ear, he weaves elaborate compositions that by their form appeal also to the mind. This side of music resembles a richer versification; it may be compared also to mathematics or to arabesques. A moving arabesque that has a vital dimension, an audible mathematics, adding sense to form, and a versification that, since it has no subject-matter, cannot do violence to it by its complex

artifices—these are types of pure living, altogether joyful and delightful things. They combine life with order, precision with spontaneity; the flux in them has become rhythmical and its freedom
has passed into a rational choice, since it has come in sight of the
eternal form it would embody. The musician, like an architect or
goldsmith working in sound, but freer than they from material
trammels, can expand for ever his yielding labyrinth; every step
opens up new vistas, every decision—how unlike those made in real
life!—multiplies opportunities, and widens the horizon before him,
without preventing him from going back at will to begin afresh at
any point, to trace the other possible paths leading thence through
various magic landscapes. Pure music is pure art. Its extreme abstraction is balanced by its entire spontaneity, and, while it has no
external significance, it bears no internal curse. It is something to
which a few spirits may well surrender themselves, sure that in a
liberal commonwealth they will be thanked for their ideal labour,
the fruits of which many may enjoy. Such excursions into ultramundane regions, where order is free, refine the mind and make it
familiar with perfection. By analogy an ideal form comes to be
conceived and desiderated in other regions, where it is not produced so readily, and the music heard, as the Pythagoreans hoped,
makes the soul also musical.

It must be confessed, however, that a world of sounds and
rhythms, all about nothing, is a by-world and a mere distraction for
a political animal. Its substance is air, though the spell of it may
have moral affinities. Nevertheless this ethereal art may be enticed
to earth and married with what is mortal. Music interests humanity
most when it is wedded to human events. The alliance comes about
through the emotions which music and life arouse in common. For
sound, in sweeping through the body and making felt there its ki-
netic and potential stress, provokes no less interest than does any
other physical event or premonition. Music can produce emotion as
directly as can fighting or love. If in the latter instances the body's
whole life may be in jeopardy, this fact is no explanation of our
concern; for many a danger is not felt and there is no magic in
the body's future condition, that it should now affect the soul.
What touches the soul is the body's condition at the moment; and
this is altered no less truly by a musical impression than by some
protective or reproductive act. If emotions accompany the latter,
they might as well accompany the former; and in fact they do. Nor

is music the only idle cerebral commotion that enlists attention and presents issues no less momentous for being quite imaginary; dreams do the same, and seldom can the real crises of life so absorb the soul, or prompt it to such extreme efforts, as can delirium in sickness, or delusion in what passes for health.

There is enough likeness, however, between musical and mundane feeling for the first to be used in entertaining the second. Hence the singular privilege of this art: to give form to what is naturally inarticulate, and express those depths of human nature which can speak no language current in the world. Emotion is primarily about nothing, and much of it remains about nothing to the end. What rescues a part of our passions from this pathological plight, and gives them some other function than merely to be, is the ideal relevance, the practical and mutually representative character, which they sometimes acquire. All experience is pathological if we consider its ground; but a part of it is also rational if we consider its import. The words I am now writing have a meaning only if this moment's product can meet and conspire with some other thought speaking of what elsewhere exists, and uttering an intuition that from time to time may be actually recovered. The art of distributing interest among the occasions and vistas of life so as to lend them a constant worth, and at the same time to give feeling an ideal object, is at bottom the sole business of education; but the undertaking is long, and much feeling remains unemployed and unaccounted for. This objectless emotion chokes the heart with its dull importunity; now it impedes right action, now it feeds and fattens illusion. Much of it radiates from primary functions which, though their operation is half known, have only base or pitiful associations in human life; so that they trouble us with deep and subtle cravings, the unclaimed *Hinterland* of life. When music, either by verbal indications or by sensuous affinities, or by both at once, succeeds in tapping this fund of suppressed feeling, it accordingly supplies a great need. It makes the dumb speak, and plucks from the animal heart potentialities of expression which might render it, perhaps, even more than human.

By its emotional range music is appropriate to all intense occasions: we dance, pray, and mourn to music, and the more inadequate words or external acts are to our predicament, the more grateful music is. As the only bond between music and life is emotion, music is out of place only where emotion itself is absent.

If it breaks in upon us in the midst of study or business it becomes an interruption or alternative to our activity, rather than an expression of it; we must either remain inattentive or pass altogether into the realm of sound (which may be unemotional enough) and become musicians for the nonce. Music brings its sympathetic ministry only to emotional moments; there it merges with common existence, and is a welcome substitute for descriptive ideas, since it co-operates with us and helps to deliver us from dumb subjection to influences which we should not know how to express otherwise. There is often in what moves us a certain ruthless persistence, together with a certain poverty of form; the power felt is out of proportion to the interest awakened, and attention is kept, as in pain, at once strained and idle. At such a moment music is a blessed resource. Without attempting to remove a mood that is perhaps inevitable, it gives it a congruous filling. Thus the mood is justified by an illustration or expression which seems to offer some objective and ideal ground for its existence; and the mood is at the same time relieved by absorption in that impersonal object. So entertained, the feeling settles. The passion to which at first we succumbed is now tamed and appropriated. We have digested the foreign substance in giving it a rational form: its energies are merged in that strength by which we freely operate.

In this way the most abstract of arts serves the dumbest emotions. Matter which cannot enter the moulds of ordinary perception, capacities which a ruling instinct usually keeps under, flow suddenly into this new channel. Music is like those branches which some trees put forth close to the ground, far below the point where the other boughs separate; almost a tree by itself, it has nothing but the root in common with its parent. Somewhat in this fashion music diverts into an abstract sphere a part of those forces which abound beneath the point at which human understanding grows articulate. It flourishes on saps which other branches of ideation are too narrow or rigid to take up. Those elementary substances the musician can spiritualise by his special methods, taking away their reproach and redeeming them from blind intensity.

There is consequently in music a sort of Christian piety, in that it comes not to call the just but sinners to repentance, and understands the spiritual possibilities in outcasts from the respectable world. If we look at things absolutely enough, and from their own point of view, there can be no doubt that each has its own ideal and does not question its own justification. Lust and frenzy, reverie or despair, fatal as they may be to a creature that has general ulterior interests, are not perverse in themselves: each searches for its own affinities, and has a kind of inertia which tends to maintain it in being, and to attach or draw in whatever is propitious to it. Feelings are as blameless as so many forms of vegetation; they can be poisonous only to a different life. Many ill-suppressed possibilities endure in matter, and peep into being through the crevices, as it were, of the dominant world. Weeds they are called by the tyrant, but in themselves they are aware of being potential gods. Why should not every impulse expand in a congenial paradise? Why should each, made evil now only by an adventitious appellation or a contrary fate, not vindicate its own ideal? If there is a piety towards things deformed, how much more should there be a piety towards things altogether lovely, when it is only space and matter that are wanting for their perfect realisation?

Philosophers talk of self-contradiction, but there is evidently no such thing, if we take for the self what is really vital, each propulsive, definite strain of being, each nucleus for estimation and for pleasure and pain. Each impulse may be contradicted, but not by itself; it may find itself opposed, in a theatre which it has entered it knows not how, by violent personages that it has never wished to encounter. The environment it calls for is congenial with it; and by that environment it could never be thwarted or condemned. Moral judgments and conflicts are possible only in the mind that represents many interests synthetically: in nature, where primary impulses collide, all conflict is physical and all will innocent.

Man possesses, for example, a native capacity for joy. There are moments, in friendship or in solitude, when joy is realised; but the occasions are often trivial and could never justify in reflection the feelings that then happen to bubble up. Nor can pure joy be long sustained: cross-currents of lassitude or anxiety, distracting incidents, irrelevant associations, trouble its course and make it languish, turning it before long into dulness or melancholy. Language cannot express a joy that shall be full and pure; for to keep the purity nothing would have to be named which carried the least suggestion of sadness with it, and, in the world that human language refers to, such a condition would exclude every situation possible. "O joy, O joy," would be the whole ditty: hence some dialecticians, whose experience is largely verbal, think whatever is pure necessarily thin. Music, on the contrary, has a more flexible measure. The joy condemned by practical exigencies to scintillate for a moment uncommunicated, and then, as it were, to be buried alive, may now find an abstract art to embody it and bring it before the public, formed into a rich and constant object called a musical composition. So art succeeds in vindicating the forgotten regions of spirit: a new spontaneous creation shows how little authority or finality the given creation has.

What is true of joy is no less true of sorrow, which, though it arises from failure in some natural desire, carries with it a sentimental ideal of its own. Even confusion can find in music an expression and a catharsis. That death or change should grieve does not follow from the material nature of these phenomena. To change or to disappear might be as normal a tendency as to move; and it actually happens, when nothing ideal has been attained, that *not to be thus* is the whole law of being. There is then a nameless satisfaction in passing on; which is the virtual ideal of pain and mere willing. Death and change acquire a tragic character when they invade a mind which is not ready for them in all its parts, so that those elements in it which are still vigorous, and would maintain somewhat longer their ideal identity, suffer violence at the hands of the others, already mastered by decay and willing to be self-destructive. Thus a man whose physiological complexion involves more poignant emotion than his ideas can absorb—one who is sentimental—will yearn for new objects that may explain, embody, and focus his dumb feelings; and these objects, if art can produce them, will relieve and glorify those feelings in the act of expressing them. Catharsis is nothing more.

There would be no pleasure in expressing pain, if pain were not dominated through its expression. To know how just a cause we have for grieving is already a consolation, for it is already a shift from feeling to understanding. By such consideration of a passion, the intellectual powers turn it into subject-matter to operate upon. Utterance is a feat—apprehension a discovery; and this intellectual victory, sounding in the midst of emotional struggles, hushes some part of their brute importunity. It is at once sublime and beneficent, like a god stilling a tempest. Melancholy can in this way be the food of art; and it is no paradox that such a material may be beautiful when a fit form is imposed upon it, since a fit form turns anything into an agreeable object; its beauty runs as deep as its fitness, and stops where its adaptation to human nature begins to fail. Whatever can interest may prompt to expression, as it may have satisfied curiosity; and the mind celebrates a little triumph whenever it can formulate a truth, however unwelcome to the flesh, or discover an actual force, however unfavourable to given interests. As meditation on death and on life make equally for wisdom, so the expression of sorrow and joy make equally for beauty. Meditation and expression are themselves congenial activities with an intrinsic value which is not lessened if what they deal with could have been abolished to advantage. If once it exists, we may understand and interpret it; and this reaction will serve a double purpose. At first, in its very act, it will suffuse and mollify the unwelcome experience by another, digesting it, which is welcome; and later, by the broader adjustment which it will bring into the mind, it will help us to elude or confront the evils thus laid clearly before us.

Catharsis has no such effect as a sophistical optimism wishes to attribute to it; it does not show us that evil is good, or that calamity and crime are things to be grateful for: so forced an apology for evil has nothing to do with tragedy or wisdom; it belongs to apologetics and an artificial theodicy. Catharsis is rather the consciousness of how evil evils are, and how besetting; and how possible goods lie between and involve serious renunciations. To understand, to accept, and to use the situation in which a mortal may find himself is the function of art and reason. Such mastery is desirable in itself and for its fruits; it does not make itself responsible for the chaos of goods and evils that it supervenes upon. Whatever writhes in matter, art strives to give form to; and however unfavourable the field may be for its activity, it does what it can there, since no other field exists in which it may labour.

Sad music pleases the melancholy because it is sad and other men because it is music. When a composer attempts to reproduce complex conflicts in his score he will please complex or disordered spirits for expressing their troubles, but other men only for the order and harmony he may have brought out of that chaos. The chaos in itself will offend, and it is no part of rational art to produce it. As well might a physician poison in order to give an antidote, or maim in order to amputate. The subject matter of art is life, life as it actually is; but the function of art is to make life better. The depth to which an artist may find current experience to be sunk in discord and confusion is not his special concern; his concern is, in some measure, to lift the spirit above them. The more barbarous his age, the more drastic and violent must be his operation. He will have to shout in a storm. His strength must needs, in such a case, be very largely physical and his methods sensational. In a gentler age he may grow nobler, and blood and thunder will no longer seem impressive. Only the weak are obliged to be violent; the strong, having all means at command, need not resort to the worst. Refined art is not wanting in power if the public is refined also. And as refinement comes only by experience, by comparison, by subordinating means to ends and rejecting what hinders, it follows that a refined mind will really possess the greater volume, as well as the subtler discrimination. Its ecstasy without grimace, and its submission without tears, will hold heaven and earth better together—and hold them better apart—than could a mad imagination.

CHAPTER 5

SPEECH AND SIGNIFICATION

MUSIC RATIONALISES sound, but a more momentous rationalising of sound is seen in language. Language is one of the most useful of things, yet the greater part of it still remains (what it must all have been in the beginning) useless and without ulterior significance. The musical side of language is its primary and elementary side. Man is endowed with vocal organs so plastic as to emit a great variety of delicately varied sounds; and by good fortune his ear has a parallel sensibility, so that much vocal expression can be registered and confronted by auditory feeling. It has been said that man's pre-eminence in nature is due to his possessing hands; his modest participation in the ideal world may similarly be due to his possessing tongue and ear. For when he finds shouting and vague moaning after a while fatiguing, he can draw a new pleasure from uttering all sorts of labial, dental, and guttural sounds. Their rhythms and oppositions can entertain him, and he can begin to use his lingual gamut to designate the whole range of his perceptions and passions.

Merely to have added a vocal designation to fleeting things would in itself have encumbered phenomena without rendering them in any way more docile to the will. But the encumbrance in this instance proved to be a wonderful preservative and means of comparison. It actually gave each moving thing its niche and cenotaph in the eternal. For the universe of vocal sounds was a field, like that of colour or number, in which the elements showed relations and transitions easy to dominate. It was a key-board over which attention could run back and forth, eliciting many implicit harmonies. Henceforth when various sounds had been idly associated with various things, and identified with them, the things could, by virtue of their names, be carried over mentally into the linguistic system; they could be manipulated there ideally, and vicariously preserved in representation. Needless to say that the things themselves remained unchanged all the while in their efficacy and mechanical succession, just as they remain unchanged in those respects when they pass for the mathematical observer into their measure or symbol; but as this reduction to mathematical form makes them calculable, so their earlier reduction to words rendered them comparable and memorable, first enabling them to figure in discourse at all.

Language had originally no obligation to subserve an end which we may sometimes measure it by now, and depute to be its proper function, namely, to stand for things and adapt itself perfectly to their structure. The vocal and musical medium is, and must always remain, alien to the spatial. Yet when sounds were attached to an event or emotion, the net of vocal relations caught that natural object as a cobweb might catch a fly, without destroying or changing it. The object's quality passed to the word at the same time that the word's relations enveloped the object; and thus a new weight and significance was added to sound, previously nothing but a dull music. A conflict at once established itself between the drift proper to the verbal medium and that proper to the designated things; a conflict which the whole history of language and thought has exemplified and which continues to this day.

Suppose an animal going down to a frozen river which he had previously visited in summer. Marks of all sorts would awaken in him an old train of reactions; he would doubtless feel premonitions of satisfied thirst and the splash of water. On finding, however, instead of the fancied liquid, a mass of something like cold stone, he would be disconcerted. His active attitude would be pulled up short and contradicted. In his fairyland of faith and magic the old river would have been simply annihilated, the dreamt-of water would have become a vanished ghost, and this ice for the moment the hard reality. He would turn away and live for a while on other illusions. When this shock was overgrown by time and it was summer again, the original habit might, however, reassert itself once more. If he revisited the stream, some god would seem to bring back something from an old familiar world; and the chill of that temporary estrangement, the cloud that for a while had made the good invisible, would soon be gone and forgotten.

If we imagine, on the contrary, that this animal could speak and had from the first called his haunt *the river*, he would have repeated its name on seeing it even when it was frozen, for he had

not failed to recognise it in that guise. The variation afterwards
noticed, upon finding it hard, would seem no total substitution, but
a *change*; for it would be the same river, once flowing, that was
now congealed. An identical word, covering all the identical qualities in the phenomena and serving to abstract them, would force
the inconsistent qualities in those phenomena to pass for accidents;
and the useful proposition could at once be framed that the same
river may be sometimes free and sometimes frozen.

This proposition is true, yet it contains much that is calculated
to offend a scrupulous dialectician. Its language and categories are
not purely logical, but largely physical and representative. The
notion that what changes nevertheless endures is a remarkable
hybrid. It arises when rigid ideal terms are imposed on evanescent
existence. Feelings, taken alone, would show no identities; they
would be lost in changing, or be woven into the infinite feeling of
change. Notions, taken alone, would allow no lapse, but would
merely lead attention about from point to point over an eternal
mosaic. Power to understand the world, logical or scientific mastery
of existence, arises only by the forced and conventional marriage of
these two essences, when the actual flux is ideally suspended and an
ideal harness is loosely flung upon things. For this purpose words
are an admirable instrument. They have dialectical relations based
on an ideal import, or tendency to definition, which makes their
essence their signification; yet they can be freely bandied about and
applied for a moment to the ambiguous things that pass through
existence.

What words add is not power of discernment or action, but a
medium of intellectual exchange. Language is like money, without
which specific relative values may well exist and be felt, but cannot be reduced to a common denominator. And as money should
have a certain intrinsic value of its own in order that its relation to
other values may be stable, so a word, by which a thing is represented in discourse, must be a part of that thing's contact with
mankind. Words, in their existence, are no more universal than
gold by nature is a standard of value in other things. Words are
a material accompaniment of phenomena, at first an idle accompaniment, but one which happens to subserve easily a universal
function. Words, just by virtue of their adventitious, detachable
status, and because they are so easily compared and manipulated in

the world of sound, were singularly well fitted for this office. They are not vague, as any common quality abstracted from things would necessarily become. It is one thing to perceive an ill-determined form and quite another to attribute to it a precise general predicate. Words, distinct in their own category and perfectly recognisable, can accordingly perform very well the function of a universal; for they can be identified in turn with many particulars and yet remain throughout particular themselves.

The psychology of nominalism is undoubtedly right where it insists that every image is particular and every term, in its existential aspect, a *flatum vocis*; but nominalists should have recognised that images may have any degree of vagueness and generality when measured by a conceptual standard. A figure having obviously three sides and three corners may very well be present to the mind when it is impossible to say whether it is an equilateral or a rectangular triangle. Functional or logical universality lies in another sphere altogether, being a matter of intent and not of existence. When we say that "universals alone exist in the mind" we mean by "mind" something unrecognised by Berkeley; not a bundle of psychoses nor an angelic substance, but quick intelligence, the faculty of discourse. Predication is an act, understanding a spiritual and transitive operation: its existential basis may well be counted in psychologically and reduced to a stream of immediate presences; but its meaning can be caught only by another meaning, as life only can exemplify life. Vague or general images are as little universal as sounds are; but a precise sound better than a flickering abstraction can serve the intellect in its operation of comparison and synthesis. Words are therefore the body of discourse, of which the soul is understanding.

The categories of discourse are in part merely representative, in part merely grammatical, and in part attributable to both spheres. Euphony and phonetic laws are principles governing language without any reference to its meaning; here speech is still a sort of music. At the other extreme lies that ultimate form of prose which we see in mathematical reasoning or in a telegraphic style, where absolutely nothing is rhetorical and speech is denuded of every feature not indispensable to its symbolic rôle. Between these two extremes lies the broad field of poetry, or rather of imaginative or playful expression, where the verbal medium is a medium indeed, having a certain transparency, a certain reference to independent facts, but at the same time elaborates the fact in expressing it, and endows it with affinities alien to its proper nature. A pun is a grotesque example of such diremption, where ambiguities belonging only to speech are used to suggest impossible substitutions in ideas. Less frankly, language habitually wrests its subject-matter in some measure from its real context and transfers it to a represented and secondary world, the world of logic and deflection. Concretions in existence are subsumed, when named, under concretions in discourse. Grammar lays violent hands upon experience, and everything becomes a prey to wit and fancy, a material for fiction and eloquence. Man's intellectual progress has a poetic phase, in which he imagines the world; and then a scientific phase, in which he sifts and tests what he has imagined.

In what measure do inflection and syntax represent anything in the subject-matter of discourse? In what measure are they an independent play of expression, a quasi-musical, quasi-mathematical veil interposed between reflection and existence? One who knows only languages of a single family can give but a biassed answer to this question. There are doubtless many approaches to correct symbolism in languages, which grammar may have followed up at different times in strangely different ways. That the medium in every art has a character of its own, a character limiting its representative value, may perhaps be safely asserted, and this intrinsic character in the medium antedates and permeates all representation. Phonetic possibilities and phonetic habits belong, in language, to this indispensable vehicle; what the throat and lips can emit easily and distinguishably, and what sequences can appeal to the ear and be retained, depend alike on physiological conditions; and no matter how convenient or inconvenient these conditions may be for signification, they will always make themselves felt and may sometimes remain predominant. In poetry they are still conspicuous. Euphony, metre, and rhyme colour the images they transmit and add a charm wholly extrinsic and imputed. In this immersion of the message in the medium and in its intrinsic movement the magic of poetry lies; and the miracle grows as there is more or less native analogy between the medium's movement and that of the subject-matter.

The structure of language, when it passes beyond the phonetic level, begins at once to lean upon existences and to imitate the structure of things. We distinguish the parts of speech, for instance, in subservience to distinctions which we make in objects. The feeling or quality represented by an adjective, the relation indicated by a verb, the substance or concretion of qualities designated by a noun, are diversities growing up in experience, by no means attributable to the mere play of sound. The parts of speech are therefore representative. Their inflection is representative too, since tenses mark important practical differences in the distribution of the events described, and cases express the respective rôles played by objects in the operation. "I struck him and he will strike me," renders in linguistic symbols a marked change that may occur; the variation in phrase is not rhetorical. Language here, though borrowed no doubt from ancestral poetry, has left all reverie far behind, and has been submerged in the Life of Reason.

The medium, however, constantly reasserts itself. An example may be found in gender, which clearly representative in a measure, cuts loose in language from all genuine representation and becomes a feature in abstract linguistic design, a formal characteristic in expression. Contrasted sentiments permeate an animal's dealings with his own sex and with the other; nouns and adjectives represent this contrast by taking on masculine and feminine forms. The distinction is indeed so important that wholly different words— duck and drake, bull and cow—stand for the best-known animals of different sex; while adjectives, where declension is extinct, as in English, often take on a connotation of gender and are applied to one sex only—as we say a beautiful woman, but a handsome man. But gender in language extends much farther than sex, and even if by some subtle analogy all the masculine and feminine nouns in a language could be attached to something suggesting sex in the objects they designate, yet it can hardly be maintained that the elaborate concordance incident upon that distinction is representative of any felt quality in the things. So remote an analogy to sex could not assert itself pervasively. Thus Horace says:

> Quis *multa* gracilis te puer in *rosa*
> perfusis liquidis urget odoribus
> *grato*, Pyrrha, sub *antro?*

Here we may perceive why the rose was instinctively made feminine, and we may grant that the bower, though the reason escape us, was somehow properly masculine; but no one would urge that a *profusion* of roses was also intrinsically feminine, or that the *pleasantness* of a bower was ever specifically masculine to sense. The epithets *multa* and *grato* take their gender from the nouns, even though the quality they designate fails to do so. Artificial concordance in gender does not express gender: it merely emphasises the grammatical links in the phrases and makes greater variety possible in the arrangement of words.

This example may prepare us to understand a general principle: that language, while essentially significant viewed in its function, is indefinitely wasteful, being automatic and tentative in its origin. It overloads itself, and being primarily music, and a labyrinth of sounds, it develops an articulation and method of its own, which only in the end, and with much inexactness, reverts to its function of designation. How great the possibilities of effect are in developing a pure medium we can best appreciate in music; but rhetoric and utility keep language going, as centrifugal and centripetal forces keep a planet in its course. Euphony, verbal analogy, grammatical fancy, poetic confusion, continually drive language afield, in its own tangential direction; while the business of life, in which language is employed, and the natural lapse of rhetorical fashions, as continually draw it back towards convenience and exactitude.

Until music is subordinated, speech has little sense. Yet if music were left behind altogether, language would pass into a sort of algebra or vocal shorthand, without literary quality; it would become wholly indicative and record facts without colouring them ideally. This medium and its intrinsic development, though they make the bane of science, make the essence of art; they give representation a new and specific value such as the object, before representation, could not have possessed. Consciousness itself is such a medium in respect to diffuse existence, which it foreshortens and elevates into synthetic ideas. Reason, too, by bringing the movement of events and inclinations to a head in single acts of reflection, thus attaining to laws and purposes, introduces into life the influence of a representative medium, without which life could never pass from a process into an art. Language acquires scope in the same way, by its kindly infidelities; its metaphors and syntax lend experience perspective. Language vitiates the experience it expresses, but thereby makes the burden of one moment relevant to that of another. The two experiences, identified roughly with the same concretion in discourse, are pronounced similar or comparable in character. Thus a proverb, by its verbal pungency and rhythm, becomes more memorable than the event it first described would ever have been if not translated into an epigram and rendered, so to speak, applicable to new cases; for by that translation the event has become an idea.

To turn events into ideas is the function of literature. Music, which in a certain sense is a mass of pure forms, must leave its "ideas" imbedded in their own medium—they are musical ideas—and cannot impose them on any foreign material, such as human affairs. Science, on the contrary, seeks to disclose the bleak anatomy of existence, stripping off as much as possible the veil of prejudice and words. Literature takes a middle course and tries to subdue music, which for its purposes would be futile and too abstract, into conformity with general experience, making music thereby significant. Literary art in the end rejects all unmeaning flourishes, all complications that have no counterpart in things or no use in expressing their relations; at the same time it aspires to digest that reality to which it confines itself, making it over into ideal substance and material for the mind. It looks at things with an incorrigibly dramatic eye, turning them into permanent unities (which they never are) and almost into persons, grouping them by their imaginative or moral affinities and retaining in them chiefly what is incidental to their being, namely, the part they may chance to play in man's adventures.

Such literary art demands a subject-matter other than the literary impulse itself. The literary man is an interpreter and hardly succeeds, as the musician may, without experience and mastery of human affairs. His art is half genius and half fidelity. He needs inspiration; he must wait for automatic musical tendencies to ferment in his mind, proving it to be fertile in devices, comparisons, and bold assimilations. Yet inspiration alone will lead him astray, for his art is relative to something other than its own formal impulse; it comes to clarify the real world, not to encumber it; and it needs to render its native agility practical and to attach its volume of feeling to what is momentous in human life. Literature has its piety, its conscience; it cannot long forget, without forfeiting all dignity, that it serves a burdened and perplexed creature, a human animal struggling to persuade the universal Sphinx to propose a more intelligible riddle. Irresponsible and trivial in its abstract impulse, man's simian chatter becomes noble as it becomes symbolic; its representative function lends it a serious beauty, its utility endows it with moral worth.

CHAPTER 6

POETRY AND PROSE

MEMORABLE NONSENSE, or sound with a certain hypnotic power, is the really primitive and radical form of poetry. Nor is such poetry yet extinct: children still love and compose it, and every genuine poet, on one side of his genius, reverts to it from explicit speech. As all language has acquired its meaning, and did not have it in the beginning, so the man who launches a new locution, the poet who creates a symbol, must do so without knowing what significance it may eventually acquire, and conscious at best only of the emotional background from which it emerged. Pure poetry is pure experiment; and it is not strange that nine-tenths of it should be pure failure. For it matters little what unutterable things may have originally gone together with a phrase in the dreamer's mind; if they were not uttered and the phrase cannot call them back, this verbal relic is none the richer for the high company it may once have kept. Expressiveness is a most accidental matter. What a line suggests at one reading, it may never suggest again even to the same person. For this reason, among others, poets are partial to their own compositions; they truly discover there depths of meaning which exist for nobody else. Those readers who appropriate a poet and make him their own fall into a similar illusion; they attribute to him what they themselves supply, and whatever he reels out, lost in his own personal reverie, seems to them, like *sortes biblicae*, written to fit their own case.

Justice has never been done to Plato's remarkable consistency and boldness in declaring that poets are inspired by a divine madness and yet, when they transgress rational bounds, are to be banished from an ideal republic, though not without some marks of Platonic regard. Instead of fillets, a modern age might assign them a coterie of flattering dames, and instead of banishment, starvation; but the result would be the same in the end.* A poet is inspired

* In America they now become professors of English in the Colleges. Author's note, 1952.

because what occurs in his brain is a true experiment in creation. His apprehension plays with words and their meanings as nature, in any spontaneous variation, plays with her own structure. An automatic force shifts the kaleidoscope; a new direction is given to growth or a new gist to signification. This inspiration, moreover, is mad, being wholly ignorant of its own issue; and though it has a confused fund of experience and verbal habit on which to draw, it draws on this fund blindly and quite at random, consciously possessed by nothing but a certain stress and pregnancy and the pains, as it were, of parturition. Finally the new birth has to be inspected critically by the public censor before it is allowed to live; most probably it is too feeble and defective to prosper in the common air, or is a monster that violates some primary rule of civic existence, tormenting itself to disturb others.

Plato seems to have exaggerated the havoc which these poetic dragons can work in the world. They are in fact more often absurd than venomous, and no special legislation is needed to abolish them. They soon die quietly of universal neglect. The poetry that ordinarily circulates among a people is poetry of a secondary and conventional sort that propagates established ideas in trite metaphors. Popular poets are the parish priests of the Muse, retailing her ancient divinations to a long since converted public. Plato's quarrel was not so much with poetic art as with ancient myth and emotional laxity: he was preaching a crusade against the established church. For naturalistic deities he wished to substitute moral symbols; for the joys of sense, austerity and abstraction. To proscribe Homer was a marked way of protesting against the frivolous reigning ideals.

Homer, indeed, was no primitive poet; he was a consummate master, the heir to generations of discipline in both life and art. This appears in his perfect prosody, in his limpid style, in his sense for proportion, his abstentions, and the frank pathos of his portraits and principles, in which there is nothing gross, subjective, or arbitrary. The inspirations that came to him never carried him into crudeness or absurdity. Every modern poet, though the world he describes may be more refined in spots and more elaborate, is less advanced in his art; for art is made rudimentary not by its date but by its irrationality. Yet even if Homer had been primitive he might well have been inspired, in the same way as a Bacchic frenzy or a mystic trance; the most blundering explosions may be justified antecedently by the plastic force that is vented in them. They may be expressive, in the physical sense of this ambiguous word; for, far as they may be from conveying an idea, they may betray a tendency and prove that something urgent is stirring in the soul. Expressiveness is often sterile; but it is sometimes fertile and capable of reproducing in representation the experience from which it sprang. As a tree in the autumn sheds leaves and seeds together, so a ripening experience comes indifferently to various manifestations, some barren and without further function, others fit to carry the parent experience over into another mind, and give it a new embodiment there. Expressiveness in the former case is dead, like that of a fossil; in the latter it is living and efficacious, recreating its original. The first is idle self-manifestation, the second rational art.

Primitive poetry is the basis of all discourse. If we open any ancient book we come at once upon an elaborate language, and on divers conventional concepts, of whose origin and history we hear nothing. We must read on, until by dint of guessing and by confronting instances we grow to understand those symbols. The writer was himself heir to a linguistic tradition which he made his own by the same process of adoption and tentative use by which we, in turn, interpret his phrases: he understood what he heard in terms of his own experience, and attributed to his predecessors (no matter what their incommunicable feelings may have been) such ideas as their words generated in his own thinking. In this way expressions continually change their sense; they can communicate a thought only by diffusing a stimulus, and in passing from mouth to mouth they will wholly transform their connotation, unless some external object or some recurring human situation lends them a constant standard, by which private aberrations may be checked. Thus in the first phrase of Genesis, "In the beginning God created the heavens and the earth," the words have a stable meaning only in so far as they are indicative and bring us back to a stable object. What "heavens" and "earth" stand for can be conveyed by gestures, by merely pointing up and down; but beyond that sensuous connotation their meaning has entirely changed since they were here written; and no two minds, even to-day, will respond to these familiar words with exactly the same images. "Beginning" and "created" have a superficial clearness, though their implications cannot be defined without precipitating the most intricate metaphysics, which would end in nothing but a proof that both terms were ambiguous. As to the word "God," all mutual understanding is impossible. It is a floating literary symbol, with a value which, if we define it scientifically, becomes quite algebraic. As no experienced object corresponds to it, it is without fixed indicative force, and admits any sense which its context in any mind may happen to give it. In the first sentence of Genesis its meaning, we may safely say, is "a masculine being by whom heaven and earth were created." To fill out this implication other instances of the word would have to be gathered, in each of which, of course, the word would appear with a new and perhaps incompatible meaning.

Whenever a word appears in a radically new context it has a radically new sense: the expression in which it so figures is a poetic figment, a fresh literary creation. Such invention is sometimes perverse, sometimes humorous, sometimes sublime; that is, it may either buffet old associations without enlarging them, or give them a plausible but impossible twist, or enlarge them to cover, with unexpected propriety, a much wider or more momentous experience. The force of perception in any moment—if we abstract it from represented values—is emotional; so that for sublime poetry what is required is to tap some reservoir of feeling. If a phrase opens the flood-gates of emotion, it has made itself most deeply significant. Its discursive range and clearness may not be remarkable; its emotional power will quite suffice. For this reason again primitive poetry may be sublime: in its inchoate phrases there is affinity to raw passion and their very blindness may serve to bring that passion back. Poetry has body; it represents the volume of experience as well as its form, and to express volume a primitive poet will rely rather on rhythm, sound, and condensed suggestion than on discursive fulness or scope.

The descent from poetry to prose is in one sense a progress. When use has worn down a poetic phrase to its external import, and rendered it an indifferent symbol for a particular thing, that phrase has become prosaic; it has also become, by the same process, transparent and purely instrumental. In poetry feeling is transferred by contagion; in prose it is communicated by bending the attention upon determinate objects; the one stimulates and the other informs. Under the influence of poetry various minds radiate from a somewhat similar core of sensation, from the same vital mood, into the most diverse and incommunicable images. Interlocutors speaking prose, on the contrary, pelt and besiege one another with a peripheral attack; they come into contact at sundry superficial points and thence push their agreement inwards, until perhaps a practical coincidence is arrived at in their thought. Agreement is produced by controlling each mind externally, through a series of checks and little appeals to possible sensation; whereas in poetry the agreement, where it exists, is vague and massive; there is an initial fusion of minds under hypnotic musical influences, from which each listener, as he awakes, passes into his own thoughts and interpretations. In prose the vehicle for communication is a conventional sign, standing in the last analysis for some demonstrable object or controllable feeling. Before this comes about, experience remains a constantly renovated dream, as poetry to the end conspires to keep it. For poetry, while truly poetical, never loses sight of initial feelings and underlying appeals; it is incorrigibly egotistic, and takes every present passion and every private dream in turn for the core of the universe. By creating new signs, or by recasting and crossing those which have become conventional, it keeps communication massive and instinctive, immersed in music, and inexhaustible by clear thought.

Lying is a privilege of poets because they have not yet reached the level on which truth and error are discernible. Veracity and exactness are not ideals for a primitive mind; we learn to value them as we learn to live, when we discover that the spirit cannot be wholly free and solipsistic. To have to distinguish fact from fancy is so great a violence to the inner man that not only poets, but theologians and philosophers, still protest against such a distinction. They urge (what is perfectly true for a rudimentary creature) that facts are mere conceptions and conceptions full-fledged facts; but this interesting embryonic lore they apply, in their intellectual weakness, to retracting or undermining those human categories which, though alone fruitful or applicable in life, are not congenial to their half-formed imagination. Retreating deeper into the inner chaos, they bring to bear the whole momentum of an irresponsible dialectic to frustrate the growth of representative ideas. In this they are genuine, if somewhat belated, poets, experimenting anew with solved problems, and fancying how creation might have moved upon other lines. The great merit that prose shares with science is that it is responsible. Its conscience is a new and wiser imagination, by which creative thought is rendered cumulative and progressive; for a man does not build less boldly or solidly if he takes the precaution of building in baked brick. Prose is in itself meagre and bodiless, merely indicating the riches of the world. Its transparency helps us to look through it to the issue, and the signals it gives fill the mind with an honest assurance and a prophetic art far surer than any ecstasy.

As men of action have a better intelligence than poets, if only their action is on a broad enough stage, so the prosaic rendering of experience has the greater value, if only the experience rendered covers enough human interests. Youth and aspiration indulge in poetry; a mature and masterful mind will often despise it, and prefer to express itself laconically in prose. It is clearly proper that prosaic habits should supervene in this way on the poetical; for youth, being as yet little fed by experience, can find volume and depth only in the soul; the half-seen, the supra-mundane, the inexpressible, seem to it alone beautiful and worthy of homage. Time modifies this sentiment in two directions. It breeds lassitude and indifference towards impracticable ideals, originally no less worthy than the practicable. Ideals which cannot be realised, and are not fed at least by partial realisations, soon grow dormant. While things impossible thus lose their serious charm, things actual reveal their natural order and variety; these not only can entertain the mind abstractly, but they can offer a thousand material rewards in observation and action. In their presence, a private dream begins to look rather cheap and hysterical. Not that existence has any dignity or prerogative in the presence of will, but that will itself, being elastic, grows definite and firm when it is fed by success; and its formed and expressible ideals then put to shame the others, which have remained vague for want of practical expression. Mature interests centre on soluble problems and tasks capable of execution; it is at such points that the ideal can be really served. The individual's dream straightens and reassures itself by merging with the dream of humanity. To dwell, as irrational poets do, on some private experience, on some emotion without representative or ulterior value, then seems a waste of time. Fiction becomes less interesting than affairs, and poetry turns into a sort of incompetent whimper, a childish foreshortening of the outspread world.

On the other hand, prose has a great defect, which is abstractness. It drops the volume of experience in finding bodiless algebraic symbols by which to measure it. The verbal form, instead of transmitting an object, seems to constitute it, in so far as there is an object suggested at all; and the ulterior situation is described only in the sense that a change is induced in the hearer which prepares him to meet that situation. Prose seems to be a use of language in the service of material life. It would tend, in that case, to undermine its own presence; for in proportion as signals for action are quick and efficacious they diminish their sensuous stimulus and fade from consciousness. Were language such a set of signals it would be something merely instrumental, which if made perfect ought to be automatic and unconscious. It would be a buzzing in the ears, not a music native to the mind. Such a theory of language would treat it as a necessary evil and would look forward hopefully to the extinction of literature, in which it would recognise nothing ideal. There is of course no reason to deprecate the use of vocables, or of any other material agency, to expedite affairs; but an art of speech, if it is to add any ultimate charm to life, has to supervene upon a mere code of signals. Prose, could it be purely representative, would be ideally superfluous. A literary prose accordingly owns a double allegiance, and its life is amphibious. It must convey intelligence, but intelligence clothed in a language that lends the message an intrinsic value, and makes it delightful to apprehend apart from its importance in ultimate theory or practice. Prose is in that measure a fine art. It might be called poetry that had become pervasively representative, and was altogether faithful to its rational function.

We may therefore with good reason distinguish prosaic form from prosaic substance. A novel, a satire, a book of speculative philosophy, may have a most prosaic exterior; every phrase may convey its idea economically; but the substance may nevertheless be poetical, since these ideas may be irrelevant to all ulterior events, and may express nothing but the imaginative energy that called them forth. On the other hand, a poetic vehicle in which there is much ornamental play of language and rhythm may clothe a dry ideal skeleton. So those tremendous positivists, the Hebrew prophets, had the most prosaic notions about the goods and evils of life. So Lucretius praised, I will not say the atoms merely, but even fecundity and wisdom. The motives, to take another example, which Racine attributed to his personages, were prosaically conceived; a physiologist could not be more exact in his calculations, for even love may be made the mainspring in a clock-work of emotions. Yet that Racine was a born poet appears in the music, nobility, and tenderness of his medium; he clothed his intelligible characters in magical and tragic robes; the aroma of sentiment rises like a sort of pungent incense between them and us, and no dramatist has ever had so sure a mastery over transports and tears.

Is there not, we may ask, some ideal form of discourse in which apperceptive life could be engaged with all its volume and transmuting power, and in which at the same time no misrepresentation should be involved? Transmutation is not erroneous when it is intentional; misrepresentation does not please for being false, but only because truth would be more congenial if it resembled such a fiction. Why should not discourse, then, have nothing but truth in its import and nothing but beauty in its form? With regard to euphony and grammatical structure there is evidently nothing impossible in such an ideal; for these radical beauties of language are independent of the subject-matter. They form the body of poetry; but the ideal and emotional atmosphere which is its soul depends on things external to language, which no perfection in the medium could modify. It might seem as if the brilliant substitutions, the magic suggestions essential to poetry, would necessarily vanish in the full light of day.

The Life of Reason involves sacrifice. What forces yearn for the ideal, being many and incompatible, have to yield and partly deny themselves in order to attain any ideal at all. There is something sad in all possible attainment so long as there is limitation to put up with, and the memory of many a defeat. Rational poetry is possible and would be infinitely more beautiful than the other; but the charm of unreason, if unreason seem charming, it certainly could not preserve. In what human fancy demands, as at present constituted, there are irrational elements. The given world seems insufficient; impossible things have to be imagined, both to extend its limits and to fill in and vivify its texture. Homer has a mythology without which experience would have seemed to him undecipherable; Dante has his allegories and his mock science; Shakespeare has his romanticism; Goethe his symbolic characters and artificial machinery. All this lumber seems to have been somehow necessary to their genius; they could not reach expression in more honest terms. If such indirect expression could be discarded, it would not be missed; but while the mind, for want of a better vocabulary, is reduced to using these symbols, it pours into them a part of its own life and makes them beautiful. Their loss is a real blow, while the incapacity that called for them endures; and the soul seems to be crippled by losing its crutches.

There are certain adaptations and abbreviations of reality which thought can never outgrow. Thought is representative; it enriches each soul and each moment with substitutes for surrounding existences. If discourse is to be significant it must transfer to its territory and reduce to its scale whatever objects it deals with: in other words, thought has a point of view and cannot see the world except in perspective. This point of view is not, for reason, locally or naturally determined; sense alone is limited in that material fashion, being seated in the body and looking thence centrifugally upon things in so far as they come into dynamic relations with that body. Intelligence, on the contrary, sallies from that physical stronghold and consists precisely in shifting and universalising the point of view, neutralising all local, temporal, or personal conditions. Yet intelligence, notwithstanding, has its own centre and point of origin, not explicitly in space or in a natural body, but in some specific interest or moral aim. It translates animal life into moral endeavour, and what figured in the first as a local existence figures in the second as a specific good. Reason accordingly has its essential bias, and looks at things as they affect the particular form of life which reason expresses: and though all reality should be ultimately swept by the eye of reason, the whole would still be surveyed by a particular method, from a particular starting-point, for a particular end; nor would it take much shrewdness to perceive that this nucleus for discourse and estimation, this ideal life, corresponds in the moral world to that animal body which gave sensuous experience its seat and centre; so that rationality is nothing but the ideal function or aspect of natural life. Reason is universal in its outlook and in its sympathies: it is the faculty of changing places ideally and representing alien points of view; but this very self-transcendence manifests a certain special method in life, an equilibrium which a far-sighted being is able to establish between itself and its comprehended conditions. Reason remains to the end essentially human and, in its momentary actuality, necessarily personal.

We have here an essential condition of discourse which renders it at bottom poetical. Selection and applicability govern all thinking, and govern it in the interests of the soul. We should not wish to know "things in themselves," even if we were able. What it concerns us to know about them is merely the service or injury they are able to do us, and in what fashion they can affect our lives. To know this would be, in so far, truly to know them; but it would be to know them through our own faculties and through their supposed effects; it would be to know them by their appearance. A singular proof of the frivolous way in which philosophers often proceed, when they think they are particularly profound, is seen in this puzzle: How is it possible to know reality, if all we can attain in experience is but appearance? The meaning of knowledge, which is an intellectual and living thing, is here forgotten, and the notion of sensation, or bodily possession, is substituted for it; so what we are really asked to consider is how, had we no understanding, we should be able to understand what we endure. It is by conceiving what we endure to be the appearance of something beyond us, that we reach knowledge that something exists beyond us, and that it plays in respect to us a determinate rôle. There could be no knowledge of reality if what conveyed that knowledge were not felt to be appearance; nor can a medium of knowledge better than appearance be by any possibility conceived. To produce such appearances is what makes realities knowable. Knowledge transcends sensation by rising to a supersensuous plane, the plane of principles and causes. These principles and causes are what we call the intelligible or the real world; and the sensations, when they have been so interpreted and underpinned, are what we call appearance.

If a poet could clarify the myths he begins with, so as to reach ultimate scientific notions of nature and life, he would still be animated by vivid feeling and its imaginative expression. Tragic, fatal, intractable, he might well feel that the truth was; but these qualities have never been absent from that half-mythical world through which poets, for want of a rational education, have hitherto wandered. A rational poet's vision would have the same moral functions which myth was asked to fulfil, and fulfilled so treacherously. Such a poet would doubtless need a robust genius. If he possessed it, and in transmuting all existence falsified nothing, giving that picture of everything which human experience in the end would have drawn, he would achieve an ideal result. In prompting mankind to imagine, he would be helping them to live. His poetry, without ceasing to be a fiction in its method and ideality, would be an ultimate truth in its practical scope. It would present in graphic images the total efficacy of surrounding things. Such a poetry would be more deeply rooted in human nature than in any casual fancy, and therefore more appealing to the heart. The images it had worked out would confront human passion more intelligibly than does the world as at present conceived, with its mechanism half ignored and its ideality half invented; they would represent vividly the uses of nature, and thereby make all natural situations seem so many incentives to art.

CHAPTER 7

PLASTIC CONSTRUCTION

WE HAVE seen how arts founded on exercise and automatic self-expression develop into music, poetry, and prose. By an indirect approach they come to represent outer conditions, till they are interwoven in a life which has in some measure gone out to meet its opportunities and learned to turn them to an ideal use. We have now to see how man's reactive habits pass simultaneously into art in a wholly different region. Spontaneous expression, such as song, comes when internal growth in an animal system vents itself, as it were, by the way. At the same time animal economy has playful manifestations concerned with outer things, such as burrowing or collecting objects. These practices are not less spontaneous than the others, and no less expressive; but they seem more external because the traces they leave on the environment are more clearly marked.

To change an object is the surest and most glorious way of changing a perception. A shift in posture may relieve the body, and in that way satisfy, but the new attitude is itself unstable. Its pleasantness, like its existence, is transient, and scarcely is a movement executed when both its occasion and its charm are forgotten. Self-expression by exercise, in spite of its pronounced automatism, is therefore something comparatively futile and inglorious. A man has hardly *done* anything when he has laughed or yawned. Even the inspired poet retains something of this futility: his work is not his, but that of a restless, irresponsible spirit passing through him, and hypnotising him for its own ends. Of the result he has no profit, no glory, and little understanding. So the mystic also positively gloats on his own nothingness, and puts his whole genuine being in a fancied instrumentality and subordination to something else. Far more virile and noble is the sense of having actually done something, and left at least the temporary stamp of one's special will on the world. To chop a stick, to catch a fly, to pile a heap of sand, is a satisfying action; for the sand stays for a while in its

345

novel arrangement, proclaiming to the surrounding level that we have made it our instrument, while the fly will never stir nor the stick grow together again in all eternity. If the impulse that has thus left its indelible mark on things is constant in our own bosom, the world will have been permanently improved and humanised by our action. Nature cannot but seem more favourable to those ideas which have already found an efficacious champion.

Plastic impulses find in this way an immediate sanction in the sense of victory and dominion which they carry with them; it is so evident a proof of power in ourselves to see things and animals bent out of their habitual form and obedient instead to our idea. But a far weightier sanction immediately follows. Man depends on things for his convenience, yet by automatic action he changes these very things so that it becomes possible that by his action he should promote his welfare. He may, of course, no less readily precipitate his ruin. The animal is more subject to vicissitudes than the plant, which makes no effort to escape them or to give chase to what it feeds upon. The greater perils of action, however, are in animals covered partly by fertility, partly by adaptability, partly by success. Sometimes, in modifying the environment, a man will improve it: which is merely to say that a change may sometimes fortify the impulse which brought it about. As soon as this retro-action is perceived and the act is done with knowledge of its ensuing benefits, plastic impulse becomes art, and the world begins actually to change in obedience to reason.

The first felt utilities by which plastic instinct is sanctioned are of course not distinctly aesthetic, much less distinctly practical; they are magical. A stone cut into some human or animal semblance fascinates the savage eye much more than would a useful tool or a beautiful idol. The man wonders at his own work, and petrifies the miracle of his art into miraculous properties in its product. Primitive art is incredibly conservative; its first creations, having once attracted attention, monopolise it henceforth and nothing else will be trusted to work the miracle. It is a sign of stupidity in general to stick to physical objects and given forms apart from their ideal functions, as when a child cries for a broken doll, even if a new and better one is at hand to replace it. Inert associations establish themselves, in such a case, with that part of a thing which is irrelevant to its value—its material substance or perhaps its name. The idol must be the self-same hereditary stock, or at least it must have the old sanctified rigidity and stare.

Idolatry is by no means incident to art; art, on the contrary, is a release from idolatry. A cloud, an animal, a spring, a stone, or the whole heaven, will serve the pure idolater's purpose to perfection; these things have existence and a certain hypnotic power, so that he may make them a focus for his dazed contemplation. When the mind takes to generalities it finds the same fascination in Being or in the Absolute, something it needs no art to discover. The more indeterminate, immediate, and unutterable the idol is, the better it induces panic self-contraction and a reduction of all discourse to the infinite intensity of zero. When idolaters pass from trying to evoke the Absolutely Existent to apostrophising the sun or an ithyphallic bull they have made an immense progress in art and religion, for now their idols represent some specific and beneficent function in nature, something propitious to ideal life and to its determinate expression. Isaiah is very scornful of idols made with hands, because they have no physical energy. He forgets that perhaps they represent something, and so have a spiritual dignity which things living and powerful never have unless they too become representative and express some ideal. The question merely is whether the sculptor's image or the prophet's stands for the greatest interest and is a more adequate symbol for the good. The noblest art will be the one, whether plastic or literary or dialectical, which creates figments most truly representative of what is momentous in human life. Similarly the least idolatrous religion would be the one which used the most perfect art, and most successfully abstracted the good from the real.

Conservatism rules also in those manufactures which are tributary to architecture and the smaller plastic arts. Utility makes small headway against custom, not only when custom has become religion, but even when it remains inert and without mythical sanction. To admit or trust anything new is to overcome that inertia which is a general law in the brain no less than elsewhere, and which may be distinguished in reflection into a technical and a social conservatism. Technical conservatism appears, for instance, in a man's handwriting, which is so seldom improved, even when admitted, perhaps, to be execrable. Every artist has his tricks of execution, every school its hereditary, irrational processes. These refractory habits are to blame for the rare and often ignored quality of genius; they limit excellence to one style and deny it to all others. The same principle goes deeper. Conception and imagination are themselves automatic and run in grooves, so that only certain forms in certain combinations will ever suggest themselves to a given designer. Every writer's style, too, however varied within limits, is single and monotonous compared with the ideal possibilities of expression. Genius at every moment is confined to the idiom it is creating.

Social inertia is due to the same causes working in the community at large. The fancy, for instance, of building churches in the shape of a cross has largely determined Christian architecture. Builders were prevented by a foregone suggestion in themselves and by their patrons' demands from conceiving any alternative to that convention. Early pottery, they say, imitates wicker-work, and painted landscape was for ages not allowed to exist without figures, although even the old masters show plainly enough in their backgrounds that they could love landscape for its own sake. When one link with humanity has been rendered explicit and familiar, people assume that by no other means can humanity be touched at all; even if at the same time their own heart is expanding to the highest raptures in a quite different region. The severer Greeks reprobated music without words; Saint Augustine complained of chants that rendered the sacred text unintelligible; the Puritans regarded elaborate music as diabolical, little knowing how soon some of their descendants would find religion in nothing else. A stupid convention still looks on material and mathematical processes as somehow distressing and ugly, and systems of philosophy, artificially mechanical, are invented to try to explain natural mechanism away; whereas in no region can the spirit feel so much at home as among natural causes, or realise so well its universal affinities, or so safely enlarge its happiness. Automatism is the source of beauty. It is not necessary to look so high as the stars to perceive this truth: the action of an animal's limbs or the movement of a waterfall will prove it to any one who has eyes and can shake himself loose from verbal prejudices, those débris of old perceptions which choke all fresh perception in the soul. Irrational hopes, irrational shames, irrational decencies, make man's chief desolation. A slight knocking of fools' heads together might be enough to break up the ossifications there and start the blood coursing again through possible channels. Art has an infinite range; nothing shifts so easily as taste and yet nothing so often misses the directions in which it might find most satisfaction.

Since construction grows rational slowly and by indirect pressure, we may expect that its most superficial merits will be the first appreciated. Of all grounds for admiration those most readily seized are size, elaboration, splendour of materials, and difficulties or cost involved. Having built or dug in the conventional way a man may hang before his door some trophy of battle or the chase, bearing witness to his prowess; just as people now, not thinking of making their rooms beautiful, fill them with photographs of friends or places they have known, to suggest and reburnish in their minds their interesting personal history, which even they, unstimulated, might tend to forget. That dwelling will seem best adorned which contains most adventitious objects; bare and ugly will be whatever is not concealed by something else. Again, a barbarous architect, without changing his model, may build in a more precious material; and his work will be admired for the evidence it furnishes of wealth and wilfulness. As a community grows luxurious and becomes accustomed to such display, it may come to seem strange and hideous to see a wooden plate or a pewter spoon. A beautiful house will need to be in marble and the sight of plebeian brick will banish all satisfaction.

Less irrational, and therefore less vulgar, is the wonder aroused by great bulk or difficulty in the work. Exertions, to produce a great result, even if it be material, must be allied to perseverance and intelligent direction. Roman bridges and aqueducts, for instance, gain a profound emotional power when we see in their monotonous arches a symbol of the mightiest enterprise in history, and in their decay an evidence of its failure. Curiosity is satisfied, historic imagination is stimulated, tragic reflection is called forth. We cannot refuse admiration to a work so full of mind, even if no great plastic beauty happens to distinguish it. It is at any rate beautiful enough, like the sea or the skeleton of a mountain. We may rely on the life it has made possible to add more positive charms and clothe it with imaginative functions. Modern engineering works often have a similar value; the force and intelligence they express merge in an aesthetic essence, and the place they hold in a portentous civilisation lends them an almost epic dignity. New York, since it took to doing business in towers, has become interesting to look at from the sea; nor is it possible to walk through the overshadowed streets without feeling a pleasing wonder. A city, when enough people swarm in it, is as fascinating as an ant-hill, and its buildings, whatever other charms they may have, are at least as curious and delightful as sea-shells or birds' nests. The purpose of improvements in modern structures may be economic, just as the purpose of castles was military; but both may incidentally please the contemplative mind by their bold forms and human associations.

An artist may be kept true to his style either by ignorance of all others or by love of his own. This fidelity is a condition of progress. Every necessary structure has its specific character and its essential associations. Taking his cue from these, an artist may experiment freely; he may emphasise the structure in the classic manner and turn its lines into ornament, adding only what may help to complete and unite its suggestions. This puritanism in design is rightly commended, but its opposite may be admirable too. We may admit that nudity is the right garment for the gods, but it would hardly serve the interests of beauty to legislate that all mortals should always go naked. The veil that conceals natural imperfections may have a perfection of its own. Maxims in art are pernicious; beauty is here the only commandment. And beauty is a free natural gift. When it has appeared, we may perceive that its influence is rational, since it both expresses and fosters a harmony of impressions and impulses in the soul; but to take any mechanism whatever, and merely because it is actual or necessary to insist that it is worth exhibiting, and that by divine decree it shall be pronounced beautiful, is to be quite at sea in moral philosophy.

To love decoration is to enjoy synthesis: in other words, it is to have hungry senses and unused powers of attention. This hunger, when it cannot well be fed by recollecting things past, relishes a profusion of things simultaneous. Nothing is so much respected by unintelligent people as elaboration and complexity. They are simply dazed and overawed at seeing at once so much more than they can master. To overwhelm the senses is, for them, the only way of filling the mind. It takes cultivation to appreciate in art, as in philosophy, the consummate value of what is simple and finite, because it has found its pure function and ultimate import in the world. What is just, what is delicately and silently adjusted to its special office, and thereby in truth to all ultimate issues, seems to the vulgar something obvious and poor.

That the ornate may be very beautiful, that in fact what is to be completely beautiful needs to be somehow rich, is a fact of experience. Decoration, by stimulating the senses, not only brings a primary satisfaction with it, independent of any that may supervene, but it furnishes an element of effect which no higher beauty can ever render unwelcome or inappropriate, since any higher beauty, in moving the mind, must give it a certain sensuous and emotional colouring. Decoration is accordingly an independent art, to be practised for its own sake, in obedience to elementary plastic instincts. It is fundamental in design, for everything structural or significant produces in the first instance some sensuous impression and figures as a spot or pattern in the field of vision. The fortunate architect is he who has, for structural skeleton in his work, a form in itself decorative and beautiful, who can carry it out in a beautiful material, and who finally is suffered to add so much decoration as the eye may take in with pleasure, without losing the expression and lucidity of the whole. The Greek temple, for instance, if we imagine it in its glory, with all its colour and furniture, was a type of human art at its best, where decoration, without in the least restricting itself, took naturally an exquisitely subordinate and pervasive form: each detail had its own splendour and refinement, yet kept its place in the whole.

In some ways the ideal Gothic church attained a similar perfection, because there too the structure remained lucid and predominant, while it was enriched by many necessary appointments—altars, stalls, screens, chantries and tombs—which, while really the *raison d'être* of the whole edifice, aesthetically regarded, served for its ornaments. It may be doubted, however, whether Gothic construction was well grounded enough in utility to be a sound and permanent basis for traditional art; and the extreme instability of Gothic style, the feverish inconstancy of architects straining after effects never, apparently, satisfactory when achieved, shows that something was vain and artificial in the circumstances. The structure, in becoming an ornament, ceased to be anything else, and could be discarded by any one whose fancy preferred a different image.

For this reason a building like the cathedral of Amiens, where a structural system is put through consistently, is far from representing mediaeval art in its full and ideal essence; it is rather an incidental achievement, a sport in which an adventitious interest is, for a moment, emphasised overwhelmingly. Intelligence here comes to the fore, and a sort of mathematical virtuosity: but it was not mathematical virtuosity nor even intelligence to which, in Christian art, the leading rôle properly belonged. What structural elucidation did for church architecture was much like what scholastic elucidation did for church dogma: it insinuated a logic into the traditional edifice which was far from representing its soul or its genuine value. To vault at such heights and to prop that vault with external buttresses was a gratuitous undertaking. The result was indeed interesting, the ingenuity and method exhibited were masterly in their way; yet the result was not proportionate in beauty to the effort required.

The true magic of that very architecture lay not in its intelligible structure but in the bewildering incidental effects which that structure permitted. The part in such churches is better than the symmetrical whole; often incompleteness and accretions alone give grace or expression to the monument. A cross vista where all is wonder, a side chapel where all is peace, strike the key-note here; not that punctilious and wooden repetition of props and arches, as a builder's model might boast to exhibit them. Perhaps the most beautiful Gothic interiors are those without aisles, if what we are considering is their proportion and majesty; elsewhere the structure, if perceived at all, is too artificial and strange to be perceived intuitively and to have the glow of a genuine beauty. There is an over-ingenious mechanism, redeemed by its colour and the thousand intervening objects, when these have not been swept way. Glazed and painted as Gothic churches were meant to be, they were no doubt exceedingly gorgeous. When we admire their structural scheme we are perhaps nursing an illusion like that which sentimental classicists once cherished when they talked about the purity of white marble statues and the ideality of their blank and sightless eyes. What we treat as a supreme quality may have been a mere means to mediaeval builders, and a mechanical expedient: their simple hearts were set on making their churches, for God's glory and their own, as large, as high, and as rich as possible. After all, an uninterrupted tradition attached them to Byzantium; and it was the sudden passion for stained glass and the goldsmith's love of intricate fineness—which the Saracens also had shown—that carried them in a century from Romanesque to flamboyant. The structure was but the inevitable underpinning for the desired display.

If these sanctuaries, in their spoliation and ruin, now show us their admirable bones, we should thank nature for that rational skeleton, imposed by material conditions on an art which in its life-time was goaded on only by a pious and local emulation, and wished at all costs to be sumptuous and astonishing.

To the architect sculpture and painting are only means of variegating a surface; light and shade, depth and elaboration, are thereby secured and aid him in distributing his masses. For this reason geometrical or highly conventionalised ornament is all the architect requires. If his decorators furnish more, if they insist on copying natural forms or illustrating history, that is their own affair. Their humanity will doubtless give them, as representative artists, a new claim on human regard, and the building they enrich in their pictorial fashion will gain a new charm, just as it would gain by historic associations or by the smell of incense clinging to its walls. When the arts superpose their effects the total impression belongs to none of them in particular; it is imaginative merely or in the broadest sense poetical. So the monumental function of Greek sculpture, and the interpretations it gave to national myths, made every temple a storehouse of poetic memories. In the same way every great cathedral became a pious story-book. Construction, by admitting applied decoration, offers a splendid basis and background for representative art. It is in their decorative function that construction and representation meet; they are able to conspire in one ideal effect by virtue of the common appeal which they unwittingly make to the senses. If construction were not decorative it could never ally itself imaginatively to decoration; and decoration in turn would never be willingly representative if the forms which illustration requires were not decorative in themselves.

CHAPTER 8

PLASTIC REPRESENTATION

IMITATION IS a fertile principle in the Life of Reason. The machinery of imitation is obscure but its prevalence is obvious. When a man involuntarily imitates other men, he does not become those other persons; he is simply modified by their presence in a manner that allows him to conceive their will and their independent existence, not without growing similar to them in some measure. He enacts what he understands, and his understanding consists precisely in knowing that he is re-enacting something which has its collateral existence elsewhere in nature. Imitation is far more than similarity, nor does its ideal function lie in bringing a flat and unmeaning similarity about. It has a representative and intellectual value because in reproducing the forms of things it reproduces them in a fresh substance to a new purpose.

If I imitate mankind by following their fashions, I add one to the million and improve nothing: but if I imitate them by representing what I do not bodily become, I preserve and enlarge my own being and make it master ideally of something else. Assimilation is a way of drifting through the flux or of letting it drift through oneself; representation, on the contrary, is a principle of progress. To grow by mastery of what you are not, and do not wish to be, is to grow in dignity. It is to be wise and prepared. It is to survey a universe without ceasing to be a mind.

A product of imitative sensibility is accordingly on a higher plane than the original existences it introduces to one another—the ignorant individual and the unknown world. Imitation in softening the body into physical adjustment stimulates the mind to ideal representation. This is the case even when the stimulus is a contagious influence or habit, though the response may then be slavish and the representation vague. Sheep jumping a wall after their leader doubtless feel that they are not alone; and though their action may have no purpose it probably has a felt sanction and reward. Men also think they invoke an authority when they

354

appeal to the *quod semper et ubique et ab omnibus*, and a conscious unanimity is a human if not a rational joy. When, however, the stimulus to imitation is not so pervasive and touches chiefly a single sense, when what it arouses is a movement of the hand or eye retracing the object, then the response becomes very definitely cognitive. It constitutes an observation of fact, an acquaintance with a thing's structure amounting to technical knowledge; for such a survey leaves behind it a power to reconstitute the process it involved. It leaves a model idea. In an idle moment, when the information thus acquired need not be put to instant use, the new-born faculty may work itself out spontaneously. The sound heard is repeated, the thing observed is sketched, the event conceived is acted out in pantomime. Then imitation rounds itself out; an uninhibited sensation has become an instinct to keep that sensation alive, and plastic representation has begun.

The secret of representative genius is simple enough. All hangs on intense, exhaustive, rehearsed sensation. To paint is a way of letting vision work; nor should the amateur imagine that while he lacks technical knowledge he can have in his possession all the ideal burden of an art. His reaction will be personal and adventitious, and he will miss the artist's real inspiration and ignore his genuine successes. You may instruct a poet about literature, but his allegiance is to emotion. You may offer the sculptor your comparative observations on style and taste; he may or may not care to listen, but what he knows and loves is the human body. Critics are in this way always one stage behind or beyond the artist; their operation is reflective and his is direct. In transferring to his special medium what he has before him his whole mind is lost in the object; as the marksman, to shoot straight, looks at the mark. How successful the result is, or how appealing to human nature, he judges afterwards, as an outsider might, and usually judges ill; since there is no life less apt to yield a broad understanding for human affairs or even for the residue of art itself, than the life of a man inspired, a man absorbed, as the genuine artist is, in his own travail. But into this travail, into this digestion and reproduction of the thing seen, a critic can hardly enter. Having himself the ulterior office of judge, he must not hope to rival nature's children in their sportiveness and intuition.

In an age of moral confusion, these circumstances may lead to a strange shifting of rôles. The critic, feeling that something in the artist has escaped him, may labour to put himself in the artist's place. If he succeeded, the result would only be to make him a biographer; he would be describing in words the very intuitions which the artist had rendered in some other medium. To understand how the artist felt, however, is not criticism; criticism is an investigation of what the work is good for. Its function may be chiefly to awaken certain emotions in the beholder, to deepen in him certain habits of apperception; but even this most aesthetic element in a work's operation does not borrow its value from the possible fact that the artist also shared those habits and emotions. If he did, and if they are desirable, so much the better for him; but his work's value would still consist entirely in its power to propagate such good effects, whether they were already present in him or not. All criticism is therefore moral, since it deals with benefits and their relative weight. Psychological penetration and reconstructed biography may be excellent sport; if they do not reach historic truth they may at least exercise dramatic talent. Criticism, on the other hand, is a serious and public function; it shows the race assimilating the individual, dividing the immortal from the mortal part of a soul.

A good way to understand schools and styles is to consider first what region of nature preoccupied the age in which they arose. Perception can cut the world up into many patterns, which it isolates and dignifies with names. It must distingish before it can reproduce and the objects which attention distinguishes are of many strange sorts. Thus the single man, the hero, in his acts of prowess or in his readiness, may be the unit and standard in discourse. It will then be his image that will preoccupy the arts. For such a task the most adequate art is evidently sculpture, for sculpture is the most complete of imitations. In no other art can apprehension render itself so exhaustively and with such recuperative force. Sculpture retains form and colour, with all that both can suggest, and it retains them in their integrity, leaving the observer free to resurvey them from any point of view and drink in their quality exhaustively.

The movement and speech which are wanting, the stage may be called upon to supply; but it cannot supply them without a terrible sacrifice, for it cannot give permanence to its expression. Acting is for this reason an inferior art, not perhaps in difficulty and certainly not in effect, but inferior in dignity, since the effort of art is to keep what is interesting in existence, to recreate it in the eternal, and this ideal is half frustrated if the representation is itself fleeting and the rendering has no firmer subsistence than the inspiration that gave it birth. By making himself, almost in his entirety, the medium of his art, the actor is morally diminished, and as little of him remains in his work, when this is good, as of his work in history. He lends himself without interest, and after being Brutus at one moment and Falstaff at another, he is not more truly himself. He is abolished by his creations, which nevertheless cannot survive him.

Being so adequate a rendering of its object, sculpture demands a perfect mastery over it and is correspondingly difficult. It requires taste and training above every other art; for not only must the material form be reproduced, but its motor suggestions and moral expression must be rendered; things which in the model itself are at best transitory, and which may never be found there if a heroic or ideal theme is proposed. The sculptor is obliged to have caught on the wing attitudes momentarily achieved or vaguely imagined; yet these must grow firm and harmonious under his hand. Nor is this enough; for sculpture is more dependent than other arts on its model. If the statue is to be ideal, *i.e.*, if it is to express the possible motions and vital character of its subject, the model must itself be refined. Training must have cut in the flesh those lines which are to make the language and eloquence of the marble. Trivial and vulgar forms, such as modern sculpture abounds in, reflect an undisciplined race of men, one in which neither soul nor body has done anything well, because the two have done nothing together. The frame has remained gross or awkward, while the face has taken on a tense expression, betraying loose and undignified habits of mind. To carve such a creature is to perpetuate a caricature. The modern sculptor is stopped short at the first conception of a figure; if he gives it its costume, it is grotesque; if he strips it, it is unmeaning and pitiful.

Greece was in all these respects a soil singularly favourable to sculpture. The success there achieved was so conspicuous that two thousand years of essential superfluity have not availed to extirpate the art. Plastic impulse is indeed immortal, and many a hand, even without classic example, would have fallen to modelling. In the middle ages, while monumental sculpture was still rudely reminiscent, ornamental carving arose spontaneously. Yet at every step the experimental sculptor would run up against disaster. What could be seen in the streets, while it offered plenty of subjects, offered none that could stimulate his talent. His patrons asked only for illustration and applied ornament; his models offered only the smirk and sad humour of a stunted life. Here and there his statues might attain a certain sweetness and grace, such as painting might perfectly well have rendered; but on the whole sculpture remained decorative and infantile.

The Renaissance brought back technical freedom and a certain inspiration, unhappily a retrospective and exotic one. The art cut praiseworthy capers in the face of the public, but nobody could teach the public itself to dance. If several great temperaments, under the auspices of fashion, could then call up a magic world in which bodies still spoke a heroic language, that was a passing dream. Society could not feed such an artificial passion, nor the schools transmit an arbitrary personal style that responded to nothing permanent in social conditions. Academies continued to offer prizes for sculpture, the nude continued to be seen in studios, and equestrian or other rhetorical statues continued occasionally to be erected in public squares. Heroic sculpture, however, in modern society, is really an anomaly and confesses as much by being a failure. No personal talent avails to rescue an art from laboured insignificance when it has no steadying function in the moral world, and must waver between caprice and convention. Where something modest and genuine peeped out was in portraiture, and also at times in that devotional sculpture in wood which still responded to a native interest and consequently kept its sincerity and colour. Pious images may be feeble in the extreme, but they have not the weakness of being merely aesthetic. The purveyor of church wares has a stated theme; he is employed for a purpose; and if he has enough technical resource his work may become truly beautiful: which is not to say that he will succeed if his conceptions are without dignity or his style without discretion. There are good *Mater dolorosas*; there is no good *Sacred Heart*.

It may happen, however, that people are not interested in subjects that demand or allow reproduction in bulk. The isolated figure or simple group may seem cold apart from its natural setting. In rendering an action you may need to render its scene, if it is the circumstance that gives it value rather than the hero. You may also wish to trace out the action through a series of episodes with many figures. In the latter case you might have recourse to a bas-relief, which, although durable, is usually a thankless work; there is little in it that might not be conveyed in a drawing with distinctness. As some artists, like Michael Angelo, have carried the sculptor's spirit into painting, many more, when painting is the prevalent and natural art, have produced carved pictures. It may be said that any work is essentially a picture which is conceived from a single quarter and meant to be looked at only in one light. Objects in such a case need not be so truly apperceived and appropriated as they would have to be in true sculpture. One aspect suffices: the subject presented is not so much constructed as dreamt.

The whole history of painting may be strung on this single thread—the effort to reconstitute impressions, first the dramatic impression and then the sensuous. A summary and symbolic representation of things is all that at first is demanded; the point is to describe something pictorially and recall people's names and actions. It is characteristic of archaic painting to be quite discursive and symbolic; each figure is treated separately and stuck side by side with the others upon a golden ground. The painter is here smothered in the recorder, in the annalist; only those perceptions are allowed to stand which have individual names or chronicle facts mentioned in the story. But vision is really more sensuous and rich than report, if art is only able to hold vision in suspense and make it explicit. When painting is still at this stage, and is employed on hieroglyphics, it may reach the maximum of decorative splendour. Whatever sensuous glow finer representations may later acquire will be not sensuous merely, but poetical; Titians, Murillos, or Turners are *colourists in representation*, and their canvases would not be particularly warm or luminous if they represented nothing human or mystical or atmospheric. A stained-glass window or a wall of tiles can outdo them for pure colour and decorative magic. Leaving decoration, accordingly, to take care of itself and be applied as sense may from time to time require, painting goes on to elaborate the symbols with which it begins, to make them symbolise more and more of what their object contains. A catalogue of persons will fall into a group, a group will be fused into a dramatic action. Conventional as the separate figures may still be, their attitudes and relations will reconstitute the dramatic impression. The event will be rendered in its own language; it will not, to be recognised, have to appeal to words. Thus a symbolic crucifixion is a crucifixion only because we know by report that it is; a plastic crucifixion would first teach us, on the contrary, what a real crucifixion might be. It only remains to supply the aerial medium and make dramatic truth sensuous truth also.

When this aerial perspective is complete the painting is essentially a landscape. It may not represent precisely the open country; it may even depict an interior, like Velasquez's Meninas. But the observer, even in the presence of men and artificial objects, has been overcome by the medium in which they swim. He is seeing the air and what it happens to hold. He is impartially recreating from within all that nature puts before him. If this physical being is wholly expressed, the humanity and morality involved will be expressed likewise, even if expressed unawares. Thus a profound and omnivorous reverie overflows the mind; it devours its objects or is absorbed into them, and the mood which this active self-alienation brings with it is called the spirit of the scene, the sentiment of the landscape.

Perception and art, in this phase, easily grow mystical; they are readily lost in primordial physical sympathies. Although at first a certain articulation and discursiveness may be retained in the picture, so that the things seen in their atmosphere and relations may still be distinguished clearly, the farther the impartial absorption in them goes, the more what is inter-individual rises and floods the individual over. All becomes light and depth and air, and those particular objects threaten to vanish which we had hoped to make luminous, breathing, and profound. The initiated eye sees so many nameless tints and surfaces, that it can no longer select any creative limits for things. There cease to be fixed outlines, continuous colours, or discrete existences in nature.

An artist, however, cannot afford to forget that even in such a case units and divisions would have to be introduced by him into his work. A man, in falling back on immediate appearance, may well feel his mind's articulate grammar losing its authority, but that grammar must evidently be reasserted if from the immediate he ever wishes to rise again to articulate mind; and art, after all, exists for the mind and must speak humanly. If we crave something else, we have not so far to go: there is always the infinite about us and the animal within us to absolve us from human distinctions.

Moreover, it is not quite true that the immediate has no real diversity. It evidently suggests the ideal terms into which we divide it, and it sustains our apprehension itself, with all the diversities this may create. To what I call right and left, light and darkness, a real opposition must correspond in any reality which is at all relevant to my experience; so that I should fail to integrate my impression, and to absorb the only reality that concerns me, if I obliterated those points of reference which originally made the world figured and distinct. Space remains absolutely dark, for all the infinite light which we may declare to be radiating through it, until this light is concentrated in one body or reflected from another; and a landscape cannot be so much as vaporous unless mists are distinguishable in it, and through them some known object which they obscure. In a word, landscape is always, in spite of itself, a collection of particular representations. It is a mass of hieroglyphics, each the graphic symbol for some definite human sensation or reaction; only these symbols have been extraordinarily enriched and are fused in representation, so that, like instruments in an orchestra, they are merged in the voluminous sensation they constitute together, a sensation in which, for attentive perception, they never cease to exist.

Impatience of such control as reality must always exercise over representation may drive painting back to a simpler function. When a designer, following his own automatic impulse, conventionalises a form, he makes a legitimate exchange, substituting fidelity to his apperceptive instincts for fidelity to his external impressions. When a landscape-painter, revolting against a tedious discursive style, studies only masses of colour and abstract systems of lines, he retains something in itself beautiful, although no longer representative, perhaps, of anything in nature. A pure impression cannot be illegitimate; it cannot be false until it pretends to represent something, and then it will have ceased to be a simple feeling, since something in it will refer to an ulterior existence, to which it ought to conform. This ulterior existence can be nothing in the end but what produced that impression. Sensuous life, however, has its value within itself; its pleasures are not significant. Representative art is accordingly in a sense secondary; beauty and expression begin farther back. They are present whenever the outer stimulus agreeably strikes an organ and thereby arouses a sustained image. An abstract design in outline and colour will amply fulfil these conditions, if sensuous and motor harmonies are preserved in it, and if a sufficient sweep and depth of reaction is secured. Stained-glass, tapestry, panelling, and in a measure all objects, by their mere presence and distribution, have a decorative function. When sculpture and painting cease to be representative they pass into the same category. Decoration in turn merges in construction; and so all art, like the whole Life of Reason, is joined together at its roots, and branches out from the vital processes of sensation and reaction.

CHAPTER 9

JUSTIFICATION OF ART

To BE bewitched is not to be saved, though all the magicians and aesthetes in the world should pronounce it to be so. Intoxication is a sad business, at least for a philosopher; for you must either drown yourself altogether, or else when sober again you will feel somewhat fooled by yesterday's joys and somewhat lost in to-day's vacancy. The man who would emancipate art from discipline and reason is trying to elude rationality, not merely in art, but in all existence. He is vexed at conditions of excellence that make him conscious of his own incompetence and failure. Rather than consider his function, he proclaims his self-sufficiency. A way foolishness has of revenging itself is to excommunicate the world.

It is in the world, however, that art must find its level. It must vindicate its function in the human commonwealth. What direct acceptable contribution does it make to the highest good? What sacrifices, if any, does it impose? What indirect influence does it exert on other activities? Our answer to these questions will be our apology for art, our proof that art belongs to the Life of Reason.

When moralists deprecate passion and contrast it with reason, they do so, if they are themselves rational, only because passion is so often "guilty," because it works havoc so often in the surrounding world and leaves, among other ruins, "a heart high-sorrowful and cloyed." Were there no danger of such after-effects within and without the sufferer, no passion would be reprehensible. Nature is innocent, and so are all her impulses and moods when taken in isolation; it is only on meeting that they blush. If it be true that matter is sinful, the logic of this truth is far from being what the fanatics imagine who commonly propound it. Matter is sinful only because it is insufficient, or is wastefully distributed. There is not enough of it to go round among the legion of hungry ideas. To express or enact an idea is the only way of making it count; but its embodiment may mutilate it, if the ma-

363

terial is not propitious. So an infant may be maimed at birth, when what injures him is not being brought forth, but being brought forth in the wrong manner. Matter has a double function in respect to spirit; essentially it enables the spirit to be, yet chokes it incidentally. Men sadly misbegotten, or those who are thwarted at every step by the times' penury, may fall to thinking of matter only by its defect, ignoring the material ground of their own aspirations. All flesh will seem to them weak, except that forgotten piece of it which makes their own spiritual strength. Every impulse, however, had initially the same authority as this censorious one, by which the others are now judged and condemned.

If a practice can point to its innocence, if it can absolve itself from concern for a world with which it does not interfere, it has justified itself to those who love it, though it may not yet have recommended itself to those who do not. Now art, more than any other considerable pursuit, more even than speculation, is abstract and inconsequential. Born of suspended attention, it ends in itself. It encourages sensuous abstraction, and nothing concerns it less than to influence the world. Nor does it really do so in a notable degree. Social changes do not reach artistic expression until after their momentum is acquired and their other collateral effects are fully predetermined. Scarcely is a school of art established, giving expression to prevailing sentiment, when this sentiment changes and makes that style seem empty and ridiculous. The expression has little or no power to maintain the movement it registers, as a waterfall has little or no power to bring more water down. Currents may indeed cut deep channels, but they cannot feed their own springs—at least not until the whole revolution of nature is taken into account.

The aesthetic interest is more than innocent, it is liberal. Not being concerned with material reality so much as with the ideal, it has no ulterior motives. In aesthetic activity we have accordingly one side of rational life; sensuous experience is dominated there as mechanical or social realities ought to be dominated in science and politics. Such dominion comes of having faculties suited to their conditions and consequently finding an inherent satisfaction in their operation. The justification of life must be ultimately intrinsic; and wherever such self-justifying experience is attained, an ideal has been in so far embodied. To have realised it in a measure helps us to realise it further; for there is a cumulative fecundity in those goods which come not by increase of force or matter, but by a better organisation and form.

Art has met, on the whole, with more success than science or morals. Beauty gives men the best hint of ultimate good which their experience as yet can offer; and the most lauded geniuses have been poets, as if people felt that those seers, rather than men of action or speculation, had lived ideally and known what was worth knowing. That such should be the case, if the fact be admitted, would indeed prove the rudimentary state of human civilisation. The truly comprehensive life should be the statesman's, for whom perception and theory might be expressed and rewarded in action. The ideal dignity of art is therefore merely symbolic and vicarious. As some people study character in novels, and travel by reading tales of adventure, because real life is not yet so interesting to them as fiction, or because they find it cheaper to make their experiments in their dreams, so art in general is a rehearsal of rational living, and recasts in idea a world which we have no present means of recasting in reality. Yet this rehearsal reveals the glories of a possible performance better than do the miserable experiments until now executed on the reality.

When we consider the present distracted state of government and religion, there is much relief in turning from them to almost any art, where what is good is altogether and finally good, and what is bad is at least not treacherous. When we consider further the senseless rivalries, the vanities, the ignominy that reign in the "practical" world, how doubly blessed it becomes to find a sphere where limitation is an excellence, where diversity is a beauty, and where every man's ambition is consistent with every other man's and even favourable to it! It is indeed so in art; for we must not import into its blameless labours the bickerings and jealousies of criticism. Critics quarrel with other critics, and that is a part of philosophy. With an artist no sane man quarrels, any more than with the colour of a child's eyes. As nature, being full of seeds, rises into all sorts of crystallisations, each having its own ideal and potential life, each a nucleus of order and a habitation for the absolute spirit, so art, though in a medium poorer than pregnant matter, and incapable of intrinsic life, generates a semblance of all conceivable beings. What nature does with existence, art does with appearance; and while the achievement leaves us, unhappily, much where we were before in all our efficacious relations, it entirely renews our vision and breeds a fresh world in fancy, where all form has the same inner justification that all life has in the real world. As no insect is without its rights and every cripple has his dream of happiness, so no artistic fact, no child of imagination, is without its small birthright of beauty. In this freer element, competition does not exist and everything is Olympian. Hungry generations do not tread down the ideal but only its spokesmen or embodiments, that have cast in their lot with other material things. Art supplies constantly to contemplation what nature seldom affords in concrete experience—the union of life and peace.

CHAPTER 10

THE CRITERION OF TASTE

DOGMATISM IN matters of taste has the same status as dogmatism in other spheres. It is initially justified by sincerity, being a systematic expression of a man's preferences; but it becomes absurd when its basis in a particuar disposition is ignored and it pretends to have an absolute or metaphysical scope. Reason, with the order which in every region it imposes on life, is grounded on an animal nature and has no other function than to serve the same; and it fails to exercise its office quite as much when it oversteps its bounds and forgets whom it is serving as when it neglects some part of its legitimate province and serves its master imperfectly, without considering all his interests.

Dialectic, logic, and morals lose their authority and become inept if they trespass upon the realm of physics and try to disclose existences; while physics is a mere idea in the realm of poetic meditation. So the notorious diversities which human taste exhibits do not become conflicts, and raise no moral problem, until their basis or their function has been forgotten, and each has claimed a right to assert itself exclusively. We might fail to understand how so preposterous an attitude could be assumed by anybody did we not remember that every young animal thinks himself absolute, and that dogmatism in the thinker is only the speculative side of greed and courage in the brute. The brute cannot surrender his appetites nor abdicate his primary right to dominate his environment. What experience and reason may teach him is merely how to make his self-assertion well balanced and successful. In the same way taste is bound to maintain its preferences but free to rationalise them. After a man has compared his feelings with the no less legitimate feelings of other creatures, he can reassert his own with more complete authority, since now he is aware of their necessary ground in his nature, and of their affinities with whatever other interests he can recognise in others and can co-ordinate with his own.

A criterion of taste is, therefore, nothing but taste itself in its more deliberate and circumspect form. Reflection refines particular sentiments by bringing them into sympathy with all rational life. There is consequently the greatest possible difference in authority between taste and taste, and while delight in drums and eagles' feathers is perfectly genuine and has no cause to blush for itself, it cannot be compared in scope or representative value with delight in a symphony or an epic. The very instinct that is satisfied by beauty prefers one beauty to another; and we have only to question and purge our aesthetic feelings in order to obtain our criterion of taste. This criterion will be natural, personal, autonomous; a circumstance that will give it authority over our own judgment—which is all moral science is concerned about—and will extend its authority over other minds also, in so far as their constitution is similar to ours.

Taste is formed in those moments when aesthetic emotion is massive and distinct; preferences then grown conscious, judgments then put into words, will reverberate through calmer hours; they will constitute prejudices, habits of apperception, secret standards for all other beauties. Half our standards come from our first masters, and the other half from our first loves. Never being so deeply stirred again, we remain persuaded that no objects save those we then discovered can have a true sublimity. These high-water marks of aesthetic life may easily be reached under tutelage. It may be some eloquent appreciations read in a book, or some preference expressed by a gifted friend, that may have revealed unsuspected beauties in art or nature; and then, since our own perception was vicarious and obviously inferior in volume to that which our mentor possessed, we shall take his judgments for our criterion, since they were the source and exemplar of all our own. Thus the volume and intensity of some appreciations, especially when nothing of the kind has preceded, makes them authoritative over our subsequent judgments. On those warm moments hang all our cold systematic opinions; and while the latter fill our days and shape our careers it is only the former that are crucial and alive.

A race which loves beauty holds the same place in history that a season of love or enthusiasm holds in an individual life. Such a race has a pre-eminent right to pronounce upon beauty and to bequeath its judgments to duller peoples. We may accordingly listen with reverence to a Greek judgment on that subject, expecting that what might seem to us wrong about it is the expression of knowledge and passion beyond our range; it will suffice that we learn to live in the world of beauty, instead of merely studying its relics, for us to understand, for instance, that imitation is a fundamental principle in art, and that any rational judgment on the beautiful must be a moral and political judgment, enveloping chance aesthetic feelings and determining their value. What painters say about painting and poets about poetry is better than lay opinion; it may reveal, of course, some petty jealousy or some partial incapacity, because a special gift often carries with it complementary defects in apprehension; yet what is positive in such judgments is founded on knowledge and avoids the romancing into which litterateurs and sentimentalists will gladly wander. The specific values of art are technical values, more permanent and definite than the adventitious analogies on which a stray observer usually bases his views. Only a technical education can raise judgments on musical compositions above impertinent autobiography. The Japanese know the beauty of flowers, and tailors and dressmakers have the best sense for the fashions. We ask them for suggestions, and if we do not always take their advice, it is not because the fine effects they love are not genuine, but because they may not be effects which we care to produce.

Good taste, besides being inwardly clear, has to be outwardly fit. It needs a material basis, a soil and situation propitious to its growth. This basis, as it varies, makes the ideal vary which is simply its expression; and therefore no ideal can be ultimately fixed in ignorance of the conditions that may modify it. It subsists, to be sure, as an eternal possibility, independently of all further earthly revolutions. Once expressed, it has revealed the inalienable values that attach to a certain form of being, whenever that form is actualised. But its expression may have been only momentary, and that eternal ideal may have no further relevance to the living world. A criterion of taste, however, looks to a social career; it hopes to educate and to judge. In order to be an applicable and a just law, it must represent the interests over which it would preside.

There are many undiscovered ideals. There are many beauties which nothing in this world can embody or suggest. There are also many once suggested or even embodied, which find later their basis gone and evaporate into their native heaven. The saddest tragedy in the world is the destruction of what has within it no inward ground of dissolution, death in youth, and the crushing out of perfection. Imagination has its bereavements of this kind. A complete mastery of existence achieved at one moment gives no warrant that it will be sustained or achieved again. The achievement may have been perfect; nature will not on that account stop to admire it. She will move on, and the meaning which was read so triumphantly in her momentary attitude will not fit her new posture. Like Polonius's cloud, she will always suggest some new ideal, because she has none of her own.

In lieu of an ideal, however, nature has a constitution, and this, which is a necessary ground for ideals, is what it concerns the ideal to reckon with. A poet, spokesman of his full soul at a given juncture, cannot consider eventualities or think of anything but the message he is sent to deliver, whether the world can then hear it or not. God, he may feel sure, understands him, and in the eternal the beauty he sees and loves immortally justifies his enthusiasm. Nevertheless, critics must view his momentary ebullition from another side. They do not come to justify the poet in his own eyes; he amply relieves them of such a function. They come only to inquire how significant the poet's expressions are for humanity at large or for whatever public he addresses. They come to register the social or representative value of the poet's soul. A work of art is a public possession; it is addressed to the world. By taking on a material embodiment, a spirit solicits attention and claims some kinship with the prevalent gods. Has it, critics should ask, the affinities needed for such intercourse? Is it humane, is it rational, is it representative? To its inherent incommunicable charms it must add a kind of courtesy. If it wants other approval than its own, it cannot afford to regard no other aspiration.

This scope, this representative faculty or wide appeal, is necessary to good taste. Force and inner consistency are gifts on which I may well congratulate another, but they give him no right to speak for me. Either aesthetic experience would have remained a chaos—which it is not altogether—or it must have tended to conciliate certain general human demands and ultimately all those interests which its operation in any way affects. The more conspicuous and permanent a work of art is, the more is such an adjustment needed. A poet or philosopher may be erratic and assure us that he is inspired; if we cannot well gainsay it, we are at least not obliged to read his works. An architect or a sculptor, however, or a public performer of any sort, that thrusts before us a spectacle justified only in his inner consciousness, makes himself a nuisance. A social standard of taste must assert itself here, or else no efficacious and cumulative art can exist at all.

There are various affinities by which art may acquire a representative or classic quality. It may do so by giving form to objects which everybody knows, by rendering experiences that are universal and primary. The human figure, elementary passions, common types and crises of fate—these are facts which pass too constantly through apperception not to acquire a normal aesthetic value. The artist who can catch that effect in its fulness and simplicity accordingly does immortal work. This sort of art immediately becomes popular; it passes into language and convention so that its aesthetic charm is apparently worn down. The old images after a while hardly stimulate unless they be presented in some paradoxical way; but in that case attention will be diverted to the accidental extravagance, and the chief classic effect will be missed. It is the honourable fate or euthanasia of artistic successes that they pass from the field of professional art altogether and become a portion of human faculty. Every man learns to be to that extent an artist; approved figures and maxims pass current like the words and idioms of a mother-tongue, themselves once brilliant inventions. The lustre of such successes is not really dimmed, however, when it becomes a part of a man's daily light; a retrogression from that habitual style or habitual insight would at once prove, by the shock it caused, how precious those ingrained apperceptions continued to be.

Both elementary and ultimate judgments contribute to a standard of taste; yet human life lies between these limits. Good taste is that taste which is a good possession, a friend to the whole man. It will not suffer him to dote on things, however seductive, which rob him of some nobler companionship. To have a foretaste of such a loss, and to reject instinctively whatever will cause it, is the very essence of refinement. Good taste comes, therefore, from experience, in the best sense of that word; it comes from having united in one's memory and character the fruit of many diverse undertakings. Mere taste is apt to be bad taste, since it regards nothing but a chance feeling. Every man who pursues an art may be presumed to have some sensibility; the question is whether he has breeding, too, and whether what he stops at is not, in the end, vulgar and offensive. Chance feeling needs to fortify itself with reasons and to find its level in the great world. When it has added fitness to its sincerity, beneficence to its passion, it will have acquired a right to live. Violence and self-justification will not pass muster in a moral society, for vipers possess both, and must nevertheless be stamped out. Citizenship is conferred only on creatures with human and co-operative instincts. A civilised imagination has to understand and to serve the world.

The great obstacle which art finds in attempting to be rational is its functional isolation. Sense and each of the passions suffers from a similar independence. The disarray of human instincts lets every spontaneous motion run too far; life oscillates between constraint and unreason. Morality too often puts up with being a constraint and even imagines such a disgrace to be its essence. Art, on the contrary, as often hugs unreason for fear of losing its inspiration, and forgets that it is itself a rational principle of creation and order. Morality is thus reduced to a necessary evil and art to a vain good, all for want of harmony among human impulses.

The joys of creating are not confined to those who create things without practical uses. The merely aesthetic, like rhyme and fireworks, is not the only subject that can engage a playful fancy or be planned with a premonition of beautiful effects. Architecture may be useful, sculpture commemorative, poetry reflective, even music, by its expression, religious or martial. In a word, practical exigencies, in calling forth the arts, give them moral functions which it is a pleasure to see them fulfil. Works may not be aesthetic in their purpose, and yet that fact may be a ground for their being doubly delightful in execution and doubly beautiful in effect. A richer plexus of emotions is concerned in producing or contemplating something humanly necessary than something idly conceived. What is very rightly called a *sense* for fitness is a vital experience, involving aesthetic satisfactions and aesthetic shocks. The more numerous the rational harmonies are which are present to the mind, the more sensible movements will be going on there to give immediate delight; for the perception or expectation of an ulterior good is a present good also. Accordingly nothing can so well call forth or sustain attention as what has a complex structure relating it to many complex interests. A work woven out of precious threads has a deep pertinence and glory; the artist who creates it does not need to surrender his practical and moral sense in order to indulge his imagination.

The truth is that mere sensation or mere emotion is an indignity to a mature human being. When we eat, we demand a pleasant vista, flowers, or conversation, and failing these we take refuge in a newspaper. The monks, knowing that men should not feed silently like stalled oxen, appointed some one to read aloud in the refectory; and the Fathers, obeying the same civilised instinct, had contrived in their theology intelligible points of attachment for religious emotion. A refined mind finds as little happiness in love without friendship as in sensuality without love; it may succumb to both, but it accepts neither. What is true of mere sensibility is no less true of mere fancy. Any absolute work of art which serves no further purpose than to stimulate an emotion has about it a certain luxurious and visionary taint. We leave it with a blank mind, and a pang bubbles up from the very fountain of pleasures. Art, so long as it needs to be a dream, will never cease to prove a disappointment. Its facile cruelty, its narcotic abstraction, can never sweeten the evils we return to at home; it can liberate half the mind only by leaving the other half in abeyance. In the mere artist, too, there is always something that falls short of the gentleman and that defeats the man.

Surely it is not the artistic impulse in itself that involves such lack of equilibrium. To impress a meaning and a rational form on matter is one of the most masterful of actions. The trouble lies in the barren and superficial character of this imposed form: fine art is a play of appearance. Appearance, for a critical philosophy, is distinguished from reality by its separation from the context of things, by its immediacy and insignificance. A play of appearance is accordingly some little closed circle in experience, some dream in which we lose ourselves by ignoring most of our interests, and from which we awake into a world in which that lost episode plays no further part and leaves no heirs. Art as mankind has hitherto practised it falls largely under this head and too much resembles an opiate or a stimulant. To exalt fine art into a truly ideal possession we should have to knit it more closely with other rational functions, so that to beautify things might render them more useful and to represent them most imaginatively might be to see them in their truth. Something of the sort has been actually attained by the noblest arts in their noblest phases. A Sophocles or a Leonardo dominates his dreamful vehicle and works upon the real world by its means. These small centres, where interfunctional harmony is attained, ought to expand and cover the whole field. Art, like religion, needs to be absorbed in the Life of Reason.

If the rendering of reality is to remain artistic, it must still study to satisfy the senses; but as this study would now accompany every activity, taste would grow vastly more subtle and exacting. Whatever any man said or did or made, he would be alive to its aesthetic quality, and beauty would be a pervasive ingredient in happiness. No work would be called, in a special sense, a work of art, for all works would be such intrinsically. Thus there would need to be no division of mankind into mechanical blind workers and half-demented poets and no separation of useful from fine art, such as people make who have understood neither the nature nor the ultimate reward of human action. All arts would be practised together and merged in the art of life, the only one wholly useful or fine among them.

CHAPTER 11

ART AND HAPPINESS

THE VALUE of art lies in making people happy, first in practising the art and then in possessing its product. This observation might seem needless, and ought to be so; but if we compare it with what is commonly said on these subjects, we must confess that it may often be denied and more often, perhaps, may not be understood. Happiness is something men ought to pursue, although they seldom do so; they are drawn away from it at first by foolish impulses and afterwards by perverse customs. To secure happiness conduct would have to remain spontaneous while it learned not to be criminal; but the fanatical attachment of men, now to a fierce liberty, now to a false regimen, keeps them barbarous and wretched. A rational pursuit of happiness—which is one thing with progress or with the Life of Reason—would embody that natural piety which leaves to the episodes of life their inherent values, mourning death, celebrating love, sanctifying civic traditions, enjoying and correcting nature's ways. To discriminate happiness is therefore the very soul of art, which expresses experience without distorting it, as those political or metaphysical tyrannies distort it which sanctify unhappiness. A free mind, like a creative imagination, rejoices at the harmonies it can find or make between man and nature; and, where it finds none, it solves the conflict so far as it may and then notes and endures it with a shudder.

A morality organised about the human heart in an ingenuous and sincere fashion would involve every fine art and would render the world pervasively beautiful—beautiful in its artificial products and beautiful in its underlying natural terrors. The closer we keep to elementary human needs and to the natural agencies that may satisfy them, the closer we are to beauty. Industry, sport, and science, with the perennial intercourse and passions of men, swarm with incentives to expression, because they are everywhere creating new moulds of being and compelling the eye to observe those forms and to recast them ideally. Art is simply an adequate industry; it arises when industry is carried out to the satisfaction of all human demands, even of those incidental sensuous demands which we call aesthetic and which a brutal industry, in its haste, may despise or ignore.

Arts responsive in this way to all human nature would be beautiful according to reason and might remain beautiful long. Poetic beauty touches the world whenever it attains some unfeigned harmony either with sense or with reason; and the more unfeignedly human happiness was made the test of all institutions and pursuits, the more beautiful they would be, having more numerous points of fusion with the mind, and fusing with it more profoundly. To distinguish and to create beauty would then be no art relegated to a few abstracted spirits, playing with casual fancies; it would be a habit inseparable from practical efficiency. All operations, all affairs, would then be viewed in the light of ultimate interests, and in their deep relation to human good. The arts would thus recover their Homeric glory; touching human fate as they clearly would, they would borrow something of its grandeur and pathos, and yet the interest that worked in them would be warm, because it would remain unmistakably animal and sincere.

The principle that all institutions should subserve happiness runs deeper than any cult for art and lays the foundation on which the latter might rest safely. If social structure were rational its free expression would be so too. Many observers, with no particular philosophy to adduce, feel that the arts among us are somehow impotent, and they look for a better inspiration, now to ancient models, now to the raw phenomena of life. A dilettante may, indeed, summon inspiration whence he will; and a virtuoso will never lack some material to keep him busy; but if what is hoped for is a genuine, native, inevitable art, a great revolution would first have to be worked in society. We should have to abandon our vested illusions, our irrational religions and patriotisms and schools of art, and to discover instead our genuine needs, the forms of our possible happiness. To call for such self-examination seems revolutionary only because we start from a sophisticated system, a system resting on traditional fashions and superstitions, by which the will of the living generation is misinterpreted and betrayed. To shake off that system would not subvert order but rather institute order for the first time; it would be an *Instauratio Magna*, a setting things again on their feet.

We in Christendom are so accustomed to artificial ideals and to artificial institutions, kept up to express them, that we hardly conceive how anomalous our situation is, sorely as we may suffer from it. We found academies and museums, as we found missions, to fan a flame that constantly threatens to die out for lack of natural fuel. Our overt ideals are parasites in the body politic, while the ideals native to the body politic, those involved in our natural structure and situation, are either stifled by that alien incubus, leaving civic life barbarous, or else force their way up, unremarked or not justly honoured as ideals. Industry and science and social amenities, with all the congruous comforts and appurtenances of contemporary life, march on their way, as if they had nothing to say to the spirit, which remains entangled in a cobweb of dead traditions. An idle pottering of the fancy over obsolete forms—theological, dramatic, or plastic—makes that by-play to the sober business of life which men call their art or their religion; and the more functionless and gratuitous this by-play is the more those who indulge in it think they are idealists. They feel they are champions of what is most precious in the world, as a sentimental lady might fancy herself a lover of flowers when she pressed them in a book instead of planting their seeds in the garden.

It is clear that gratuitous and functionless habits cannot bring happiness; they do not constitute a pursuit at once spontaneous and beneficent, such as noble art is an instance of. Those habits may indeed give pleasure; they may bring extreme excitement, as madness notably does, though it is in the highest degree functionless and gratuitous. Nor is such by-play without consequences, some of which might conceivably be fortunate. What is functionless is so called for being worthless from some ideal point of view, and not conducing to the particular life considered. But nothing real is dissociated from the universal flux; everything—madness and all unmeaning cross-currents in being—count in the general process and discharge somewhere, not without effect, the substance they have drawn for a moment into their little vortex. So our vain arts and unnecessary religions are not without real effects and not without a certain internal vitality. When life is profoundly disorganised it may well happen that only in detached episodes, only in moments snatched for dreaming in, can men see the blue or catch a glimpse of something like the ideal. In that case their esteem for their irrelevant visions may be well grounded, and their thin art and far-fetched religion may really constitute what is best in their experience. In a pathetic way these poor enthusiasms may be justified, but only because the very conception of a rational life lies entirely beyond the horizon.

It is no marvel, when art is a brief truancy from rational practice, that the artist himself should be a vagrant, and at best, as it were, an infant prodigy. The wings of genius serve him only for an escapade, enabling him to skirt the perilous edge of madness and of mystical abysses. But such an erratic workman does not deserve the name of artist or master; he has burst convention only to break it, not to create a new convention more in harmony with nature. His originality, though it may astonish for a moment, will in the end be despised and will find no thoroughfare. He will meantime be wretched himself, torn from the roots of his being by that cruel, unmeaning inspiration; or, if too rapt to see his own plight, he will be all the more pitied by practical men, who cannot think it a real blessing to be lost in joys that do not strengthen the character and yield nothing for posterity.

Art, in its nobler acceptation, is an achievement, not an indulgence. It prepares the world in some sense to receive the soul, and the soul to master the world; it disentangles those threads in each that can be woven into the other. That the artist should be eccentric, homeless, dreamful may almost seem a natural law, but it is none the less a scandal. An artist's business is not really to cut fantastical capers or be licensed to play the fool. His business is simply that of every keen soul to build well when it builds, and to speak well when it speaks, giving the treatment everywhere the greatest possible affinity to the theme and the most delicate adjustment to every faculty it affects. The wonder of an artist's performance grows with the range of his penetration, with the instinctive sympathy that makes him, in his mortal isolation, considerate of other men's fate and a great diviner of their secret, so that his work speaks to them kindly, with a deeper assurance than they could have spoken with to themselves. And the joy of his great sanity, the power of his adequate vision, is not the less intense because he can lend it to others and has borrowed it from a faithful study of the world.

If happiness is the ultimate sanction of art, art in turn is the best instrument of happiness. In art more directly than in other activities man's self-expression is cumulative and finds an immediate reward; for it alters the material conditions of sentience so that sentience becomes at once more delightful and more significant. In industry man is still servile, preparing the materials he is to use in action. In action itself, though he is free, he exerts his influence on a living and treacherous medium and sees the issue at each moment drift farther and farther from his intent. In science he is an observer, preparing himself for action in another way, by studying its results and conditions. But in art he is at once competent and free; he is creative. He is not troubled by his materials, because he has assimilated them and may take them for granted; nor is he concerned with the chance complexion of affairs in the actual world, because he is making the world over, not merely considering how it grew or how it will consent to grow in future. Nothing, accordingly, could be more delightful than genuine art, nor more free from remorse and the sting of vanity. Art springs so completely from the heart of man that it makes everything speak to him in his own language; it reaches, nevertheless, so truly to the heart of nature that it co-operates with her, becomes a parcel of her creative material energy, and builds by her instinctive hand. If the various formative impulses afoot in the world never opposed stress to stress and made no havoc with one another, nature might be called an unconscious artist. In fact, just where such a formative impulse finds support from the environment, a consciousness supervenes. If that consciousness is adequate enough to be prophetic, an art arises. Thus the emergence of arts out of instincts is the token and exact measure of nature's success and of mortal happiness.

V

REASON IN SCIENCE

CHAPTER 1

TYPES AND AIMS OF SCIENCE

SCIENCE IS so new a thing and so far from final, it seems to the layman so hopelessly accurate and extensive, that a moralist may well feel some diffidence in trying to estimate its achievements and promises at their human worth. The morrow may bring some great revolution in science, and is sure to bring many a correction and many a surprise. Religion and art have had their day; indeed a part of the faith they usually inspire is to believe that they have long ago revealed their secret. A critic may safely form a judgment concerning them; for they have run their course through in various ages and climes with results which anybody is free to estimate if he has an open mind and sufficient interest in the subject. Science, on the contrary, which apparently cannot exist where intellectual freedom is denied, has flourished only twice in recorded times: once for some three hundred years in ancient Greece, and again for about the same period in modern Christendom. Its fruits have scarcely begun to appear; the lands it is discovering have not yet been circumnavigated, and there is no telling what its ultimate influence will be on human practice and feeling.

The true contrast between science and myth is roughly indicated when we say that science alone is capable of verification. Some ambiguity, however, lurks in this phrase, since verification comes to a method only vicariously, when the particulars it prophesies are realised in sense. To verify a theory as if it were not a method but a divination of occult existences would be to turn the theory into a myth and then to discover that what the myth pictured had, by a miracle, an actual existence also. There is accordingly a sense in which myth admits substantiation of a kind that science excludes. The Olympic hierarchy might conceivably exist bodily; but gravitation and natural selection, being schemes of relation, can never exist substantially and on their own behoof.

Nevertheless, the Olympic hierarchy, even if it happened to exist, could not be proved to do so unless it were a part of the natural world open to sense; while gravitation and natural selection, without being existences, can be verified at every moment by concrete events occurring as those principles require. A hypothesis, being a discursive device, gains its utmost possible validity when its discursive value is established. It *is* not, it merely *applies*; and every situation in which it is found to apply is a proof of its truth.

A chief characteristic of science, then, is that in supplementing given facts it supplements them by adding other facts belonging to the same sphere, and eventually discoverable by tracing the given object in its own plane through its continuous transformations. Science expands speculatively, by the aid of merely instrumental hypotheses, objects given in perception until they compose a congruous, self-supporting world, all parts of which might be observed consecutively. What a scientific hypothesis interpolates among the given facts—the atomic structure of things, for instance —might come in time under the direct fire of attention, fixed more scrupulously, longer, or with better instruments upon those facts themselves. Otherwise the hypothesis that assumed that structure would be simply false, just as a hypothesis that the interior of the earth is full of molten fire would be false if on inspection nothing were found there but solid rock. Science does not merely prolong a habit of inference; it verifies and solves the inference by reaching the fact inferred.

The contrast with myth at this point is very interesting; for in myth the facts are themselves made vehicles, and knowledge is felt to terminate in an independent existence on a higher or deeper level than any immediate fact; and this circumstance is what makes myth impossible to verify and, except by laughter, to disprove. If I attributed the stars' shining to the diligence of angels who lighted their lamps at sunset, lest the upper reaches of the world should grow dangerous for travellers, and if I made my romance elaborate and ingenious enough, I might possibly find that the stars' appearance and disappearance could continue to be interpreted in that way. My myth might always suggest itself afresh and might be perennially appropriate. But it would never descend, with its charming figures, into the company of its evidences. It would never prove that what it terminated in was a fact, as in my metaphysical faith I had deputed and asserted it to be. The angels would remain notional, while my intent was to have them exist; so that the more earnestly I held to my fable the more grievously should I be deceived. For even if seraphic choirs existed in plenty on their own emotional or musical plane of being, it would not have been their hands—if they had hands—that would have lighted the stars I saw; and this, after all, was the gist and starting-point of my whole fable and its sole witness in my world. A myth might by chance be a revelation, did what it talks of have an actual existence somewhere else in the universe; but it would need to be a revelation in order to be true at all.

Science is a half-way house between private sensation and universal vision. We should not forget to add, however, that the universal vision in question, if it were to be something better than private sensation or passive feeling in greater bulk, would have to be intellectual, just as science is; that is, it would have to be practical and to survey the flux from a given standpoint, in a perspective determined by special and local interests. Otherwise the whole world, when known, would merely be re-enacted in its blind immediacy without being understood or subjected to any purpose. The critics of science, when endowed with any speculative power, have always seen that what is hypothetical and abstract in scientific method is somehow servile and provisional; science being a sort of telegraphic wire through which a meagre report reaches us of things we would fain observe and live through in their full reality. This report may suffice for approximately fit action; it does not suffice for ideal knowledge of the truth nor for adequate sympathy with the reality. What commonly escapes speculative critics of science, however, is that in transcending hypothesis and reaching immediacy again we should run a great risk of abandoning knowledge and sympathy altogether; for if we *became* what we now represent so imperfectly, we should evidently no longer represent it at all. We should not, at the end of our labours, have enriched our own minds by adequate knowledge of what surrounds us, nor made our wills just in view of alien but well-considered interests. We should have lost our own essence and substituted for it, not something higher than indiscriminate being, but only indiscriminate being in its flat, blind, and selfish infinity. The ideality, the representative faculty, would have gone out in our souls, and our perfected humanity would have brought us back to protoplasm.

In transcending science, therefore, we must not hope to transcend knowledge, nor in transcending selfishness to abolish finitude. Finitude is the indispensable condition of unselfishness as well as of selfishness, and of speculative vision no less than of hypothetical knowledge. The defect of science is that it is inadequate or abstract, that the account it gives of things is not full and sensuous enough; but its merit is that, like sense, it makes external being present to a creature that is concerned in adjusting itself to its environment, and informs that creature about things other than itself. Science, if brought to perfection, would not lose its representative or ideal essence. It would still survey and inform, but it would survey everything at once and inform the being it enlightened about all that could affect its interests. It would thus remain practical in effect and speculative in character. In losing its accidental limitations it would not lose its initial bias, its vital function. It would continue to be a rational activity, guiding and perfecting a natural being.

Perfect knowledge of things would be as far as possible from identifying the knower with them, seeing that for the most part—even when we call them human—they have no knowledge of themselves. Science, accordingly, even when imperfect, is a tremendous advance on absorption in sense and a dull immediacy. It begins to enrich the mind and gives it some inkling, at least, of that ideal dominion which each centre of experience might have if it had learned to regard all others, and the relation connecting it with them, both in thought and in action. Ideal knowledge would be an inward state corresponding to a perfect adjustment of the body to all forces affecting it. If the adjustment was perfect the inward state would regard every detail in the objects envisaged, but it would see those details in a perspective of its own, adding to sympathetic reproduction of them a consciousness of their relation to its own existence and perfection.

The fact that science expresses the character and relation of objects in their own terms has a further important consequence, which serves again to distinguish science from metaphorical thinking. If a man tries to illustrate the nature of a thing by assimilating it to something else which he happens to have in mind at the same time, it is obvious that a second man, whose mind is differently furnished, may assimilate the same object to a quite different idea: so myths are centrifugal, and the more elaborate and delicate they are the more they diverge, like well-developed languages. The rude beginnings of myth in every age and country bear a certain resemblance, because the facts interpreted are similar and the minds reading them have not yet developed their special grammar of representation. But two highly developed mythical systems—two theologies, for instance, like the Greek and the Indian—will grow every day farther and farther apart. Science, on the contrary, whatever it may start with, runs back into the same circle of facts, because it follows the lead of the subject-matter, and is attentive to its inherent transformations.

Men asleep, said Heraclitus, live each in his own world, but awake they live in the same world together. To be awake is nothing but to be dreaming under control of the object; it is to be pursuing science to the comparative exclusion of mere mental vegetation and spontaneous myth. Thus if our objects are the same, our science and our waking lives will coincide; or if there is a natural diversity in our discoveries, because we occupy different points in space and time and have a varying range of experience, these diversities will nevertheless supplement one another; the discovery that each has made will be a possible discovery for the others also. So a geographer in China and one in Babylonia may at first make wholly unlike maps; but in time both will take note of the Himalayas, and the side each approaches will slope up to the very crest approached by the other. So science is self-confirming, and its most disparate branches are mutually illuminating; while in the realm of myth, until it is surveyed scientifically, there can be nothing but mutual repulsion and incapacity to understand. Languages and religions are necessarily rivals, but sciences are necessarily allies.

Science is not absolutely single but springs up in various places at once, as a certain consistency or method becomes visible in this or that direction. These independent sciences might, conceivably, never meet at all; each might work out an entirely different aspect of things and cross the other, as it were, at a different level. This actually happens, for instance, in mathematics as compared with history or psychology, and in morals as compared with physics. Nevertheless, the fact that these various sciences are all human, and that here, for instance, we are able to mention them in one breath and to compare their natures, is proof that their spheres touch somehow, even if only peripherally. Since common knowledge, which knows of them all, is itself an incipient science, we may be sure that some continuity and some congruity obtains between their provinces. Some aspect of each must coincide with some aspect of some other, else nobody who pursued any one science would so much as suspect the existence of the rest. Great as may be the aversion of learned men to one another, and comprehensive as may be their ignorance, they are not positively compelled to live in solitary confinement, and the key of their prison cells is at least in their own pocket.

Some sciences, like chemistry and biology, or biology and anthropology, are parted only, we may presume, by accidental gaps in human knowledge; a more minute and better directed study of these fields would doubtless disclose their continuity with the fields adjoining. But human understanding has used from the beginning a double method of surveying and arresting ideally the irreparable flux of being. One expedient has been to notice and identify similarities of character, recurrent types, in the phenomena that pass before it or in its own operations; the other expedient has been to note and combine in one complex object characters which occur and reappear together. The latter feat which is made easy by the fact that when various senses are stimulated at once the inward instinctive reaction—which is felt by a primitive mind more powerfully than any external image—is one and not consciously divisible.

The first expedient imposes on the flux what we call ideas, which are concretions in discourse, terms employed in thought and language. The second expedient separates the same flux into what we call things, which are concretions in existence, complexes of qualities subsisting in space and time, having definable dynamic relations there and a traceable history. Carrying out this primitive diversity in reflection science has moved in two different directions. By refining concretions in discourse it has attained to mathematics, logic, and the dialectical developments of ethics; by tracing concretions in existence it has reached the various natural and historical sciences. Following ancient usage, I shall take the liberty of calling the whole group of sciences which elaborates ideas *dialectic*, and the whole group that describes existences *physics*.

The contrast between ideal science or dialectic and natural science or physics is as great as the understanding of a single experience could well afford; yet the two kinds of science are far from independent. They touch at their basis and they co-operate in their results. Were dialectic made clearer or physics deeper than it commonly is, these points of contact would doubtless be multiplied; but even as they stand they furnish a sufficient illustration of the principle that all science develops objects in their own category and gives the mind dominion over the flux of matter by discovering its form.

That physics and dialectic touch at their basis may be shown by a double analysis. In the first place, it is clear that the science of existence, like all science, is itself discourse, and that before concretions in existence can be discovered, and groups of coexistent qualities can be recognised, these qualities themselves must be arrested by the mind, noted, and identified in their recurrences. But these terms, bandied about in scientific discourse, are so many essences and pure ideas: so that the inmost texture of natural science is logical, and the whole force of any observation made upon the outer world lies in the constancy and mutual relations of the terms it is made in. If down did not mean down and motion motion, Newton could never have taken note of the fall of his apple. Now the constancy and relation of meanings is something *meant*, it is something created by insight and intent and is altogether dialectical; so that the science of existence is a portion of the art of discourse.

On the other hand discourse, in its operation, is a part of existence. That truth or logical cogency is not itself an existence is obvious to any one who sees for a moment what truth means, especially if he remembers at the same time that all existence is mutable, which it is the essence of truth not to be. But the knowledge or discovery of truth is an event in time, an incident in the flux of existence, and therefore a matter for natural science to study.

Furthermore, every term which dialectic uses is originally given embodied; in other words, it is given as an element in the actual flux, it comes by illustration. Though meaning is the object of an ideal function, and signification is inwardly appreciable only in terms of signification, yet the ideal leap is made from a material datum: that in which signification is seen is a fact. Or to state the matter somewhat differently, truth is not self-generating; if it were it would be a falsehood. Its eternity, and the infinitude of propositions it contains, remain potential and unapproachable until their incidence is found in existence. Form cannot of itself decide which of all possible forms shall be real; in their ideality, and without reference to their illustration in things, all consistent propositions would be equally valid and equally trivial. Important validity is truth about something; and although a single datum might suffice to give foothold and pertinence to an infinity of truths, as one atom would posit all geometry, geometry, if there were no space, would be, if I may say so, all of the fourth dimension, and arithmetic, if there were no pulses or chasms in being, would be all algebra. Truth depends upon facts for its perspective, since facts select truths and decide which truths shall be mere possibilities and which shall be the eternal forms of actual things. The dialectical world would be a trackless desert if the existent world had no arbitrary constitution. Living dialectic comes to clarify existence; it turns into meanings the actual forms of things by reflecting upon them, and by making them intended subjects of discourse.

Dialectic and physics, thus united at their basis, meet again in their results. In mechanical science, which is the best part of physics, mathematics, which is the best part of dialectic, plays a predominant rôle; it furnishes the whole method of understanding wherever there is any real understanding at all. In psychology and history, too, although dialectic is soon choked by the cross-currents of nature, it furnishes the little perspicuousness which there is. We understand actions and mental developments when the purposes or ideas contained in any stage are carried out logically in the sequel; it is when conduct and growth are rational, that is, when they are dialectical, that we think we have found the true secret and significance of them. It is the evident ideal of physics, in every department, to attain such an insight into causes that the effects actually given may be thence *deduced*; and deduction is another name for dialectic. To be sure, the dialectic applicable to material processes and to human life is one in which the terms and the categories needed are still exceedingly numerous and vague: a little logic is all that can be read into the cataract of events. But the hope of science, a hope which is supported by every success it scores, is that a simpler law than has yet been discovered will be found to connect units subtler than those yet known; and that in these finer terms the universal mechanism may be exhaustively rendered. Mechanism is the ideal of physics, because it is the infusion of a maximum of mathematical necessity into the flux of real things. It is the aspiration of natural science to be as dialectical as possible, and thus, in their ideal, both branches of science are brought together.

That the ideal of dialectic is to apply to existence and thereby to coincide with physics is in a sense no less true, although dialecticians may be little inclined to confess it. The direct purpose of deduction is to elucidate an idea, to develop an import, and nothing can be more irrelevant in this science than whether the conclusion is verified in nature or not. But the direct purpose of dialectic is not its ultimate justification. Dialectic is a human pursuit and has, at bottom, a moral function; otherwise, at bottom, it would have no value. And the moral function and ultimate justification of dialectic is to further the Life of Reason, in which human thought has the maximum practical validity, and may enjoy in consequence the richest ideal development. If dialectic takes a turn which makes it inapplicable in physics, which makes it worthless for mastering experience, it loses all its dignity: for abstract cogency has no dignity if the subject-matter into which it is introduced is trivial. In fact, were dialectic a game in which the counters were not actual data and the conclusions were not possible principles for understanding existence, it would not be a science at all. It would resemble a counterfeit paper currency, without intrinsic value and without commercial convenience. Just as a fact without implications is not a part of science, so a method without application would not be.

The free excursions of dialectic into non-natural regions may be wisely encouraged when they satisfy an interest which is at bottom healthy and may, at least indirectly, bring with it excellent fruits. As musicians are an honour to society, so are dialecticians that have a single heart and an exquisite patience. But somehow the benefit must redound to society and to practical knowledge, or these abstracted hermits will seem at first useless and at last mad. The logic of nonsense has a subtle charm only because it can so easily be turned into the logic of common sense. Empty dialectic is, as it were, the ballet of science: it runs most neatly after nothing at all.

Both physics and dialectic are contained in common knowledge, and when carried further than men carry them in daily life, these sciences remain essentially inevitable and essentially fallible. If science deserves respect, it is not for being oracular but for being useful and delightful, as seeing is. Understanding is nothing but seeing under and seeing far. There is indeed a great mystery in knowledge, but this mystery is present in the simplest memory or presumption. The sciences have nothing to supply more fundamental than vulgar thinking or, as it were, preliminary to it. They are simply elaborations of it; they accept its presuppositions and carry on its ordinary processes. A pretence on the philosopher's part that he could get behind or below human thinking, that he could underpin, so to speak, his own childhood and the inherent conventions of daily thought, would be pure imposture. A philosopher can of course investigate the history of knowledge, he can analyse its method and point out its assumptions; but he cannot know by other authority than that which the vulgar know by, nor can his knowledge begin with other unheard-of objects or deploy itself in advance over an esoteric field. Every deeper investigation presupposes ordinary perception and uses some at least of its data. Every possible discovery *extends* human knowledge. None can base human knowledge anew on a deeper foundation or prefix an ante-experimental episode to experience. We may construct a theory as disintegrating as we please about the dialectical or empirical conditions of the experience given; we may disclose its logical stratification or physical antecedents; but every idea and principle used in such a theory must be borrowed from current knowledge as it happens to lie in the philosopher's mind.

If these speculative adventures do not turn out well, the scientific man is free to turn about and become the critic and satirist of his foiled ambitions. He may exhaust scepticism and withdraw into the citadel of immediate feeling, yielding bastion after bastion to the assaults of doubt. When he is at last perfectly safe from error and reduced to speechless sensibility, he will perceive, however, that he is also washed clean of every practical belief: he would declare himself universally ignorant but for a doubt whether there be really anything to know. This metaphysical exercise is simply one of those "fallings from us, vanishings, blank misgivings of a creature moving about in worlds not realised" which may visit any child. So long as the suspension of judgment lasts, knowledge is surely not increased; but when we remember that the enemy to whom we have surrendered is but a ghost of our own evoking, we easily reoccupy the lost ground and fall back into an ordinary posture of belief and expectation. This recovered faith has no new evidences to rest on. We simply stand where we stood before we began to philosophise, only with a better knowledge of the lines we are holding and perhaps with less inclination to give them up again for no better reason than the undoubted fact that, in a speculative sense, it is always possible to renounce them.

Science, then, is the attentive consideration of common experience; it is common knowledge extended and refined. Its validity is of the same order as that of ordinary perception, memory, and understanding. Its test is found, like theirs, in actual intuition, which sometimes consists in perception and sometimes in intent. The flight of science is merely longer from perception to perception, and its deduction more accurate of meaning from meaning and purpose from purpose. It generates in the mind, for each vulgar observation, a whole brood of suggestions, hypotheses, and inferences. The sciences bestow, as is right and fitting, infinite pains upon that experience which in their absence would drift by unchallenged or misunderstood. They take note, infer, and prophesy. They compare prophecy with event, and altogether they supply—so intent are they on reality—every imaginable background and extension for the present dream.

CHAPTER 2

HISTORY

THE LEAST artificial extension of common knowledge is history. Personal recollection supplies many an anecdote, anecdotes collected and freely commented upon make up memoirs, and memoirs happily combined make not the least interesting sort of history. When a man recalls any episode in his career, describes the men that flourished in his youth, or laments the changes that have since taken place, he is an informal historian. He would become one in a formal and technical sense if he supplemented and controlled his memory by ransacking papers, and taking elaborate pains to gather evidence on the events he wished to relate. This systematic investigation, especially when it goes back to first sources, widens the basis for imaginative reconstruction. It buttresses somewhat the frail body of casual facts that in the first instance may have engaged an individual's attention.

History is nothing but assisted and recorded memory. It might almost be said to be no science at all, if memory and faith in memory were not what science necessarily rests on. In order to sift evidence we must rely on some witness, and we must trust experience before we proceed to expand it. The line between what is known scientifically and what has to be assumed in order to support that knowledge is impossible to draw. Memory itself is an internal rumour; and when to this hearsay within the mind we add the falsified echoes that reach us from others, we have but a shifting and unseizable basis to build upon. The picture we frame of the past changes continually and grows every day less similar to the original experience which it purports to describe.

It is true that memory sometimes, as in a vision, seems to raise the curtain upon the past and restore it to us in its pristine reality. We may imagine at such moments that experience can never really perish, but, though hidden by chance from the roving eye, endures eternally in some spiritual sphere. Such bodily recovery of the past, however, like other telepathic visions, can never prove its own truth. A lapse into by-gone perception, a sense of living the past over with all its vivid minutiae and trivial concomitants, might involve no true repetition of anything that had previously existed. It might be a fresh experience altogether. The sense of knowing constitutes only a working presumption for experiment to start with; until corroboration comes that presumption can claim no respect from the outsider.

While memory remains a private presumption, therefore, it can be compared with nothing else that might test its veracity. Only when memory is expressed and, in the common field of expression, finds itself corroborated by another memory, does it rise somewhat in dignity and approach scientific knowledge. Two presumptions, when they coincide, make a double assurance. While memory, then, is the basis of all historical knowledge, it is not called history until it enters a field where it can be supported or corrected by evidence. This field is that natural world which all experiences, in so far as they are rational, envisage together. Assertions relating to events in that world can corroborate or contradict one another—something that would be impossible if each memory, like the plot of a novel, moved in a sphere of its own. For memory to meet memory, the two must present objects which are similar or continuous: then they can corroborate or correct each other and help to fix the order of events as they really happened—that is, as they happened independently of what either memory may chance to claim. Thus even the most miraculous and direct recovery of the past needs corroboration if it is to be systematically credited; but to receive corroboration it must refer to some event in nature, in that common world in space and time to which other memories and perceptions may refer also. In becoming history, therefore, memory becomes a portion of natural science. Its assertions are such that any natural science may conceivably support or contradict them.

The consolidation of legend is not intentional. It is ingenuous and for the most part inevitable. When we muse about our own past we are conscious of no effort to give it dramatic unity; on the contrary, the excitement and interest of the process consist in seeming to discover the hidden eloquence and meaning of the events themselves. When a man of experience narrates the wonders he has seen, we listen with a certain awe, and believe in him for his miracles as we believe in our own memory for its

arts. A bard's mechanical and ritualistic habits usually put all judgment on his own part to sleep; while the sanctity attributed to
the tale, as it becomes automatically more impressive, precludes
tinkering with it intentionally. Especially the allegories and mar-
vels with which early history is adorned are not ordinarily invented with malice prepense. They are rather discovered in the
mind, like a foundling, between night and morning. They are
divinely vouchsafed. Each time the tale is retold it suffers a variation which is not challenged, since it is memory itself that has
varied. The change is discoverable only if some record of the
narrative in its former guise, or some physical memorial of the
event related, survives to be confronted with the modified version.
The modified version itself can make no comparisons. It merely
inherits the name and authority of its ancestor. The innocent poet
believes his own lies.

Legends consequently acquire a considerable eloquence and dramatic force. These beauties accrue spontaneously, because rhythm
and ideal pertinence, in which poetic merit largely lies, are natural
formative principles for speech and memory. As symmetry in
material structures is a ground for strength, and hills by erosion
are worn to pyramids, so it is in thoughts. Yet the stability attained is not absolute, but only such stability as the circumstances
require. Dramatic effect is not everywhere achieved, nor is it missed
by the narrator where it is wanting, so that even the oldest and
best-pruned legends are full of irrelevant survivals, contradictions,
and scraps of nonsense. These literary blemishes are like embedded fossils and tell of facts which the mechanism of reproduction, for some casual reason, has not obliterated. The recorder
of verbal tradition religiously sets down its inconsistencies and
leaves in the transfigured chronicle many tell-tale incidents and
remarks which, like atrophied organs in an animal body, reveal
its gradual formation. Art and a deliberate pursuit of unction or
beauty would have thrown over this baggage. The automatic and
pious minstrel carries it with him to the end.

For these reasons there can be no serious history until there
are archives and preserved records, although sometimes a man in
a privileged position may compose interesting essays on the events
and persons of his own time, as his personal experience has presented them to him. Archives and records, moreover, do not absolve a speculative historian from paying the same toll to the

dramatic unities and making the same concessions to the laws of
perspective which, in the absence of documents, turn tradition so
soon into epic poetry. The principle that elicits histories out of
records is the same that breeds legends out of remembered events.
In both cases the facts are automatically foreshortened and made
to cluster, as it were providentially, about a chosen interest. The
historian's politics, philosophy, or romantic imagination furnishes
a vital nucleus for reflection. All that falls within that particular
vortex is included in the mental picture, the rest is passed over
and tends to drop out of sight. It is not possible to say, nor to
think, everything at once; and the private interest which guides
a man in selecting his materials imposes itself inevitably on the
events he relates and especially on their grouping and significance.

History is always written wrong, and so always needs to be
rewritten. The conditions of expression and even of memory dra-
goon the facts and put a false front on diffuse experience. What
is interesting is brought forward as if it had been central and
efficacious in the march of events, and harmonies are turned into
causes. Kings and generals are endowed with motives appropriate
to what the historian values in their actions; plans are imputed
to them prophetic of their actual achievements, while the thoughts
that really preoccupied them remain buried in absolute oblivion.
Such falsification is inevitable, and an honest historian is guilty of
it only against his will. He would wish, as he loves the truth, to
see and to render it entire. But the limits of his book and of his
knowledge force him to be partial. It is only a very great mind,
seasoned by large wisdom, that can lend such an accent and such
a carrying-power to a few facts as to make them representative of
all reality.

Some historians, indeed, are so frankly partisan or cynical that
they avowedly write history with a view to effect, either political
or literary. Moralising historians belong to this school, as well
as those philosophers who worship evolution. They sketch every
situation with malice and twist it, as if it were an argument, to
bring out a point, much as fashionable portrait-painters sometimes
surcharge the characteristic, in order to make a bold effect at a
minimum expense of time and devotion. And yet the truly memorable aspect of a man is that which he wears in the sunlight of
common day, with all his generic humanity upon him. His most
interesting phase is not that which he might assume under the

lime-light of satirical or literary comparisons. The characteristic is after all the inessential. It marks a peripheral variation in the honest and sturdy lump. To catch only the heartless shimmer of individuality is to paint a costume without the body that supports it. Therefore a broad and noble historian sets down all within his apperception. His literary interests are forgotten; he is wholly devoted to expressing the passions of the dead. His ideal, emanating from his function and chosen for no extraneous reason, is to make his heroes think and act as they really thought and acted in the world.

We may conveniently distinguish in history, as it is perforce written by men, three distinct elements, which we may call historical investigation, historical theory, and historical romance.

Historical investigation is the natural science of the past. The circumstance that its documents are usually literary may somewhat disguise the physical character and the physical principles of this science; but when a man wishes to discover what really happened at a given moment, even if the event were somebody's thought, he has to read his sources, not for what they say, but for what they imply. In other words, the witnesses cannot be allowed merely to speak for themselves, after the gossiping fashion familiar in Herodotus; their testimony has to be interpreted according to the laws of evidence. The past needs to be reconstructed out of reports, as in geology or archaeology it needs to be reconstructed out of stratifications and ruins. A man's memory or the report in a newspaper is a fact justifying certain inferences about its probable causes according to laws which such phenomena betray in the present when they are closely scrutinised. This reconstruction is often very difficult, and sometimes all that can be established in the end is merely that the tradition before us is certainly false; somewhat as a perplexed geologist might venture on no conclusion except that the state of the earth's crust was once very different from what it is now.

A natural science dealing with the past labours under the disadvantage of not being able to appeal to experiment. The facts it terminates upon cannot be recovered, so that they may verify in sense the hypothesis that had inferred them. The hypothesis can be tested only by current events; it is then turned back upon the past, to give assurance of facts which themselves are hypothetical and remain hanging, as it were, to the loose end of the hypothesis itself. A hypothetical fact is a most dangerous creature, since it lives on the credit of a theory which in turn would be bankrupt if the fact should fail. Inferred past facts are more deceptive than facts prophesied, because while the risk of error in the inference is the same, there is no possibility of discovering that error; and the historian, while really as speculative as the prophet, can never be found out.

Most facts known to man, however, are reached by inference, and their reality may be wisely assumed so long as the principle by which they are inferred, when it is applied in the present, finds complete and constant verification. Presumptions involved in memory and tradition give the first hypothetical facts we count upon; the relations which these first facts betray supply the laws by which facts are to be concatenated; and these laws may then be used to pass from the first hypothetical facts to hypothetical facts of a second order, forming a background and congruous extension to those originally assumed. This expansion of discursive science can go on for ever, unless indeed the principles of inference employed in it involve some present existence, such as a skeleton in a given tomb, which direct experience fails to verify. Then the theory itself is disproved and the whole galaxy of hypothetical facts which clustered about it forfeit their credibility.

The profit of studying history lies in something else than in a dead knowledge of what happens to have happened. A seductive alternative might be to say that the profit of it lies in *understanding* what has happened, in perceiving the principles and laws that govern social evolution, or the meaning which events have. We are hereby launched upon a region of physico-ethical speculation where any man with a genius for quick generalisation can swim at ease. To find the one great cause why Rome fell, especially if no one has ever thought of it before, or to expound the true import of the French Revolution, or to formulate in limpid sentences the essence of Greek culture—what could be more tempting or more purely literary? It would ill become the author of this book to decry allegorical expressions, or a cavalierlike fashion of dismissing whole periods and tendencies with a verbal antithesis. We must have exercises in apperception, a work of imagination must be taken imaginatively, and a landscape painter must be suffered to be, at his own risk, as impressionistic as he will. If Raphael, when he was designing the *School of Athens*, had said to himself that Aristotle should point down to a fact and Plato up to a meaning, or when designing the *Disputa* had conceived that the proudest of intellects, weary of argument and learning, should throw down his books and turn to revelation for guidance, there would have been much historical pertinence in those conceptions; yet the figures would have been allegorical, contracting into a decorative design events that had been dispersed through centuries and emotions that had only cropped up here and there, with all manner of variations and alloys, when the particular natural situation had made them inevitable. So the Rennaissance might be spoken of as a person and the Reformation as her stepsister, and something might be added about the troubles of their home life; but would it be needful in that case to enter a warning that these units were verbal merely, and that the phenomena and the forces really at work had been multitudinous and infinitesimal?

In fine, historical terms mark merely rhetorical unities, which have no dynamic cohesion, and there are no historical laws which are not at bottom physical, like the laws of habit—those expressions of Newton's first law of motion. An essayist may play with historical apperception as long as he will and always find something new to say, discovering the ideal nerve and issue of a movement in a different aspect of the facts. The truly proportionate, constant, efficacious relations between things will remain material. Physical causes traverse the moral units at which history stops, determining their force and duration, and the order, so irrelevant to intent, in which they succeed one another. Even the single man's life and character have subterranean sources; how should the outer expression and influence of that character have sources more superficial than its own? Yet we cannot trace moral development down to the more stable units composing a personal organism, and much less, therefore, to those composing a complex social evolution. We accordingly translate the accidents, obviously lurking under life's commonplace yet unaccountable shocks, into verbal principles, names for general impressive results, that play some rôle in our ideal philosophy. Each of these idols of the theatre is visible only on a single stage and to duly predisposed spectators. The next passion affected will throw a differently coloured light on the same pageant, and there will be no end of rival evolutions and incompatible ideal principles crossing one another at every interesting event.

Such a manipulation of history, when made by persons who un-derestimate their imaginative powers, ends in asserting that events have directed themselves prophetically upon the interests which they arouse. Apart from the magic involved and this mockery of all science, there is a difficulty here which even a dramatic idealist ought to feel. The interests affected are themselves many and contrary. If history is to be understood teleologically, which of all the possible ends it might be pursuing shall we think really en-dowed with regressive influence and responsible for the movement that is going to realise it? Did Columbus, for instance, discover America so that George Washington might exist or that some day football and the Church of England may prevail throughout the world? Or was it (as has been seriously maintained) in order that the converted Indians of South America might console Saint Peter for the defection of the British and Germans? Or was America, as Hegel believed, ideally superfluous, the absolute having become self-conscious enough already in Prussia? Or shall we say that the real goal is at an infinite distance and unimaginable by us, and useless, therefore, for understanding anything?

There is a sense, of course, in which definite political plans and moral aspirations may well be fulfilled by events. Our ancestors, sharing and anticipating our natures, may have had in many re-spects our actual interests in view, as we may have those of pos-terity. Such ideal co-operation extends far, where primary interests are concerned; it is rarer and more qualified where a fine and fragile organisation is required to support the common spiritual life. Even in these cases, the aim pursued and attained is not the force that operates, since the result achieved had many other con-ditions besides the worker's intent, and that intent itself had causes which it knew nothing of. Every "historical force" pompously appealed to breaks up on inspection into a cataract of miscellaneous natural processes and minute particular causes. It breaks into its mechanical constituents and proves to have been nothing but an *effet d'ensemble* produced on a mind whose habits and categories are essentially rhetorical.

This sort of false history or philosophy of history might be purified, like so many other things, by self-knowledge. If the philosopher in reviewing events confessed that he was scrutinising them in order to abstract from them whatever tended to illustrate his own ideals, as he might look over a crowd to find his friends, the operation would become a perfectly legitimate one. The events themselves would be left for scientific inference to discover, where credible reports did not testify to them directly; and the causes of events would be left to some theory of natural evolution, to be stated, according to the degree of knowledge attained, in terms more and more exact and mechanical. In the presence of the past so defined imagination and will, however, would not abdicate their rights, and a sort of retrospective politics, an estimate of events in reference to the moral ideal which they embodied or betrayed, might supervene upon positive history. This estimate of evolution might well be called a philosophy of history, since it would be a higher operation performed on the results of natural science, to give a needful basis and illustration to the chosen ideal. The present work is an essay in that direction.

The ideal which in such a review would serve as the touchstone for estimation, if it were an enlightened ideal, would recognise its own natural basis, and therefore would also recognise that under other conditions other ideals, no less legitimate, may have arisen and may have been made the standard for a different judgment on the world. Historical investigation, were its resources adequate, would reveal to us what these various ideals have been. Every animal has his own, and whenever individuals or nations have become reflective they have known how to give articulate expression to theirs. That all these ideals could not have been realised in turn or together is an immense misfortune, the irremediable half-tragedy of life, by which we also suffer. In estimating the measure of success achieved anywhere a liberal historian, who does not wish to be bluntly irrational, will of course estimate it from *all* these points of view, considering all real interests affected, in so far as he can appreciate them. This is what is meant by putting the standard of value, not in some arbitrary personal dogma but in a variegated omnipresent happiness.

It is by no means requisite, therefore, in disentangling the Life of Reason, to foresee what ultimate form the good might some day take, much less to make the purposes of the philosopher himself, his time, or his nation the test of all excellence. This test is the perpetual concomitant ideal of the life it is applied to. As all could not be well in the world if my own purposes were defeated, so the general excellence of things would be heightened if other men's purposes also had been fulfilled. Each will is a true centre for universal estimation. As each will, therefore, comes to expression, real and irreversible values are introduced into the world, and the historian, in estimating what has been hitherto achieved, needs to make himself the spokesman for all past aspirations.

If the Egyptian poets sang well, though that conduces not at all to our advantage, and though all those songs are now dumb, the Life of Reason was thereby increased once for all in pith and volume. Brief erratic experiments made in living, if they were somewhat successful in their day, remain successes always: and this is the only kind of success that in the end can be achieved at all. The philosopher that looks for what is good in history and measures the past by the scale of reason need be no impertinent dogmatist on that account. Reason would not be reason but passion if it did not make all passions in all creatures constituents of its own authority. The judgments it passes on existence are only the judgments which existence, so far, has passed on itself, and these are indelible and have their proportionate weight though others of many different types may surround or succeed them.

To inquire what everybody has thought about the world, and into what strange shapes every passionate dream would fain have transformed existence, might be merely a part of historical investigation. These facts of preference and estimation might be made to stand side by side with all other facts in that absolute physical order which the universe must somehow possess. In the reference book of science they would all find their page and line. But it is not for the sake of making vain knowledge complete that historians are apt to linger over heroic episodes and commanding characters in the world's annals. It is not even in the hope of discovering just to what extent and in how many directions experience has been a tragedy. The mathematical balance of failure and success, even if it could be drawn with accuracy, would not be a truth of moral importance, since whatever that balance might be for the world at large, success and benefit here, from the living point of view, would be equally valid and delightful; and however good or however bad the universe may be it is always worth while to make it better.

What engages the historian in the reconstruction of moral life, such as the past contained, is that he finds in that life many an illustration of his own ideals, or even a necessary stimulus in defining what his ideals are. Where his admiration and his sympathy are awakened, he sees noble aims and great achievements, worthy of being minutely studied and brought vividly before later generations. Very probably he will be led by moral affinities with certain phases of the past to attribute to those phases, in their abstraction and by virtue of their moral dignity, a material efficacy which they did not really have; and his interest in history's moral will make him turn history itself into a fable. This abuse may be abated, however, by having recourse to impartial historical investigation, that will restore to the hero all his circumstantial impotence, and to the glorious event all its insignificant causes. Certain men and certain episodes will retain, notwithstanding, their intrinsic nobility; and the historian, who is often a politician and a poet rather than a man of science, will dwell on those noble things so as to quicken his own sense for greatness and to burnish in his soul ideals that may have remained obscure for want of scrutiny or may have been tarnished by too much contact with a sordid world.

History so conceived has the function of epic or dramatic poetry. The moral life represented may actually have been lived through; but that circumstance is incidental merely and what makes the story worth telling is its pertinence to the political or emotional life of the present. To revive past moral experience is indeed wellnigh impossible unless the living will can still covet or dread the same issues; historical romance cannot be truthful or interesting when profound changes have taken place in human nature. The reported acts and sentiments of early peoples lose their tragic dignity in our eyes when they lose their pertinence to our own aims. So that a recital of history with an eye to its dramatic values is possible only when that history is, so to speak, our own, or when we assimilate it to ours by poetic license.

The various functions of history have been generally carried on simultaneously and with little consciousness of their profound diversity. Since historical criticism made its appearance, the romantic interest in the past, far from abating, has fed eagerly on all the material incidents and private gossip of remote times. This sort of petty historical drama has reflected contemporary interests, which have centred so largely in material possessions and personal careers; while at the same time it has kept pace with the knowedge of minutiae attained by archaeology. When historical investigation has reached its limits a period of ideal reconstruction may very likely set in. Indeed were it possible to collect in archives exhaustive accounts of everything that has ever happened, so that the curious man might always be informed on any point of fact that interested him, historical imagination might grow free again in its movements. Not being suspected of wishing to distort facts which could so easily be pointed to, it might become more conscious of its own moral function, and it might turn unblushingly to what was important and inspiring in order to put it with dramatic force before the mind. Such a treatment of history would reinstate that epic and tragic poetry which has become obsolete; it might well be written in verse, and would at any rate be frankly imaginative; it might furnish a sort of ritual, with scientific and political sanctions, for public feasts. Tragedies and epics are such only in name if they do not deal with the highest interests and destinies of a people; and they could hardly deal with such ideals in an authoritative and definite way, unless they found them illustrated in that people's traditions.

Historic romance is a work of art, not of science, and its fidelity to past fact is only an expedient, often an excellent and easy one, for striking the key-note of present ideals. The insight attained, even when it is true insight into what some one else felt in some other age, draws its force and sublimity from current passions, passions potential in the auditor's soul. Mary Queen of Scots, for instance, doubtless repeated, in many a fancied dialogue with Queen Elizabeth, the very words that Schiller puts into her mouth in the central scene of his play, "*Denn ich bin Euer König!*" Yet the dramatic force of that expression, its audacious substitution of ideals for facts, depends entirely on the scope which we lend it. Different actors and different readers would interpret it differently. Some might see in it nothing but a sally in a woman's quarrel, reading it with the accent of mere spite and irritation. Then the tragedy, not perhaps without historic truth, would be reduced to a loud comedy. Other interpreters might find in the phrase the whole feudal system, all the chivalry, legality, and foolishness of the Middle Ages. Then the drama would become more interesting, and the poor queen's cry, while that of a mind sophisticated and fanatical, would have great pathos and keenness. To reach sublimity, however, that moment would have to epitomise ideals which we deeply respected. We should have to believe in the sanctity of canon law and in the divine right of primogeniture. That a woman may have been very unhappy or that a state may have been held together by personal allegiance does not raise the fate of either to the tragic plane, unless "laws that are not of to-day nor yesterday," aspirations native to the heart, shine through those legendary misfortunes.

It would matter nothing to the excellence of Schiller's drama which of these interpretations might have been made by Mary Stuart herself at any given moment; doubtless her attitude toward her rival was coloured on different occasions by varying degrees of political insight and moral fervour. The successful historical poet would be he who caught the most significant attitude which a person in that position could possibly have assumed, and his Mary Stuart, whether accidentally resembling the real woman or not, would be essentially a mythical person. So Electra and Antigone and Helen of Troy are tragic figures absolved from historical accuracy, although possibly if the personages of heroic times were known to us we might find that our highest imagination had been anticipated in their pride.

Of the three parts into which the pursuit of history may be divided—investigation, theory, and story-telling—not one attains ideal finality. Investigation is merely useful, because its intrinsic ideal—to know every detail of everything—is not rational, and its acceptable function can only be to offer accurate information upon such points as are worth knowing for some ulterior reason. Historical theory, in turn, is a falsification of causes, since no causes are other than automatic; it is an arbitrary foreshortening of physics, and it dissolves in the presence either of adequate knowledge or of clear ideals. Finally, historical romance passes, as it grows mature, into epics and tragedies, where the moral imagination disengages itself from all allegiance to particular past facts. Thus history proves to be an imperfect field for the exercise of reason; it is a provisional discipline; its values, with the mind's progress, would empty into higher activities. The function of history is to lend materials to politics and to poetry. These arts need to dominate past events, the better to dominate the present situation and the ideal one. A good book of history is one that helps the statesman to formulate and to carry out his plans, or that helps the tragic poet to conceive what is most glorious in human destiny. Such a book, as knowledge and ignorance are now mingled, will have to borrow something from each of the methods by which history is commonly pursued. Investigation will be necessary, since the needful facts are not all indubitably known; theory will be necessary too, so that those facts may be conceived in their pertinence to public interests, and the latter may thereby be clarified; and romance will not be wholly excluded, because the various activities of the mind about the same matter cannot be divided altogether, and a dramatic treatment is often useful in summarising a situation, when all the elements of it cannot be summoned up in detail before the mind.

Fragmentary, arbitrary, and insecure as historical conceptions must remain, they are nevertheless highly important. In human consciousness the indispensable is in inverse ratio to the demonstrable. Sense is the foundation of everything. Without sense memory would be both false and useless. Yet memory rather than sense is knowledge in the pregnant acceptation of the word; for in sense object and process are hardly distinguished, whereas in memory significance inheres in the datum, and the present vouches for the absent. Similarly history, which is derived from memory, is superior to it; for while it merely extends memory artificially it shows a higher logical development than memory has and is riper for ideal uses. Trivial and useless matter has dropped out. Inference has gone a step farther, thought is more largely representative, and testimony conveyed by the reports of others or found in monuments leads the speculative mind to infer events that must have filled the remotest ages. This information is not passive or idle knowledge; it truly *informs* or shapes the mind, giving it new aptitudes. As an efficacious memory modifies instinct, by levelling it with a wider survey of the situation, so a memory of what human experience has been, a sense of what it is likely to be under specific circumstances, gives the will a new basis. Great interests are a gift which history makes to the heart.

CHAPTER 3

MECHANISM

A RETROSPECT over human experience, if a little extended, can
hardly fail to come upon many interesting recurrences. The seasons make their round and the generations of men, like the forest
leaves, repeat their career. In this its finer texture history undoubtedly repeats itself. A study of it, in registering so many recurrences, leads to a description of habit, or to natural history.
To observe a recurrence is to divine a mechanism. It is to analyse
a phenomenon, distinguishing its form, which alone recurs, from
its existence, which is irrevocable; and that the flux of phenomena
should turn out, on closer inspection, to be composed of a multitude of recurring forms, regularly interwoven, is the ideal of
mechanism. The forms, taken ideally and in themselves, are what
reflection first rescues from the flux and makes a science of; they
constitute that world of eternal relations with which dialectic is
conversant. To note here and there some passing illustration of
these forms is one way of studying experience. The observer, the
poet, the historian merely *define* what they see. But these incidental illustrations of form (called by Plato phenomena) may
have a method in their comings and goings, and this method may
in turn be definable. It will be a new sort of constant illustrated
in the flux; and this we call a law. If events could be reduced
to a number of constant forms moving in a constant medium according to a constant law, a maximum of constancy would be
introduced into the flux, which would thereby be proved to be
mechanical.

The form of events, abstracted from their material presence,
becomes a general mould to which we tend to assimilate new observations. Whatever in particular instances may contravene the
accredited rule, we attribute without a qualm to unknown variations in the circumstances, thus saving our faith in order at all
hazards and appealing to investigation to justify the same. Only
when another rule suggests itself which leaves a smaller margin

unaccounted for in the phenomena do we give up our first generalisation. Not even the rudest superstition can be criticised or dislodged scientifically save by another general rule, more exact and trustworthy than the superstition. The scepticism which comes from distrust of abstraction and disgust with reckoning of any sort is not a scientific force; it is an intellectual weakness.

Generalities are indeed essential to understanding, which is apt to impose them hastily upon particulars. Confirmation is not needed to create prejudice. It suffices that a vivid impression should once have cut its way into the mind and settled there in a fertile soil. Prejudices, however refractory to new evidence, evolve inwardly of themselves. The mental soil in which they lie is in a continual ferment and their very vitality will extend their scope and change their application. Generalisations, therefore, when based on a single instance, will soon forget it and shift their ground, as unchecked words shift their meaning. But when a phenomenon actually recurs the generalisations founded on it are reinforced and kept identical, and prejudices so sustained by events make man's knowledge of nature.

Natural science consists of general ideas which look for verification in events, and which find it. The particular instance, once noted, is thrown aside like a squeezed orange, its significance in establishing some law having once been extracted. Science, by this flight into the general, lends immediate experience an interest and scope which its parts, taken blindly, could never possess; since if we remained sunk in the moments of existence and never abtracted their character from their pulsation, we should never know that they had any relation to one another. We should feel their incubus without being able to distinguish their dignities or to give them names. By analysing what we find and abstracting what recurs from its many vain incidents we can discover a sustained structure within, which enables us to foretell what we may find in future. Science thus articulates experience and reveals the skeleton of events.

Skeletons are not things particularly congenial to poets, unless it be for the sake of having something truly horrible to shudder at: and so a certain school of philosophers exhaust their rhetoric in convincing us that the objects known to science are artificial and dead, while the living reality is infinitely rich and absolutely unutterable. This is merely an ungracious way of describing the office of thought and bearing witness to its necessity. A body is none the worse for having some bones in it, even if they are not all visible on the surface. They are certainly not the whole man, who nevertheless runs and leaps by their leverage and smooth turning in their sockets; and a surgeon's studies in dead anatomy help him excellently to set a living joint. The abstractions of science are extractions of truths. Truths cannot of themselves constitute existence with its irrational concentration in time, place, and person, its hopeless flux, and its vital exuberance; but they can be true of existence; they can disclose that structure by which its parts cohere materially and become ideally inferable from one another.

Science becomes demonstrable in proportion as it becomes abstract. It becomes in the same measure applicable and useful, as mathematics witnesses, whenever the abstraction is judiciously made and has seized the profounder structural features in the phenomenon. These features are often hard for human eyes to discern, buried as they may be in the internal infinitesimal texture of things. Things accordingly seem to move on the world's stage in an unaccountable fashion, and to betray magic affinities to what is separated from them by apparent chasms. Any chance conjunction, any incidental harmony, will start a hypothesis about the nature of the universe and be the parent image of a whole system of philosophy. In self-indulgent minds most of these standard images are dramatic, and the cue men follow in unravelling experience is that offered by some success or failure of their own. The sanguine, having once found a pearl in a dunghill, feel a glorious assurance that the world's true secret is that everything in the end is ordered for everybody's benefit—and that is optimism. The atrabilious, being ill at ease with themselves, see the workings everywhere of insidious sin, and conceive that the world is a dangerous place of trial. A somewhat more observant intellect may decide that what exists is a certain number of definite natures, each striving to preserve and express itself; and in such language we still commonly read political events and our friend's actions. At the dawn of science a Thales, observing the ways and the conditions of things somewhat more subtly, will notice that rain, something quite adventitious to the fields, is what covers them with verdure, that the slime breeds life, that a liquid will freeze to stone and evaporate to air; and his shrewd conclusion will be that everything is water in one disguise or another. It is only after long accumulated observation that we can reach any exact law of nature; and this law we hardly think of applying to living things. These have not yet revealed the secret of their structure, and clear insight is vouchsafed us only in such regions as that of mathematical physics, where cogency in the ideal system is combined with adequacy to explain the phenomena.

These exact sciences cover in the gross the field in which human life appears, the antecedents of this life, and its instruments. To a speculative mind, that had retained an ingenuous sense of nature's inexhaustible resources and of man's essential continuity with other natural things, there could be no ground for doubting that similar principles (could they be traced in detail) would be seen to preside over all man's action and passion. A thousand indications, drawn from introspection and from history, would be found to confirm this speculative presumption. It is not only earthquakes and floods, summer and winter, that bring human musings sharply to book. Love and ambition are unmistakable blossomings of material forces, and the more intense and poetical a man's sense is of his spiritual condition the more loudly will he proclaim his utter dependence on nature and the identity of the moving principle in him and in her.

Mankind and all its works are undeniably subject to gravity and to the law of projectiles; yet what is true of these phenomena in bulk seems to a superficial observation not to be true of them in detail, and a person may imagine that he subverts all the laws of physics whenever he wags his tongue. Only in inorganic matter is the ruling mechanism open to human inspection: here changes may be seen to be proportionate to the elements and situation in which they occur. Habit here seems perfectly steady and is called necessity, since the observer is able to deduce it unequivocally from given properties in the body and in the external bodies acting upon it. In the parts of nature which we call living and to which we impute consciousness, habit, though it be fatal enough, is not so exactly measurable and perspicuous. Physics cannot account for that minute motion and pullulation in the earth's crust of which human affairs are a portion. Human affairs have to be surveyed under categories lying closer to those employed in memory and legend. These looser categories are of every sort—grammatical, moral, magical—and there is no knowing when any of them will apply or in what measure. Between the matters covered by the exact sciences and vulgar experience there remains, accordingly, a wide and nebulous gulf. Where we cannot see the mechanism involved in what happens we have to be satisfied with an empirical description of appearances as they first fall together in our apprehension; and this want of understanding in the observer is what popular philosophy calls intelligence in the world.

That this gulf is apparent only, being due to inadequacy and confusion in human perception rather than to incoherence in things, is a speculative conviction altogether trustworthy. Any one who can at all catch the drift of experience—moral no less than physical—must feel that mechanism rules the whole world. There are doubleness and diversity enough in things to satiate the greatest lover of chaos; but that a cosmos nevertheless underlies the superficial play of sense and opinion is what all practical reason must assume and what all comprehended experience bears witness to. A cosmos does not mean a disorder with which somebody happens to be well pleased; it means a regularity from which every one must draw his happiness. Mechanical processes are not like mathematical relations, because they *happen*. What they express the form of is a flux, not a truth or an ideal necessity. The situation may therefore always be new, though produced from the preceding situation by rules which are invariable, since the preceding situation was itself novel.

Mechanism might be called the dialectic of the irrational. It is such a measure of intelligibility as is compatible with flux and with existence. Existence itself being irrational and change unintelligible, the only necessity they are susceptible of is a natural or empirical necessity, impinging at both ends upon brute matters of fact. The existential elements, their situation, number, affinities, and mutual influence all have to be begged before calculation can begin. When these surds have been accepted at their face value, inference may set to work among them; yet the inference that mechanism will continue to reign will not amount to certain knowledge until the event inferred has come to give it proof. Calculation in physics differs from pure dialectic in that the ultimate object it looks to is not ideal. Theory here must revert to the observable flux for its sanction, whereas dialectic is a centrifugal emanation from existence and never returns to its point of origin. It remains suspended in the ether of those eternal relations which forms have, even when found embedded in matter.

If the total flux is continuous and naturally intelligible, why is the part felt by man so disjointed and opaque? An answer to this question may perhaps be drawn from the fact that consciousness apparently arises to express the functions only of extremely complicated organisms. The basis of thought is vastly more elaborate than its deliverance. It takes a wonderful brain and exquisite senses to produce a few stupid ideas. The mind starts, therefore, with a tremendous handicap. Its existence is intermittent and its visions unmeaning. It fails to conceive its own interests or the situations that might support or defeat those interests. If it pictures anything clearly, it is only some phantastic image in no way adequate to its own complex basis. Thus the parasitical human mind, finding what clear knowledge it has laughably insufficient to interpret its destiny, takes to neglecting knowledge altogether and to hugging instead various irrational ideas. On the one hand it lapses into dreams which, while obviously irrelevant to practice, express the mind's vegetative instincts; hence poetry and mythology, which substitute play-worlds for the real one on correlation with which human prosperity and dignity depend. On the other hand, the mind becomes wedded to conventional objects which mark, perhaps, the turning-points of practical life and plot the curve of it in a schematic and disjointed fashion, but which are themselves entirely opaque and, as we say, material. Now as matter is commonly a name for things not understood, men materially minded are those whose ideas, while practical, are meagre and blind, so that their knowledge of nature, if not invalid, is exceedingly fragmentary. This grossness in common sense, like irrelevance in imagination, springs from the fact that the mind's representative powers are out of focus with its controlling conditions.

CHAPTER 4

PSYCHOLOGY

IF PSYCHOLOGY is a science, many things that books of psychology contain should be excluded from it. One is social imagination. Nature, besides having a mechanical form and wearing a garment of sensible qualities, makes a certain inner music in the beholder's mind, inciting him to enter into other bodies and to fancy the new and profound life which he might lead there. Who, as he watched a cat basking in the sun, has not passed into that vigilant eye and felt all the leaps potential in that luxurious torpor? Who has not attributed some little romance to the passer-by? Who has not sometimes exchanged places even with things inanimate, and drawn some new moral experience from following the movement of stars or of daffodils? All this is idle musing or at best poetry; yet our ordinary knowledge of what goes on in men's minds is made of no other stuff. True, we have our own mind to go by, which presumably might be a fair sample of what men's minds are; but unfortunately our notion of ourselves is of all notions the most biassed and idealistic. If we attributed to other men only such obvious reasoning, sound judgment, just preferences, honest passions, and blameless errors as we discover in ourselves, we should take but an insipid and impractical view of mankind.

In fact, we do far better: for what we impute to our fellow-men is suggested by their conduct or by an instant imitation of their gesture and expression. These manifestations, striking us in all their novelty and alien habit, and affecting our interests in all manner of awkward ways, create a notion of our friends' natures which is extremely vivid and seldom extremely flattering.

Such romancing has the cogency proper to dramatic poetry; it is persuasive only over the third person, who has never had, but has always been about to have, the experience in question. Drawn from the potential in one's self, it describes at best the possible in others. The thoughts of men are incredibly evanescent, merely the foam of their labouring natures; and they doubtless vary much more than our trite classifications allow for. This is what makes passions and fashions, religions and philosophies, so hard to conceive when once the trick of them is a little antiquated. Languages are hardly more foreign to one another than are the thoughts uttered in them. We should give men credit for originality at least in their dreams, even if they have little of it to show elsewhere; and as it was discovered but recently that all memories are not furnished with the like material images, but often have no material images whatever, so it may have to be acknowledged that the disparity in men's soliloquies is enormous, and that some races, perhaps, live content without soliloquising at all.

Nevertheless, in describing what happens, or in enforcing a given view of things, we constantly refer to universal experience as if everybody was agreed about what universal experience is and had personally gathered it all since the days of Adam. In fact, each man has only his own, the remnant saved from his personal acquisitions. On the basis of this his residual endowment, he has to conceive all nature, with whatever experiences may have fallen there to the lot of others. Universal experience is a comfortable fiction, a distinctly ideal construction, and no fund available for any one to draw from; which of course is not to deny that tradition and books, in transmitting materially the work of other generations, tend to assimilate us also to their mind. The result of their labours, in language, learning, and institutions, forms a hot-house in which to force our seedling fancy to a rational growth; but the influence is physical, the environment is material, and its ideal background or significance has to be inferred by us anew, according to our imaginative faculty and habits. Past experience, apart from its monuments, is fled for ever out of mortal reach. It is now a figment of the ineffectual truth about what once was. To know it we must evoke a notion of it within ourselves, starting from its inadequate expressions still extant in the world. This reconstruction is highly speculative and, as Spinoza noted, better evidence of what we are than of what other men have been.

When we appeal to general experience, then, what we really have to deal with is our interlocutor's power of imagining that experience; for the real experience is dead and ascended into heaven, where it can neither answer nor hear. Our agreements or divergences in this region do not touch science; they concern only friendship and unanimity. All our proofs are, as they say

in Spain, pure conversation; and as the purpose and best result
can be only to kindle intelligence and propagate an ideal art, the
method should be Socratic, genial, literary. In these matters, the
alternative to imagination is not science but sophistry. We may
perhaps entangle our friends in their own words, and force them
for the moment to say what they do not mean, and what it is not
in their natures to think; but the bent bow will spring back, perhaps somewhat sharply, and we shall get little thanks for our
labour. There would be more profit in taking one another frankly
by the arm and walking together along the outskirts of real knowledge, pointing to the material facts which we all can see, nature,
the monuments, the texts, the actual ways and institutions of men;
and in the presence of such a stimulus, with the contagion of a
common interest, the plastic mind would respond of itself to the
situation, and we should be helping one another to understand
whatever lies within the range of our fancy, be it in antiquity
or in the human heart. That would be a true education; and while
the result could not possibly be a science, not even a science of
people's states of mind, it would be a deepening of humanity in
ourselves and a wholesome knowledge of our ignorance.

In what is called psychology this loose, imaginative method
is often pursued, although the field covered may be far narrrower.
Any generic experience of which a writer pretends to give an
exact account must be reconstructed *ad hoc*; it is not the experience that necessitates the description, but the description that recalls
the experience, defining it in a novel way. When La Rochefoucauld
says, for instance, that there is something about our friend's troubles that secretly pleases us, many circumstances in our own lives,
or in other people's, may suddenly recur to us to illustrate that
aperçu; and we may be tempted to say, There is a truth. But is
it a scientific truth? Or is it merely a bit of satire, a ray from a
literary flashlight, giving a partial clearness for a moment to
certain jumbled memories? If the next day we open a volume
of Adam Smith, and read that man is naturally benevolent,
that he cannot but enact and share the vicissitudes of his fellow-
creatures, and that another man's imminent danger or visible torment will cause in him a distress little inferior to that felt by the
unfortunate sufferer, we shall probably think this is a truth also, and
a more normal and a profounder truth than the other. But is
it a law? Is it a scientific discovery that can lead us to definite

inferences about what will happen or help us to decompose a single event, accurately and without ambiguity, into its component forces? Not only is such a thing impossible, but the Scotch philosopher's amiable generalities, perhaps largely applicable to himself and to his friends of the eighteenth century, may fail altogether to fit an earlier or a later age; and every new shade of brute born into the world will ground a new "theory of the moral sentiments."

The whole cogency of such psychology, therefore, lies in the ease with which the hearer, on listening to the analysis, recasts something in his own past after that fashion. These endless rival apperceptions regard facts that, until they are referred to their material ground, show no continuity and no precision in their march. The apperception of them, consequently, must be doubly arbitrary and unstable, for there is no method in the subject-matter and there is less in the treatment of it. The views, however, are far from equal in value. Some may be more natural, eloquent, enlightening, than others; they may serve better the essential purpose of reflection, which is to pick out and bring forward continually out of the past what can have a value for the present. The spiritual life in which this value lies is practical in its associations, because it understands and dominates what touches action; yet it is contemplative in essence, since successful action consists in attempting what you can find yourself achieving. Plan and performance will alike appeal to imagination and be appreciated through it; so that what trains imagination refines the very stuff that life is made of. Science is instrumental in comparison, since the chief advantage that comes of knowing accurately is to be able, with safety, to imagine freely. But when it is science and accurate knowledge that we pursue, we should not be satisfied with literature.

When discourse on any subject would be persuasive, it appeals to the interlocutor to think in a certain dynamic fashion, inciting him, not without leading questions, to give shape to his own sentiments. Knowledge of the soul, insight into human nature and experience, are no doubt requisite in such an exercise; yet this insight is in these cases a vehicle only, an instinctive method, while the result aimed at is agreement on some further matter, conviction and enthusiasm, rather than psychological information. Thus if I declare that the storms of winter are not so unkind as benefits forgot, I say something which if true has a certain psychological value, for it could be inferred from that assertion that resentment is generally not proportionate to the injury received but rather to the surprise caused, so that it springs from our own foolishness more than from other people's bad conduct. Yet my observation was not made in the interest of any such inferences: it was made to express an emotion of my own, in hopes of kindling in others a similar emotion. It was a judgment which others were invited to share. There was as little exact science about it as if I had turned it into frank poetry and exclaimed, "Blow, blow, thou winter's wind!" Knowledge of human nature might be drawn even from that apostrophe, and a very fine shade of human feeling is surely expressed in it, as Shakespeare utters it; but to pray or to converse is not for that reason the same thing as to pursue science.

There is a second constituent of current psychology which is indeed a science, but not a science of matters of fact—I mean the dialectic of ideas. The character of father, for example, implies a son, and this relation, involved in the ideas both of son and of father, implies further that a transmitted essence or human nature is shared by both. Every idea, if its logical texture is reflected upon, will open out into a curious world constituted by distinguishing the constituents of that idea more clearly and making explicit its implicit structure and relations. When an idea has practical intent and is a desire, its dialectic is even more remarkable. If I love a man I thereby love all those who share whatever makes me love him, and I thereby hate whatever tends to deprive him of this excellence. If it should happen, however, that those who resembled him most in amiability—say by flattering me no less than he did—were precisely his mortal enemies, the logic of my affections would become somewhat involved. I might end either by striving to reconcile the rivals or by discovering that what I loved was not the man at all, but only an office exercised by him in my regard which any one else might also exercise.

Spinoza's account of the passions is a beautiful example of dialectical psychology, beautiful because it shows so clearly the possibilities and impossibilities in such a method. Spinoza began with self-preservation, which was to be the principle of life and the root of all feelings. The violence done to physics appears in this beginning. Self-preservation, taken strictly, is a principle not illustrated in nature, where everything is in flux, and where habits destructive or dangerous to the body are as conspicuous as protective instincts. Physical mechanism requires reproduction, which implies death, and it admits suicide.

A man suffered by destiny to maintain for ever a single unchanged emotion might indeed think out its multifarious implications much in Spinoza's way. It is in that fashion that parties and sects, when somewhat stable, come to define their affinities and to know their friends and enemies all over the universe of discourse. Suppose, for instance, that I feel some titillation on reading a proposition concerning the contrast between Paul's idea of Peter and Peter's idea of himself, a titillation which is accompanied by the idea of Spinoza, its external cause. Now he who loves an effect must proportionately love its cause, and titillation accompanied by the idea of its external cause is, Spinoza has proved, what men call love. I therefore find that I love Spinoza. Having got so far, I may consider further, referring to another demonstration in the book, that if some one gives Spinoza joy— Hobbes, for instance—my delight in Spinoza's increased perfection, consequent upon his joy and my love of him, accompanied by the idea of Hobbes, its external cause, constitutes love on my part for the redoubtable Hobbes as well. Thus the periphery of my affections may expand indefinitely, till it includes the infinite, the ultimate external cause of all my titillations. But how these interesting discoveries are interrupted before long by a desire for food, or by an indomitable sense that Hobbes and the infinite are things I do *not* love, is something that my dialectic cannot deduce; for it was the values radiating from a given impulse, the implications of its instant object, that were being explicated, not at all the natural forces that carry a man through that impulse and beyond it to the next phase of his dream, a phase which if it continues the former episode must continue it spontaneously, by grace of mechanical forces.

When dialectic is thus introduced into psychology, an intensive knowledge of the heart is given out for distributive knowledge of events. Such a study, when made by a man of genius, may furnish good spiritual reading, for it will reveal what our passions mean and what sentiments they would lead to if they could remain fixed and dictate all further action. This insight may make us aware of strange inconsistencies in our souls, and seeing how contrary some of our ideals are to others and how horrible, in some cases, would be their ultimate expression, we may be shocked into setting our house in order; and in trying to understand ourselves we may actually develop a self that can be understood. Meantime this inner discipline will not enlighten us about the march of affairs. It will not give us a key to evolution, either in ourselves or in others. Even while we refine our aspirations, the ground they sprang from will be eaten away beneath our feet. Instead of developing yesterday's passion, to-day may breed quite another in its place; and if, having grown old and set in our mental posture, we are incapable of assuming another, and are condemned to carrying on the dialectic of our early visions into a newborn world, to be a schoolmaster's measuring-rod for life's infinite exuberance, we shall find ourselves at once in a foreign country, speaking a language that nobody understands. No destiny is more melancholy than that of the dialectical prophet, who makes more rigid and tyrannous every day a message which every day grows less applicable and less significant.

That remaining portion of psychology which is a science, and a science of matters of fact, is physiological; it belongs to natural history and constitutes the biology of man. Soul, which was not originally distinguished from life, is there studied in its natural operation in the body and in the world. Psychology then remains what it was in Aristotle's *De Anima*—an ill-developed branch of natural science, pieced out with literary terms and perhaps enriched by occasional dramatic interpretations. The specifically mental or psychic element consists in the feeling which accompanies bodily states and natural situations. This feeling is discovered and distributed at the same time that bodies and other material objects are defined; for when a man begins to decipher permanent and real things, and to understand that they are merely material, he thereby sets apart, in contrast with such external objects, those images and emotions which can no longer enter into the things' texture. The images and emotions remain, however, attached to those things, for they are refractions of them through bodily organs, or effects of their presence on the will, or passions fixed upon them as their object.

In parts of biology which do not deal with man observers do not hesitate to refer in the same way to the pain, the desire, the intention, which they may occasionally read in an animal's aspect. Darwin, for instance, constantly uses psychical language: his birds love one another's plumage and their aesthetic charms are factors in natural selection. Such little fables do not detract from the scientific value of Darwin's observations, because we see at once what the fables mean. The description keeps close enough to the facts observed for the reader to stop at the latter, rather than at the language in which they are stated. In the natural history of man such interpretation into mental terms, such microscopic romance, is even easier and more legitimate, because language allows people, perhaps before their feelings are long past, to describe them in terms which are understood to refer directly to mental experience. The sign's familiarity, to be sure, often hides in these cases a great vagueness and unseizableness in the facts; yet a beginning in defining distinctly the mental phase of natural situations has been made in those small autobiographies which introspective writers sometimes compose, or which are taken down in hospitals and laboratories from the lips of "subjects." What a man under special conditions may say he feels or thinks adds a constituent phase to his natural history; and were these reports exact and extended enough, it would become possible to enumerate the precise sensations and ideas which accompany every state of body and every social situation.

This advantage, however, is the source of that confusion and sophistry which distinguish the biology of man from the rest of physics. Attention is there arrested at the mental term, in forgetfulness of the situation which gave it warrant, and an invisible world, composed of these imagined experiences, begins to stalk behind nature and may even be thought to exist independently. This metaphysical dream may be said to have two stages: the systematic one, which is called idealism, and an incidental one which pervades ordinary psychology, in so far as mental facts are uprooted from their basis and deprived of their expressive or spiritual character, in order to be made elements in a dynamic scheme. This battle of feelings, whether with atoms or exclusively with their own cohorts, might be called a primitive materialism, rather than an idealism, if idealism were to retain its Platonic sense; for forms and realisations are taken in this system for substantial elements, and are made to figure either as a part or as the whole of the world's matter.

Phenomena specifically mental certainly exist, since natural phenomena and ideal truths are concentrated and telescoped in apprehension, besides being weighted with an emotion due to their effect on the person who perceives them. This variation, which reality suffers in being reported to perception, turns the report into a mental fact distinguishable from its subject-matter. When the immediate flux is partly understood and the natural world has become a constant presence, the whole flux itself, as it flowed originally, comes to be called a mental flux, because its elements and method are seen to differ from the elements and method embodied in material objects or in ideal truth. The primitive phenomena are now called mental because they all deviate from the realities to be ultimately conceived. To call the immediate mental is therefore correct and inevitable when once the ultimate is in view; but if the immediate were all, to call it mental would be unmeaning.

Mental facts, moreover, are highly selective; especially does this appear in respect to the dialectical world, which is in itself infinite, while the sum of human logic and mathematics, though too long for most men's patience, is decidedly brief. If we ask ourselves on what principle this selection and foreshortening of logic takes place in the mind, we may perhaps come upon the real bond and the deepest contrast between mind and its environment. The infinity of formal truth is disregarded in human thought when it is irrelevant to practice and to happiness; the infinity of nature is represented there in violent perspective, centring about the body and its interests. The seat and starting-point of every mental survey is a brief animal life. A mind seems, then, to be a consciousness of the body's interests, expressed in terms of what affects that body, as if in the Babel of nature a man heard only the voices that pronounced his name. A mind is a private view; it is gathered together in proportion as physical sensibility extends its range and makes one stretch of being after another tributary to the animal's life, and in proportion also as this sensibility is integrated, so that every organ in its reaction enlists the resources of every other organ as well. A personal will and intelligence thus arise; and they direct action from within with a force and freedom which are exactly proportionate to the material forces, within and without the body, which the soul has come to represent.

In other words, mind raises to an actual existence that *form* in material processes which, had the processes remained wholly material, would have had only ideal or imputed being—as the stars would not have been divided into the signs of the Zodiac but for the fanciful eye of astrologers. Automata might arise and be destroyed without any value coming or going; only a form-loving observer could say that anything fortunate or tragic had occurred, as poets might at the budding or withering of a flower. Some of nature's automata, however, love themselves, and comment on the form they achieve or abandon; these constellations of atoms are genuine beasts. Their consciousness and their interest in their own individuality rescues that individuality from the realm of discourse and from having merely imputed limits.

That the basis of mind lies in the body's interests rather than in its atoms may seem a doctrine somewhat too poetical for psychology; yet may not poetry, superposed on material existence and supported by it, be perhaps the key to mind? Such a view hangs well together with the practical and prospective character of consciousness, with its total dependence on the body, its cognitive relevance to the world, and its formal disparity from material being. Mind does not accompany body like a useless and persistent shadow; it is significant and it is intermittent. Much less can it be a link in physiological processes, processes irrelevant to its intent and incompatible with its immaterial essence. Consciousness seems to arise when the body assumes an attitude which, being an attitude, supervenes upon the body's elements and cannot be contained within them. This attitude belongs to the whole body in its significant operation, and the report of this attitude, its expression, requires survey, synthesis, appreciation—things which constitute what we call mentality. This remains, of course, the mentality of that material situation; it is the voice of that particular body in that particular pass. The mind therefore represents its basis, but this basis (being a *form* of material existence and not matter itself) is neither vainly reduplicated by representation nor used up materially in the process.

Representation is far from idle, since it brings to focus those mechanical unities which otherwise would have existed only potentially and at the option of a roving eye. In evoking consciousness nature makes this delimination real and unambiguous; there are henceforth actual centres and actual interests in the automatic flux. The flux continues to be automatic, but the representation of it supervening has created values which, being due to imputation, could not exist without being imputed, while at the same time they could not have been imputed without being attached to one object or event rather than to another. Material dramas are thus made moral and raised to an existence of their own by being expressed in what we call the souls of animals and men; a mind is the entelechy of an organic body.* It is a region where form breeds an existence to express it, and destiny becomes important by being felt. Mind adds to being a new and needful witness so soon as the constitution of being gives foothold to apperception of its movement, and offers something in which it is possible to ground an interest.

Understanding has to be described in terms of its potential outcome, since the incandescent process itself, as it exists only in transit, will not suffer stable terms to define it. Potentiality is something which each half of reality reproaches the other with; things are potential to feeling because they are not life, and feelings are potential to science because they elude definition. To understand, therefore, is to know what to do and what to say in the sign's presence; and this practical knowledge is far deeper than any echo casually awakened in fancy at the same time. Instinctive recognition has those echoes for the most superficial part of its effect. Because I understand what "horse" means, the word can make me recall some episode in which a horse once figured. This understanding is instinctive and practical and, if the phrase may be pardoned, it is the body that understands. It is the body, namely, that contains the habit and readiness on which understanding hangs; and the sense of understanding, the instant rejection of whatever clashes and makes nonsense in that context, is but a transcript of the body's education. Actual mind is all above board; it is all speculative, vibrant, the fruit and gift of those menial subterranean processes. Some generative processes may be called psychic in that they minister to mind and lend it what little continuity it can boast of; but they are not processes in consciousness. Processes in consciousness are aesthetic or dialectical processes, focussing a form rather than ushering in an existence.

This placing of mental facts is made easy by the mental facts themselves, since the connection of mind with nature is double,

* Aristotle called the soul the first entelechy of such a body. This first entelechy is what we should call life, since it is possessed by a man asleep. The French I know but do not use is in its first entelechy; the French I am actually speaking is in its second. Consciousness is therefore the second or actualised entelechy of its body.

and even when the derivation of a feeling is obscure we have but to study its meaning, allowing it to tell us what it is interested in, for a roundabout path to lead us safely back to its natural basis. It is superfluous to ask a third person what circumstances produce hunger: hunger will lead you unmistakably enough to its point of origin, and its extreme interest in food will not suffer you long to believe that want of nourishment has nothing to do with its cause. And it is not otherwise with higher emotions and ideas. Nothing but sophistry can put us in doubt about what conscience represents; for conscience does not say, square the circle, extinguish mankind so as to stop its sufferings, or steal so as to benefit your heirs. It says, Thou shalt not kill, and it also says, Thou shalt worship the Lord thy God who brought thee out of the land of Egypt. So that conscience, by its import and incidence, clearly enough declares what it springs from—a social tradition; and what it represents—the interests, real or imaginary, of the community in which you were reared.

Where psychology depends on literature, where both its units and its method are poetical, there can be no talk of science. We may as justly, or as absurdly, speak of the spirit of an age or of a religion as of a man's character or a river's god. Particulars in illustration may have good historic warrant, but the unities superimposed are ideal. Such metaphors may be very useful, for a man may ordinarily be trusted to continue his practices and a river its beneficent or disastrous floods; and since those rhetorical forms have no existence in nature we may continue to frame them as may be most convenient for discourse.

"Reality" is an ambiguous term. What, for instance, is the reality of Napoleon? Is it what a telepathic poet, a complete Browning, might reconstruct? Is it Napoleon's life-long soliloquy? Or to get at the reality should we have to add, as scientific psychology would, the conditions under which he lived, and their relation to his casual feelings? Obviously if Napoleon's thoughts had had no reference to the world we should not be able to recover them; or if by chance such thoughts fell some day to our share, we should attribute them to our own mental luxuriance, without suspecting that they had ever visited another genius. Our knowledge of his life, even where it is imaginative, depends upon scientific knowledge for its projection; and his fame and immortality depend on the degree to which his thoughts, being rooted in the structure of the world and pertinent to it, can be rationally reproduced in others and attributed to him. Napoleon's consciousness might perhaps be more justly identified with the truth or reality of him than could that of most people, because he seems to have been unusually cognisant of his environment and master of the forces at work in it and in himself. He understood his causes and function, and knew that he had *arisen*, like all the rest of history, and that he stood for the transmissible force and authority of greater things. Such a consciousness can be known in proportion as we, too, possess knowledge, and is worth the pains; something which could not be said of the absolute sentience of Dick or Harry, which has only material being, brute existence, without relevance to anything nor understanding of itself.

The circumstances, open to science, which surround consciousness are thus real attributes of a man by which he is truly known and distinguished. Appearances are the qualities of reality, else realities would be without place, time, character, or interrelation. In knowing that Napoleon was a Corsican, a short man with a fine countenance, we actualise appearances only; but these appearances are true of the reality. And if the presumable inner appearances, Napoleon's long soliloquy, were separated from the others, those inner appearances would not belong to Napoleon nor have any home in the knowable world. That which physics, with its concomitant psychology, might discover in a man is the sum of what is true about him, seeing that a man is a concretion in existence, the fragment of a world, and not a definition. Appearances define the constituent elements of his reality, which could not be better known than through their means.

CHAPTER 5

THE NATURE OF INTENT

EXISTENCE NATURALLY precedes any idealisation of it which men can contrive (since they, at least, must exist first), yet in the order of values knowledge of existence is subsidiary to knowledge of ideals. If it be true that a good physics is as yet the predominant need in science, and that man is still most troubled by his ignorance of matters of fact, this circumstance marks his illiberal condition. Without knowledge of existence nothing can be done; but nothing is really done until something else is known also, the use or excellence that existence may have. It is a great pity that those finer temperaments that are naturally addressed to the ideal should have turned their energies to producing bad physics, or to preventing others from establishing natural truths; for if physics were established on a firm basis the idealists would for the firt time have a free field. They might then recover their proper function of expressing the mind honestly, and disdain the sorry attempt to prolong confusion and to fish in troubled waters.

Perhaps if physical truth had not been so hugely misrepresented in men's faith and conduct, it would not need to be minutely revealed or particularly emphasised. When the conditions surrounding life are not rightly faced by instinct they are inevitably forced upon reflection through painful shocks; and for a long time the new habit thus forced upon men brings to consciousness not so much the movement of consciousness itself as the points at which its movement impinges on the external world and feels checks and frictions. Physics thus becomes inordinately conspicuous (as when philology submerges the love of letters) for lack of a good disposition that should allow us to take physics for granted. Much in nature is delightful to know and to keep in mind, but much also (the whole infinite remainder) is obscure and uninteresting; and were we practically well adjusted to its issue we might gladly absolve ourselves from studying its processes. In a world that in extent and complexity so far outruns human en-

427

ergies, physical knowledge ought to be largely virtual; that is, nature ought to be represented by a suitable attitude toward it, by the attitude which reason would dictate were knowledge complete, and not by explicit ideas.

The ancients were happily inspired when they imagined that beyond the gods and the fixed stars the cosmos came to an end, for the empyrean beyond was nothing in particular, nothing to trouble one's self about. Many existences are either out of relation to man altogether or have so infinitesimal an influence on his experience that they may be sufficiently represented there by an atom of star-dust; and it is probable that if, out of pure curiosity, we wished to consider very remote beings and had the means of doing so, we should find the detail of existence in them wholly incommensu-rable with anything we can conceive. Such beings could be known virtually only, in that we might speak of them in the right key, representing them in appropriate symbols, and might move in their company with the right degree of respectful indifference.

The present situation of science, however, reverses the ideal one. Physics, in so far as it exists, is explicit, and at variance with our acquired attitude toward things; so that we may justly infer, by the shock our little knowledge gives us, that our presumptions and assumptions have been so egregious that more knowledge would give us still greater shocks. Meantime dialectic, or knowl-edge of ideal things, remains merely virtual. The ideal usually comes before us only in revulsions which we cannot help feeling against some scandalous situation or some intolerable muddle. We have no time or genius left, after our agitated soundings and balings, to think of navigation as a fine art, or to consider freely the sea and sky or the land we are seeking. The proper occupation of the mind is gone, or rather not initiated.

A further bad consequence of this illiberal state is that, among many who have, in spite of the times, adoration in their souls, to adore physics, to worship Being, seems a philosophical religion, whereas, of course, it is the essence of idolatry. The true God is an object of intent, an ideal of excellence and knowledge, not a term belonging to sense or to probable hypothesis or to the pru-dent management of affairs. After we have squared our accounts with nature and taken sufficient thought for our bodily necessities, the eyes can be lifted for the first time to the eternal. The rest was superstition and the quaking use of a false physics. That appeal to the supernatural which while the danger threatens is but forlorn medicine, after the blow has fallen may turn to sublime wisdom. This wisdom has cast out the fear of material evils, and dreads only that the divine should not come down and be worthily entertained among us. In art, in politics, in that form of religion which is superior, and not inferior, to politics and art, we define and embody intent; and the intent embodied dignifies the work and lends interest to its conditions. So, in science, it is dialectic that makes physics speculative and worthy of a free mind. The baser utilities of material knowledge would leave life itself perfectly vain, if they did not help it to take on an ideal shape. Ideal life, in so far as it constitutes science, is dialectical. It consists in seeing how things hang together perspicuously and how the later phases of any process fill out—as in good music—the tendency and promise of what went before. This derivation may be mathematical or it may be moral; but in either case the data and problem define the result, dialectic being insight into their inherent correspondence.

Intent is one of many evidences that the intellect's essence is practical. Intent is action in the sphere of thought; it corresponds to transition and derivation in the natural world. Analytic psychology is obliged to ignore intent, for it is obliged to regard it merely as a feeling; but while the feeling of intent is a fact like any other, intent itself is an aspiration, a passage, the recognition of an object which not only is not a part of the feeling given but is often incapable of being a feeling or a fact at all. What happened to motion under the Eleatic analysis happens to intent under an anatomising reflection. The parts do not contain the movement of transition which makes them a whole. Moral experience is not expressible in physical categories, because while you may give place and date for every feeling that something is important or is absurd, you cannot so express what these feelings have discovered and have wished to confide to you. The importance and the absurdity have disappeared. Yet it is this pronouncement concerning what things are absurd or important that makes the intent of those judgments. To touch it you have to enter the moral world; that is, you have to bring some sympathetic or hostile judgment to bear on those you are considering and to meet intent, not by noting its existence, but by estimating its value, by collating it with your own intent. If some one says two and two are five, you are no counter-mathematician when you conscientiously put it down that he said so. Your science is not relevant to his intent until you run some risk yourself in that arena and say, No: two and two are four.

Feelings and ideas, when plucked and separately considered, do not retain the intent that made them cognitive or living; yet in their native medium something certainly lived and knew. If this ideality or transcendence seems a mystery, it is such only in the sense in which every initial or typical fact is mysterious. Every category would be unthinkable if it were not actually used. The mystery in this instance has, however, all that can best serve to make a mystery homely and amiable. It is supported by a strong analogy to other familiar mysteries. The fact that intellect has intent, and does not constitute or contain what it envisages, is like the fact that time flows, that bodies gravitate, that experience is gathered, or that existence is suspended between being and not being. Propagation in animals is mysterious and familiar in the same fashion. Cognition, too, is an expedient for vanquishing instability. As reproduction circumvents mortality and preserves a semblance of permanence in the midst of change, so intent regards what is not yet, or not here, or what exists no longer. Thus the pulverisation proper to existence is vanquished by thought, which in a moment announces or commemorates other moments, together with the manner of their approach or recession. The mere image of what is absent constitutes no knowledge of it; a dream is not knowledge of a world like it existing elsewhere; it is simply another more fragile world. What renders the image cognitive is the intent that projects it and deputes it to be representative. It is cognitive only in use, when it is the vehicle of an assurance which may be right or wrong, because it takes something ulterior for its standard.

We may give intent a somewhat more congenial aspect if we remember that thought comes to animals in proportion to their docility in the world and to their practical competence. The more plastic a being is to experience, so long as he retains vital continuity and a cumulative structure, the more intelligent he becomes. Intelligence is an expression of adaptation, of impressionable and prophetic structure. What wonder, then, that intelligence should speak of the things that inspire it and that lend it its oracular and practical character, namely, of things at that moment not possess but merely posited, in other words, of the surrounding world? Mere feeling might suffice to translate into consciousness each particle of protoplasm in its isolation; but to translate the relations of that particle to what is not itself and to express its response to those environing presences, intent and conscious signification are required. Intellect transcends the given and means the absent because life, of which intellect is the fulfilment or entelechy, is itself absorbed from without and radiated outward. As life depends on an equilibrium of material processes which reach far beyond the individual they sustain in being, so intent is a recognition of outlying existences which sustain in being that very sympathy by which they are recognised. Intent and life are more than analogous. If we use the word life in an ideal sense, the two are coincident, for, as Aristotle says, the act proper to intellect is life.* The flux is so pervasive, so subtle in its persistency, that even those miracles which suspend it must somehow share its destiny. Intent bridges many a chasm, but only by leaping across. The life that is sustained for years, the political or moral purpose that may bind whole races together, is condemned to be partly a memory and partly a plan and wholly an ideal. Its scope is nothing but the range to which it can continually extend its sympathies and its power of representation. Its moments have nothing in common except their loyalties and a conspiring interest in what is not themselves.

This moral energy, so closely analogous to physical interplay, is of course not without a material basis. Spiritual sublimation does not consist in not using matter but in using it up, in making it all useful. When life becomes rational it continues to be mechanical and to dramatize room and energy in the natural world. In its most intimate and supernatural functions intellect has natural conditions. In dreams and madness intent is confused and wayward, in idiocy it is suspended altogether; nor has discourse any other pledge that it is addressing kindred interlocutors except that which it receives from the disposition and habit of bodies. People who have not yet been born into the world have not yet begun to think about it.

There is, of course, an inner dialectical relevance among all propositions that have the same ideal theme, no matter how re-

* Cf. the motto on the title-page.

mote or unknown to one another those who utter the propositions may be; but the medium in which this infinite dialectical network is woven is out of time, and indifferent to the direction in which thought might traverse it; in other words, it is not discourse or intelligence but eternal truth. From the point of view of experience this prior dialectical relation of form to form is merely potential; for the thoughts between which it would obtain need never exist or be enacted. There is society only among incarnate ideas; and it is only by expressing some material situation that an idea is selected out of the infinity of not impossible ideas and promoted to the temporal dignity of actual thought.

Moreover, even if the faculty of intelligence were disembodied and could exist in a vacuum, it would still be a vain possession if no data were given for it to operate upon and if no particular natural structure, animal, social, or artistic, were at hand for intelligence to ally itself to and defend. Reason would in that case die of inanition; it would have no subject-matter and no sanction, as well as no seat. Intelligence is not a substance; it is a principle of order and of art; it requires a given situation and some particular natural interest to bring it into play. In fact, it is nothing but a name for the empire which conscious, but at bottom irrational, interests attain over the field in which they operate; it is the fruition of life, the token of successful operation.

Every theme or motive in the Life of Reason expresses some instinct rooted in the body and incidental to natural organisation. The intent by which memory refers to past or reported experience, or the intent by which perception becomes recognition, is a transcript of relations in which events actually stand to one another. Such intent represents modifications of structure and action important to life, modifications that have responded to forces on which life is dependent. Both desire and meaning translate into cognitive or ideal energy, into intent, material relations subsisting in nature. These material relations give practical force to the thought that expresses them, and the thought in turn gives significance and value to the forces that subserve it. Fulfilment is mutual, in one direction bringing material potentialities to the light and making them actual and conscious, and in the other direction embodying intent in the actual forms of things and manifesting reason. Nothing could be more ill-considered than the desire to disembody reason. Reason cries aloud for reunion with the material world which she needs not only for a basis but, what concerns her even more, for a theme.

In private and silent discourse, when words and grammar are swathed in reverie, the material basis and reference of thought may be forgotten. Desire and intent may then seem to disport themselves in a purely ideal realm; moral or logical tensions alone may seem to determine the whole process. Meditative persons are even inclined to regard the disembodied life which they think they enjoy at such times as the true and native form of existence; all organs, applications, and expressions of thought they deprecate and call accidental. As some pious souls reject dogma to reach pure faith and suspend prayer to enjoy union, so some mystical logicians drop the world in order to grasp reality. It is an exquisite suicide; but the energy and ideal that sustain such a flight are annihilated by its issue, and the soul drops like a paper balloon consumed by the very flame that wafted it. No thought is found without an organ; none is conceivable without a verbal expression which is that organ's emanation; and none would be significant without a subject-matter lying in the world of which that organ is a part.

Significant language forms a great system of ideal tensions, contained in the mutual relations of parts of speech, and of clauses in propositions. Of these tensions the intent in a man's mind at any moment is a living specimen. Experience at that moment may have a significance, a transitive force, that asks to be enshrined in some permanent expression; the more acute and irrevocable the crisis is, the more urgent the need of transmitting to other moments some cognisance of what was once so great. But were this experience to exhale its spirit in a vacuum, using no conventional and transmissible medium of expression, it would be foiled in its intent. It would leave no monument and achieve no immortality in the world of representation; for the experience and its expression would remain identical and perish together, just as a perception and its object would remain identical and perish together if there were no intelligence to discover the material world, to which the perplexing shifts of sensation may be habitually referred. Spontaneous expression, if it is to be recognisable and therefore in effect expressive, labours under the necessity of subordinating itself to an ideal system of expressions, a permanent language in which its spontaneous utterances may be embedded. By virtue of such adoption into a common medium expression becomes interpretable; a later moment may then reconstruct the past out of its surviving memorial.

Intent, besides the form it has in language, where it makes the soul of grammar, has many other modes of expression, in mathematical and logical reasoning, in action, and in those contemplated and suspended acts which we call estimation, policy, or morals. Moral philosophy, the wisdom of Socrates, is merely a consideration of intent. In intent we pass over from existence to ideality, the nexus lying in the propulsive nature of life which could not have been capped by any form of knowledge which was not itself in some way transitive and ambitious. Intent, though it looks away from existence and the actual, is the most natural and pervasive of things. Physics and dialectic meet in this: that the second brings to fruition what the first describes, namely, existence, and that both have their transcendental root in the flux of being. Matter cannot exist without some form, much as by shedding every form in succession it may proclaim its aversion to fixity and its radical formlessness or infinitude. Nor can form, without the treacherous aid of matter, pass from its ideal possibility into selected and instant being.

In order to live—if such a myth may be allowed—the Titan Matter was eager to disguise his incorrigible vagueness and pretend to be something. He accordingly addressed himself to the beautiful company of Forms, sisters whom he thought all equally beautiful, though their number was endless, and equally fit to satisfy his heart. He wooed them hypocritically, with no intention of wedding them; yet he uttered their names in such seductive accents (called by mortals intelligence and toil) that the virgin goddesses offered no resistance—at least such of them as happened to be near or of a facile disposition. They were presently deserted by their unworthy lover; yet they, too, in that moment's union, had tasted the sweetness of life. The heaven to which they returned was no longer an infinite mathematical paradise. It was crossed by memories of earth, and a warmer breath lingered in some of its lanes and grottoes. Henceforth its nymphs could not forget that they had awakened a passion, and that, unmoved themselves, they had moved a strange indomitable giant to art and love.

CHAPTER 6

DIALECTIC

THE ADVANTAGE which the mechanical sciences have over history is drawn from their mathematical form. Mathematics has somewhat the same place in physics that conscience has in action; it seems to be a directive principle in natural operations where it is only a formal harmony. The formalistic school, which treats grammar in all departments as if it were the ground of import rather than a means of expressing it, takes mathematics also for an oracular deliverance, springing full-armed out of the brain, and setting up a canon which all concrete things must conform to. Thus mathematical science has become a mystery which a myth must be constructed to solve. For how can it happen, people ask, that pure intuition, retreating into its cell, can evolve there a prodigious system of relations which it carries like a measuring-rod into the world and lo! everything in experience submits to be measured by it? What pre-established harmony is this between the spinning cerebral silkworm and nature's satins and brocades?

If we but knew, so the myth runs, that experience can show no patterns but those which the prolific Mind has woven, we should not wonder at this necessary correspondence. The Mind having decreed of its own motion, while it sat alone before the creation of the world, that it would take to dreaming mathematically, it evoked out of nothing all formal necessities; and later, when it felt some solicitation to play with things, it imposed those forms upon all its toys, admitting none of any sort into the nursery. In other words, perception perfected its grammar before perceiving any of its objects, and having imputed that grammar to the materials of sense, it was able to perceive objects for the first time and to legislate further about their relations.

The most obvious artifices of language are often the most deceptive and bring on epidemic prejudices. What is this Mind, this machine existing prior to existence? The mind that exists is only a particular department or focus of existence; its principles cannot

435

be its own source, much less the source of anything in other beings. Mathematical principles in particular are not imposed on existence or on nature *ab extra*, but are found in and abstracted from the subject-matter and march of experience. To exist things have to wear some form, and the form they happen to wear is largely mathematical. This being the case, the mind in shaping its barbarous prosody somewhat more closely to the nature of things, learns to note and to abstract the form that so strikingly defines them. Once abstracted and focussed in the mind, these forms, like all forms, reveal their dialectic; but that things conform to that dialectic (when they do) is not wonderful, seeing that it is the obvious form of things that the mind has singled out, not without practical shrewdness, for more intensive study.

The difference between ideal and material knowledge does not lie in the ungenerated oracular character of one of them in opposition to the other; in both the data are inexplicable and irrational, and in both investigation is tentative, observant, and subject to control by the subject-matter. The difference lies, rather, in the direction of speculation. In physics, which is at bottom historical, we study what happens; we make inventories and records of events, of phenomena, of juxtapositions. In dialectic, which is wholly intensive, we study what is; we strive to clarify and develop the essence of what we find, bringing into focus the inner harmonies and implications of forms—forms which our attention or purpose has defined initially. The intuitions from which mathematical deduction starts are highly generic notions suggested by the given forms of things. The lines and angles of geometers are ideals, and their ideal context is entirely independent of what may be their context in the world; but we read them into the world, and their ideals are suggested by very common sensations. Had they been invented, by some inexplicable parthenogenesis in thought, it would indeed have been a marvel had they found application. Philosophy has enough notions of this inapplicable sort—usually, however, not very recondite in their origin—to show that dialectic, when it seems to control existence, must have taken more than one hint from the subject world, and that in the realm of logic, too, nothing submits to be governed without representation.

When dialectic is employed, as in ethics and metaphysics, upon highly complex ideas—concretions in discourse which cover large blocks of existence—the dialectician in defining and in deducing often reaches notions which cease to apply in some important respect to the object originally intended. Thus Socrates, taking "courage" for his theme, treats it dialectically and expresses the intent of the word by saying that courage must be good, and then develops the meaning of good, showing that it means the choice of the greater benefit; and finally turns about and ends by saying that courage is consequently the choice of the greater benefit and identical with wisdom. Here we have a process of thought ending in a paradox which, frankly, misrepresents the original meaning. For "courage" meant not merely something desirable but something having a certain animal and psychological aspect. The emotion and gesture of it had not been excluded from the idea. So that while the argument proves to perfection that unwise courage is a bad thing, it does not end with an affirmation really true of the original concept. The instinct which we call courage, with an eye to its psychic and bodily quality, is not always virtuous or wise. Dialectic, when it starts with confused and deep-dyed feelings, like those which ethical and metaphysical terms generally stand for, is thus in greater danger of proving unsatisfactory and being or seeming sophistical.

The mathematical dialectician has no such serious dangers to face. When, having observed the sun and sundry other objects, he frames the idea of a circle and tracing out its intent shows that the circle meant cannot be squared, there is no difficulty in reverting to nature and saying that the sun's circle cannot be squared. For there is no difference in intent between the circularity noted in the sun and that which is the subject of the demonstration. The geometer has made in his first reflection so clear and violent a transcript of the sun's actual bulk and qualities that he will never imagine himself to be speaking of anything but a concretion in discourse. The concretion in nature is never legislated about nor so much as thought of except possibly when, under warrant of sense, it is chosen to illustrate the concept investigated dialectically. It does not even occur to a man to ask if the sun's circle can be squared, for every one understands that the sun is circular only in so far as it conforms to the circle's ideal nature; which is as if Socrates and his interlocutors had clearly understood that the *virtue* of courage in an intemperate villain meant only whatever in his mood or action was rational and truly desirable, and had then said that courage, so understood, was identical with wisdom or with the truly rational and desirable rule of life.

The applicability of mathematics is not vouched for by mathematics but by sense, and its application in some distant part of nature is not vouched for by mathematics but by inductive arguments about nature's uniformity, or by the character which the notion, "a distant part of nature," already possesses. Inapplicable mathematics, we are told, is perfectly thinkable, and systematic deductions, in themselves valid, may be made from concepts which contravene the facts of perception. We may suspect, perhaps, that even these concepts are framed by definition out of suggestions found in sense, so that some symbolic relevance or proportion is kept, even in these dislocated speculations, to the matter of experience. It is like a new mythology; the purely fictitious idea has a certain parallelism and affinity to nature and moves in a human and familiar way. Both data and method are drawn from applicable science, elements of which even myth, whether poetic or mathematical, may illustrate by a sort of variant or fantastic reduplication.

The great glory of mathematics, like that of virtue, is to be useful while remaining free. Number and measure furnish an inexhaustible subject-matter which the mind can dominate and develop dialectically as it is the mind's inherent office to develop ideas. At the same time number and measure are the grammar of sense; and the more this inner logic is cultivated and refined the greater subtlety and sweep can be given to human perception. Astronomy on the one hand and mechanical arts on the other are fruits of mathematics by which its worth is made known even to the layman, although the born mathematician would not need the sanction of such an extraneous utility to attach him to a subject that has an inherent cogency and charm. Ideas, like other things, have pleasure in propagation, and even when allowance is made for birth-pangs and an occasional miscarriage, their native fertility will always continue to assert itself. The more ideal and frictionless the movement of thought is, the more perfect must be the physiological engine that sustains it. The momentum of that silent and secluded growth carries the mind, with a sense of pure disembodied vision, through the logical labyrinth; but the momentum is vital, for the truth itself does not move.

Whether the airy phantoms thus brought into being are valued and preserved by the world is an ulterior point of policy which the pregnant mathematician does not need to consider in bringing to light the legitimate burden of his thoughts. But were mathematics incapable of application, did nature and experience, for instance, illustrate nothing but Parmenides' Being or Hegel's Logic, the dialectical cogency which mathematics would of course retain would not give this science a very high place in the Life of Reason. Mathematics would be an amusement, and though apparently innocent, like a game of patience, it might even turn out to be a wasteful and foolish exercise for the mind; because to deepen habits and cultivate pleasures irrelevant to other interests is a way of alienating ourselves from our general happiness. Distinction and a curious charm there may well be in such a pursuit, but this quality is perhaps traceable to affinities and associations with other more substantial interests, or is due to the ingenious temper it denotes, which touches that of the wit or magician. Mathematics, if it were nothing more than a pleasure, might conceivably become a vice. Those addicted to it might be indulging an atavistic taste at the expense of their humanity. It would then be in the position now occupied by mythology and mysticism. Even as it is, mathematicians share with musicians a certain partiality in their characters and mental development. Masters in one abstract subject, they may remain children in the world; exquisite manipulators of the ideal, they may be erratic and clumsy in their earthly ways. Immense as are the uses and wide the applications of mathematics, its texture is too thin and inhuman to employ the whole mind or render it harmonious. It is a science which Socrates rejected for its supposed want of utility; but perhaps he had another ground in reserve to justify his humorous prejudice. He may have felt that such a science, if admitted, would endanger his thesis about the identity of virtue and knowledge.

Mathematical method has been the envy of philosophers, perplexed and encumbered as they are with the whole mystery of existence, and they have attempted at times to emulate mathematical cogency. Now the lucidity and certainty found in mathematics are not inherent in its specific character as the science of number or dimension; they belong to dialectic as a whole which is essentially elucidation. The effort to explain meanings is in most cases abortive because these meanings melt in our hands— a defeat which Hegel would fain have consecrated, together with all other evils, into necessity and law. But the merit of mathematics is that it is so much less Hegelian than life; that it holds its own while it advances, and never allows itself to misrepresent its original intent. In all it finds to say about the triangle it never comes to maintain that the triangle is really a square. The privilege of mathematics is simply to have offered the mind, for dialectical treatment, a material to which dialectical treatment could be honestly applied. This material consists in certain general aspects of sensation—its extensity, its pulsation, its distribution into related parts. The wakefulness that originally makes these abstractions is able to keep them clear, and to elaborate them infinitely without contradicting their essence.

The question in dialectic is always what is correct, what can be said, about *this*; and the demonstrative pronoun, indicating an act of selective attention, raises the object it selects to a concretion in discourse, the relations of which in the universe of discourse it then proceeds to formulate. At the same time this dialectical investigation may be full of surprises. Knowledge may be so truly enriched by it that *knowledge*, in an ideal sense, only begins when dialectic has given some articulation to being. Without dialectic an animal might follow instinct, he might have vivid emotions, expectations, and dreams, but he could hardly be said to know anything or to guide his life with conscious intent. The accretions that might come empirically into any field of vision would not be new predicates to be added to a known thing, unless the logical and functional mantle of that thing fell upon them and covered them. While the right of particulars to existence is their own, granted them by the free grace of heaven, their ability to enlarge our knowledge on any particular subject—their relevance or incidence in discourse—hangs on their fulfilling the requirements which that subject's dialectical nature imposes on all its expressions.

So long as in using terms there is no fixed intent, no concretion in discourse with discernible predicates, controversy will rage as conceptions waver and will reach no valid result. But when the force of intellect, once having arrested an idea amid the flux of perceptions, avails to hold and examine that idea with perseverance, not only does a flash of light immediately cross the mind, but deeper and deeper vistas are opened there into ideal implication. The principle of dialectic is intelligence itself; and as no part of man's economy is more vital than intelligence (since intelligence is what makes life aware of its destiny), so no part has a more delightful or exhilarating movement. To understand is pre-eminently to live, moving not by stimulation and external compulsion, but by inner direction and control. Dialectic is related to observation as art is to industry; it uses what the other furnishes; it is the fruition of experience. It is not an alternative to empirical pursuits but their perfection; for dialectic, like art, has no special or private subject-matter, nor any obligation to be useless. Its subject-matter is all things, and its function is to compare them in form and worth, giving the mind speculative dominion over them. It profits by the flux to fix its signification. This is precisely what mathematics does for the abstract form and multitude of sensible things; it is what dialectic might do everywhere, with the same incidental utility, if it could settle its own attitude and learn to make the passions steadfast and calm in the consciousness of their ultimate objects.

The sincere dialectician, the genuine moralist, must stand upon human, Socratic ground. Though art be long, it must take a short life for its basis and an actual interest for its guide. The liberal dialectician has the gift of conversation; he does not pretend to legislate from the throne of Jehovah about the course of affairs, but asks the ingenuous heart to speak for itself, guiding and checking it only in its own interest. The result is to express a given nature and to cultivate it; so that whenever any one possessing such a nature is born into the world he may use this calculation, and more easily understand and justify his mind. Of course, if experience were no longer the same, and faculties had entirely varied, the former interpretation could no longer serve. Where nature shows a new principle of growth the mind must find a new method of expression, and move toward other goals. Ideals are not forces stealthily undermining the will; they are possible forms of being that would frankly express it. These forms are invulnerable, eternal, and free; and he who finds them divine and congenial and is able to embody them at least in part and for a season, has to that extent transfigured life, turning it from a fatal process into a liberal art.

CHAPTER 7

PRE-RATIONAL MORALITY

PRE-RATIONAL MORALITY is vigorous because it is sincere. Actual interests, rooted habits, appreciations the opposite of which is inconceivable and contrary to the current use of language, are embodied in special precepts; or they flare up of themselves in impassioned judgments. It is hardly too much to say indeed, that prerational morality is morality proper. Rational ethics, in comparison, seems a kind of politics or wisdom, while postrational systems are essentially religions. If we thus identify morality with prerational standards, we may agree also that morality is no science in itself, though it may become, with other matters, a subject for the science of anthropology; and Hume, who had never come to close quarters with any rational or postrational ideal, could say with perfect truth that morality was not founded on reason. Instinct is of course not founded on reason, but *vice versa*; and the maxims enforced by tradition or conscience are unmistakably founded on instinct. They might, it is true, become materials for reason, if they were intelligently accepted, compared, and controlled; but such a possibility reverses the partisan and spasmodic methods which Hume and most other professed moralists associate with ethics. Hume's own treatises on morals, it need hardly be said, are pure psychology. It would have seemed to him conceited, perhaps, to inquire what ought really to be done. He limited himself to asking what men tended to think about their doings.

The chief expression of rational ethics which a man in Hume's world would have come upon lay in the Platonic and Aristotelian writings; but these were not then particularly studied nor vitally understood. The chief illustration of postrational morality that could have fallen under his eyes, the Catholic religion, he would never have thought of as a philosophy of life, but merely as a combination of superstition and policy, well adapted to the lying and lascivious habits of Mediterranean peoples. Under such circumstances ethics could not be thought of as a science; and whatever gradual definition of the ideal, whatever prescription of what ought to be and to be done, found a place in the thoughts of such philosophers formed a part of their politics or religion and not of their reasoned knowledge.

There is, however, a dialectic of the will; and that is the science which, for want of a better name, we must call ethics or moral philosophy. The interweaving of this logic of practice with various natural sciences that have man or society for their theme, leads to much confusion in terminology and in point of view. Is the good, we may ask, what anybody calls good at any moment, or what anybody calls good on reflection, or what all men agree to call good, or what God calls good, no matter what all mankind may think about it? Or is true good something that perhaps nobody calls good nor knows of, something with no other characteristic or relation except that it is simply good?

Various questions are involved in such perplexing alternatives; some are physical questions and others dialectical. Why any one values anything at all, or anything in particular, is a question of physics; it asks for the causes of interest, judgment, and desire. To esteem a thing good is to express certain affinities between that thing and the speaker; and if this is done with self-knowledge and with knowledge of the thing, so that the felt affinity is a real one, the judgment is invulnerable and cannot be asked to rescind itself. Thus if a man said hemlock was good to drink, we might say he was mistaken; but if he explained that he meant good to drink in committing suicide, there would be nothing pertinent left to say: for to adduce that to commit suicide is not good would be impertinent. To establish that, we should have to go back and ask him if he valued anything—life, parents, country, knowledge, reputation; and if he said no, and was sincere, our mouths would be effectually stopped—that is, unless we took to declamation. But we might very well turn to the bystanders and explain what sort of blood and training this man possessed, and what had happened among the cells and fibres of his brain to make him reason after that fashion. The causes of morality, good or bad, are physical, seeing that they are causes.

The science of ethics, however, has nothing to do with causes, not in that it need deny or ignore them but in that it is their fruit and begins where they end. Incense rises from burning coals, but it is itself no conflagration, and will produce none. What ethics asks is not why a thing is called good, but whether it is good or not, whether it is right or not so to esteem it. Goodness, in this ideal sense, is not a matter of opinion, but of nature. For intent is at work, life is in active operation, and the question is whether the thing or the situation responds to that intent. So if I ask, Is four really twice two? the answer is not that most people say so, but that, in saying so, I am not misunderstanding myself. To judge whether things are *really* good, intent must be made to speak; and if this intent may itself be judged later, that happens by virtue of other intents comparing the first with their own direction.

Hence good, when once the moral or dialectical attitude has been assumed, means not what is called good but what is so; that is, what *ought* to be called good. For intent, beneath which there is no moral judgment, sets up its own standard, and ideal science begins on that basis, and cannot go behind it to ask why the obvious good is good at all. Naturally, there is a reason, but not a moral one; for it lies in the physical habit and necessity of things. The reason is simply the propulsive essence of animals and of the universal flux, which renders forms possible but unstable, and either helpful or hurtful to one another. That nature should have this constitution, or intent this direction, is not a good in itself. It is esteemed good or bad as the intent that speaks finds in that situation a support or an obstacle to its ideal. As a matter of fact, nature and the very existence of life cannot be thought wholly evil, since no intent is wholly at war with these its conditions; nor can nature and life be sincerely regarded as wholly good, since no moral intent stops at the facts; nor does the universal flux, which infinitely overflows any actual synthesis, altogether support any intent it may generate.

Philosophers would do a great discourtesy to estimation if they sought to justify it. It is all other acts that need justification by this one. The first philosophers were accordingly sages. They were statesmen and poets who knew the world and cast a speculative glance at the heavens, the better to understand the conditions and limits of human happiness. Before their day, too, wisdom had spoken in proverbs. *It is better*, every adage began: *Better this than that*. Images or symbols, mythical or homely events, of course furnished subjects and provocations for these judgments; but the residuum of all observation was a settled estimation of things, a direction chosen in thought and life because it was better. Such was philosophy in the beginning and such is philosophy still.

To one brought up in a sophisticated society, or in particular under an ethical religion, morality seems at first an external command, a chilling and arbitrary set of requirements and prohibitions which the young heart, if it trusted itself, would not reckon at a penny's worth. Yet while this rebellion is brewing in the secret conclave of the passions, the passions themselves are prescribing a code. They are inventing gallantry and kindness and honour; they are discovering friendship and paternity. With maturity comes the recognition that the authorised precepts of morality were essentially not arbitrary; that they expressed the genuine aims and interests of a practised will; that their alleged alien and supernatural basis (which if real would have deprived them of all moral authority) was but a mythical cover for their forgotten natural springs. Virtue is then seen to be admirable essentially, and not merely by conventional imputation. If traditional morality has much in it that is out of proportion, much that is unintelligent and inert, nevertheless it represents on the whole the verdict of reason. It speaks for a typical human will chastened by a typical human experience.

Gnomic wisdom, however, is notoriously polychrome, and proverbs depend for their truth entirely on the occasion they are applied to. Almost every wise saying has an opposite one, no less wise, to balance it; so that a man rich in such lore, like Sancho Panza, can always find a venerable maxim to fortify the view he happens to be taking. In respect to foresight, for instance, we are told, Make hay while the sun shines, A stitch in time saves nine, Honesty is the best policy, Murder will out, Woe unto you, ye hypocrites, Watch and pray, Seek salvation with fear and trembling, and *Respice finem.* But on the same authorities exactly we have opposite maxims, inspired by a feeling that mortal prudence is fallible, that life is shorter than policy, and that only the present is real; for we hear, A bird in the hand is worth two in the bush, *Carpe diem, Ars longa, vita brevis,* Be not righteous overmuch, Enough for the day is the evil thereof, Behold the lilies of the field, Judge not, that ye be not judged, Mind your own business, and It takes all sorts of men to make a world. So when some particularly shocking thing happens one man says, *Cherchez la femme*, and another says, Great is Allah.

That these maxims should be so various and partial is quite intelligible when we consider how they spring up. Every man, in moral reflection, is animated by his own intent; he has something in view which he prizes, he knows not why, and which wears to him the essential and unquestionable character of a good. With this standard before his eyes, he observes easily—for love and hope are extraordinarily keen-sighted—what in action or in circumstances forwards his purpose and what thwarts it; and at once the maxim comes, very likely in the language of the particular instance before him. Now the interests that speak in a man are different at different times; and the outer facts or measures which in one case promote that interest may, where other less obvious conditions have changed, altogether defeat it. Hence all sorts of precepts looking to all sorts of results.

Prescriptions of this nature differ enormously in value; for they differ enormously in scope. By chance, or through the insensible operation of experience leading up to some outburst of genius, intuitive maxims may be so central, so expressive of ultimate aims, so representative, I mean, of all aims in fusion, that they merely anticipate what moral science would have come to if it had existed. This happens much as in physics ultimate truths may be divined by poets long before they are discovered by investigators; the *vivida vis animi* taking the place of much recorded experience, because much unrecorded experience has secretly fed it. Such, for instance, is the central maxim of Christianity, Love thy neighbour as thyself. On the other hand, what is usual in intuitive codes is a mixture of some elementary precepts, necessary to any society, with others representing local traditions or ancient rites: so Thou shalt not kill, and Thou shalt keep holy the Sabbath day, figure side by side in the Decalogue. When Antigone, in her sublimest exaltation, defies human enactments and appeals to laws which are not of to-day nor yesterday, no man knowing whence they have arisen, she mixes various types of obligation in a most instructive fashion; for a superstitious horror at leaving a body unburied—something decidedly of yesterday—gives poignancy in her mind to natural affection for a brother —something indeed universal, yet having a well-known origin.

The passionate assertion of right is here, in consequence, more dramatic than spiritual; and even its dramatic force has suffered somewhat by the change in ruling ideals.

The disarray of intuitive ethics is made painfully clear in the conflicts which it involves when it has fostered two incompatible growths in two centres which lie near enough to each other to come into physical collision. Such ethics has nothing to offer in the presence of discord except an appeal to force and to ultimate physical sanctions. It can instigate, but cannot resolve, the battle of nations and the battle of religions. Precisely the same zeal, the same patriotism, the same readiness for martyrdom fires adherents to rival societies, and fires them especially in view of the fact that the adversary is no less uncompromising and fierce. It might seem idle, if not cruel and malicious, to wish to substitute one historical allegiance for another, when both are equally arbitrary, and the existing one is the more congenial to those born under it; but to feel this aggression to be criminal demands some degree of imagination and justice, and sectaries would not be sectaries if they possessed it.

Truly religious minds, while eager perhaps to extirpate every religion but their own, often rise above national jealousies; for spirituality is universal, whatever churches may be. Similarly politicians often understand very well the religious situation; and of late it has become again the general practice among prudent governments to do as the Romans did in their conquests, and to leave people free to exercise what religion they have, without pestering them with a foreign one. On the other hand the same politicians are the avowed agents of a quite patent iniquity; for what is their ideal? To substitute their own language, commerce, soldiers, and tax-gatherers for the tax-gatherers, soldiers, commerce, and language of their neighbours; and no means is thought illegitimate, be it fraud in policy or bloodshed in war, to secure this absolutely nugatory end. Is not one country as much a country as another? Is it not as dear to its inhabitants? What then is gained by oppressing its genius or by seeking to destroy it altogether?

Here are two flagrant instances where prerational morality defeats the ends of morality. Viewed from within, each religious or national fanaticism stands for a good; but in its outward operation it produces and becomes an evil. It is possible, no doubt, that its agents are really so far apart in nature and ideals that, like men and mosquitoes, they can stand in physical relations only, and if they meet can meet only to poison or to crush one another. More probably, however, humanity in them is no merely nominal essence; it is definable ideally, as essences are defined, by a partially identical function and intent. In that case, by studying their own nature, they could rise above their mutual opposition, and feel that in their fanaticism they were taking too contracted a view of their own souls and were hardly doing justice to themselves when they did such great injustice to others.

How prerational morality may approach the goal, and miss it, is well illustrated in the history of Hellenism. Greek morals may be said to have been inspired by two prerational sentiments, a naturalistic religion and a local patriotism. Could Plato have succeeded in making that religion moral, or Alexander in universalising that patriotism, perhaps Greece might have been saved and we might all be now at a very different level of civilisation. Both Plato and Alexander failed, in spite of the immense and lasting influence of their work; for in both cases the after-effects were spurious, and the new spirit was smothered in the dull substances it strove to vivify.

Greek myth was an exuberant assertion of the rights of life in the universe. Existence could not but be joyful and immortal, if it had once found, in land, sea, or air, a form congruous with that element. Such congruity would render a being stable, efficient, beautiful. He would achieve a perfection grounded in skilful practice and in a thorough rejection of whatever was irrelevant. These things the Greeks called virtue. The gods were perfect models of this kind of excellence; for of course the amours of Zeus and Hermes' trickery were, in their hearty fashion, splendid manifestations of energy. This natural divine virtue carried no sense of responsibility with it, but it could not fail to diffuse benefit because it radiated happiness and beauty. The worshipper, by invoking those braver inhabitants of the cosmos, felt he might more easily attain a corresponding beauty and happiness in his paternal city.

The source of myth had been a genial sympathy with nature. The observer, at ease himself, multiplied ideally the potentialities of his being; but he went farther in imagining what life might yield abroad, freed from every trammel and necessity, than in deepening his sense of what life was in himself, and of what it ought to be. This moral reflection, absent from mythology, was

supplied by politics. The family and the state had a soberer antique religion of their own; this hereditary piety, together with
the laws, prescribed the citizen's education, customs, and duties.
The city drew its walls close about the heart, and while it fostered friendship and reason within, without it looked to little but
war. A splendid physical and moral discipline was established to
serve a suicidal egoism. The city committed its crimes, and the
individual indulged his vices of conduct and estimation, hardly
rebuked by philosophy and quite unrebuked by religion. Nevertheless, religion and philosophy existed, together with an incomparable literature and art, and an unrivalled measure and simplicity
in living. A liberal fancy and a strict civic regimen, starting with
different partial motives and blind purposes, combined by good
fortune into an almost rational life.

It was inevitable, however, when only an irrational tradition
supported the state, and kept it so weak amid a world of enemies,
that this state should succumb; not to speak of the mean animosities, the license in life, and the spirit of mockery that inwardly
infested it. The myths, too, faded; they had expressed a fleeting
moment of poetic insight, as patriotism had expressed a fleeting
moment of unanimous effort; but what force could sustain such
accidental harmonies? The patriotism soon lost its power to inspire sacrifice, and the myth its power to inspire wonder; so that
the relics of that singular civilisation were scattered almost at once
in the general flood of the world.

The Greek ideal has fascinated many men in all ages, who have
sometimes been in a position to set a fashion, so that the world
in general has pretended also to admire. But the truth is Hellas,
in leaving so many heirlooms to mankind, has left no constitutional benefit; it has taught the conscience no lesson. We possess
a great heritage from Greece, but it is no natural endowment.
An artistic rennaissance in the fifteenth century and a historical
one in the nineteenth have only affected the trappings of society.
The movement has come from above. It has not found any response in the people. While Greek morality, in its contents or in
the type of life it prescribes, comes nearer than any other pre-
rational experiment to what reason might propose, yet it has been
less useful than many other influences in bringing the Life of
Reason about. The Christian and the Moslem, in refining their
more violent inspiration, have brought us nearer to genuine good-

ness than the Greek could by his idle example. Classic perfection is a seedless flower, imitable only by artifice, not reproducible by generation. It is capable of influencing character only through the intellect, the means by which character can be influenced least. It is a detached ideal, responding to no crying and actual demand in the world at large. It never passed, to win the right of addressing mankind, through a sufficient novitiate of sorrow.

The Hebrews, on the contrary, who in comparison with the Greeks had a barbarous idea of happiness, showed far greater moral cohesion under the pressure of adversity. They integrated their purposes into a fanaticism, but they integrated them; and the integrity that resulted became a mighty example. It constituted an ideal of character not the less awe-inspiring for being merely formal. We need not marvel that abstract commandments should have impressed the world more than concrete ideals. To appreciate an ideal, to love and serve it in the full light of science and reason, would require a high intelligence, and, what is rarer still, noble affinities and renunciations which are not to be looked for in an undisciplined people. But to feel the truth and authority of an abstract maxim (as, for instance, Do right and shame the devil), a maxim applicable to experience on any plane, nothing is needed but a sound wit and common honesty. Men know better what is right and wrong than what is ultimately good or evil; their conscience is more vividly present to them than the fruits which obedience to conscience might bear; so that the logical relation of means to ends, of methods to activities, eludes them altogether. What is a necessary connection between the given end, happiness, and the normal life naturally possessing it, appears to them as a miraculous connection between obedience to God's commands and enjoyment of his favour. The evidence of this miracle astonishes them and fills them with zeal. They are strengthened to persevere in righteousness under any stress of misfortune, in the assurance that they are being put to a temporary test and that the reward promised to virtue will eventually be theirs.

As the happiness secured by virtue may be remote and may demand more virtue to make it appreciable, the mere rationality of a habit gives it no currency in the world and but little moral glow in the conscience. We should not, therefore, be too much offended at the illusions which play a part in moral integration. Imagination is often more efficacious in reaching the gist and meaning of experience than intelligence can be, just because imagination is less scrupulous and more instinctive. Even physical discoveries, when they come, are the fruit of divination, and Columbus had to believe he might sail westward to India before he could actually hit upon America. Reason cannot create itself, and nature, in producing reason, has to feel her way experimentally. Habits and chance systems of education have to arise first and exercise upon individuals an irrational suasion favourable to rational ends. Organs long exist before they reach their perfect function. The fortunate instincts of a race destined to long life and rationality express themselves in significant poetry before they express themselves in science.

The service which Hebraism has rendered to mankind has been instrumental, as that rendered by Hellenism has been imaginative. Hebraism has put earnestness and urgency into morality, making it a matter of duty, at once private and universal, rather than what paganism had left it, a mass of local allegiances and legal practices. The Jewish system has, in consequence, a tendency to propaganda and intolerance; a tendency which would not have proved nefarious had this religion always remained true to its moral principle; for morality is coercive and no man, being autonomous, has a right to do wrong. Conscience, thus reinforced by religious passion, has been able to focus a general abhorrence on certain great scandals—slavery and sodomy could be practically suppressed among Christians, and drunkenness, among Moslems. The Christian principle of charity also owed a part of its force to Hebraic tradition. For the law and the prophets were full of mercy and loving kindness toward the faithful. What Moses had taught his people Christ and his Hellenising disciples had the beautiful courage to preach to all mankind. Yet this virtue of charity, on its subtler and more metaphysical side, belongs to the spirit of redemption, to that ascetic and quasi-Buddhistic element in Christianity to which we shall presently revert. The pure Jews can have no part in such insight, because it contradicts the positivism of their religion and character and their ideal of worldly happiness.

As the human body is said to change all its substance every seven years, and yet is the same body, so the Hebraic conscience might change all its tenets in seven generations and be the same conscience still. Could this abstract moral habit, this transferable earnestness, be enlisted in rational causes, the Life of Reason would have gained a valuable instrument. Men would possess the "single eye," and the art, so difficult to an apelike creature with loose moral feelings, of acting on principle. Could the vision of an adequate natural ideal fall into the Hebraising mind, already aching for action and nerved to practical enthusiasm, that ideal vision might become efficacious and be largely realised in practice. The abstract power of self-direction, if enlightened by a larger experience and a more fertile genius, might give the Life of Reason a public embodiment such as it has not had since the best days of classic antiquity. Thus the two prerational moralities out of which European civilisation has grown, could they be happily superposed, would make a rational polity.

The objects of human desire, then, until reason has compared and experience has tested them, are a miscellaneous assortment of goods, unstable in themselves and incompatible with one another. It is a happy chance if a tolerable mixture of them recommends itself to a prophet or finds an adventitious acceptance among a group of men. Intuitive morality is adequate while it simply enforces those obvious and universal laws which are indispensable to any society, and which impose themselves everywhere on men under pain of quick extinction—a penalty which many an individual and many a nation continually prefers to pay. But when intuitive morality ventures upon speculative ground and tries to guide progress, its magic fails. Ideals are tentative and have to be critically viewed. A moralist who rests in his intuitions may be a good preacher, but hardly deserves the name of philosopher. He cannot find any authority for his maxims which opposite maxims may not equally invoke. To settle the relative merits of rival authorities and of hostile consciences it is necessary to appeal to the only real authority, to experience, reason, and human nature in the living man. No other test is conceivable and no other would be valid; for no good man would ever consent to regard an authority as divine or binding which essentially contradicted his own conscience. Yet a conscience which is irreflective and incorrigible is too hastily satisfied with itself, and not conscientious enough: it needs cultivation by dialectic. It neglects to extend to all human interests that principle of synthesis and justice by which conscience itself has arisen. And so soon as the conscience summons its own dicta for revision in the light of experience and of universal sympathy, it is no longer called conscience, but reason. So, too, when the spirit summons its traditional faiths, to subject them to a similar examination, that exercise is not called religion, but philosophy. It is true, in a sense, that philosophy is the purest religion and reason the ultimate conscience; but so to name them would be misleading. The things commonly called by those names have seldom consented to live at peace with sincere reflection. It has been felt vaguely that reason could not have produced them, and that they might suffer sad changes by submitting to it; as if reason could be the *ground* of anything, or as if everything might not find its consummation in becoming rational.

CHAPTER 8

RATIONAL ETHICS

ETHICS, IF it is to be a science and not a piece of arbitrary legislation, cannot pronounce it sinful in a serpent to be a serpent; it cannot even accuse a barbarian of loving a wrong life, except in so far as the barbarian is supposed capable of accusing himself of barbarism. If he is a perfect barbarian he will be inwardly, and therefore morally, justified. The notion of a barbarian will then be accepted by him as that of a true man, and will form the basis of whatever rational judgments or policy he attains. It may still seem dreadful to him to be a serpent, as to be a barbarian might seem dreadful to a man imbued with liberal interests. But the degree to which moral science, or the dialectic of will, can condemn any type of life depends on the amount of disruptive contradiction which, at any reflective moment, that life brings under the unity of apperception. The discordant impulses therein confronted will challenge and condemn one another; and the court of reason in which their quarrel is ventilated will have authority to pronounce between them.

The physical repulsion, however, which everybody feels to habits and interests which he is incapable of sharing is no part of rational estimation, large as its share may be in the fierce prejudices and superstitions which prerational morality abounds in. The strongest feelings assigned to the conscience are not moral feelings at all; they express merely physical antipathies.

Toward alien powers a man's true weapon is not invective, but skill and strength. An obstacle is an obstacle, not a devil; and even a moral life, when it actually exists in a being with hostile activities, is merely a hostile power. It is not hostile, however, in so far as it is moral, but only in so far as its morality represents a material organism, physically incompatible with what the thinker has at heart.

Material conflicts cannot be abolished by reason, because reason is powerful only where they have been removed. Yet where

454

opposing forces are able mutually to comprehend and respect one another, common ideal interests at once supervene, and though the material conflict may remain irrepressible, it will be overlaid by an intellectual life, partly common and unanimous. In this lies the chivalry of war, that we acknowledge the right of others to pursue ends contrary to our own. Competitors who are able to feel this ideal comity, and who leading different lives in the flesh lead the same life in imagination, are incited by their mutual understanding to rise above that material ambition, perhaps gratuitous, that has made them enemies. They may ultimately wish to renounce that temporal good which deprives them of spiritual goods in truth infinitely greater and more appealing to the soul—innocence, justice, and intelligence. They may prefer an enlarged mind to enlarged frontiers, and the comprehension of things foreign to the destruction of them. They may even aspire to detachment from those private interests which, as Plato said,* do not deserve to be taken too seriously; the fact that we must take them seriously being the ignoble part of our condition.

Perhaps the art of politics, if it were practised scientifically, might obviate open war, religious enmities, industrial competition, and human slavery; but it would certainly not leave a free field for all animals nor for all monstrosities in men. There is tragedy in perfection, because the universe in which perfection arises is itself imperfect. Accidents will always continue to harass the most consummate organism; they will flow in both from the outer world and from the interstices, so to speak, of its own machinery; for a rational life touches the irrational at its core as well as at its periphery. In both directions it meets physical force and can subsist only by exercising physical force in return. The range of rational ethics is limited to the intermediate political zone, in which existences have attained some degree of natural unanimity.

It should be added, perhaps, that the frontiers between moral and physical action are purely notional. Real existences do not lie wholly on one or the other side of them. Every man, every material object, has moral affinities enveloping an indomitable vital nucleus or brute personal kernel; this moral essence is enveloped in turn by untraceable relations, radiating to infinity over the natural world. The stars enter society by the light and knowledge they afford, the time they keep, and the ornament they lavish;

* Laws. VII. 803. B.

but they are mere dead weights in their substance and cosmological puzzles in their destiny. You and I possess manifold ideal bonds in the interests we share; but each of us has his poor body and his irremediable, incommunicable dreams. Beyond the little span of his foresight and love, each is merely a physical agency, preparing the way quite irresponsibly for undreamt-of revolutions and alien lives.

A truly rational morality, or social regimen, has never existed in the world and is hardly to be looked for. What guides men and nations in their practice is always some partial interest or some partial disillusion. A rational morality would imply perfect self-knowledge, so that no congenial good should be needlessly missed—least of all practical reason or justice itself; so that no good congenial to other creatures would be needlessly taken from them. The total value which everything had from the agent's point of view would need to be determined and felt efficaciously; and, among other things, the total value which this point of view, with the conduct it justified, would have for every foreign interest which it affected. Such knowledge, such definition of purpose, and such perfection of sympathy are clearly beyond man's reach. All that can be hoped for is that the advance of science and commerce, by fostering peace and a rational development of character, may bring some part of mankind nearer to that goal; but the goal lies, as every ultimate ideal should, at the limit of what is possible, and must serve rather to measure achievements than to prophesy them.

In lieu of a rational morality, however, we have rational ethics; and this mere idea of a rational morality is something valuable. While we wait for the sentiments, customs, and laws which should embody perfect humanity and perfect justice, we may observe the germinal principle of these ideal things; we may sketch the ground-plan of a true commonwealth. This sketch constitutes rational ethics, as founded by Socrates, glorified by Plato, and sobered and solidified by Aristotle. It sets forth the method of judgment and estimation which a rational morality would apply universally and express in practice. The method, being very simple, can be discovered and largely illustrated in advance, while the complete self-knowledge and sympathy are still wanting which might avail to embody that method in the concrete and to discover unequivocally where absolute duty and ultimate happiness may lie.

This method, the Socratic method, consists in accepting any

estimation which any man may sincerely make, and in applying dialectic to it, so as to let the man see what he really esteems. What he really esteems is what ought to guide his conduct; for to suggest that a rational being ought to do what he feels to be wrong, or ought to pursue what he genuinely thinks is worthless, would be to impugn that man's rationality and to discredit one's own. With what face could any man or god say to another: Your duty is to do what you cannot know you ought to do; your function is to suffer what you cannot recognise to be worth suffering? Such an attitude amounts to imposture and excludes society; it is the attitude of a detestable tyrant, and any one who mistakes it for moral authority has not yet felt the first heart-throb of philosophy.

More even than natural philosophy, moral philosophy is something Greek: it is the appanage of freemen. The Socratic method is the soul of liberal conversation; it is compacted in equal measure of sincerity and courtesy. Each man is autonomous and all are respected; and nothing is brought forward except to be submitted to reason and accepted or rejected by the self-questioning heart. Indeed, when Socrates appeared in Athens mutual respect had passed into democracy and liberty into license; but the stalwart virtue of Socrates saved him from being a sophist, much as his method, when not honestly and sincerely used, might seem to countenance that moral anarchy which the sophists had expressed in their irresponsible doctrines. Their sophistry did not consist in the private *seat* which they assigned to judgment; for what judgment is there that is not somebody's judgment at some moment? The sophism consisted in ignoring the living moment's *intent*, and in suggesting that no judgment could refer to anything ulterior, and therefore that no judgment could be wrong: in other words that each man at each moment was the theme and standard, as well as the seat, of his judgment.

Socrates escaped this folly by force of honesty, which is what saves from folly in dialectic. He built his whole science precisely on that intent which the sophists ignored; he insisted that people should declare sincerely what they meant and what they wanted; and on that living rock he founded the persuasive and ideal sciences of logic and ethics, the necessity of which lies all in free insight and in actual will. This will and insight they render deliberate, profound, unshakable, and consistent. Socrates, by his genial midwifery, helped men to discover the truth and excellence to which they were naturally addressed. This circumstance rendered his doctrine at once moral and scientific; scientific because dialectical, moral because expressive of personal and living aspirations. His ethics was not like what has since passed under that name—a spurious physics, accompanied by commandments and threats. It was a pliant and liberal expression of ideals, inwardly grounded and spontaneously pursued. It was an exercise in self-knowledge.

Socrates' liberality was that of a free man ready to maintain his will and conscience, if need be, against the whole world. The sophists, on the contrary, were sycophants in their scepticism, and having inwardly abandoned the ideals of their race and nation— which Socrates defended with his homely irony—they dealt out their miscellaneous knowledge, or their talent in exposition, at the beck and for the convenience of others. Their theory was that each man having a right to pursue his own aims, skilful thinkers might, for money, furnish any fellow-mortal with instruments fitted to his purpose. Socrates, on the contrary, conceived that each man, to achieve his aims must first learn to distinguish them clearly; he demanded that rationality, in the form of an examination and clarification of purposes, should precede any selection of external instruments. For how should a man recognise anything useful unless he first had established the end to be subserved and thereby recognised the good? True science, then, was that which enabled a man to disentangle and attain his natural good; and such a science is also the art of life and the whole of virtue.

The autonomous moralist differs from the sophist or ethical sceptic in this: that he retains his integrity. In vindicating his ideal he does not recant his human nature. In asserting the initial right of every impulse in others, he remains the spokesman of his own. Knowledge of the world, courtesy, and fairness do not neutralise his positive life. He is thoroughly sincere, as the sophist is not; for every man, while he lives, embodies and enacts some special interest; and this truth, which those who confound psychology with ethics may think destructive of all authority in morals, is in fact what alone renders moral judgment possible and respectable. If the sophist declares that what his nature attaches him to is not "really" a good, because it would not be a good, perhaps, for a different creature, he is a false interpreter of his own heart, and rather discreditably stultifies his honest feelings and actions by those theoretical valuations which, in guise of a mystical ethics, he gives out to the world. Socratic liberality, on the contrary, is consistent with itself, as Spinozistic naturalism is also; for it exercises that right of private judgment which it concedes to others, and avowedly builds up the idea of the good on that natural inner foundation on which everybody who has it at all must inevitably build it. This functional good is accordingly always relative and good for something; it is the ideal which a vital and energising soul carries with it as it moves. It is identical, as Socrates constantly taught, with the useful, the helpful, the beneficent. It is the complement needed to perfect every art and every activity after its own kind.

Rational ethics is an embodiment of volition, not a description of it. It is the expression of living interest, preference, and categorical choice. It leaves to psychology and history a free field for the description of moral phenomena. It has no interest in slipping far-fetched and incredible myths beneath the facts of nature, so as to lend a non-natural origin to human aspirations. It even recognises, as an emanation of its own force, that uncompromising truthfulness with which science assigns all forms of moral life to their place in the automatic system of nature. But the rational moralist is not on that account reduced to a mere spectator, a physicist acknowledging no interest except the interest in facts and in the laws of change. His own spirit, small by the material forces which it may stand for and express, is great by its prerogative of surveying and judging the universe; surveying it, of course, from a mortal point of view, and judging it only by its kindliness or cruelty to some actual interest, yet, even so, determining unequivocally a part of its constitution and excellence. The rational moralist represents a force energising in the world, discovering its affinities there and clinging to them to the exclusion of their hateful opposites. He represents, over against the chance facts, an ideal embodying the particular demands, possibilities, and satisfactions of a specific being.

This dogmatic position of reason is not uncritically dogmatic; on the contrary, it is the sophistical position that is uncritically neutral. All criticism needs a dogmatic background, else it would lack objects and criteria for criticism. The sophist himself, without confessing it, enacts a special interest. He bubbles over with convictions about the pathological and fatal origin of human beliefs, as if that could prevent some of them from being more trustworthy and truer than others. He is doubtless right in his psychology; his own ideas have their natural causes and their chance of signifying something real. His scepticism may represent a wider experience than do the fanaticisms it opposes. But this sceptic also lives. Nature has sent her saps abundantly into him, and he cannot but nod dogmatically on that philosophical tree on which he is so pungent a berry. His imagination is unmistakably fascinated by the pictures it happens to put together. His judgment falls unabashed, and his discourse splashes on in its dialectical march, every stepping-stone an unquestioned idea, every stride a categorical assertion. Does he deny this? Then his very denial, in its promptness and heat, audibly contradicts him and makes him ridiculous. Honest criticism consists in being consciously dogmatic, and conscientiously so, like Descartes when he said, "I am." It is to sift and harmonise all assertions so as to make them a faithful expression of actual experience and inevitable thought.

Now will, no less than that reason which avails to render will consistent and far-reaching, animates natural bodies and expresses their functions. It has a radical bias, a foregone, determinate direction, else it could not be a will nor a principle of preference. The knowledge of what other people desire does not abolish a man's own aims. Sympathy and justice are simply an expansion of the soul's interests, arising when we consider other men's lives so intently that something in us imitates and re-enacts their experience, so that we move partly in unison with their movement, recognise the reality and initial legitimacy of their interests, and consequently regard their aims in our action, in so far as our own status and purposes have become identical with theirs. We are not less ourselves, nor less autonomous, for this assimilation, since we assimilate only what is in itself intelligible and congruous with our mind and obey only that authority which can impose itself on our reason.

The case is parallel to that of knowledge. To know all men's experience and to comprehend their beliefs would constitute the most cogent and settled of philosophies. Thought would then be reasonably adjusted to all the facts of history, and judgment would grow more authoritative and precise by virtue of that enlightenment. So, too, to understand all the goods that any man, nay, that any beast or angel, may ever have pursued, would leave man still necessitous of food, drink, sleep, and shelter; he would still love; the comic, the loathsome, the beautiful would still affect him with unmistakable direct emotions. His taste might no doubt gain in elasticity by those sympathetic excursions into the polyglot world; the plastic or dramatic quality which had enabled him to feel other creatures' joys would grow by exericse and new overtones would be added to his gamut. But the foundations of his nature would stand; and his possible happiness, though some new and precious threads might be woven into it, would not have a texture fundamentally different.

The radical impulses at work in any animal must continue to speak while he lives, for they are his essence. A true morality does not have to be adopted; the parts of it best practised are those which are never preached. To be "converted" would be to pass from one self-betrayal to another. It would be to found a new morality on a new artifice. The morality which has genuine authority exists inevitably and speaks autonomously in every common judgment, self-congratulation, ambition, or passion that fills the vulgar day. The pursuit of those goods which are the only possible or fitting crown of a man's life is predetermined by his nature; he cannot choose a law-giver, nor accept one, for none who spoke to the purpose could teach him anything but to know himself. Rational life is an art, not a slavery; and terrible as may be the errors and the apathy that impede its successful exercise, the standard and goal of it are given intrinsically. Any task imposed externally on a man is imposed by force only, a force he has the right to defy so soon as he can do so without creating some greater impediment to his natural vocation.

Rational ethics, then, resembles prerational precepts and half-systems in being founded on impulse. It formulates a natural morality. It is a settled method of achieving ends to which man is drawn by virtue of his physical and rational constitution. By this circumstance rational ethics is removed from the bad company of all artificial, verbal, and unjust systems of morality, which in absolving themselves from relevance to man's endowment and experience merely show how completely irrelevant they are to life. Once, no doubt, each of these arbitrary systems expressed (like the observance of the Sabbath) some practical interest or some not unnatural rite; but so narrow a basis of course has to be disowned when the precepts so originating have been swollen into universal tyrannical laws. A rational ethics reduces them at once to their slender representative rôle; and it surrounds and buttresses them on every side with all other natural ideals.

Rational ethics thus differs from the prerational in being conclusive. There is one impulse which intuitive moralists ignore: the impulse ot reflect. Human instincts are ignorant, multitudinous, and contradictory. To satisfy them as they come is often impossible, and often disastrous, in that such satisfaction prevents the satisfaction of other instincts inherently no less fecund and legitimate. When we apply reason to life we immediately demand that life be consistent, complete, and satisfactory when reflected upon and viewed as a whole. This view, as it presents each moment in its relations, extends to all moments affected by the action or maxim under discussion; it has no more ground for stopping at the limits of what is called a single life than at the limits of a single adventure. To stop at selfishness is not particularly rational. The same principle that creates the ideal of a self creates the ideal of a family or an institution.

The conflict between selfishness and altruism is like that between any two ideal passions that in some particular may chance to be opposed; but such a conflict has no obstinate existence for reason. For reason the person itself has no obstinate existence. The *character* which a man achieves at the best moment of his life is indeed something ideal and significant; it justifies and consecrates all his coherent actions and preferences. But *the man's life*, the circle drawn by biographers around the career of a particular body, from the womb to the charnel-house, and around the mental flux that accompanies that career, is no significant unity. All the substances and efficient processes that figure within it come from elsewhere and continue beyond; while all the rational objects and interests to which it refers have a transpersonal status. Self-love itself is concerned with public opinion; and if a man concentrates his view on private pleasures, these may qualify the fleeting moments of his life with an intrinsic value, but they leave the life itself shapeless and infinite, as if sparks should play over a piece of burnt paper.

If pleasure, because it is commonly a result of satisfied instinct, may by a figure of speech be called the aim of impulse, happiness, by a like figure, may be called the aim of reason. The direct aim of reason is harmony; yet harmony, when made to rule in life, gives reason a noble satisfaction which we call happiness. Happiness is impossible and even inconceivable to a mind without scope and without pause, a mind driven by craving, pleasure, and fear. The moralists who speak disparagingly of happiness are less sublime than they think. In truth their philosophy is too lightly ballasted, too much fed on prejudice and quibbles, for happiness to fall within its range. Happiness implies resource and security; it can be achieved only by discipline. Your intuitive moralist rejects discipline, at least discipline of the conscience; and he is punished by having no lien on wisdom. He trusts to the clash of blind forces in collision, being one of them himself. He demands that virtue should be partisan and unjust; and he dreams of crushing the adversary in some physical cataclysm.

Such groping enthusiasm is often innocent and romantic; it captivates us with its youthful spell. But it has no structure with which to resist the shocks of fortune, which it goes out so jauntily to meet. It turns only too often into vulgarity and worldliness. A snow-flake is soon a smudge, and there is a deeper purity in the diamond. Happiness is hidden from a free and casual will; it belongs rather to one chastened by a long education and unfolded in an atmosphere of sacred and perfected institutions. It is discipline that renders men rational and capable of happiness, by suppressing without hatred what needs to be suppressed to attain a beautiful naturalness. Discipline discredits the random pleasures of illusion, hope, and triumph, and substitutes those which are self-reproductive, perennial, and serene, because they express an equilibrium maintained with reality. So long as the result of endeavour is partly unforeseen and unintentional, so long as the will is partly blind, the Life of Reason is still swaddled in ignominy and the animal barks in the midst of human discourse. Wisdom and happiness consist in having recast natural energies in the furnace of experience. Nor is this experience merely a repressive force. It enshrines the successful expressions of spirit as well as the shocks and vetoes of circumstance; it enable a man to know himself in knowing the world and to discover his ideal by the very ring, true or false, of fortune's coin.

With this brief account we may leave the subject of rational ethics. Its development is impossible save in the concrete, when a legislator, starting from extant interests, considers what practices serve to render those interests vital and genuine, and what external alliances might lend them support and a more glorious expression. The difficulty in carrying rational policy very far comes partly from the refractory materials at hand, and partly from the narrow range within which moral science is usually confined. The materials are individual wills naturally far from unanimous, lost for the most part in frivolous pleasures, rivalries, and superstitions, and little inclined to listen to a law-giver that, like a new Lycurgus, should speak to them of unanimity, simplicity, discipline, and perfection. Devotion and singlemindedness, perhaps possible in the cloister, are hard to establish in the world; yet a rational morality requires that all lay activities, all sweet temptations, should have their voice in the conclave. Morality becomes rational precisely by refusing either to accept human nature, as it sprouts, altogether without harmony, or to mutilate it in the haste to make it harmonious. The condition, therefore, of making a beginning in good politics is to find a set of men with well-knit character and cogent traditions, so that there may be a firm soil to cultivate and that labour may not be wasted in ploughing the quicksands.

CHAPTER 9

POST-RATIONAL MORALITY

WHEN SOCRATES and his two great disciples composed a system
of rational ethics they were hardly proposing practical legislation
for mankind. One by his irony, another by his frank idealism, and
the third by his preponderating interest in history and analysis,
showed clearly enough how little they dared to hope. They were
merely writing an eloquent epitaph on their country. They were
publishing the principles of what had been its life, gathering
piously its broken ideals, and interpreting its momentary achievement. The spirit of liberty and co-operation was already dead.
The private citizen, debauched by the largesses and petty quarrels of his city, had become indolent and mean-spirited. He had
begun to question the utility of religion, of patriotism, and of justice. Having allowed the organ for the ideal to atrophy in his
soul, he could dream of finding some sullen sort of happiness in
unreason. He felt that the austere glories of his country, as a
Spartan regimen might have preserved them, would not benefit
that baser part of him which alone remained. Political virtue
seemed a useless tax on his material profit and freedom. The
tedium and distrust proper to a disintegrated society began to
drive him to artificial excitements and superstitions. Democracy
had learned to regard as enemies the few in whom public interest
was still represented, the few whose nobler temper and traditions
still coincided with the general good. These last patriots were
gradually banished or exterminated, and with them died the spirit
that rational ethics had expressed. Philosophers were no longer
suffered to have illusions about the state. Human activity on the
public stage had shaken off all allegiance to art or reason.

Life is older and more persistent than reason, and the failure
of a first experiment in rationality does not deprive mankind of
that mental and moral vegetation which they possessed for ages in
a wild state before the advent of civilisation. They merely revert
to their uncivil condition and espouse whatever imaginative ideal

comes to hand, by which some semblance of meaning and beauty may be given to existence without the labour of building this meaning and beauty systematically out of its positive elements.

Not to study these imaginative ideals, partial and arbitrary as they are, would be to miss one of the most instructive points of view from which the Life of Reason may be surveyed: the point of view of its satirists. For moral ideals may follow upon philosophy, just as they may precede it. When they follow, at least so long as they are consciously embraced in view of reason's failure, they have a quite particular value. Aversion to rational ideals does not then come, as the intuitionist's aversion does, from moral incoherence or religious prejudice. It does not come from lack of speculative power. On the contrary, it may come from undue haste in speculation, from a too ready apprehension of the visible march of things. The obvious irrationality of nature as a whole, too painfully brought home to a musing mind, may make it forget or abdicate its own rationality. In a decadent age, the philosopher who surveys the world and sees that the end of it is even as the beginning, may not feel that the intervening episode, in which he and everything he values after all figure, is worth consideration; and he may cry, in his contemplative spleen, that *all* is vanity.

If you should still confront him with a theory of the ideal, he would not be reduced, like the pre-rational moralists in a similar case, to mere inattention and bluster. If you told him that every art and every activity involves a congruous good, and that the endeavour to realise the ideal in every direction is an effort of which reason necessarily approves, since reason is nothing but the method of that endeavour, he would not need to deny your statements in order to justify himself. He might admit the naturalness, the spontaneity, the ideal sufficiency of your conceptions; but he might add, with the smile of the elder and the sadder man, that he had experience of their futility.

Such a position may be turned dialectically by invoking whatever positive hopes or convictions the critic may retain, who while he lives cannot be wholly without them. But the position is specious and does not collapse, like that of the intuitionist, at the first breath of criticism. Pessimism, and all the moralities founded on despair, are not pre-rational but post-rational. They are the work of men who more or less explicitly have conceived the Life of Reason, tried it at least imaginatively, and found it wanting. These systems are a refuge from an intolerable situation: they are experiments in redemption. As a matter of fact, animal instincts and natural standards of excellence are never eluded in them, for no moral experience has other terms; but the part of the natural ideal which remains active appears in opposition to all the rest and, by an intelligible illusion, seems to be no part of that natural ideal because, compared with the commoner passions on which it reacts, it represents some simpler or more attenuated hope—the appeal to some very humble or very much chastened satisfaction, or to an utter change in the conditions of life.

Post-rational morality thus constitutes, in intention if not in fact, a criticism of all experience. It thinks it is not, like pre-rational morality, an arbitrary selection from among co-ordinate precepts. It is an effort to subordinate all precepts to one, that points to some single eventual good. For it occurs to the founders of these systems that by estranging oneself from the world, or resting in the moment's pleasure, or mortifying the passions, or enduring all sufferings in patience, or studying a perfect conformity with the course of affairs, one may gain admission to some sort of residual mystical paradise; and this thought, once conceived, is published as a revelation and accepted as a panacea. It becomes in consequence (for such is the force of nature) the foundation of elaborate institutions and elaborate philosophies, into which the contents of the worldly life are gradually reintroduced.

Socrates was still living when a school of post-rational morality arose among the Sophists, which after passing quickly through various phases, settled down into Epicureanism and has remained the source of a certain consolation to mankind, which if somewhat cheap, is none the less genuine. The pursuit of pleasure may seem simple selfishness, with a tendency to debauchery; and in this case the pre-rational and instinctive character of the maxim retained would be very obvious. Pleasure, to be sure, is not the direct object of an unspoiled will; but after some experience and discrimination, a man may actually guide himself by a foretaste of the pleasures he has found in certain objects and situations. The criticism required to distinguish what pays from what does not pay may not often be carried very far; but it may sometimes be carried to the length of suppressing every natural instinct and natural hope, and of turning the philosopher, as it turned Hegesias the Cyrenaic, into a eulogist of death.

The post-rational principle in the system then comes to the fore, and we see clearly that to sit down and reflect upon human life, picking out its pleasant moments and condemning all the rest, is to initiate a course of moral retrenchment. It is to judge what is worth doing, not by the innate ambition of the soul, but by experience of incidental feelings, which to a mind without constructive ideas may seem the only objects worthy of pursuit. That life ought to be accompanied by pleasure and exempt from pain is certain; for this means that what is agreeable to the whole process of nature would have become agreeable also to the various partial impulses involved—another way of describing organic harmony and physical perfection. But such a desirable harmony cannot be defined or obtained by picking out and isolating from the rest those occasions and functions in which it may already have been reached. These partial harmonies may be actual arrests or impediments in the whole which is to be made harmonious; and even when they are innocent or helpful they cannot serve to determine the form which the general harmony might take on. They merely illustrate its principle. The organism in which this principle of harmony might find pervasive expression is still potential, and the ideal is something of which, in its concrete form, no man has had experience. It involves a propitious material environment, perfect health, perfect arts, perfect government, a mind enlarged to the knowledge and enjoyment of all its external conditions and internal functions. Such an ideal is lost sight of when a man cultivates his garden-plot of private pleasures, leaving it to chance and barbarian fury to govern the state and quicken the world's passions.

Even Aristippus, the first and most delightful of hedonists, who really enjoyed the pleasures he advocated and was not afraid of the incidental pains—even Aristippus betrayed the post-rational character of his philosophy by abandoning politics, mocking science, making his peace with all abuses that fostered his comfort, and venting his wit on all ambitions that exceeded his hopes. A great temperament can carry off a rough philosophy. Rebellion and license may distinguish honourable souls in an age of polite corruption, and a grain of sincerity is better, in moral philosophy, than a whole harvest of conventionalities. The violence and shamelessness of Aristippus were corrected by Epicurus; and a balance was found between utter despair and utter irresponsibility. Epicureanism retrenched much: it cut off politics, religion, enterprise and passion. These things it convicted of vanity, without stopping to distinguish in them what might be inordinate from what might be rational. At the same time it retained friendship, freedom of soul, and intellectual light. It cultivated unworldliness without superstition and happiness without illusion. It was tender toward simple and honest things, scornful and bitter only against pretence and usurpation. It thus marked a first halting-place in the retreat of reason, a stage where the soul had thrown off only the higher and more entangling part of her burden and was willing to live, in somewhat reduced circumstances, on the remainder. Such a philosophy expresses well the genuine sentiment of persons, at once mild and emancipated, who find themselves floating on the ebb-tide of some civilisation, and enjoying its fruits, without any longer representing the forces that brought that civilisation about.

The same emancipation, without its mildness, appeared in the Cynics, whose secret it was to throw off all allegiance and all dependence on circumstance, and to live entirely on inner strength of mind, on pride and inflexible humour. The renunciation was far more sweeping than that of Epicurus, and indeed wellnigh complete; yet the Stoics, in underpinning the Cynical self-sufficiency with a system of physics, introduced into the life of the sect a contemplative element which very much enlarged and ennobled its sympathies. Nature became a sacred system, the laws of nature being eulogistically called rational laws, and the necessity of things, because it might be foretold in auguries, being called providence. There was some intellectual confusion in all this; but contemplation, even if somewhat idolatrous, has a purifying effect, and the sad and solemn review of the cosmos to which the Stoic daily invited his soul, to make it ready to face its destiny, doubtless liberated it from many an unworthy passion. The impressive spectacle of things was used to remind the soul of her special and appropriate function, which was to be rational. This rationality consisted partly in insight, to perceive the necessary order of things, and partly in conformity, to perceive that this order, whatever it might be, could serve the soul to exercise itself upon, and to face with equanimity.

Despair, in this system, flooded a much larger area of human life; everything, in fact, was surrendered except the will to endure whatever might come. The concentration was much more marked, since only a formal power of perception and defiance was retained and made the sphere of moral life; this rational power, at least in theory, was the one peak that remained visible above the deluge. But in practice much more was retained. Some distinction was drawn, however unwarrantably, between external calamities and human turpitude, so that absolute conformity and acceptance might not be demanded by the latter; although the chief occasion which a Stoic could find to practise fortitude and recognise the omnipresence of law was in noting the universal corruption of the state and divining its ruin. The obligation to conform to nature (which, strictly speaking, could not be disregarded in any case) was interpreted to signify that every one should perform the offices conventionally attached to his station. In this way a perfunctory citizenship and humanity were restored to the philosopher. But the restored life was merely histrionic: the Stoic was a recluse parading the market-place and a monk disguised in armour. His interest and faith were centred altogether on his private spiritual condition. He cultivated the society of those persons who, he thought, might teach him some virtue. He attended to the affairs of state so as to exercise his patience. He might even lead an army to battle, if he wished to test his endurance and make sure that philosophy had rendered him indifferent to the issue.

The strain and artifice of such a discipline, with merely formal goals and no hope on earth or in heaven, could not long maintain itself; and doubtless it existed, at a particular juncture, only in a few souls. Resignation to the will of God, says Bishop Butler, is *the whole of piety*; yet mere resignation would make a sorry religion and the negation of all morality, unless the will of God was understood to be quite different from his operation in nature. To turn Stoicism into a workable religion we need to qualify it with some pre-rational maxims. Islam, for instance, which boasts that in its essence it is nothing but the primitive and natural religion of mankind, consists in abandoning oneself to the will of God or, in other words, in accepting the inevitable. This will of God is learned for the most part by observing the course of nature and history, and remembering the fate meted out habitually to various sorts of men. Were this all, Islam would be a pure Stoicism, and Hebraic religion, in its ultimate phase, would be simply the eloquence of physics. It would not, in that case, be a moral inspiration at all, except as contemplation and the sense of one's nothingness might occasionally silence the passions and for a moment bewilder the mind. On recovering from this impression, however, men would find themselves enriched with no self-knowledge, armed with no precepts, and stimulated by no ideal. They would be reduced to enacting their incidental impulses, as the animals are, quite as if they had never perceived that in doing so they were fulfilling a divine decree. Enlightened Moslems, accordingly, have often been more Epicurean than Stoical; and if they have felt themselves (not without some reason) superior to Christians in delicacy, in *savoir vivre*, in kinship with all natural powers, this sense of superiority has been quite rationalistic and purely human. Their religion contributed to it only because it was simpler, freer from superstition, nearer to a clean and pleasant regimen in life. Resignation to the will of God being granted, expression of the will of man might more freely begin.

What made Islam, however, a positive and contagious novelty was the assumption that God's will might be incidentally revealed to prophets before the event, so that past experience was not the only source from which its total operation might be gathered. In its opposition to grosser idolatries Islam might appeal to experience and challenge those who trusted in special deities to justify their worship in face of the facts. The most decisive facts against idolaters, however, were not yet patent, but were destined to burst upon mankind at the last day—and most unpleasantly for the majority. Where Mohammed speaks in the name of the universal natural power he is abundantly scornful toward that fond paganism which consists in imagining distinct patrons for various regions of nature or for sundry human activities. In turning to such patrons the pagan regards something purely ideal or, as the Koran shrewdly observes, worships his own passions. Allah, on the contrary, is overwhelmingly external and as far as possible from being ideal. He is indeed the giver of all good things, as of all evil, and while his mercies are celebrated on every page of the Koran, these mercies consist in the indulgence he is expected to show to his favourites, and the exceeding reward reserved for them after their earthly trials. Allah's mercy does not exclude all those senseless and unredeemed cruelties of which nature is daily guilty; nay, it shines all the more conspicuously by contrast with his essential irresponsibility and wanton wrath, a part of his express purpose being to keep hell full of men and demons.

The tendency toward enlightenment which Islam represents, and the limits of that enlightenment, may be illustrated by the precept about unclean animals. Allah, we are told, being merciful and gracious, made the world for man's use, with all the animals in it. We may therefore justly slaughter and devour them, in so far as comports with health; but, of course, we may not eat animals that have died a natural death, nor those offered in sacrifice to false gods, nor swine; for to do so would be an abomination.

Unfortunately religious reformers triumph not so much by their rational insight as by their halting, traditional maxims. Mohammed felt the unity of God like a philosopher; but people listened to him because he preached it like a sectary. God, as he often reminds us, did not make the world for a plaything; he made it in order to establish distinctions and separate by an immense interval the fate of those who conform to the truth from the fate of those who ignore it. Human life is indeed beset with enough imminent evils to justify this urgent tone in the Semitic moralist and to lend his precepts a stern practical ring, absent from merely Platonic idealisms. But this stringency, which is called positivism when the conditions of welfare are understood, becomes fanaticism when they are misrepresented. Had Mohammed spoken only of the dynamic unity in things, the omnipresence of destiny, and the actual conditions of success and failure in the world, he would not have been called a prophet or have had more than a dozen intelligent followers, scattered over as many centuries; but the weakness of his intellect, and his ignorance of nature, made the success of his mission. It is easier to kindle righteous indignation against abuses when, by abating them, we further our personal interests; and Mohammed might have been less zealous in denouncing false gods had his own God been altogether the true one. But, in the heat of his militancy, he descends so far as to speak of *God's interests* which the faithful embrace, and of fighting in *God's cause*. By these notions, so crudely pre-rational, we are allowed to interpret and discount the pantheistic sublimities with which in most places we are regaled; and in order that a morality, too weak to be human, may not wither altogether in the fierce light of the Absolute, we are led to humanise the Absolute into a finite force, needing our support against independent enemies. So complete is the bankruptcy of that Stoic morality which thinks to live on the worship of That which Is.

As extremes are said to meet, so we may say that a radical position is often the point of departure for opposite systems. Pantheism, or religion and morality abdicating in favour of physics, may, in practice, be interpreted in contrary ways. To be in sympathy with the Whole may seem to require us to outgrow and discard every part; yet, on the other hand, there is no obvious reason why Being should love its essence in a fashion that involves hating every possible form of Being. The worshipper of Being accordingly assumes now one, now the other, of two opposite attitudes, according as the society in which he lives is in a pre-rational or a post-rational state of culture. Pantheism is interpreted pre-rationally, as by the early Mohammedans, or by the Hegelians, when people are not yet acquainted, or not yet disgusted, with worldliness; the Absolute then seems to lend a mystical sanction to whatever existences or tendencies happen to be afoot. Morality is reduced to sanctioning reigning conventions, or reigning passions, on the authority of the universe. Thus the Moslems, by way of serving Allah, could extend their conquests and cultivate the arts and pleasures congenial to a self-sufficing soul, at once indolent and fierce; while the transcendentalists of our times, by way of accepting their part in the divine business, have merely added a certain speculative loftiness to the maxims of some sect or the chauvinism of some nation.

To accept everything, however, is not an easy nor a tolerable thing, unless you are naturally well pleased with what falls to your share. However the Absolute may feel, a moral creature has to hate some forms of being; and if the age has thrust these forms before a man's eyes, and imposed them upon him, not being suffered by his pantheism to blame the Absolute he will (by an inconsistency) take to blaming himself. It will be his finitude, his inordinate claims, his enormous effrontery in having any will or any preference in particular, that will seem to him the source of all evil and the single blot on the infinite lucidity of things. Pantheism, under these circumstances, will issue in a post-rational morality. It will practise asceticism and look for a mystical deliverance from infinite existence.

Under these circumstances myth is inevitably reintroduced. Without it, no consolation could be found except in the prospect of death and, awaiting that, in incidental natural satisfactions; whereby absorption in the Absolute might come to look not only impossible but distinctly undesirable. To make retreat out of human nature seem a possible vocation, this nature itself must, in some myth, be represented as unnatural; the soul that this life stifles must be said to come from elsewhere and to be fitted to breathe some element far rarer and finer than this sublunary fog.

A curious foothold for such a myth was furnished by the Socratic philosophy. Plato, wafted by his poetic vision too far, perhaps, from the utilitarianism of his master, had eulogised concretions in discourse at the expense of existences and had even played with cosmological myths, meant to express the values of things, by speaking as if these values had brought things into being. The dialectical terms thus contrasted with natural objects, and pictured as natural powers, furnished the dogmas needed at this juncture by a post-rational religion. The spell which dialectic can exercise over an abstracted mind is itself great; and it may grow into a sacred influence and a positive revelation when it offers a sanctuary from a weary life in the world. Out of the play of notions carried on in a prayerful dream wonderful mysteries can be constructed, to be presently announced to the people and made the core of sacramental injunctions. When the tide of vulgar superstition is at the flood and every form of quackery is welcome, we need not wonder that a theosophy having so respectable a core—something, indeed, like a true logic misunderstood—should gain many adherents. Out of the names of things and of virtues a mystic ladder could be constructed by which to leave the things and the virtues themselves behind; but the sagacity and exigencies of the school would not fail to arrange the steps in this progress—the end of which was unattainable except, perhaps, in a momentary ecstasy—so that the obvious duties of men would continue, for the nonce, to be imposed upon them. The chief difference made in morals would be only this: that the positive occasions and sanctions of good conduct would no longer be mentioned with respect, but the imagination would be invited to dwell instead on mystical issues.

Neo-Platonic morality, through a thousand learned and vulgar channels, permeated Christianity and entirely transformed it. Original Christianity was, though in another sense, a religion of redemption. The Jews, without dreaming of original sin or of any inherent curse in being infinite, had found themselves often in the sorest material straits. They hoped, like all primitive peoples, that relief might come by propitiating the deity. They knew that the sins of the fathers were visited upon the children even to the third and fourth generation. They had accepted this idea of joint responsibility and vicarious atonement, turning in their unphilosophical way this law of nature into a principle of justice. Meantime the failure of all their cherished ambitions had plunged them into a penitential mood. Though in fact pious and virtuous to a fault, they still looked for repentance—their own or the world's—to save them. This redemption was to be accomplished in the Hebrew spirit, through long-suffering and devotion to the Law, with the Hebrew solidarity, by vicarious attribution of merits and demerits within the household of the faith.

Such a way of conceiving redemption was far more dramatic, poignant, and individual than the Neo-Platonic; hence it was far more popular and better fitted to be a nucleus for religious devotion. However much, therefore, Christianity may have insisted on renouncing the world, the flesh, and the devil, it always kept in the background this perfectly Jewish and pre-rational craving for a delectable promised land. The journey might be long and through a desert, but milk and honey were to flow in the oasis beyond. Had renunciation been fundamental or revulsion from nature complete, there would have been no much-trumpeted last judgment and no material kingdom of heaven. The renunciation was only temporary and partial; the revulsion was only against incidental evils. Despair touched nothing but the present order of the world, though at first it took the extreme form of calling for its immediate destruction. This was the sort of despair and renunciation that lay at the bottom of Christian repentance; while hope in a new order of this world, or of one very like it, lay at the bottom of Christian joy. A temporary sacrifice, it was thought, and a partial mutilation would bring the spirit miraculously into a fresh paradise. The pleasures nature had grudged or punished, grace was to offer as a reward for faith and patience. The earthly life which was vain as an experience was to be profitable as a trial. Normal experience, appropriate exercise for the spirit, would thereafter begin.

Christianity is thus a system of postponed rationalism, a rationalism intercepted by a supernatural version of the conditions of happiness. Its moral principle is reason—the only moral principle there is; its motive power is the impulse and natural hope to be and to be happy. Christianity merely renews and reinstates these universal principles after a first disappointment and a first assault of despair, by opening up new vistas of accomplishment, new qualities and measures of success. The Christian field of action being a world of grace enveloping the world of nature, many transitory reversals of acknowledged values may take place in its code. Poverty, chastity, humility, obedience, self-sacrifice, ignorance, sickness, and dirt may all acquire a religious worth which reason, in its direct application, might scarcely have found in them; yet these reversed appreciations are merely incidental to a secret rationality, and are justified on the ground that human nature, as now found, is corrupt and needs to be purged and transformed before it can safely manifest its congenital instincts and become again an authoritative criterion of values. In the kingdom of God men would no longer need to do penance, for life there would be truly natural and there the soul would be at last in her native sphere.

This submerged optimism exists in Christianity, being a heritage from the Jews; and those Protestant communities that have rejected the pagan and Platonic elements that overlaid it have little difficulty in restoring it to prominence. Not, however, without abandoning the soul of the gospel; for the soul of the gospel, though expressed in the language of Messianic hopes, is really post-rational. It was not to marry and be given in marriage, or to sit on thrones, or to unravel metaphysical mysteries, or to enjoy any of the natural delights renounced in this life, that Christ summoned his disciples to abandon all they had and to follow him. There was surely a deeper peace in his self-surrender. It was not a new thing even among the Jews to use the worldly promises of their exoteric religion as symbols for inner spiritual revolutions; and the change of heart involved in genuine Christianity was not a fresh excitation of gaudy hopes, nor a new sort of utilitarian, temporary austerity. It was an emptying of the will, in respect to all human desires, so that a perfect charity and contemplative justice, falling like the Father's gifts ungrudgingly on the whole creation, might take the place of ambition, petty morality, and earthly desires. It was a renunciation which, at least in Christ himself and in his more spiritual disciples, did not spring from disappointed illusion or lead to other unregenerate illusions even more sure to be dispelled by events. It sprang rather from a native speculative depth, a natural affinity to the divine fecundity, serenity, and sadness of the world. It was the spirit of prayer, the kindliness and insight which a pure soul can fetch from contemplation.

This mystical detachment, supervening on the dogged old Jewish optimism, gave Christianity a double aspect, and had some curious consequence in later times. Those who were inwardly convinced—as most religious minds were under the Roman Empire—that all earthly things were vanity, and that they plunged the soul into an abyss of nothingness if not of torment, could, in view of brighter possibilities in another world, carry their asceticism and their cult of suffering farther than a purely negative system, like the Buddhistic, would have allowed. For a discipline that is looked upon as merely temporary can contradict nature more boldly than one intended to take nature's place. The hope of unimaginable benefits to ensue could drive religion to greater frenzies than it could have fallen into if its object had been merely to silence the will. Christianity persecuted, tortured, and burned. Like a hound it tracked the very scent of heresy. It kindled wars, and nursed furious hatreds and ambitions. It sanctified, quite like Mohammedanism, extermination and tyranny. All this would have been impossible if, like Buddhism, it had looked only to peace and the liberation of souls. It looked beyond; it dreamt of infinite blisses and crowns it should be crowned with before an electrified universe and an applauding God. These were rival baits to those which the world fishes with, and were snapped at, when seen, with no less avidity. Man, far from being freed from his natural passions, was plunged into artificial ones quite as violent and much more disappointing. Buddhism had tried to quiet a sick world with anaesthetics; Christianity sought to purge it with fire.

Another consequence of combining, in the Christian life, postrational with pre-rational motives, a sense of exile and renunciation with hopes of a promised land, was that esoteric piety could choose between the two factors, even while it gave a verbal assent to the dogmas that included both. Mystics honoured the postrational motive and despised the pre-rational; positivists clung to the second and hated the first. To the spiritually minded, whose religion was founded on actual insight and disillusion, the joys of heaven could never be more than a symbol for the intrinsic worth of sanctity. To the worldling those heavenly joys were nothing but a continuation of the pleasures and excitements of this life, serving to choke any reflections which, in spite of himself, might occasionally visit him about the vanity of human wishes. So that Christianity, even in its orthodox forms, covers various kinds of morality, and its philosophical incoherence betrays itself in disruptive movements, profound schisms, and total alienation on the part of one Christian from the inward faith of another. Trappist or Calvinist may be practising a heroic and metaphysical self-surrender while the busy-bodies of their respective creeds are fostering, in God's name, all their hot and miscellaneous passions.

This contradiction, present in the overt morality of Christendom, cannot be avoided, however, by taking refuge again in pure asceticism. There is, let us say, a law of Karma, by which merit and demerit accruing in one incarnation pass on to the next and enable the soul to cruise continuously through a series of stages. Thus the world, though called illusory, is not wholly intractable. It provides systematically for an exit out of its illusions. On this rational ordinance of phenomena, which is left standing by an imperfect nihilism, Buddhist morality is built. Rational endeavour remains possible because experience is calculable and fruitful in this one respect, that it dissolves in the presence of goodness and knowledge.

Similarly in Christian ethics, the way of the cross has definite stations and a definite end. However negative this end may be thought to be, the assurance that it may be attained is a remnant of natural hope in the bosom of pessimism. A complete disillusion would have involved the neglect of such an assurance, the denial that it was possible or at least that it was to be realised under specific conditions. That conversion and good works lead to something worth attaining is a new sort of positivistic hope. A complete scepticism would involve a doubt, not only concerning the existence of such a method of salvation, but also (what is more significant) concerning the importance of applying it if it were found. For to assert that salvation is not only possible but urgently necessary, that every soul is now in an intolerable condition and should search for an ultimate solution to all its troubles, a restoration to a normal and somehow blessed state—what is this but to assert that the nature of things has a permanent constitution, by conformity with which man may secure his happiness? Moreover, we assert in such a faith that this natural constitution of things is discoverable in a sufficient measure to guide our action to a successful issue. Belief in Karma, in prayer, in sacraments, in salvation is a remnant of a natural belief in the possibility of living successfully. The remnant may be small and "expressed in fancy." Transmigration or an atonement may be chimerical ideas. Yet the mere fact of reliance upon something, the assumption that the world is steady and capable of rational exploitation, even if in a supernatural interest and by semi-magical means, amounts to an essential loyalty to postulates of practical reason, an essential adherence to natural morality.

The pretension to have reached a point of view from which *all* impulse may be criticised is accordingly an untenable pretension. It is abandoned in the very systems in which it was to be most thoroughly applied. The instrument of criticism must itself be one impulse surviving the wreck of all the others; the vision of salvation and of the way thither must be one dream among the rest. A single suggestion of experience is thus accepted while all others are denied; and although a certain purification and revision of morality may hence ensue, there is no real penetration to a deeper principle than spontaneous reason, no revelation of a higher end than the best possible happiness. One sporadic growth of human nature may be substituted for its whole luxuriant vegetation; one negative or formal element of happiness may be preferred to the full entelechy of life. We may see the Life of Reason reduced to straits, made to express itself in a niggardly and fantastic environment; but we have, in principle and essence, the Life of Reason still, empirical in its basis and rational in its method, its substance impulse and its end happiness.

Post-rational systems accordingly mark no real advance and offer no genuine solution to spiritual enigmas. The saving force each of them invokes is merely some remnant of that natural energy which animates the human animal. Faith in the supernatural is a desperate wager made by man at the lowest ebb of his fortunes; it is as far as possible from being the source of that normal vitality which subsequently, if his fortunes mend, he may gradually recover. Under the same religion, with the same posthumous alternatives and mystic harmonies hanging about them, different races, or the same race at different periods, will manifest the most opposite moral characteristics. Belief in a thousand hells and heavens will not lift the apathetic out of apathy or hold back the passionate from passion; while a newly planted and ungalled community, in blessed forgetfulness of rewards or punishments, of cosmic needs or celestial sanctions, will know how to live cheerily and virtuously for life's own sake, putting to shame those thin vaticinations. To hope for a second life, to be had gratis, merely because this life has lost its savour, or to dream of a different world, because nature seems too intricate and unfriendly, is in the end merely to play with words. What keeps supernatural morality, in its better forms, within the limits of sanity is the fact that it reinstates in practice, under novel associations and for motives ostensibly different, the very natural virtues and hopes which, when seen to be merely natural, it had thrown over with contempt. The new dispensation itself restores the authority of those human ideals which it expresses in a fable.

The extent of this moral restoration, the measure in which nature is suffered to bloom in the sanctuary, determines the value of post-rational moralities. They may preside over a good life, personal or communal, when their symbolism, though cumbrous, is not deceptive; when the supernatural machinery brings man back to nature through mystical circumlocutions, and becomes itself a poetic echo of experience and a dramatic impersonation of reason. The peculiar accent and emphasis which it will not cease to impose on the obvious lessons of life need not then repel the wisest intelligence. True sages and true civilisations can accordingly flourish under a dispensation nominally supernatural; for that supernaturalism may have become a mere form in which imagination clothes a rational and humane wisdom.

CHAPTER 10

THE VALIDITY OF SCIENCE

THE SAME despair or confusion which, when it overtakes human purposes, seeks relief in arbitrary schemes of salvation, when it overtakes human knowledge, may breed arbitrary substitutes for science. There are post-rational systems of nature as well as of duty. Most of these are myths hardly worth separating from the post-rational moralities they adorn, and have been sufficiently noticed in the last chapter; but a few aspire to be critical revisions of science, themselves scientific. It may be well, in bringing this book to a close, to review these proposed revisions. The validity of science is at stake, and with it the validity of that whole Life of Reason which science crowns, and justifies to reflection.

There are many degrees and kinds of this critical retractation. Science may be accepted bodily, while its present results are modified by suggesting speculatively what its ultimate results might be. This is natural philosophy or legitimate metaphysics. Or science may be accepted in part, and in part subjected to control by some other alleged vehicle of knowledge. This is traditional or intuitive theology. Or science may be retracted and withdrawn altogether, on the ground that it is but methodological fiction, its facts appearances merely, and its principles tendencies to feign. This is transcendentalism; whereupon a dilemma presents itself. We may be invited to abstain from all hypostasis or hearty belief in anything, and to dwell only on the consciousness of imaginative activity in a vacuum—which is radical idealism. Or we may be assured that, science being a dream, we may awake from it into another cosmos, built upon principles quite alien to those illustrated in nature or applicable in practice—which is idealism of the mythical sort. Finally it may occur to us that the criticism of science is an integral part of science itself, and that a transcendental method of survey, which marshals all things in the order of their discovery, far from invalidating knowledge can only serve to separate it from incidental errors and to disclose the relative importance of

481

truths. Science would then be rehabilitated by criticism. The primary movement of the intellect would not be condemned by that subsequent reflection which it makes possible, and which collates its results. Science, purged of all needless realism and seen in its relation to human life, would continue to offer the only conception of reality which is pertinent or possible to the economic mind.

We may now proceed to discuss these various attitudes in turn.

A first and quite blameless way of criticising science is to point out that science is incomplete. That it grows fast is indeed its commonest boast; and no man of science is so pessimistic as to suppose that its growth is over. To wish to supplement science and to regard its conclusions as largely provisional is therefore more than legitimate. It is actually to share the spirit of inquiry and to feel the impulse toward investigation. When new truths come into view, old truths are thereby reinterpreted and put in a new light; so that the acquisitions of science not only admit of revision but loudly call for it, not wishing for any other authority or vindication than that which they might find in the context of universal truth.

To revise science in this spirit would be merely to extend it. No new method, no transverse philosophy, would be requisite or fitted for the task. Knowledge would be transformed by more similar knowledge, not by some verbal manipulation. Yet while waiting for experience to grow and accumulate its lessons, a man of genius, who had drunk deep of experience himself, might imagine some ultimate synthesis. He might venture to carry out the suggestions of science and anticipate the conclusions it would reach when completed. The game is certainly dangerous, especially if the prophecy is uttered with any air of authority; yet with good luck and a fine instinct, such speculation may actually open the way to discovery and may diffuse in advance that virtual knowledge of physics which is enough for moral and poetic purposes. Verification in detail is needed, not so much for its own sake as to check speculative errors; but when speculation is by chance well directed and hits upon the substantial truth, it does all that a completed science would do for mankind; since science, if ever completed, would immediately have to be summed up again and reduced to generalities. Under the circumstances of human life, ultimate truth must forego detailed verification and must remain speculative. The curse of modern philosophy is only that it has not drawn its inspiration from science; as the misfortune of science is that it has not yet saturated the mind of philosophers and recast the moral world. The Greek physicists, puerile as was their notion of natural mechanism, had a more integral view of things. They understood nature's uses and man's condition in an honest and noble way. If no single phenomenon had been explained correctly by any philosopher from Thales to Lucretius, yet by their frank and studious contemplation of nature they would have liberated the human soul.

Unfortunately the supplements to science which most philosophers supply in our day are not conceived in a scientific spirit. Instead of anticipating the physics of the future they cling to the physics of the past. They do not stimulate us by a picture, however fanciful, of what the analogies of nature and politics actually point to; they seek rather to patch and dislocate current physics with some ancient myth, once the best physics obtainable, from which they have not learned to extricate their affections.

Sometimes these survivals are intended to modify scientific conceptions but slightly, and merely to soften a little the outlines of a cosmic picture to which religion and literature are not yet accustomed. There is a school of political conservatives who, with no specific interest in metaphysics, cannot or dare not break with traditional modes of expression, with the customs of their nation, or with the clerical classes. They accordingly append to current knowledge certain sentimental postulates, alleging that what is established by tradition and what appeals to the heart must somehow correspond to something which is needful and true. But their conventional attachment to a religion which in its original essence was perhaps mystical and revolutionary, scarcely modifies, in their eyes, the sum of practical assurances or the aim of human life. As language exercises some functions which science can hardly assume (as, for instance, in poetry and communication) so theology and metaphysics, which to such men are nothing but languages, might provide for inarticulate interests, and unite us to much that lies in the dim penumbra of our workaday world. Ancient revelations and mysteries, however incredible if taken literally, might therefore be suffered to flourish undisturbed, so long as they did not clash with any clear fact or natural duty. They might continue to decorate with a mystical aureole the too prosaic kernel of known truth.

Mythology and ritual, with the sundry divinations of poets,

might in fact be kept suspended with advantage over human passion and ignorance, to furnish them with decent expression. But
once indulged, divination is apt to grow arrogant and dogmatic.
When its oracles have become traditional they are almost inevitably mistaken for sober truths. Hence the second kind of supplement offered to science, so that revelations with which moral life
has been intertwined may find a place beside or beyond science.
The effort is honest, but extraordinarily short-sighted. Whatever
value those revelations may have they draw from actual experience
or inevitable ideals. When the ground of that experience and
those ideals is disclosed by science, nothing of any value is lost; it
only remains to accustom ourselves to a new vocabulary and to
shift somewhat the associations of those values which life contains
or pursues. Revelations are necessarily mythical and subrational;
they express natural forces and human interests in a groping way,
before the advent of science. To stick in them, when something
more honest and explicit is available, is inconsistent with caring
for attainable welfare or understanding the world. It is to be
stubborn and negligent under the cloak of religion. These prejudices are a drag on progress, moral no less than material; and the
sensitive conservatism that fears they may be indispensable is entangled in a pathetic delusion. It is conservatism in a shipwreck.
It has not the insight to embrace the fertile principles of life,
which are always ready to renew life after no matter what natural catastrophe. The good laggards have no courage to strip for
the race. Rather than live otherwise, and live better, they prefer
to nurse the memories of youth and to die with a retrospective
smile upon their countenance.

    Far graver than the criticism which shows science to be incom-
plete is that which shows it to be relative. The fact is undeniable,
though the inferences made from it are often rash and gratuitous.
We have seen that science is nothing but developed perception,
interpreted intent, commonsense rounded out and minutely articulated. It is therefore as much an instinctive product, as much a
stepping forth of human courage in the dark, as is any inevitable
dream or impulsive action. Like life itself, like any form of determinate existence, it is altogether autonomous and unjustifiable from
the outside. It must lean on its own vitality; to sanction reason
there is only reason, and to corroborate sense there is nothing
but sense. Inferential thought is a venture not to be approved of,

save by a thought no less venturesome and inferential. This is once for all the fate of a living being—it is the very essence of spirit—to be ever on the wing, borne by inner forces toward goals of its own imagining, confined to a passing apprehension of a represented world. Mind, which calls itself the organ of truth, is a permanent possibility of error. The encouragement and corroboration which science is alleged to receive from moment to moment may, for aught it knows, be simply a more ingenious self-deception, a form of that cumulative illusion by which madness can confirm itself, creating a whole world, with an endless series of martyrs, to bear witness to its sanity.

To insist on this situation may seem idle, since no positive doctrine can gain thereby in plausibility, and no particular line of action in reasonableness. Yet this transcendental exercise, this reversion to the immediate, may be recommended by way of a cathartic, to free the mind from ancient obstructions and make it hungrier and more agile in its rational faith. Scepticism is harmless when it is honest and universal; it clears the air and is a means of reorganising belief on its natural foundations. Belief is an inevitable accompaniment of practice and intent, both of which it will cling to all the more closely after a thorough criticism. When all beliefs are challenged together, the just and necessary ones have a chance to step forward and to re-establish themselves alone. The doubt cast on science, when it is an ingenuous and impartial doubt, will accordingly serve to show what sort of thing science is, and to establish it on a sure foundation. Science will then be seen to be tentative, genial, practical, and humane, full of ideality and pathos, like every great human undertaking.

Unfortunately a searching disintegration of dogma, a conscientious reversion to the immediate, is seldom practised for its own sake. So violent a disturbance of mental habits needs some great social upheaval or some revolutionary ambition to bring it about. The transcendental philosophy might never have been put forward at all, had its authors valued it for what it can really accomplish. The effort would have seemed too great and the result too nugatory. Their criticism of knowledge was not freely undertaken, with the ·pure speculative motive of understanding and purifying human science. They were driven on by the malicious psychology of their predecessors, by the perplexities of a sophistical scepticism, and by the imminent collapse of traditional metaphysics. They were enticed at the same time by the hope of finding a new basis for the religious myths associated with that metaphysics. In consequence their transcendentalism was not a rehearsal of the Life of Reason, a retrospect criticising and justifying the phases of human progress. It was rather a post-rational system of theology, the dangerous cure to a harmless disease, inducing a panic to introduce a fable. The panic came from the assumption (a wholly gratuitous one) that a spontaneous constructive intellect cannot be a trustworthy instrument, that appearances cannot be the messengers of reality, and that things cannot be what science finds that they are. We were forbidden to believe in anything we might discover or to trust in anything we could see. The artificial vacuum thus produced in the mind ached to be filled with something, and of course a flood of rhetorical commonplaces was at hand, which might rush in to fill it.

The most heroic transcendentalists were but men, and having imagined that logic obliged them to abstain from every sort of hypostasis, they could not long remain true to their logic. For a time, being of a buoyant disposition, they might feel that nothing could be more exhilarating than to swim in the void, altogether free from settled conditions, altogether the ignorant creators of each moment's vision. Such a career evidently affords all sorts of possibilities, except perhaps the possibility of being a career. When a man has strained every nerve to maintain an absolute fluidity, the episodes of experience, not being due to any conceivable machinery beneath, might come of mere willing, or at the waving of a dialectical wand. We are released from all dogma and reinstated in the primordial assurance that we are all there is, but without understanding what we are, and without any means of controlling our destiny, though cheered by the magnificent feeling that we create it.

It is intelligible that a pure transcendentalism of this sort should not be either stable or popular. It may be admired for its analytic depth and its persistency in tracing all supposed existences back to the experience that vouches for them. Yet a spirit that finds its only exercise in gloating on the consciousness that it is a spirit, one that has so little skill in expression that it feels all its embodiments to be betrayals and all its symbols to be misrepresentations, is a spirit evidently impotent and confused. We may admire a school that has done one original task so thoroughly

as transcendentalism has done its examination of the cognitive conscience, even if it has failed to do something else to which it did
not distinctly address itself and for which it had no aptitude—
namely, to discover what is really true. But it becomes necessary
to note this limitation, especially when it is virtually disallowed,
and when science is systematically disparaged in favour of a method
that is merely disintegrating and incapable of establishing a single
positive truth.

The legitimacy of the transcendental method is so obvious
that it is baffling when unfamiliar and trifling when understood.
It is somewhat like the scientific discovery that man is an animal;
for in spite of its pompous language and unction, transcendentalism, when not transcended, is a stopping short at the vegetative
and digestive stage of consciousness, where nothing seems to be
anything but a play of variations in the immediate. That is what
science has risen from; it is the primordial slime. But to stop there
and make life consist in hearing the mind work is illiberal and
childish. Maturity lies in taking reason at its word and learning
to believe and to do what it bids us. Inexperience, pedantry, and
mysticism—three obstacles to wisdom—were not absent from those
academic geniuses by whom transcendentalism was first brought
forth.

The dethronement of empirical knowledge which these philosophers announced was occasioned by the discovery that empirical knowledge was ideal and hypothetical; that its terms, like all
terms in thought, were thrown out during the fission or crystallisation of a growing experience. Science accordingly was merely a
set of ideas; its subject-matter seemed to be sucked in and absorbed by the theory that presented it, so that when the history
of science was written the whole substance and meaning of science
was exhausted. This damaging implication, that what is ideal is
imaginary and that what is inferred exists only in the fooled mind
that infers it, would, if it were allowed, make short work of all
philosophy. Theology would fare no better than science, and it is
hard to see how transcendental idealism itself could stand, if it
pretended to constitute an articulate theory of reality. All faith
would be invalidated, since it would be proved to be faith only,
having no real object. But then history itself is a science; and to
represent a series of events or related phenomena in time would be
to pretend to impossible knowledge. It would become necessary

to retract and withdraw the alleged evolution of thought itself, in which science was to figure as an imaginative device and a passing episode. History and experience would be nothing but the idea of them; and the Absolute Ego or Absolute Life also, in so far as anything could be said of it, would be simply an integral term in the discourse that described it. And this discourse, this sad residuum of reality, would remain an absolute datum without a ground, and without an object.

It suffices, therefore, to take the supposed negative implication in transcendentalism a little seriously to see that it leaves nothing standing but negation and imbecility; so that we may safely conclude that such a negative implication is gratuitous, and also that in taking the transcendental method for an instrument of reconstruction its professors were radically false to it. They took the starting-point of experience, on which they had fallen back, for its ultimate deliverance, and in reverting to protoplasm they thought they were rising to God. The transcendental method is merely retrospective; its use is to recover more systematically conceptions already extant and inevitable. It invalidates nothing in science; much less does it carry with it any rival doctrine of its own. Every philosophy, even materialism, may find a transcendental justification, if experience as it develops will yield no other terms. What has reason to tremble at a demand for its credentials is surely not natural science; it is rather those mystical theologies or romantic philosophies of history which aspire to take its place. This nemesis is inevitable; for the mind must be inhabited, and the ideas with which science peoples it are simply its involuntary perceptions somewhat more clearly arranged.

That the relativity of science—its being an emanation of human life—is nothing against its validity appears best, perhaps, in the case of dialectic. Dialectic is valid by virtue of an intended meaning and felt congruity in its terms; but these terms, which intent fixes, are eternal and independent in their ideal nature, and the congruity between them is not created by being felt but, whether incidentally felt or not, is inherent in their essence. Mathematical thinking is the closest and most intimate of mental operations, nothing external being called in to aid; yet mathematical truth is as remote as possible from being personal or psychic. It is absolutely self-justified and is necessary before it is discovered to be so. Here, then, is a conspicuous region of truth, disclosed to the human intellect by its own internal exercise, whose theme is nevertheless altogether independent, being eternal and indefeasible, while the thought that utters it is ephemeral.

The validity of material science, not being warranted by pure insight, cannot be so quickly made out; nevertheless it cannot be denied systematically, and the misunderstood transcendentalism which belittles physics contradicts its own basis. For how are we supposed to know that what we call facts are mere appearances and what we call objects mere creations of thought? We know this by physics. It is physiology, a part of physics, that assures us that our senses and brains are conditions of our experience. Were it not for what we know of the outer world and of our place in it, we should be incapable of attaching any meaning to subjectivity. The flux of things would then go on in their own medium, not in our minds; and no suspicion of illusion or of qualification by mind would attach to any event in nature. So it is in a dream; and it is our knowledge of physics, our reliance on the world's material coherence, that marks our awakening, and that constitutes our discovery that we exist as minds and are subject to dreaming. It is quite true that the flux, as it exists in men, is largely psychic; but only because the events it contains are effects of material causes and the images in it are flying shadows cast by solid external things. This is the meaning of psychic existence, and its differentia. Mind is an expression, weighted with emotion, of natural relations among bodies.

The validity of science in general is accordingly established merely by establishing the truth of its particular propositions, in dialectic on the authority of intent and in physics on that of experiment. It is impossible to base science on a deeper foundation or to override it by a higher knowledge. What is called metaphysics, if not an anticipation of natural science, is a confusion of it with dialectic or a mixture of it with myths. If we have the faculty of being utterly sincere and of disintegrating the conventions of language and religion, we must confess that knowledge is only a claim we put forth, a part of that unfathomable compulsion by force of which we live and hold our painted world together for a moment. If we have any insight into mind, or any eye for human history, we must confess at the same time that the oracular substitutes for knowledge to which, in our perplexities, we might be tempted to fly, are pathetic popular fables, having no other sanctity than that which they borrow from the natural impulses they play upon. To live by science requires intelligence and faith, but not to live by it is folly.

If science thus contains the sum total of our rational convictions and gives us the only picture of reality on which we should care to dwell, we have but to consult the sciences in detail to ascertain, as far as that is possible, what sort of a universe we live in. The result is as yet far from satisfactory. The sciences have not joined hands and made their results coherent, showing nature to be, as it doubtless is, all of one piece. The moral sciences especially are a mass of confusion. Negative, I think, must be the attitude of reason, in the present state of science, upon any hypothesis far outrunning the recorded history and the visible habitat of the human race. Yet exactly the same habits and principles that have secured our present knowledge are still active within us, and promise further discoveries. It is more desirable to clarify our knowledge within these bounds than to extend it beyond them. For while the reward of action is contemplation or, in more modern phrase, experience and consciousness, there is nothing stable or interesting to contemplate except objects relevant to action—the natural world and the mind's ideals.

Both the conditions and the standards of action lie well within the territory which science, after a fashion, already dominates. But there remain unexplored jungles and monster-breeding lairs within our nominal jurisdiction which it is the immediate task of science to clear. The darkest spots are in man himself, in his fitful, irrational disposition. Could a better system prevail in our lives a better order would establish itself in our thinking. It has not been for want of keen senses, or personal genius, or a constant order in the outer world, that mankind have fallen back repeatedly into barbarism and superstition. It has been for want of good character, good example, and good government. There is a pathetic capacity in men to live nobly, if only they would give one another the chance. The ideal of political perfection, vague and remote as it yet seems, is certainly approachable, for it is as definite and constant as human nature. The knowledge of all relevant truth would be involved in that ideal, and no intellectual dissatisfaction would be felt with a system of ideas that should express and illumine a perfect life.

INDEX

forms of, 15; psychology of, 17; successive, 18; recurrent, 22-3; come and go, 31; of objects, 46 ff.

Peter, Saint, 225, 401

Peter, the Great, 122

Petrarch, 63-4

Pharisees, 237

Philosophy, beneficence and importance of, 76

Physics, as whole group of sciences that describe existences, 388; contrasted and compared with dialectic, 388 ff.; contained in common knowledge, 391; need of firm basis for, 427; explicit, 428; adoration of, essence of idolatry, 428

Piety (see III, Chap. 10); defined in Roman sense, 258; true objects of, 258 ff., 262 ff.; spirit's acknowledgment of its incarnation by, 260; pathetic and noble, 261; patriotism a form of, 261; accidental expression of morality, 262; mankind not factually object of, 262; retrospective, 264; toward the lovely, 321

Pilgrim Fathers, 162

Pindar, 68

Plastic construction (see IV, Chap. 7); of tools, 346; of idols, 346-7; conservatism in, 347 ff.; social inertia in, 348; wonder and admiration aroused by, 349 ff.; decoration in, 350; the Gothic, 351-2; architectural, 351-3

Plastic impulse (instinct), sanction of, 346; becomes art, 346; immortal, 357

Plastic representation, begins in imitation, 355 (see IV, Chap. 8)

Plato, 57-8, 80, 89, 98, 101, 103, 184, 241 ff., 246-7, 334-5, 400, 408, 448, 455-6, 474

Platonic writings, 442

Platonism, 57

Plato's Republic, 70, 131, 272

Poetry, passion perfect soil for, 81; where its magic lies, 329 (see IV, Chap. 6); primitive and radical form of, 334, 336 ff.; when pure is pure experiment, 334-5; inspiration in, 334 ff.; represents volume and form of experience, 336; stimulation of, 337-8; embodiment of ideals, 339; appeal of, 339; aspects of, in prose, 340-1; beauties of language form body of, 341; possibility of rational, 341 ff.

Poets, inspired by divine madness, 334 ff.; popular, 335; lying a privilege of, 338; in relation to myths, 343-4; a vision of the rational, 343-4

Prayer (see III, Chap. 3); expresses need, 197 ff.; a magic, 198; accomplishments of, 198 ff.; constitutes something spiritual, 200-1

Prejudices, evolve inwardly of themselves, 409

Prince of Peace, 235 (see Christ)

Prometheus, 176, 250

Prophets, The, 211 ff.

Prose, function to inform, 337-8; responsible, 338; appeals of, 339; great defect of, 339-40; owns double allegiance, 340; in a measure a fine art, 340; aspects of poetry in, 340-1

Protestant communities, 476

Protestantism, spirit and inward inspiration of, 236 ff.; Teutonic origins of, 236-7; characteristics of, 237, 239; gospel relations of, 237-8; the Reformation and, 239-40; assumes form of German speculative philosophy, 239-40; becomes more pale and rationalistic, 255

Protestants, The, 241

Proverbs, truth of, 445-6; value of, 446

Providence, 202

Prudence, equated with knowledge, 50, 52

Prussia, 401

Puritans, 237, 348

Psychology (see V, Chap. 4); social imagination should be excluded from, 414 ff.; loose imaginative method in, 416 ff.; dialectic of ideas in, 418 ff.; as science, physiological,